The Riel Problem

Canada,
the Métis,
and a
Resistant
Hero

The Riel Problem

ALBERT BRAZ

UNIVERSITY of ALBERTA PRESS

Published by

University of Alberta Press
1-16 Rutherford Library South
11204 89 Avenue NW
Edmonton, Alberta, Canada T6G 2J4
amiskwaciwâskahikan | Treaty 6 |
Métis Territory
ualbertapress.ca | uapress@ualberta.ca

Copyright © 2024 Albert Braz

LIBRARY AND ARCHIVES CANADA
CATALOGUING IN PUBLICATION

Title: The Riel problem : Canada, the Métis, and a resistant hero / Albert Braz.
Names: Braz, Albert, 1957- author.
Description: Includes bibliographical references and index.
Identifiers: Canadiana (print) 20230551513 | Canadiana (ebook) 20230551661 | ISBN 9781772127331 (softcover) | ISBN 9781772127485 (EPUB) | ISBN 9781772127492 (PDF)
Subjects: LCSH: Riel, Louis, 1844-1885. | LCSH: Métis—History. | LCSH: Métis—Prairie Provinces—Biography. | LCSH: Métis—Historiography. | LCSH: Canada—History. | LCSH: Canada—Historiography.
Classification: LCC FC3217.1.R53 B73 2024 | DDC 971.05/1092—dc23

First edition, first printing, 2024.
First printed and bound in Canada by Houghton Boston Printers, Saskatoon, Saskatchewan.
Copyediting and proofreading by Alicia Hibbert.
Indexing by Adrian Mather.
Map by Eric Leinberger.

All rights reserved. No part of this publication may be reproduced, stored in a retrieval system, or transmitted in any form or by any means (electronic, mechanical, photocopying, recording, generative artificial intelligence [AI] training, or otherwise) without prior written consent. Contact University of Alberta Press for further details.

University of Alberta Press supports copyright. Copyright fuels creativity, encourages diverse voices, promotes free speech, and creates a vibrant culture. Thank you for buying an authorized edition of this book and for complying with the copyright laws by not reproducing, scanning, or distributing any part of it in any form without permission. You are supporting writers and allowing University of Alberta Press to continue to publish books for every reader.

This book has been published with the help of a grant from the Federation for the Humanities and Social Sciences, through the Awards to Scholarly Publications Program, using funds provided by the Social Sciences and Humanities Research Council of Canada.

University of Alberta Press gratefully acknowledges the support received for its publishing program from the Government of Canada, the Canada Council for the Arts, and the Government of Alberta through the Alberta Media Fund.

Canada,
the Métis,
and a
Resistant
Hero

The Riel Problem

ALBERT BRAZ

UNIVERSITY *of* **ALBERTA** PRESS

Published by

University of Alberta Press
1-16 Rutherford Library South
11204 89 Avenue NW
Edmonton, Alberta, Canada T6G 2J4
amiskwaciwâskahikan | Treaty 6 |
Métis Territory
ualbertapress.ca | uapress@ualberta.ca

Copyright © 2024 Albert Braz

LIBRARY AND ARCHIVES CANADA
CATALOGUING IN PUBLICATION

Title: The Riel problem : Canada, the Métis, and a resistant hero / Albert Braz.
Names: Braz, Albert, 1957- author.
Description: Includes bibliographical references and index.
Identifiers: Canadiana (print) 20230551513 | Canadiana (ebook) 20230551661 | ISBN 9781772127331 (softcover) | ISBN 9781772127485 (EPUB) | ISBN 9781772127492 (PDF)
Subjects: LCSH: Riel, Louis, 1844-1885. | LCSH: Métis—History. | LCSH: Métis—Prairie Provinces—Biography. | LCSH: Métis—Historiography. | LCSH: Canada—History. | LCSH: Canada—Historiography.
Classification: LCC FC3217.1.R53 B73 2024 | DDC 971.05/1092—dc23

First edition, first printing, 2024.
First printed and bound in Canada by Houghton Boston Printers, Saskatoon, Saskatchewan.
Copyediting and proofreading by Alicia Hibbert.
Indexing by Adrian Mather.
Map by Eric Leinberger.

All rights reserved. No part of this publication may be reproduced, stored in a retrieval system, or transmitted in any form or by any means (electronic, mechanical, photocopying, recording, generative artificial intelligence [AI] training, or otherwise) without prior written consent. Contact University of Alberta Press for further details.

University of Alberta Press supports copyright. Copyright fuels creativity, encourages diverse voices, promotes free speech, and creates a vibrant culture. Thank you for buying an authorized edition of this book and for complying with the copyright laws by not reproducing, scanning, or distributing any part of it in any form without permission. You are supporting writers and allowing University of Alberta Press to continue to publish books for every reader.

This book has been published with the help of a grant from the Federation for the Humanities and Social Sciences, through the Awards to Scholarly Publications Program, using funds provided by the Social Sciences and Humanities Research Council of Canada.

University of Alberta Press gratefully acknowledges the support received for its publishing program from the Government of Canada, the Canada Council for the Arts, and the Government of Alberta through the Alberta Media Fund.

For my parents

God curse them, Louis. They will regret this!

Regret hanging you

    —MARILYN DUMONT, *The Pemmican Eaters*

Contents

Preface xi

Map xv

Introduction xvii
The National Metamorphosis of Louis Riel

1 | I, the Prophet 1
Riel's Image and His Self-Fashioning

2 | The Precursors 39
John Coulter, Joseph Kinsey Howard, and the New Riel

3 | Singing *Louis Riel* 73
The Centennial Quest for Representative Canadian Heroes

4 | The Bard's Apocryphal Song 99
Rudy Wiebe, Pierre Falcon, and Riel

5 | Consecrating Canada's Icon 127
The Projet Riel Project

6 | The Naked Martyr 155
Sculpture and the Shifting Image of Riel

7 | The Problematic Patriot 181
Chester Brown's Louis Riel *and Canadian Nationalism*

8 | Confronting the Hero 201
Contemporary Métis Engagements with Riel

Conclusion 241
Louis Riel in the Twenty-First Century

Appendix 255
Variations on the "Riel" Artistic Prophecy

Works Cited 257

Index 291

Preface

The Riel Problem: Canada, the Métis, and a Resistant Hero builds on my 2003 book *The False Traitor: Louis Riel in Canadian Culture*. In that earlier monograph, a comprehensive survey of the cultural representations of Riel, I endeavoured to cover the totality of the discourse on him from the 1860s to the end of the twentieth century. I showed that he has such a multifaceted image that he has been portrayed variously as a traitor to Canada, a Franco-Catholic martyr, an Indigenous hero, a deluded mystic, a Prairie political maverick, and a Father of Confederation. In contrast, *The Riel Problem* focuses just on his Canadianization, mostly since the Centennial in 1967, and on the attempt by contemporary Métis to claim Riel as a strictly Indigenous hero—two developments that are often resisted by his writings. From the outset, it is implicit that historical truth is highly unstable, as illustrated by the fact that someone hanged as a traitor by a country can be transformed into a hero by that country. For the same reason, no current scholarly consensus exists on Riel's place in Canadian history. Throughout my study, I strive to show how Riel viewed himself and the world, particularly Canada and the Métis, and I analyze cultural and academic celebrations of him as a Canadian or Métis hero in light of his poetry and prose, which I examine in detail.

Because of historical fluidity, nomenclature can pose a challenge in a work like this one. Riel is best known for his role in two political-military conflicts between the Métis and Canada at Red River in 1869–1870 and at Batoche in 1885, both having borne a series of negative monikers such as *rebellion* or *uprising*. Given that, at the time Canada had no title to Red River, the event has become generally known as the *Red River Resistance*, a practice I follow. The 1885 clash is now also frequently called the North-West Resistance. However, there is a critical legal-political difference between the two conflicts in that, by 1885, Canada had stewardship of the territory. As well, Riel never questioned the constitutional legitimacy of the United States, which, like Canada, is a settler state. Consequently, I will use the less judgmental *North-West War* to describe the second confrontation between Riel and Canada. In addition, Québec has been called New France, Lower Canada, and Canada East, whereas Ontario has been known as Upper Canada and Canada West. For the sake of simplicity, I usually refer to the two as Québec and Ontario. I also continue to employ the term Halfbreed(s), despite its having become increasingly problematic. My justification is that in the nineteenth century, Métis and Halfbreed referred to two distinct communities or peoples, reflected in the fact that the two movements led by Riel were mainly composed of French-speaking Métis. No less important, some descendants of the historical Halfbreeds feel that they have been unwittingly absorbed under the umbrella term *Métis*, erasing their own history, not the least their relationship with English-speaking Canada. I should also note that the posthumous Canadianization of Riel is largely an English-speaking project. For ethnocultural and religious reasons, Québec historically tended to be sympathetic to Riel, viewing him as a victim of Anglo-Protestant bigotry. Unsurprisingly, it has not been invested in the acclamation of the Métis leader as a pan-Canadian hero.

| Although this book is my sole responsibility, it has benefited tremendously from the assistance of family, friends, and even complete strangers. I am grateful to Paul D. Morris and Tracy Ware for reading individual chapters and to Matthew Tétreault for reading the whole manuscript. During my academic career, I profited from the numerous discussions I had with colleagues and students about Riel and his place in both Canadian and Métis culture. This is especially true of the interactions I was privileged to have while

supervising three PHD dissertations on the Métis by Katherine Durnin, Danielle Monica Lamb, and Matthew Tétreault. I also wish to express my thanks to the staff at the University of Alberta Press, notably Acquisitions Editor Michelle Lobkowicz, for her unstinting support of my project. Similarly, I am much obliged to Karen Nugent and Timothy Long for an invaluable guided viewing of John Nugent's Riel sculptures housed in the vaults of the MacKenzie Art Gallery; to the University of Regina Archives and Special Collections for scanning their holdings on John Nugent for me; and to the University of Calgary Rare Books and Special Collections Librarian Annie Murray for inviting me to attend the reception for her exhibition "Devotion: Louis Riel Writes Home." In addition, I am extremely grateful for the unanticipated contributions made by two anonymous reviewers who not only did close readings of my manuscript but also generously suggested ways to improve it. One provided me with insights on how to expand my analysis of the musical elements in the Centennial opera, an area that is outside my field of expertise. The other showed that my book demanded a more explicit focus on the way Riel's writings trouble not only his Canadianization but also the attempts by Métis writers, visual writers, and scholars to portray him as a champion of pan-Indigenous rights. To both individuals, I am deeply indebted.

As usual, this book would not have been possible without the support of my family. To begin with, I wish to thank my wife and first auditor, the biologist Carolyn Kapron, who has been compelled to share my interest in Riel for over three decades. Likewise, I would like to thank our children Jon and Ali, their partners, and the indispensable Penny. Finally, I would like to express my boundless gratitude to two people whose conduct and love have always been an inspiration: my parents, João Braz and Rosa Raimundo Braz. *Muito obrigado, mãe; muito obrigado, pai.*

An early version of the second part of chapter 1 appeared in my 2020 article (Braz, "The Continentalist Classic"). Chapter 2 is a much-revised version of a book chapter bearing the same title (Braz, "Singing Louis Riel"). An earlier version of chapter 4 appeared in the *Journal of Canadian Studies* (Braz, "Consecrating Canada's Icon"). Parts of chapter 7 appeared under the same title, "The Problematic Patriot: Chester Brown's *Louis Riel* and Canadian Nationalism," in *De Pierre-Esprit Radisson à Louis Riel: voyageurs et métis / From Pierre-Esprit Radisson to Louis Riel: Voyageurs and Métis* (Braz, "The Problematic Patriot"). I would like to express my sincere thanks to the respective editors and publishers. I wish as well to thank Marilyn Dumont for authorizing me to use as my epigraph part of her poem "Our Prince"; Karen Nugent and the MacKenzie Art Gallery for giving me permission to reproduce photographs of two John Nugent sculptures; and David Garneau for allowing me to include reproductions of two of his paintings. Finally, I thank the Awards to Scholarly Publications Program of the Federation for the Humanities and Social Sciences for awarding my monograph a Publication Grant.

Map

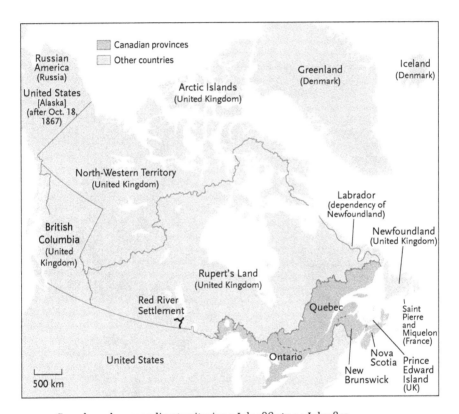

Canada and surrounding territories, 1 July 1867 to 14 July 1870.

Introduction
The National Metamorphosis of Louis Riel

> *Forgetting, I would even say historical error, is essential to the creation of a nation.*
> —ERNEST RENAN, *Qu'est-ce qu'une nation? / What Is a Nation?*

THE MOST PARADOXICAL ASPECT of nationalism is arguably the way it can transform former enemies into compatriots. Over time, individuals who had battled a given country are turned into icons of the very polity they opposed and that vanquished them. This is what has happened to Louis Riel in Canada. After having been hanged for high treason by the Canadian state in 1885, the Métis political leader, poet, and mystic has emerged as nothing less than the quintessential Canadian hero. For decades after his death, Riel was perceived by most Canadians as either demented or a rebel, when he was discussed at all. But his image started to change after the Second World War, and by the late 1960s, he had become one of the most popular figures in Canadian culture, easily eclipsing the country's founding prime minister and his nemesis, Sir John A. Macdonald. Riel has been the subject of endless poems, novels, films, sculptures, and even a world-class opera (Braz, *False Traitor*).

This book maps out his national metamorphosis from a wicked foe of Canada to the epitome of Canadianness. It does so mainly by examining a series of watershed cultural and scholarly commemorations of Riel since 1967, from a large-scale opera about his life, through his published extant writings, to several statues in his honour. In the process, it shows that a country's conversion of a former enemy into a national icon is never innocent. At the least, it requires that the country efface its earlier defenders or caricature them for their now ostensibly anachronistic worldviews. To further complicate matters, the new hero's writings may resist the fraternal embrace, as may the hero's ethnonational progeny. This is what has transpired in Canada, as contemporary Métis writers, visual artists, and scholars pointedly ask what was the nation (and nationalism) championed by Riel. Yet, while exposing the constructedness of the Canadian nation-state and the magnitude of the current Canadian historical revisionism when dealing with Riel, today's Métis artists and intellectuals reveal much discomfort about the politics of their historical leader. As I will show particularly in the later part of the book, through his writings, Riel can be as much of a problem for Métis as for Canadians in general.

The selective fashioning of a national past is neither a new phenomenon nor restricted to Canada. Nation-building is necessarily an exercise in myth-making, and historical truth is just one of its many casualties. As the French historian Ernest Renan posited in his seminal 1882 lecture on nationhood, "Forgetting, I would even say historical error, is essential to the creation of a nation, which is why the advance of historical study often poses a threat to nationality" (19). Speaking of his own country, only three years before Riel's death, Renan remarked that in order to adopt the idea of collective oneness, "every French citizen must have forgotten the Saint Barthélemy massacre [of 1572] or the massacres of the Midi in the thirteenth century" (21), both reminders of the cultural and religious heterogeneity that France did not allow to flourish within its borders. The theoretician of nationalism Benedict Anderson underlines that such amnesia is what enables military conflicts between enemies to be transmuted into "reassuringly fratricidal wars" between compatriots, blotting out both killers and killed (200). This is what has occurred in the Canadian response to Riel, who has gone from being condemned as an "apostle of insurrection and unrest" in the 1880s (Collins 5) to being extolled as someone who is "first and foremost a patriotic Canadian" in the 1970s (Charlebois 9). By 2010, even such an eminent figure as the then Chief Justice of the Supreme Court of Canada, Beverley McLachlin, could declare that "Riel fought against Canada in the name of values that Canada now proudly embraces: respect and accommodation for pluralism" (11; see also Reid 224). That is, Confederation's one-time scourge not only has been incorporated into the Canadian family but somehow personifies the truest of Canadian values, principles that the country's founders presumably did not share. The complication with this reversal is that, unlike the Albigenses and France's other erstwhile enemies, the Métis have not vanished. On the contrary, the Métis—and Indigenous people as a whole—have a much greater presence in today's Canada than they have ever had since 1867. Moreover, some of them are now contesting Canada's right to claim their historical leader as its own (Gaudry, "Métis-ization"), a development that perhaps should have been anticipated by Riel's contemporary Canadian advocates.

Louis Riel was born to a French-speaking and devoutly Catholic Métis family in 1844 in what is now the Winnipeg neighbourhood of St. Boniface, which was then part of the Red River Settlement, itself administered by the London-based Hudson's Bay Company (HBC), along with the rest of Rupert's Land. He grew up in the adjacent village of St. Vital and received his primary education in St. Boniface, the future Catholic Mother Church of Western Canada. After training for the priesthood in Montréal (Stanley, *Louis Riel* 21–30), Riel first gained prominence when he led the Métis opposition to Canada's acquisition of what would become the Canadian Prairies (and much of the North) during the Red River Resistance of 1869–1870. Although Riel and the Métis were overwhelmed by the Canadian forces, he was instrumental in bringing Manitoba into Confederation. But his reputation was besmirched by his sanctioning of the execution of an obscure Protestant Anglo-Canadian expansionist named Thomas Scott, chiefly for impudence (Bumsted, *Thomas Scott's Body* 208–09). Because of the events at Red River, Riel was banished from Canada for five years and fled into exile in the United States. While visiting Washington, DC, late in 1875, he experienced an epiphany during Mass at St. Patrick's Catholic Church and became convinced that God had anointed him the Prophet of the New World, among whose tasks was to relocate the Holy See from the Vatican to his hometown of St. Vital. Except for his surreptitious internment in two Québec mental hospitals in the late 1870s (Flanagan, *Louis "David" Riel* 62–76), Riel would remain south of the border, even becoming a citizen of the United States in 1883. He was working as a schoolteacher at a Jesuit mission in Montana Territory in 1884 when a delegation from the Saskatchewan Valley, headed by the legendary Métis buffalo hunter Gabriel Dumont, invited him to help them prepare their myriad grievances against the federal government. Riel accepted the entreaty and travelled north with his wife and their two young children, a fateful journey that culminated in the North-West War of 1885. Following the Métis defeat at Batoche, Riel was subjected to what is widely considered a political trial (Salhany) and was hanged for treason in Regina on November 16 of that year.

Even without broaching the always delicate matter of Riel's mental state, his posthumous Canadianization raises a series of issues. The most daunting of these is Riel's Métis nationalism, which is at the heart of his clashes with Canada. The Métis are a post-contact Indigenous people. Of mixed First Nations and European ancestry, they emerged toward the end of the eighteenth century and came of age as a collectivity in the nineteenth, naming themselves *La Nouvelle Nation*, or the New Nation. There are five pivotal events in their national history: the 1816 Battle of Seven Oaks (*La Grenouillère*), in present-day Winnipeg, when the Métis established their identity as a nation; the 1849 Guillaume Sayer affair which challenged the HBC's monopoly on trading furs, and in which Riel's father played a key role; the 1851 Battle of the Grand Coteau, in today's North Dakota, in which they attained dominance of the prairie buffalo hunt; the Red River Resistance of 1869–1870, also around Winnipeg, where they consolidated their sense of nationhood; and the 1885 North-West War, in what is now north-central

Riel at approximately age fourteen, soon after he arrived in Montréal.
(Photo by Joseph-Napoléon Laprés and Jules Renaud Lavergne, 1858, University of Manitoba Archives and Special Collections).

The defendant Riel addressing the jury at his Regina treason trial in 1885.
(Photo by Oliver B. Buell, Library and Archives Canada.)

Saskatchewan, which marked the beginning of the end of their dream of living as an autonomous people.

There is another event that perhaps should be considered paramount in Métis history, specifically when it comes to their legal status. In the *Constitution Act, 1982*, Canada proclaimed that its Aboriginal peoples include "the Indian, Inuit and Métis" (Canada, "Section 35"), making it the first country in the world to recognize "a mixed-people as 'Aboriginal'" (Teillet, "Winds of Change" 61). Among other impacts, Canada's historic acceptance of the Métis as an Indigenous people has led to "an astonishing and demographically improbable" upsurge in the country's Métis population (Andersen, "From Nation" 347, 359). This boom, in turn, has precipitated much contestation as to who really has the right to call oneself Métis (Andersen, "Métis"; Bouchard, Malette, and Marcotte; Dubé 20), with the resurgence of the "born-again brown" (Vermette, *Strangers* 110). What the controversy about who counts as Métis also elucidates is how the Métis have transformed themselves from a predominantly

French-speaking collectivity into an English-speaking one. Similarly, they have drifted away from the Catholicism that once defined them, especially in opposition to their English-speaking and Protestant cousins, the Halfbreeds, whose descendants today are not even allowed to identify "officially" by that name (Dahl 127). But while the Métis may not have a territory of their own, they continue to exhibit a distinct national consciousness, usually linked to Riel.

The Métis, though, were not the sole collectivity with whom Riel identified. Prior to his return to Red River from Montréal in 1868, he perceived himself primarily as a member of the larger French Canadian family. Throughout his life, he also identified strongly with France, whom he considered his "mère" (Riel, *Collected Writings* 2: 118). More surprisingly, Riel had substantial affinities with the United States. He not only maintained that his acquisition of U.S. citizenship had "éffacé" the border between the North-West and the United States (*Collected Writings* 3: 307), but even attempted to persuade U.S. President Grover Cleveland of "the advantage of annexing the Northwest to the great american republic" (3: 187)—although Riel's spelling can be quite idiosyncratic, particularly capitalization, I reproduce his texts as they appear in his *Collected Writings*. In contrast, Riel was rather ambivalent about the First Nations. He also evinced little sympathy toward Canada, underscoring Red River's right not to join the "immense fraud and... dreadfull tyranny" that is the Canadian Confederation (3: 187). Needless to say, the fact Riel did not display much enthusiasm toward Canada has not precluded contemporary Canadian artists, scholars, and politicians from claiming him as one of their own, even if they themselves often betray their awareness of the extent of the revisionism involved.

At the unveiling of a statue of Riel in front of the Saskatchewan Legislature in 1968, Prime Minister Pierre Elliott Trudeau asserted that no other figure in "Canadian history suffered as many reversals of fortune during his life" as did the Métis leader. Trudeau added that, from a Canadian perspective, none of those changes would likely be as decisive as "the reversal of official and public opinion" symbolized by the erection of a monument to "a convicted traitor" on the grounds of a Canadian legislature (109). It was also during his Regina address that Trudeau made his famous pronouncement that "we must never forget that, in the long run, a democracy is judged by the way the majority treats the minority" (110). For Trudeau, Riel's lesson was precisely about the verdict of history—on Canada and Canadians. As he confided to the enormous crowd gathered by Regina's serene Wascana Lake, "How many of us are willing to concede that future historians, in chronicling the events of our lives, may choose to emphasize and applaud the activities, not of the privileged majority, but of some little-known leader of an unpopular minority?" (109). Trudeau seemed to recognize that the Canadian commemorations of Riel are less about him and the Métis people than about Canada, which may explain the frequent interventions by leading Canadian politicians on the Riel question, particularly one of Trudeau's predecessors, Prime Minister Louis St. Laurent.

In 1951, St. Laurent caused a political "storm" when he gave a speech in Battleford, Saskatchewan, one of the sites of the North-West War, in which he praised Riel (W. Mitchell 7). The incident followed a visit to the North-West Mounted Police Museum in Fort Battleford, during which St. Laurent was shocked to find the terms "'rebels' and 'rebellion' splashed all over the place." He complained to the head of the museum, J.D. Herbert, that "the word 'rebellion' was unfortunately chosen to describe the events of 1885" and that it "should be dropped and [the conflict] should be properly referred to as simply an uprising" (qtd. in McCullough 172)—a view that Macdonald came to embrace, arguing that it was "a mere domestic trouble, and ought not to be elevated to the rank of a rebellion" (Macdonald, *Correspondence* 355). In a letter to the minister in charge of the country's historic sites and monuments, the French-speaking and Catholic St. Laurent expanded that "there are a great many Canadians of my race and religion who resent as cowardly the conduct of Sir John A. Macdonald and his government in allowing Riel to be hanged" (qtd. in McCullough 173). Whatever the St. Laurent controversy may say about Riel, it reveals that there are still unresolved issues in Canadian society that are evoked by the

Métis leader and the two military-political conflicts associated with his name. It also highlights the instability of historical truth, as exemplified by official acts of remembering.

The historian Alan McCullough has deftly captured the impact of the embroilments by St. Laurent and other Canadians on the memorialization of Riel, evident in the tentativeness of the title of his article "Parks Canada and the 1885 Rebellion/Uprising/Resistance." In his study of how Parks Canada has interpreted the North-West War since the 1920s, McCullough makes a cogent argument that, regardless of their ostensible authoritativeness, the "bronze plaque texts...have proven surprisingly malleable and subject to change" (162). McCullough is supportive of this trend, since it is a response to regional complaints about misrepresentation and questions the notion that there is a single way of construing historical events. As he concludes, with what appears to be a self-consciously Canadian metaphor but which turns out to be a rather Darwinian one: "The past is not a unitary state but an unstable federation of competing concepts, each with its supporters struggling for their place in the sun" (190). Historical truth, one infers, is whatever the dominant discursive group manages to impose on the rest of the world.

However, not everyone was satisfied with the idea that historical truth—by which I mean an independent analysis of the available evidence—is determined by the volubility of discourse. The justification that St. Laurent provided for having the word rebellion replaced by uprising to describe the 1885 clash was that "the people involved on both sides of the affair were equally interested in the democratic process" (qtd. in McCullough 172). If this is true, the logical deduction is that the fighting was really a war of competing democratic visions. By the end of the last millennium, one person who was not enthralled by the elasticity of the textual content on the plaques at Canada's historic sites was the director general of the National Historic Sites Directorate. Writing in 1997, Christina Cameron was blunt about what she branded the "insidious influence" of political correctness among Parks Canada historians (29). An example she offers to support her stance is from the brochures at Lower Fort Garry, some 30 km north of Winnipeg and of the Red River Métis provisional government's headquarters at Upper Fort Garry. "The 1960 version" of the brochure, observes Cameron, "states that 'the Lower Fort was also "raided" once by Riel and some followers'; by 1969, the text has been modified to indicate that 'Riel himself, with a number of his followers, made a surprise visit to the Fort'" (30). But if Riel's presence at Lower Fort Garry merely constituted a visit, one is tempted to query why this warrants commemoration.

Cameron's critique of the evolution of the interpretation of the events memorialized at Canadian historic sites associated with Riel underlines the challenges of "interpreting the history of a heterogeneous country from a homogeneous national viewpoint" (C. Taylor 3), suggesting that historical truth may not be better served today than it was in the past. As the recent representations of Thomas Scott demonstrate, we do not have more narratives, only different ones (Braz, "Orange Devil" 52). There are also indications that the new status quo entails much-institutionalized forgetting, often accompanied by the outright denigration of early figures from whom many Canadians now wish to distance themselves. Cameron cautions that if today's scholars "have contempt for the work of our predecessors, we breed a climate whereby our contemporaries as well as our successors may have contempt for ours" (34). But there may be another reason why contemporary Canadians should resist indulging in facile denunciations of those who came before, which is that it is a transparently disingenuous exercise. As the historian Desmond Morton quips in his introduction to the transcript of Riel's trial, "To test one's ancestors by one's own wisdom and morality is to emerge a certain winner" ("Introduction" xxix), making one wonder if our collective desire to forget is not linked to the suspicion that we are complicit in that past.

The question of a people's motivation to forget is triggered by the awareness that even events once deemed foundational in a country's history can be consigned to oblivion. In 1985, there were no fewer than four conferences devoted to Riel across Canada, the best known of which took place at the University of Guelph, approximately 100 km west of Toronto. Titled "The Image of Riel in Canadian Culture," the Guelph gathering is notable because it was not only bilingual and included the participation of both scholars and writers but also of actors and singers, who performed excerpts from plays about Riel and the Centennial opera ("*Man They Could Not Hang*" 2; see also Hathorn and Holland i). While commenting on the conference at the time, the University of Guelph English professor Elizabeth Waterston remarked that she found it striking that in "a year in which we could be celebrating the one-hundredth anniversary of the completion of the CPR [Canadian Pacific Railway], celebrating the great visible link that first united us, the focus has been on Riel, someone who represents the potential of all our divisions" (qtd. in "*Man They Could Not Hang*" 1). Waterston, who was born in Montréal in 1922, added that when she was in grade school, she had been taught that "Riel was 'just a rebel'" and she attributed the new respect for the Métis leader to the fact "we understand more now about invisible unities than we did" when she was a girl (2). The implication is that the embrace of Riel over his antagonists is a sign of the growing sophistication of Canadians, a view that the historical record does not necessarily support.

There was one conference on both Riel and the CPR in 1985, but significantly it did not take place in Canada. That year the British Association for Canadian Studies held its annual meeting in Edinburgh on the centenary of the two events. Yet even across the Atlantic, there was little doubt which narrative was on the ascent. As the Alberta poet and novelist Robert Kroetsch noted in his Edinburgh paper, "In 1885 the completion of the railway seemed the dominant narrative, an expression of, as the journalists would have it, the national dream." But a century later, it is "the Riel story [that] has become the stuff of our imaginative life" ("Disunity" 21). Kroetsch elaborated that in a hundred years, the main architect of Confederation, Macdonald, "becomes a failure, even a villain," whereas "Riel, the outcast," is transformed into "the stuff of myth" (23–24). Kroetsch at least pointed to the irony of the development, as if such an outcome is not usually expected. Also, the volume of the discourse on Riel notwithstanding, it is not clear that most

Canadians no longer believe in the centrality of the transcontinental railroad, a project that has been called the new Hudson's Bay Company (Stanley, "Louis Riel" 17) and which, like "most other transportation systems" in Canada, supposedly "followed routes already blazed by Metis pioneers" (H. Daniels 4).

The contributions of various prime ministers to the debate on Riel's place in Canadian history and culture intimate that some nineteenth-century visions of Canada coexist with more recent ones. In the mid-1970s, John Diefenbaker had no qualms about broadcasting that he believed Riel was "not...a martyr" and had "been built up as a hero in consequence of publicity and politics" (26). An unabashed admirer of Dumont, whom he considered "a military genius" and "a military strategist of the highest quality" (26), Diefenbaker did not think so highly of Dumont's political leader. According to the Member of Parliament for Prince Albert, Riel "hanged himself" at his trial, despite having "the best of lawyers." By insisting on addressing the court, against the supplications of his counsel, Riel provided "the most powerful refutation of his insanity" (27; see also Salhany 206). In the early 1990s, Joe Clark justified his involvement in the campaign to have Riel declared a founder of Manitoba and a father of Confederation by stressing the need for Canadians "to demonstrate respect for aboriginal people" (81). Yet, in the mid-1990s, while a member of the opposition Reform Party, Stephen Harper made a methodical case as to why Riel did not merit to have his conviction for treason revoked. After identifying Riel as "the greatest leader ever produced by the Metis," the future prime minister enumerated his copious "tragic flaws." Among these was "his monumental vanity," which led Riel to style himself as the David of the New World and to have the Batoche Council vote him "their official prophet with a right 'to direct the priests'" (Canada, *House* 5454). More germane, Harper charged that "Riel encouraged his followers to rebel against the crown"; that he had "mixed" motives for fomenting the North-West War, being ready to give up the struggle if Ottawa agreed to "pay him a large sum of money" (5454); that he turned to violence after learning the federal government had begun to address "the real grievances of the local people," which threatened "his own future as a political leader"; and that "Riel got a fair trial within the context of his own time and place" (5454, 5455). For Harper, there were no grounds for revising history by rescinding his conviction.

Riel evokes conflicting responses not only from different people, but sometimes from the same person. In the very paragraph in which Diefenbaker states that Riel refuted his insanity during his trial, unaware of the contradiction, he also affirms that "Riel was insane" (27; see also Deane 23, 222). No less compelling than the fact Canadians remain divided about Riel is that we are so captivated by him. In *The False Traitor: Louis Riel in Canadian Culture*, I suggested that the fascination with Riel, at least by Canadians of European descent, may be due to his ethnocultural background, which enables him to serve as "the ideal human bridge between Euro-Canadians and not just the First Nations but Canada itself" (203). My view clashes with the position held by the organizers of the Guelph conference, Ramon Hathorn and Patrick Holland, who contend that Riel does not "occupy" the role that one would expect of him "as bridge, as mediator," but that it is "this failure... that gives him continuing life while historians and creative writers alike search for Riel's fixed 'middle' place" (v–vi). But there may be a more pragmatic explanation for the Métis leader's appeal to non-Indigenous Canadians, which is that so little cost is exacted by the reclamations of historical figures. The anarchist thinker (and anti-nationalist) George Woodcock was suspicious of the motivation for the Canadianization of Riel. Writing in the early 1980s, he claimed that "such official tributes often seem to have the facility and falseness of belated amends to the past that can be made at no cost to the present." The reason for Woodcock's skepticism was that he felt "the condition of the Métis people has not changed materially as a result of this shift in national mythology" ("Prairie Writers" 94, 95). It is worth bearing in mind that it was not in the unenlightened nineteenth century, but well into the twenty-first, that Indigenous Canadians accounted for nearly a third of all inmates in the country's prisons, although they comprise only four percent of the population (Malakieh). Among women, the situation is even more dismal, with Indigenous women making up "half of the female population in federal penitentiaries" (White). Considering that the Truth and Reconciliation Commission concluded that "the relationship between the federal government and Aboriginal peoples is deteriorating" (Truth and Reconciliation, *Final Report* 8), and that there is still a hidden "fear" of Indigenous people among the general populace (Cariou, *Lake* 102), the popularity of the reclamations of Riel suggests that we are more comfortable addressing national inequities and transgressions in the past than in the present.

The political scientist Anthony Marx writes that, contrary to the common perception, much of the power of nationalism does not reside in the fact it imagines a group of people as a "community of inclusion" but rather of "exclusion," a divide "encouraged or enforced to serve the explicit requirements for solidifying core loyalty to the nation" (21). That is, nationalism is a less utopian concept than its proponents boast, necessitating that members of an ethnonational group imagine themselves as incompatible with their neighbours. This is especially true of large countries like Canada, where geographic and cultural diversity is bound to accentuate a polity's lack of cohesiveness. Thus, political figures have "learned that exclusion of a group could serve to unify and cohere a sufficient core constituency to preserve the state and make it governable" (74). Or as the literary scholar Jonathan Kertzer writes, "If the easiest way to love one's country is to hate the stranger within the gates, then an alien presence must continually be found and feared in order to defend national purity" (*Worrying* 171–72). Nationalism, though, is an extremely fluid force and, through history, polities can reconfigure themselves in radically different ways. The example of Riel and the Métis illustrates not only how oppositional political figures and ethnocultural groups can be integrated into the collectivity that battled them in order to enable that collectivity to fashion its own identity but also how their presumed values can be appropriated by the victorious side. More startling, a nation's historical defenders can be othered by their own descendants. As Prime Minister Justin Trudeau declared on the anniversary of Riel's death in 2021, thanks to his struggle for "equality, social justice, and minority language rights," Riel has "left a lasting impact on Confederation and paved the way for a more inclusive country" ("Statement"), raising the question of what the Canada for which Riel's opponents fought stood for and what has happened to it.

These are among the central issues explored in *The Riel Problem: Canada, the Métis, and a Resistant Hero*. Chapter 1, "I, the Prophet: Riel's Image and His Self-Fashioning," attempts to situate Riel in space and time by showing how his writings often complicate the ways he is portrayed. The second chapter, "The Precursors: John Coulter, Joseph Kinsey Howard, and the New Riel," examines the pioneering works by the two authors most responsible for making possible the transformation of the Métis leader from a rebel into a potential Canadian hero. Chapter 3, "Singing *Louis Riel*: The Centennial Quest for Representative Canadian Heroes," traces the Métis leader's national journey from being hanged for treason to becoming the subject of an opera designed to celebrate the country that sacrificed him. The fourth chapter, "The Bard's Apocryphal Song: Rudy Wiebe, Pierre Falcon, and Riel," scrutinizes how an award-winning white writer appropriates Riel as an ancestor in the sketching of a Prairie tradition. Chapter 5, "Consecrating Canada's Icon: The Projet Riel Project," documents and analyzes the history of the monumental bilingual initiative that resulted in the publication of Riel's extant poetry and prose, *The Collected Writings of Louis Riel / Les écrits complets de Louis Riel*. The sixth chapter, "The Naked Martyr: Sculpture and the Shifting Image of Riel," investigates the conflicted struggle to memorialize Riel in stone and concrete. Chapter 7, "The Problematic Patriot: Chester Brown's *Louis Riel* and Canadian Nationalism," dissects the contradictory treatment of the Métis leader in the bestselling graphic memoir. The eighth chapter, "Confronting the Hero: Contemporary Métis Engagements with Riel," probes the contrasting ways in which recent Métis writers, visual artists, and scholars have responded to their historical leader. The book then closes with some reflections on Riel's image in the twenty-first century. In particular, the conclusion ponders the significance of the perplexing ambiguity that permeates so many cultural representations of Riel—an equivocation that is most evident in the reluctance of their creators to peruse his widely available writings, which may be an indirect acknowledgement that they suspect their purported hero resists such interpretations.

1 I, the Prophet
Riel's Image and His Self-Fashioning

> To the end, Riel remained maddeningly ambiguous.
> —THOMAS R. BERGER, "Louis Riel and the New Nation"

ONE OF THE MOST momentous events in the Canadianization of Riel was the publication of his extant poetry and prose, *The Collected Writings of Louis Riel / Les écrits complets de Louis Riel*, under the general editorship of the historian George F.G. Stanley, a name that appears frequently throughout this study. Since the bulk of this collection was not available in print until 1985, the centenary of Riel's death, I will discuss it in chapter 5. Riel did not write an autobiography. Yet several commentators, including two of his editors, have asserted that from his texts readers "can draft their own biography" of the Métis leader (Stanley, "Foreword" xxxii; see also "General Editor's Remarks" 2). One of them, Raymond Huel, actually maintains that what makes Riel's writings so valuable is that they "permit us to fathom his complex personality and character," for through them he "might reveal himself 'tel qu'il est'" ("Introduction" xl, xlix). In this chapter, I will not attempt to produce a biography of Riel. What I will do instead is dissect his writings to show how he perceived himself and the world. More specifically, I will trace and analyze how Riel fashions himself as both a political leader and the Prophet of the New World. I will argue that his career was always a heady mix of politics and religion, albeit the religious component became more pronounced in the later stages, and that his multiple collective identities make it difficult to associate him with a single nationalism, including the Métis one.

Needless to say, it is impossible to reconstruct the life story of another person without moulding it. Even though the primary texts I examine in this chapter were written by Riel, I cannot help but shape them in the process of turning them into a narrative. After all, not only am I a third party, but I am writing almost 140 years after he died—Riel himself would construct a very different autobiography today than he would have during his lifetime. The assembling of a sketch of Riel from his writings is further complicated by the unusually high number of gaps in his story. "Few events inspire more speculation," opines the paleontologist Stephen Jay Gould about Charles Darwin, "than long and unexplained pauses in the activities of famous people" (21). This is definitely true of Riel. Not only have many of the documents he composed likely vanished but he was also prone to long silences, protracted periods during which he does not seem to have written to anyone, including his mother and siblings. In such instances, there is little that one can do beyond identifying the hiatuses and, possibly, speculating about what might account for them. Riel also circulated largely in traditional Franco-Catholic circles across North America, from Red River through Québec to New England, New York, and Washington, DC. Thus, the bulk of his correspondence was with politically and theologically conservative Catholics, which could not help but delimit the nature and range of the topics raised. By necessity, most of the recipients of his letters and poems were also literate. Given that Riel belonged to what was "an oral culture until the beginning of the twentieth century" (Teillet, *North-West* xxii), he may not be very representative of the people he has come to embody. The extent to which the Métis continue to be identified with Riel is underlined by Jean Teillet's 2019 book *The North-West Is Our Mother: The Story of Louis Riel's People, the Métis Nation*, in which the title is taken from a statement made by Riel at his Regina trial and the subtitle categorizes the Métis as his people. The legal scholar Paul L.A.H. Chartrand, likewise, restricts the Métis to "'Riel's people'; 'the new nation'" ("Constitutional Status" 120–24, 128; see also Saunders, "Métis Political Identity"). That said, I will make every effort possible to convey a fair sense of the life of Riel as he depicts it.

While Riel did not produce a full autobiography, he did write some short texts detailing his life. On 17 November 1885, the day after Riel was hanged, the Toronto *Globe* published his "Autobiographical Notes." Just under 1,000 words, and written sometimes in the first person and sometimes in the third, the single-paragraph text covers Riel's life from his birth in St. Boniface in 1844, through his first confession and his Catholic schooling locally with the Grey Nuns and the Christian Brothers and then with the Sulpician Priests at the Collège de Montréal, to the announcement of his prophetic "mission...in writing by the late Archbishop [Ignace] Bourget" in 1875 (*Collected Writings* 3: 264). In addition, Riel conveys his gratitude to his many "kind and generous benefactors," the most notable of whom is Archbishop Alexandre-Antonin Taché, who "never paid a visit to Montreal during my studies without coming and seeing me at the College" (3: 263). He also writes that he left the Collège de Montréal in 1865 and the city the following year and that, after spending two more years living in Minnesota and Dakota Territory, he arrived back in St. Boniface in the summer of 1868. This was just in time to assume the leadership of the predominantly Métis forces that were resisting Canada's acquisition of the Red River Settlement and the rest of Rupert's Land, being "acknowledged and elected President [of the provisional government] by the whole people" (3: 264). Following the arrival of Colonel Garnet Wolseley's troops, with their "threat and determination to fight notwithstanding peace guaranteed by treaty," Riel was forced to flee to the United States. Because of his popularity in the community, over the next few years, he was chosen three times to represent the Conservative Party in the Canadian Parliament. But after being "expelled" from the House of Commons in 1875, he was "banished from British possessions" (3: 264), including Red River.

The *Globe*'s editors introduced "Autobiographical Notes" by stating that, at the request of his confessor Father Alexis André, Riel "had begun writing out a résumé of his life, which was not complete at the time of his death, extending only to 1875" (qtd. in Riel, *Collected Writings* 3: 264). However, there are two earlier drafts of the piece. The first consists of a few sentences, but the second is considerably longer than the version that appeared in the *Globe*—a newspaper founded by the expansionist George Brown and historically not sympathetic to either Catholics or French speakers. Apart from stressing Bourget's announcement "in writing [of] his grand Mission," Riel avows that "God anointed him with his divine gifts and fruits of his Spirit, as prophet of the new world" at St. Patrick's Church in Washington, DC, on 8 December 1875, and that he was committed to two Québec asylums between 1876 and 1878, his "communication with God beeing continual and taken for insanity" (3: 261). Riel also remarks that he "had the great sorrow and misfortune" of losing his father in 1864 (3: 260), when he was nineteen years old and living far away from his family in Montréal. Lastly, he writes that, besides getting married, he had received his "naturalization papers" as a United States citizen in 1883, and the following year, he arrived in Batoche at the invitation of an official Saskatchewan Valley delegation that solicited his assistance (3: 261, 262), carrying his story all the way to 1884.

Presumably, the reason that the version of Riel's "Autobiographical Notes" published in the *Globe* is much shorter than the previous draft is the intervention by Father André. In his editorial comments on the piece, Thomas Flanagan makes the perceptive observation that the text was "probably edited by Father André" in an attempt "to remove anything after 1875, since much of it concerned Riel's religious 'mission'" (Riel, *Collected Writings* 3: 262, 264). But it is not only André, whom Riel had just appointed his literary executor (3: 256), who was guilty of omissions. Riel himself fails to explain why it takes him over two years to make the five-week trip from Montréal to St. Boniface, particularly given that his father had died and his mother was raising her large family on her own. In her biography of Riel, Maggie Siggins rationalizes the delay by stating that "it was necessary for the eldest son and head of the household to earn some hard cash before he returned to the Northwest" and that Riel "may well have been trying to establish himself in business as a trader" (69, 71). But she provides no evidence for these claims, certainly no evidence from Riel. Even more curious, Riel writes that he is not able to live safely in Manitoba at the end of the Red River disturbances partly because "the Ontario Legislature offered to give $1,000 for my capture" (*Collected Writings* 3: 264). Yet he does not say a word about his role in the controversial execution of the Orangeman Thomas Scott, widely perceived as "the great miscalculation" of his political career (Bumsted, *Louis Riel* 225). As well, Riel says nothing about his family, including his being the oldest of eleven children—two of whom died in infancy—or that his father, also named Louis Riel, was a respected Métis farmer and civic leader and his mother, Julie Lagimodière Riel, was the daughter of the Québec voyageur Jean-Baptiste Lagimodière and of Marie-Anne Gaboury, the first white woman to settle in what is now Western Canada (Stanley, *Louis Riel* 1-3, 14-17). He also does not mention that his father played a leading role not only in the free-trade Sayer affair of 1849 but also in the 1859 collusive "kidnapping" of two teacher-nuns after their order recalled them back to Ottawa, so that they would continue to teach at Red River (Eddington 43). Much less does Riel point out that he and his siblings grew up near the Gaboury-Lagimodières and were very close to their maternal grandparents, who were viewed as "Selkirk sympathizers" and "Hudson's Bay Company loyalists" (Siggins 18, 20). In fact, Jean-Baptiste Lagimodière acquired his familial plot of land as "a reward" for undertaking an epic journey on foot to Montréal to warn the Scottish philanthropist and HBC stockholder Thomas Douglas, Lord Selkirk, of the impending attacks on his colonists by the North West Company and its Métis allies during the conflict that led to the Battle of Seven Oaks (Stanley, *Louis Riel* 1).

Still, not the least of the merits of the last two drafts of "Autobiographical Notes" is that they draw attention to two central (if polemical) figures in Riel's life, St. Boniface's Archbishop Taché and Archbishop Bourget of Montréal. It was Taché, while a bishop, who made it possible for Riel and two other Métis boys (Daniel McDougall and Louis Schmidt) to travel to Québec to study for the priesthood. This is a gesture that Riel never forgets, coming to see the prelate as nothing less than "la figure et le portrait de Jésus Christ!" (*Collected Writings* 2: 58). His appreciation entails matters spiritual as well as educational. In a long poem titled "L'Archevêque de Saint Boniface," written in 1884, Riel praises Taché for enabling Métis families to make more "progrès" in thirty or forty years under his guidance than they had in the previous century and for helping many Métis to become educated (*Collected Writings* 4: 345). Taché, affirms Riel, is the fulcrum of the Catholic faith around whom "Métis canadiens et français / Viennent s'amalgamer sans cesse et sans réplique" (4: 346), and is instrumental in helping the Métis become a modern people.

Riel, though, is most grateful for what Taché has done for his most famous pupil, Riel. He declares that he owes everything to the Québec-born cleric, most preciously his writings:

> Si ma poésie est oeuvre de bon poète,
> Je l'offre à votre Grâce, et j'en ai du plaisir,
> Ma langue, Monseigneur, serait presque muette
> Si vous ne m'aviez pas aimé pour me choisir
> Comme vous l'avez fait d'une manière aimable
> Lorsque j'avais douze ans... (*Collected Writings* 4: 352)

There are contemporary scholars who casually allege that "Riel was plucked from his home by a patronizing order of priests and placed in a foreign institution" (LaRocque 83), which is an odd charge to make in light of his familial background and his own testimony. Riel's parents, who were part of the settled Métis class and who both had deep Québec roots, were renowned for their fervent religiosity. His father had briefly studied for the Catholic priesthood, and his mother hesitated to marry because she was intent on becoming a nun (Stanley, *Louis Riel* 2–3). As late as 1885, Riel writes to Taché that the Christian virtues were inculcated into him as an infant by his beloved parents, principally in "le lait dont ma mère m'a nourri" (*Collected Writings* 3: 142). Riel's sister Sara, too, reminds their mother that it was "on your lap that I learned to listen to the voice of God," and thanks her for having "made me a Sister of Charity," or Grey Nun (qtd. in Erickson 119). Sara further interprets her becoming the first Métis missionary nun not just as a personal achievement but as the manifestation of God's "love for our family" (S. Riel 73). This sense of being part of the elect is also evident when Louis thanks Taché for leading him to "le noble pays" of New France and saving him "de l'ignorance / Et des profondeurs de sa nuit..." (*Collected Writings* 4: 352). The reason Riel is so boundlessly beholden to his "Très vénérée Bienfaitrice" Sophie Masson, the Québec patrician Taché had persuaded to pay for part of his education, is that he is aware she had done "la même faveur" to his father (*Collected Writings* 1: 8, 9; see also Braz, *False Traitor* 21).

Judging by Riel's writings, Taché is not the future Métis leader's oppressor but his liberator, his mental emancipator. Furthermore, this emancipation is as much intellectual as spiritual, being effected through writing. As Riel reminds his mentor:

> Mais sans votre protection,
> Sans la brillante instruction
> Dont les prêtres que je vénère
> M'ont fait don sous le toit de leur beau séminaire,
> Ah! sans vos bienfaits, Monseigneur,
> Comment aurais-je pus m'élever à l'honneur
> D'écrire mon nom dans l'histoire? (*Collected Writings* 4: 353)

Riel is explicit that he owes not just his fame but his very voice to Taché. Yet, after he became President of the Red River provisional government and Taché agreed to serve as an emissary for the Canadian government, Riel had no misgivings about placing the bishop under house arrest since "we have to be careful" and "not rush blindly into the hands of any Commissioners" (*Collected Writings* 1: 61; see also Huel, *Archbishop* 108–09). Riel's treatment of Taché undercuts the popular thesis that his "true constituency in 1869 was the Catholic Church" (Ens, "Prologue" 116)—even if a local nun vouched that Riel was manifestly "l'élu de Dieu" to save his country (qtd. in Moissac 215, 223, 228). It also signals that, for the young Métis, gratitude had its limits when it came to matters of state, or when he felt that his power was being threatened.

Riel's relationship with Bourget was more strictly ideological, both men being drawn together by their mutual ultramontanism. Bourget, who was the Bishop of Montréal between 1840 and 1876 and was awarded the honorary title of Archbishop of Marcianopolis upon retiring, was a leading Canadian exponent of the international Catholic movement that opposed the attempts by nation-states to gain supremacy over the Vatican. But unlike most of their counterparts around the world, Québec ultramontanes were nationalists. As Stanley writes, "Confronting an alien authority which wanted to assimilate the French Canadians culturally and religiously, church and nation stood shoulder to shoulder in self-defence" (*Louis Riel* 214). Riel befriended Bourget during his exile years in the mid-1870s, and the "sense of mission" that he developed later was "greatly stimulated" by the Montréal ecclesiastic (216). Indeed, there are many times when even Riel's revelations appear to be subordinate to the written pronouncements by Bourget.

The most important event in Riel's spiritual life, if not his life in general, occurred on 8 December 1875 when God purportedly appeared to him in Washington, DC, and consecrated him the Prophet of the New World. It was on that fateful day in the capital of the United States, Riel writes, that "le Saint Esprit" deigned to take full possession of his heart and his whole being (*Collected Writings* 2: 49). He also notes that since his mystical experience, which occurred on the day Adam and Eve left purgatory (*Collected Writings* 3: 489), the world "me trouve fou" and "se rit de moi" (*Collected Writings* 2: 96, 163; *Collected Writings* 4:140). Like so many other aspects of his life, Riel's views of his mental state are multilayered. On the one hand, Riel asserts that "I have always believed that I was put in the asylum without reason" (*Queen* 316), as people mistook his hypermysticism for mental instability. Yet, on the other hand, he charges that "Les anglais m'ont tant malmené / Que je m'en trouve aliéné" (*Collected Writings* 4: 247). There is no denying that there is a link between Riel's religious visions and the perception that he was at least intermittently afflicted by mental illness. His friends became increasingly troubled by his heterodox claims about Catholic doctrine, to say nothing of his advocacy of "Biblical" practices like incest and nudity, and his disruptive public behaviour. As well, it was his intimates who had Riel incarcerated in Québec mental institutions under the guise that he would receive proper treatment to "rétablir [sa] santé" (Riel, Collected Writings 2: 62). What Riel does not divulge is that his hospitalization may also have been linked to his failure to persuade U.S. President Ulysses S. Grant to help him wrest from Canada's "hands the government of Manitoba and of the Northwest," as his stalwart Franco-American ally Edmond Mallet suggests (Riel, Collected Writings 2: 14; see also Stanley, Louis Riel 222). More perplexing, Riel then proceeds to attempt to establish the authenticity of his prophetic visions, not based on what God imparts to him but on a letter by Bourget.

Bourget's letter became almost a talisman for Riel, "le livre de ma guidance" (Collected Writings 2: 35). As he later apprises the cleric, whom he considers nearly a thousand times "plus saint" than Saint Ignatius of Loyola, he carries the missive above his heart during the day, places it at his bedside at night, and "médite continuellement vos paroles" (2: 355, 35). Written on 14 July 1875—close to five months prior to the epiphany in Saint Patrick's Church—Bourget's letter is extremely vague. It simply assures Riel that God, who has always guided and assisted him, has given him "une mission qu'il vous faudra accomplir en tous points" (Bourget 492). Unsurprisingly, Riel's reliance on a written text for the confirmation of an otherworldly communication was bound to generate complications. When Riel informed Father Frederick Eberschweiler of the contents of the letter, the Montana priest felt that Riel had "pas compris" the text and, as penitence, demanded that he ask Bourget what he had meant (qtd. in Riel, Collected Writings 2: 315). In his response, Bourget attested that, as Riel paraphrases him, "il n'avait jamais cru et qu'il ne croyait pas encore à la mission que j'étais persuadé avoir reçue du ciel" (2: 355). In other words, Bourget avers that Riel has misread him by projecting onto the letter things its author had never written, an assessment that is hard to dispute. As Gilles Martel comments, it would be fascinating to know Riel's "réactions" upon receiving Bourget's clarification and, if he replied to the bishop, what sort of arguments he employed ("Introduction" xxxvi).

Riel's exaltation of Bourget's "mission" letter is intriguing for several reasons. Besides the fact that his reliance on a human for the interpretation of a mystical experience appears unnecessary, it highlights the degree to which he prizes writing; namely, he does not fully trust the spoken word even when it is enunciated by God. Most salient, his fetishization of Bourget's letter reveals the extent to which an oppositional figure like Riel appeals to the authority of the Catholic hierarchy to demonstrate the truth of his claims. This is a phenomenon that is never more conspicuously illustrated than in his account of his adoption of the name David.

The version of Riel's "Autobiographical Notes" that was published in the *Globe* at the end of 1885 opens with the statement: "Louis David Riel [was] born at St. Boniface Oct. 23, 1844" (*Collected Writings* 3: 263). Setting aside the fact that his mother and one of his sisters insisted he was born on October 22 (3: 206), this information is technically incorrect in the sense that David was not part of his birth, or baptismal, name. Riel did not start using the name David until May 1876 (*Collected Writings* 2: 75), the year he would turn thirty-two and months after his Washington mystical experience. He usually also placed "David" in quotation marks, showing that by 1885, even an orthodox priest like Father André accepted Riel's identification with David. As well, this transformation had been quite slow. Unless one accepts the contention by the novelist Joseph Boyden that Riel was "by God baptized David" (54), his adoption of a new name may have been influenced by the example of his sister Sara, the sibling closest in age to him. After suffering a massive hemorrhage late in 1872, Sara Riel attributed her miraculous recovery to her prayers to Marguerite-Marie [Margaret Mary] Alacoque and decided to rename herself after the seventeenth-century French nun and mystic (a devotee of the Sacred Heart of Jesus who had been beatified by the Catholic Church in 1864 and would be canonized as a saint in 1920). Sara was conscious of the symbolism of "bury[ing] my name with my life under the snow," as she wrote to her brother while asking him to no longer address his letters to her as Sister Riel but "Sister Marguerite-Marie" (S. Riel 73, 74). Sara begged Louis not to "be hurt; I have never been ashamed of my name; God knows how dear it is to me" (74). Nevertheless, she stressed that she felt compelled to express her gratitude to God not only for saving her life but for enabling her to become a new person.

Louis's account of his renaming is different from the one associated with his sister but no less dramatic. When Riel travelled to Ottawa to take his seat as a Member of Parliament late in 1873, his associates persuaded him that his "journey must be kept a secret" and he must assume a different name (Stanley, *Louis Riel* 194; see also Riel, *Collected Writings* 2: 44). At his trial, Riel testified that it was his friend the future judge and politician Joseph Dubuc "who gave [him] the name of David" in order for him to be able to travel safely outside Manitoba and for the two of them to correspond (*Queen* 363). It was also for his protection—and that of his allies—that he was hospitalized at Montréal's Longue-Pointe Asylum under the pseudonym Louis R. David, as he would be subsequently at the Beauport Asylum (Charlebois 111). This was an alias that he at first resisted vehemently (Flanagan, *Louis "David" Riel* 67–68), but to which before long he would come to attach much import.

Riel's attitude toward the name David changed drastically over time. In a 20 April 1876 letter to Bourget from Longue-Pointe Asylum, Riel writes, "Ici on veut que je me nomme David" (*Collected Writings* 2: 40), implying that the moniker is being imposed on him by some functionary or functionaries. But by 22 May, after being transferred to the Beauport Asylum, near Québec City, he is signing his name "Louis 'David' Riel," and claiming to be God's "prophète, Pontife infaillible, Prêtre-Roi" (2: 75). Later that year, he writes Taché that during his convalescence he had been counselled to seek the protection of the Holy King David, to whom he promised that one day he would place himself under his "patronage, en prenant son nom" (2: 93). Then in March 1877, Riel asks Taché for permission to "prendre un de mes noms de baptême, le nom David" (2: 105). Yet on the back of the certificate of his marriage to the Montana Métisse Marguerite Monet, which took place in March 1882, there is a note written and signed by Father Joseph Damiani, the priest who officiated at the ceremony: "The name David has been added on the marriage day according [to] the custom of some Catholic Country'" (2: 243). This view is reinforced by Riel in a June 1883 letter to the United States consul in Winnipeg, James Wickes Taylor, to clarify why his Declaration of Intention to become a U.S. citizen "bears the name of Louis Riel" whereas his "naturalization paper bears the name of Louis David Riel." Riel states that the name "David has been added, on the wedding day, according to a custom of some catholic countries, as explains the priest who gave my marriage its Religious and Legal Status" (2: 292, see also 242–43). However, when Riel writes to Bourget in early 1884 to inform him of his marriage, he asserts that he asked the priest who blessed his nuptials if he would permit him to "prendre à cette occasion le surnom de David" (2: 319). In short, his adoption of the name David is not the consequence of some obscure Catholic tradition but Riel's own choice, a choice that, for whatever reason, he finds difficult to own up to.

The equivocation by Riel about his embrace of the name David has strong echoes in his romantic relationships, more precisely, in his explanation of why he marries the Red River-born Marguerite Monet. Excluding his potential relationship with one or two of the Marion sisters of Saint Joseph, Dakota Territory, in 1879 (G. Campbell, "Femmes" 23, 29–30; G. Campbell and Flanagan, "Romantic Interests" 6–8), Riel is known to have been romantically involved with three different women: Marie-Julie Guernon, Évelina Barnabé, and Monet. He met Guernon during his student days at the Collège de Montréal. She was a neighbour of his paternal aunt Lucie Riel Lee and her husband John Lee, and it is surmised the two youths fell in love while he was visiting the Lees. Riel and Guernon went as far as signing a marriage contract in 1866, in which they stipulated that they would not have any "communauté de biens" (Riel, *Collected Writings* 1: 479). But Guernon's parents allegedly disapproved of the match for racial reasons, and the engagement was terminated (Stanley, *Louis Riel* 33). Although there are no extant letters between Riel and Guernon, several of his early poems seem to have been inspired by their relationship. The best known of these, written in the mid-1860s in the voice of a fictional young woman's mother, captures the ethnoracial animosity that might have precluded a union such as theirs:

> Ma fille est trop tranquille
> Pour avoir un bandit
> Elle est bien trop gentille
> Pour vous, sans contredit.
>
> Elle est bien trop gentille
> Pour vous, sans contredit
> Ainsi pour ma Cécile
> Comptez-vous interdit. (4: 19)

The most common assumption is that the Guernons opposed their daughter's marriage to Riel because of his mixed ancestry, a decision that reflects their "pure bigotry" (Siggins 62). But this interpretation is not completely convincing, since the Guernons were friends with the Lees and Lucie Lee was also Métis. It is plausible that the fact Riel was being groomed for the priesthood and not only hailed from distant Red River but had no economic prospects were factors.

Incidentally, the relationship between Riel and Guernon may have produced an offspring. In 2018, during the process of trying to publish their joint article "Louis Riel's Romantic Interests" in the journal *Manitoba History* (now *Prairie History*), Glen Campbell and Thomas Flanagan learned that Riel might have had a "love child" with Guernon, a boy named Léon-Noël-Ernest Guernon (4). An anonymous reviewer for the journal revealed that a member of the Guernon family had informed the Société historique de Saint-Boniface that he and his relatives believe Marie-Julie became pregnant by Riel before he left Montréal in 1866 and later gave birth to the boy. Thanks to the Société historique, Campbell and Flanagan were able to contact current members of the Guernon family, who confirmed the story. After conducting further investigation, the two authors concluded that the theory Riel had a child with Marie-Julie Guernon "has elements of plausibility," in light of his abrupt departure from Montréal and his frequent references to "his 'falls' as a young man" (Flanagan, "Appendix" 11), notably his failing to "step...up to the altar" and become a priest (S. Riel 74). But, in the end, Campbell and Flanagan agreed with their reviewer that the case cannot be resolved until there is conclusive "DNA evidence" (qtd. in "Romantic Interests" 10), and hope that more research will be done on the story.

Riel's second love interest was Évelina Barnabé, the sister of the pastor of the northern New York hamlet of Keeseville, Fabien Barnabé. Father Barnabé, who like his younger sibling hailed from Québec, became one of Riel's great champions, seeing the Métis expatriate as "a devoted friend, a loved brother" (qtd. in Stanley, Louis Riel 198). After Riel was released from the Beauport Asylum in 1878, he spent several months recovering in Keeseville, where Father Barnabé lived with Évelina and their mother. Thanks to Father Barnabé's financial assistance, Riel was able to turn himself into a "cultivateur," growing potatoes and Indian corn on three acres of land that he rented (Riel, Collected Writings 2: 194). Meanwhile, he and Évelina became involved in a very discreet romantic relationship, trading love poems with each other. In one of those poems, Riel writes Évelina that he has asked God to "nous unir" as soon as possible (Collected Writings 4: 214), to which she replies that life moves painfully slowly when she is far from "mon Louis! que j'aime si tendrement" (qtd. in Riel, Collected Writings 4: 216). Riel refers to Évelina as "ma fiancée...ma soeur" (4: 219), and she reciprocates by describing herself as his "intimate friend and little sister" (qtd. in Charlebois 112). More unexpectedly, he reminds her of how the Biblical David's son "Ammon commit l'inceste / Avec sa soeur Thamar" (Collected Writings 4: 213). In the just quoted couplet, Riel appears determined to impress upon his sweetheart that modern people could learn from their Old

Testament antecedents. But before those lines, he cautions Évelina that it takes wisdom for the Christian woman who wishes to serve God to escape the world and its dangers. Even the sanctuary of the family, he underlines, is "souillé / Plus Souvent qu'on le croit, même entre soeur et frère" (4: 213). Given the context, critics have postulated that Riel must be alluding to incest either between him and his sister Sara, aka Sister Marguerite-Marie (Flanagan, *Louis "David" Riel* 93), or between Évelina and her brother Fabien (Siggins 273-74). But since there is no evidence that either pair committed incest, the discussion has never gone beyond speculation. All that can be said with any certitude is that this is a most unusual subject for a love poem.

At some point, Riel and Évelina became secretly engaged. Yet they continued to maintain a considerable degree of formality in their correspondence, addressing each other as "vous," instead of the more intimate "tu." When Riel decided to begin a new life in the western United States, Évelina stayed behind until he could afford to send for her, as she divulges while asking him not to mention their union in the letters he writes to the Barnabés, but to wait until "vos moyens vous permettent de la contracter" (qtd. in Riel, *Collected Writings* 2: 265). Although Riel eventually ceased writing to her, Évelina was not overly concerned. But when she read in a newspaper about his marriage to Monet, she became indignant and sent him a letter demanding if he were "capable d'une telle infamie?" (qtd. in Riel, *Collected Writings* 2: 265). She threatened that if he failed to respond, he would bring upon himself "the greatest curses God can utter, for having destroyed forever the future of one who has only one regret…of having known and loved you" (qtd. in Stanley, *Louis Riel* 239; see also Charlebois 112-13). Riel's reaction was characteristic, admonishing Évelina that she had been the one who wrote him that it would be difficult for her to consent to marry him until he had "un domicile" of his own and the financial means to enable her to "vivre convenablement" (*Collected Writings* 2: 264; see also *Collected Writings* 4: 198-99). Unfortunately, continued Riel, he had not managed to acquire much material wealth, a setback that persuaded him she would find his "pauvreté" discouraging. This is why he stopped his correspondence, since she was apparently expecting "lettres indifférentes" and he was incapable of producing such missives (2: 264). Regarding his marriage to Monet, he closed the letter by stating that his confessor "m'a conseillé de me marier. J'ai retardé pendant quelques temps. Enfin pour lui obéir, je me suis marié; étant très pauvre" (2: 265, see also 450). That is, he married Monet, not because he loved her, but because he was a dutiful Catholic who obediently followed his priest's commands.

Like his prevarication about the source of the name David, Riel's parting letter to Évelina exposes either an extraordinary lack of self-knowledge or a proclivity for self-deception. His own writings demonstrate that his assertion he married Monet because he was advised to do so by a priest is false. In a 9 August 1882 letter to his mother, unearthed after the publication of his *Collected Writings*, Riel informs Julie Riel that he has been "marié depuis plus d'un an" to a young "Métisse canadienne française" originally from Manitoba's White Horse Plains (Letter to J. Riel 279). He adds that he did not have his marriage blessed until March of that year because "par ici nous n'avons pas [l'occasion] de voir le prêtre plus qu'une fois par [an]" (279; see also Riel, *Collected Writings* 2: 254, 255). As well, in a poem about Monet, Riel writes that he lives with his betrothed, "Mais je ne vous ai pas encor / Mariée en face de l'église" (*Collected Writings* 4: 275). If Riel weds Monet country-style months before the act was blessed by a priest, then the priest could not have counselled him to marry. At the most, the priest sanctified what had already been transacted. Therefore, one cannot help but wonder why someone with the mental fortitude to break with a global institution like the Catholic Church is too timid to explain why he wishes to adopt the name David or, more importantly, to inform his fiancée why his economic circumstances do not allow him to marry her, as he had intended.

Even without addressing Riel's disingenuous explanation of why he married Monet, his handling of his breakup with Évelina does not reflect well on him. An otherwise adulatory commentator like Siggins is bewildered that "Riel could be so insensitive,

indeed cruel, to a woman who loved him" (309). His forsaking of
Évelina is puzzling since she is considered his "grande passion"
(Campbell, "Femmes" 29). Politically as much as spiritually, they
shared the same loves and the same hatreds. As Évelina discloses
in her response to one of Riel's letters after he decides to settle in
Montana, she is delighted to learn that "your aim in going out west
was not only to recover your health but also to create an Indian
movement. If it please God that you succeed, don't hold back from
massacres until no more of that infamous [Orange] race remains
in your country" (qtd. in Flanagan, *Louis "David" Riel* 113). Also, his
marriage to Monet, who was sixteen years his junior, does not seem
to have been a meeting of minds. Riel certainly implies that it was
not well received by the people around him, even if it is possible
that the sensitive intellectual misreads ribbing as an insult. In
an 1881 poem, he writes that every guy in the world is allowed to
pursue a love interest. Yet his compatriots begrudge the fact that
he, too, has a girlfriend and mock him:

> Ma nation que j'aime
> S'amuse à m'insulter
> On prend un trouble extrême
> Pour me déconcerter.
> On veut me faire un crime
> De l'amour juste et doux
> de cet amour sublime
> Que Dieu fait naître vous. (*Collected Writings* 4: 273)

As well, there are indications that, at the outset, Riel did not
perceive Monet as his soul mate. In a poem that his editors tentatively date much earlier, but which appears to deal with his marriage,
Riel castigates himself for having "follement pris une femme. / Avant
que de pouvoir la faire subsister" (4: 194), and now because of his
"extrême indigence," his children go hungry (4: 195). He expands
that his wife has succumbed to a deep unhappiness for his "coeur
ne bat plus assez fort pour le sien" and refers to Évelina as his "très
aimable blonde" (4: 196, 198), which suggests that he may not have

been over his earlier relationship. One of his biographers ventures that Évelina "perhaps...intimidated" Riel intellectually and "may have appreciated this fact" (Bumsted, *Louis Riel* 232). Whether or not this is so, it is telling that he kept her letters until the day he died (Stanley, *Louis Riel* 239; see also Charlebois 116; Siggins 308).

What Riel's amorous entanglements also reveal is the downward spiral of his life. For someone who deems education the ultimate symbol of a people's progress, it is hard not to notice how Riel goes from being romantically involved with the urbanite Marie-Julie Guernon, through nearly marrying the educated sister of a priest, Évelina Barnabé, to wedding the illiterate daughter of a buffalo hunter, Marguerite Monet—or "Margarita Monete," as her name is Hispanicized in their marriage certificate (Charlebois 117; see also Riel, *Collected Writings* 2: 242). Interestingly, it is only during his Montana years, starting when he is already in his mid-thirties, that Riel becomes involved in the traditional life of the Métis. Siggins even attributes his heartless treatment of Évelina to his having "become absorbed in the culture of the Montana buffalo hunter" (309). This is a peculiar argument, given how Siggins portrays the behaviour of Riel's maternal grandfather, Jean-Baptiste Lagimodière, toward his wife. Siggins writes that after Marie-Anne Gaboury arrived in the North-West from Québec, she discovered not only that her husband had three daughters with a Cree woman but also that his "country wife" lived in the area. Siggins describes Lagimodière's actions as "unnecessarily insensitive and cruel" (7), which are almost the same words she uses to characterize Riel's breakup with Évelina (309). So Riel's conduct toward his Keeseville paramour may be less the result of his brief exposure to the lifestyle of the buffalo hunter than a continuation of a male family tradition. In any case, there is no escaping the impression of how unenviable his socioeconomic circumstances are in Montana, where, as Riel confides to his mother, he remains "toujours pauvre mais pas plus découragé qu'avant" (Letter to J. Riel 279; see also *Collected Writings* 2: 313, 327). His impecuniousness, even after becoming a school teacher, may also account for his enthusiastic response to the 1884 invitation to travel north to Batoche.

In light of Riel's iconic image as the quintessential Métis or Canadian hero, another unanticipated aspect of his self-construction in his writings is his articulation of multiple nationalisms. His dominant collective identity is predictably with Red River. Throughout his poetry and prose, Riel writes with much affection about his birthplace and its people, especially the Métis. In his first published text, a 1 February 1870 letter to the editor of the Montréal ultramontane newspaper *Le Nouveau Monde*, Riel establishes his authority to challenge (and ridicule) the claim by the Anglo-Canadian nationalist poet Charles Mair that he knows Red River just by stating, "je suis métis moi" (*Collected Writings* 1: 14). Riel exudes even more pride in being Métis in his celebrated 1870 poem "La Métisse," which the contemporary Manitoba poet Di Brandt calls a "haunting ballad" and whose opening stanza is reproduced here in the English translation by L. Verrault, "Song of the Métis Maiden":

> I am a maid of the small Métis nation
> And with great pride this heritage I share;
> I know that God when He shaped His creation
> Made every race with equal love and care.
> Though the Métis are not many in number,
> Great is the destiny which they command;
> Proud of the hate that the world heaps upon them,
> Yet they have played a great role in this land. (Riel, "Song" 54)

The penultimate line of the French original is exceptionally revealing: "Etre haïs comme ils sont les honore" (*Collected Writings* 4: 88), indicating that Riel believes the Métis associate their glory with being loathed by others. Thus, even after the invasion of his homeland by Protestant Ontario, he remains confident about its future. When Riel is about to go into exile, following his banishment from Canada, he writes his mother that he has just one request to make of the "Métis: rester Métis, devenir plus Métis que jamais!" (*Collected Writings* 1: 467). For him, group solidarity is essential and, if the Métis believe in themselves, they will prevail.

His love of Red River is also perceptible in an 1878 poem that Riel composes about crossing Minnesota, the "pays" adjoining his own. The farther north he travels, he writes, the more joyous he becomes because he can gaze from a close distance at his "patrie / Chérie," Manitoba, which he loves and adores as one does "une épouse. / L'orangiste te tient: mon âme en est jalouse" (*Collected Writings* 4: 221). Riel expands that he has laboured ceaselessly for the province and finds it "encor plus aimable et plus belle" than Solomon found the Queen of Sheba (4: 222). After an absence of five years, he is distressed that it is now in foreign hands and entertains "plans sinistres" that will make "sang clair rougir l'eau" of the Assiniboine and Red rivers (4: 222). He is also concerned that Manitoba no longer has an army. But since he knows that Providence is "maîtresse de tout" (4: 223), he is confident that God will liberate his homeland.

Curiously, in his early writings, Riel expressed little identification with either Red River or the Métis. Until he left Montréal in 1866, his sympathies were primarily with the wider French Canadian world. In three linked epistolary poems that he writes to George-Étienne Cartier, all of which he signs enigmatically as J.B.A. Louis Riel (*Collected Writings* 4: 69, 72, 77), Riel attempts to gain an audience with the railway promoter extraordinaire and soon-to-be Father of Confederation by obsequiously praising him. He imparts to Cartier that he wishes to see him in the top ranks of "nos célébrités," as behooves someone whose political responsibilities have forced him to quit "notre beau Montréal" for Ottawa (4: 70) and who has become "l'honneur des Canadiens français" (4: 71). While noting that he is a nobody, Riel conveys the impression that he and a "noble Canadien" like Cartier belong to the same family (4: 71)—a view he would reverse years later when he brands Cartier a hypocrite and a liar, a practitioner of the "politique anglaise" (4: 127). In "O Québec," written late in 1870 and after the rise and fall of Red River's Métis provisional government, Riel refers to Québec as "Mère Colonie" and to the Métis as your "enfants chéris" (4: 95). As he addresses the province, "O Québec! Malgré toi, jamais notre pays!" (4: 96; see also *Collected Writings*

1: 426). Most stunning, in a December 1869 letter to the Québec notary and poet Eustache Prud'homme, discovered after the publication of *The Collected Writings*, Riel attempts to persuade his former Collège de Montréal schoolmate to migrate to Red River. He emphasizes that not only would Prud'homme make "de l'argent" and render a great service to the Métis, but he would be with his own kind. "Tout ce que je sais," declares Riel, "c'est qu'avant tout Je suis Canadien Français!" (Letter to Prud'homme 266), evoking Cartier's famous poem "Avant tout je suis Canadien," which became "the marching song" during Lower Canada's 1837 Rebellion (Cartier; Wade, *French Canadians* 310). Again, Riel's national family can be rather heterogeneous, comprising distinct collectivities.

Moreover, Riel's Frenchness is not limited to his bonds to the society along the St. Lawrence River, but goes all the way back to the heart of Europe. To know him, Riel writes, people must realize that almost all his "sang vient de la France" (*Collected Writings* 2: 72). He asserts that not only is most of his blood Gallic, but it is royal blood, for through his mother, "Julie de la Gimodière," he is one of the "princes descendants de Louis XI" (*Collected Writings* 3: 209). Or as Riel testifies in one of his poems, his mother is of "race guerrière," possessing "pur sang français" (*Collected Writings* 4: 267, 429). Such ethnocultural (and aristocratic) lineage is evident in the links that Riel establishes among the three societies. He states that as God bestowed on French Canada the task of carrying on France's "belle mission" in the New World, it is now the turn of the Métis to accept "l'héritage" of Lower Canada and continue its heroic work (*Collected Writings* 2: 119, 120). This belief in pan-French exceptionalism sheds some light on Riel's limited identification with the First Nations, including his own ancestors. It also elucidates why Riel spurs the Métis to be "fiers d'être français" and to be "métis-canadiens-français" (2: 301). Along with Catholicism, it is the French language that unifies all three peoples.

Considering the biocultural connections among the Métis, Québec, and France, it is not difficult to understand why Riel would develop "national" feelings toward all of them. But there is no parallel tie when it comes to his other major national affiliation, that with the United States. As mentioned in relation to his adoption of the name David, Riel became a U.S. citizen in 1883 (*Collected Writings* 2: 266–67). Such a step did not have to be imbued with political symbolism, since he was an exile and politically disenfranchised. Yet Riel makes it unequivocal that his U.S. citizenship is critically important to him, perhaps because he had to "swet" for it (*Collected Writings* 4: 305). By the time he arrives in the village of Batoche in the summer of 1884, he describes himself as "an american, of french and half-breed descent" and later states that he speaks as an "aboriginal, as an american" (*Collected Writings* 3: 9, 319). Also, during his treason trial, he challenges the legitimacy of the judicial case against him because of his U.S. citizenship, the fact he has "two countries," in the same way that he has "two hands" and "two sides to [his] head" (*Queen* 357). This is why, throughout the proceedings, he appeals to the United States government to ensure he has a fair trial and to protect him from Canada (Riel, *Collected Writings* 3: 107, 134–35).

More revealing, Riel contends that his taking U.S. citizenship has effaced the border between the North-West and the United States, and he is not speaking metaphorically. As a "citoyen de la République," he wants the United States to erase the international line all the way from Lake Superior to the Pacific Ocean (*Collected Writings* 3: 307), a wish that he says has been transmitted to him by God (3: 312, 349). Riel's admiration for his adopted country is most explicit in his "Memoir on the Indian Question." Written in the early 1880s, the four-part manuscript is a paean to the United States, a "well named" country whose appellation "expresses well the union of our varied and beautiful provinces" (*Collected Writings* 2: 361). For Riel, the United States comprise an amalgamation of the moral contributions of nationalities from around the world and are "essentially progressive and generous. It is why they have spared nothing to play out the difficult problem of slavery; calling away the africans to come and enjoy the great american union" (2: 361–62). Likewise, the United States "are always busy, at sparing magnanimously the Indians and in many cases are trying actively to improve the conditions of their existence" (2: 363). Riel singles out the Republican Party as most deserving to be commended for having "put all races on a perfect footing of equality before the White House" (*Collected Writings* 3: 362). But the country as a whole should be celebrated for its "cause...is the cause of civilization; the cause of humanity itself" (*Collected Writings* 2: 369). Riel has some reservations about the place of the "Mongolian race" in the United States, since as "heathens" and "pagans" its members "have not yet any moral state to present the Union with" (2: 370). Otherwise, just about every ethnonational group is welcome in a country that purportedly transcends the national by incorporating the nations of the world into its identity.

Riel's U.S. nationalism is striking, not the least because the Métis did not enjoy any more rights below the forty-ninth parallel than they did above it. This is also true of Catholics. It is worth noting that one of the principal clauses in Riel's 1875 memorial to President Grant specifies that the Métis-dominated North-West would receive "all the french Canadian and Irish american citizens who would be willing to share our fortune" (*Collected Writings* 2: 7). Riel writes that a northward migration would have such appeal to those two groups because "all over the united States the Irish would long for a province of their own" (2:10, 211–13) and the French Canadians do not have "la quotte-part" of the public jobs to which they are entitled (*Collected Writings* 3: 380). The implication is that, due to their Catholicism, the Irish and French Canadians are not at home in the United States. Yet Riel is grateful that the Divine Essence discloses to him that "le Nord ouest passe aux Etats-Unis" (3: 467) and that God has chosen the United States to "protéger la Nouvelle-France et le nord contre les Pouvoirs qui voudront les gouverner d'une façon malveillante" (3: 493). In view of the ignoble history that Riel documents, one has to wonder what sort of assistance he expects.

What Riel's fiery U.S. nationalism also underlines is his lack of self-identification with Canada, as well as his dissimilar conceptions of the place of the Métis in the two countries. The only plausible explanation for his affability toward the United States is as a counterweight to what he views as an oppressive, if not malevolent, Canada. Riel does not disguise his contempt for both Macdonald and Confederation. He calls the Prime Minister an "homme sans parole" and an "homme vulgaire" (*Collected Writings* 4: 234) and Ottawa that "Ville damnée" (4: 120). Confederation itself is an evil force whose driving ambition is to "détruire" the Métis, and he cautions Macdonald that if he does not treat his "fière race" as it deserves, it will soon part company with Canada (4: 118). For Riel, Canada is the enemy. So he embraces the United States as the defender of the Métis, despite knowing that the Métis have to play a subordinate role in this highly unbalanced relationship. Paradoxically, when dealing with Canada, Riel forcefully asserts his people's collective rights, starting with the right of a colony of not being "forcée à entrer dans la confédération" (*Collected Writings* 1: 106). But when interacting with the United States, he begs for accommodation, like when he petitions the U.S. government to create "a special reservation" in Montana Territory "for the halfbreeds, as, scattered amongst other settlers" (*Collected Writings* 2: 224; see also Pannekoek, *Snug* 3–4). It is as if Riel envisages the Métis as a British North American (but not Canadian) entity, with territorial rights north of the international boundary that they do not have south of it.

Riel's emotional attachment to the United States is perplexing because he is often extremely critical of the country and its values. To begin with, Riel tends to see the United States essentially as an Anglo-Saxon polity, like Great Britain and Canada (*Collected Writings* 3: 440, 494). This is the reason that he contends Washington should support the emigration of its Irish and French Canadian citizens to the North-West, since it would leave its territory "plus exclusivement, plus entièrement aux écossais, à la race Anglo-saxonne du nouveau Monde" (*Collected Writings* 4: 311), what he terms "Pure americans" (*Collected Writings* 2: 307). Also, while praising the United States as the guardian of the Métis and the North-West, he betrays profound discontent about his experiences in the country. As he writes in his Batoche "Journal" of 1884–1885:

Oh my God! Save me from the misfortune of getting involved
with the United States. Let the United States protect us indi-
rectly, spontaneously through an act of Your Holy Providence,
but not through any commitment or agreement on our part.

I used to live wretchedly in the United States among
serpents, amid poisonous vipers. I was so surrounded that
wherever I wished to set foot I saw them teeming. The ground
was crawling with them. The United States are hell for an honest
man. A respectable family is in disrepute there. It is ridiculed,
scoffed at. Oh, what a great misfortune it is to be obliged to
seek refuge in the United States. (*Diaries* 78; see also *Collected
Writings* 3: 404)

Such feelings may explain why, as the date of his hanging
approaches, Riel does not express a desire to be buried in the
United States, not even in Montana's "médicinal" prairie soil
(*Collected Writings* 2: 206). Instead, he entrusts Father André with
the task of having his body transported to St. Boniface (*Collected
Writings* 3: 192). But that request generates some complications of
its own. Riel's wish to be interred in his birthplace is not merely
the result of a longing for Red River but also of his concerns about
his afterlife. In one of his Regina prophecies, he writes that he
must "mourir près de Saint Boniface, pour y ressusciter" (3: 247,
256–57). His hanging thus may not be as terminal as one might
think, merely marking the end of his initial earthly existence.

Riel's nonchalant statement that he will rise from the dead
prompts questions about both his mental state and the nature of
his writings. Beyond acknowledging that people associated his
mystical visions with his purported delusions, Riel rarely conceded
that he may have struggled with mental illness. This is why he
preferred that the Regina court condemn him to death rather than
judge him "insane...a lunatic" (*Queen* 316, 351), a verdict he believed
would delegitimize his cause. The matter of Riel's mental state
continues to trouble Métis, who tend to either downplay it or deny
it outright. His great-grandniece and Indigenous rights lawyer
Jean Teillet, for one, claims both that "Riel's sanity has never been

particularly relevant" for the Métis (*North-West* 7–8) and that "Riel's sanity is a touchy issue," but only because "it is an obsession with Canadian historians" (365, 367). The Manitoba Métis leader David Chartrand goes further and finds proof of Riel's mental balance in his handwriting. As Chartrand remarks upon seeing one of Riel's original manuscripts, "look at the penmanship—it's beautiful. He's not somebody who's mad, or angry or shaken up" (CBC News; see also Saunders 68). By that criterion, one would have to deduce that Riel's one-time hero Cartier was a raving maniac, since "he wrote a shocking hand" (Pope 404).

The sensitivity of Métis elites about Riel's mental state is most discernible in the edict that the Union nationale métisse's Historical Committee issued to the author of its chronicle to "ne pas toucher" its historical leader's "'folie'" (qtd. in Bocquel 268), a subject that will be discussed in more detail in chapter 8. But it is not only Métis who fear that Riel's possible struggle with psychological disorders would taint his fight for Métis rights, as shown by M. Max Hamon's *The Audacity of His Enterprise: Louis Riel and the Métis Nation That Canada Never Was, 1840–1875*. Hamon points out that he ends his 2019 biographical study of Riel ten years before his death in order to "decolonize history," which requires a new periodization (11). He asserts that he does not judge Riel's life after 1875 "an unfortunate postscript" to his success at Red River (12), but his words hint otherwise, and the cause is the matter of Riel's mental stability. Hamon describes the last decade of his subject's life as "a tragic story. Frustrated and perhaps insane, Riel was forced into an asylum [two, actually] by his friends," and the North-West War "appears as a failed spiritual quest for redemption—or, more cynically, the 'madness' of his mission is defeated by modern colonial forces" (11–12). Since the last ten years of Riel's life might undermine his early achievements, reasons Hamon, scholars should pretend that they did not take place.

There is a delectable irony in Hamon's reconstruction of the life of Riel, which is that it follows the same timeline as in his "Autobiographical Notes." It seems that a twenty-first-century "decolonial" historian can be as unsettled by Riel's religious visions as the nineteenth-century Catholic Church. Hamon's rationale for stopping his monograph in 1875 is that, within such a time frame, "Riel makes sense" (*Audacity* 13). The question that one is bound to ask is, to whom does this Riel make sense? It clearly does to Hamon, but does it to the historical Riel? If not, how rigorous is such a project? I can fathom why Hamon might favour the political Riel over the mystical one and conclude that "1875 was climactic in his career as a political leader" (12). But 1875 was also the year in which Riel experienced his transformative Washington epiphany and became convinced that God had anointed him the Prophet of the New World. Even in a study that privileges politics, can one ignore that Riel the political leader is also a mystic? Hamon explains that he decided not to address the North-West conflict because the 1885 events have "cast a shadow on the rest of Riel's life and are an obstacle to our understanding of the complexity of the past" (13). He evidently would not agree with the Métis legal scholar Darren O'Toole that to discern the complexity of Riel, one must examine the totality of his life, not just "those aspects that are comfortable or convenient" (65). So Hamon excises whatever muddles his version of the Riel story. Besides, he is not content to embrace a reduced Riel, positing that all scholars "should not read Riel's spiritual awakening, or madness, back into the years he was at school" (*Audacity* 13; see also Dummitt, "In the Eye" 25–26). Hamon believes not only that the post-1875 Riel is a different person but also that there is no continuity between his later self and his early one, especially when it comes to his mental state.

The problem with Hamon's approach is that there are indications those close to Riel occasionally found his behaviour anomalous since his early adulthood. His uncle John Lee was deeply disturbed by Riel's overemotional despondency after his father's death, an "extraordinary sorrow" that propelled the nineteen-year-old to throw "himself into excesses of piety" (qtd. in Flanagan, *Louis "David" Riel* 13). Lee would witness even more distressing behaviour by Riel. Following what Mallet calls the "failure" of his audience with Grant in December 1875 (qtd. in Martel, "Introduction" xxxiv), Riel had a nervous breakdown.

Unable to provide his guest with the continuous attention he needed, Mallet sought the assistance of a network of supportive French Canadian priests in the eastern United States, a process that eventually took Riel to Father Barnabé in Keeseville. But even in such amiable surroundings, the exile remained out of control. As Siggins relates, Riel was unable to sleep and, day and night, "he cried and howled so horribly that the priest's mother was terrified of him and wouldn't go near him" (257). Father Barnabé had to turn for help to Lee, who soon realized the severity of the situation, listening for hours as "his beloved nephew roared like a bull" (257). Riel kept drawing attention to himself with his bellowing during the train ride to Montréal, which was politically dangerous as his amnesty was conditional on his banishment from Canada until the end of 1879, meaning that he was in the country illegally. The situation did not improve after they reached the Lee residence, and Riel "locked himself in his room, stripped naked and tore all his clothes and bed coverings to shreds" (257), leaving Lee and his wife Lucie little choice but to commit him to a mental hospital. Also, this was already the second time that Riel had a recorded mental breakdown. In late February 1870, the Red River journalist and historian Alexander Begg wrote in his journal that Riel had been "taken very ill...with an attack of brain fever" (321; see also Bumsted, *Reporting* 261). Since the ailment manifested itself less than two weeks before Riel elected not to stop the execution of Scott, one cannot help but speculate if there is a link between the two incidents.

Given that Riel was positive he was utterly rational, he seldom acknowledged any struggles with mental health, even during his internment in Québec asylums. But there are other instances that intimate he may have been afflicted by bouts of mental instability. The most dramatic of these involve his relations with his North-West secretary, Will Jackson, and his family. In the summer of 1882, the Ontario-born William Henry Jackson left his studies at the University of Toronto to join his parents, brother, and sister in Prince Albert, where they had settled two years earlier (D.B. Smith 24). The Liberal Jacksons were militantly antagonistic toward Macdonald and the Conservative Party and, soon after arriving,

Will immersed himself in political agitation. He founded a newssheet called *The Voice of the People* and became the secretary of the newly-formed Settlers' Rights Association, which had been inspired by Riel's actions at Red River (Stanley, *Birth* 301–02). Unusually for the time, Will was a passionate defender of both settler and Indigenous rights, viewing the subjugation of the First Nations as "the crying sin of the white race in America" (qtd. in D.B. Smith 36). He also had long been an admirer of Riel. Therefore, once Will learned that the latter had arrived in the Batoche area in the summer of 1884, he went to meet him. The connection was instantaneous. Will declared himself a disciple of Riel, and the two men became almost inseparable, even if there were missteps.

Presumably because of his friendship with Will, Riel was invited to dinner at the Jackson home the following winter. But the occasion did not go well, as Riel informed his mother, without identifying his hosts. The meat that was served to the visitor was covered with pepper and other condiments, and he was unable to swallow the first bite. Fearing that one of the Jacksons was trying to "empoisonner" him, Riel abruptly got up from the table and refused to sit down again (Riel, *Collected Writings* 3: 98). But Will's sister Cicely provides a more innocuous explanation for the alleged gastronomic attempt on Riel's life. She says that the reason the meat the Jacksons served Riel looked suspect was because of the bitter cold that year (Deane 183–84); the temperature inside the house was so low that "the salt and pepper on the outside did not melt" (D.B. Smith 46), suggesting that Riel could be assailed by both real and imaginary enemies.

Despite such setbacks, Will Jackson remained a staunch believer in Riel's cause and, while serving as the secretary of the Settlers' Rights Association, agreed to become Riel's unofficial secretary. Moreover, Will's affinities with Riel were not just political but also religious. After moving to Batoche, he announced his intention to convert to Catholicism. Will, whose parents were both children of Methodist ministers, imagined himself as a bridge between the English-speaking settlers and the Métis. But if he believed that his conversion would contribute to the reconciliation between the two groups, he made a serious miscalculation. The decision was very poorly received by his parents, who made separate trips to Batoche to appeal to him not to join the Church of Rome—his father's "secret dream" being for the Methodist Church to send missionaries "to convert" the Métis (D.B. Smith 48). But it was all to no avail, as Will persisted with his plan and was baptized into the Catholic faith, adopting the name Joseph—and later calling himself Honoré Jaxon.

Will Jackson's conversion to Catholicism, though, was not the only momentous religious event that occurred at Batoche on the eve of the North-West War. Within weeks of leading Will to enter the Catholic Church, Riel shocked his acolyte by informing him that he was breaking with the Vatican and starting a more ecumenical creed. Will was initially resistant, but eventually "accepted Riel's new religion" (D.B. Smith 58), the Holy Catholic, Apostolic, and Vital Church of the New World (Riel, *Collected Writings* 3: 406). Yet even that did not fully make him a member of the community at Batoche. Riel and his Métis followers became "convinced that he was a lunatic" and arrested him (Siggins 389), but Will never lost faith in Riel. In letters to both his family and the authorities, he continued to express his unconditional support for the Métis leader and his ideas, political as well as religious. After he was sent to prison at Lower Fort Garry, following his acquittal for treason felony for reasons of insanity, he created the first known bust of Riel (D.B. Smith 62; see also the frontispiece of Riel, *Collected Writings* 3). Still, Riel's mercurial treatment of Will Jackson raises serious issues about his own mental state. In response to his father's death, Riel attempted to comfort his mother and siblings by telling them that they should derive solace from the knowledge the family's patriarch was now "au ciel, au moins bien près du ciel." But he then interpreted their loss as a reminder by an omnibenevolent God that here on earth "rien n'est stable" (*Collected Writings* 1: 4). This would seem to be true of humans, such as the self-proclaimed New World decoder of God's prophecies.

Riel's letters to his family document how he might have been psychologically affected by the formidable challenges he faced throughout his life. Not the least daunting of these obstacles were financial. Until the early 1880s, after he moved to Montana, Riel never had a steady source of income. This forced him to rely on the support of his French Canadian friends across North America and his family, especially his mother. One of the most poignant texts produced by Riel is his 9 June 1885 letter from the Regina jail to Julie Riel, which appears to have been the first time he had written to her since returning to Canada a year earlier. Riel reassured his mother that he was well and requested that she propose to his brothers and sisters the family "priez en commun" for him, both mornings and evenings (*Collected Writings* 3: 97). Upon informing her that he left Batoche "en souliers mous" and is in "nu-pieds," he asked her to do him a great favour and send him a hat and shoes, and "quelques schillings," so that he could pay for envelopes and stamps (3: 98). Also, this was only the latest instalment in a pattern of financial dependency that punctuated his life, most recently when he needed "un peu d'argent" to relocate to the western United States (*Collected Writings* 2: 172,178). To the end of his days, the former president of the Red River and North-West provisional governments relied on his widowed mother for the most basic economic needs. This dependence even transcended his death, as his last will enumerated considerable "dettes" to a number of individuals across Canada and the United States, including his father-in-law and Father Barnabé, to whom he owed $250, with interest, since 1878 (*Collected Writings* 3: 228).

By the way, it is in that 9 June 1885 letter that Riel charges that some Saskatchewan personages attempted to kill him by poisoning his food. It is also in the same letter that he confides to Julie Riel that it was neither the Métis nor the Canadian government that precipitated the North-West War. Rather, it was "*des* gens opposés au gouvernement et ennemis de nos droits, qui, on été, à mon avis la principale cause du conflit," as they feared the possibility of an "entente" between the Métis and the government (*Collected Writings* 3: 97). Or as he writes to Prime Minister Macdonald a few weeks later, it is the last two leaders of the Liberal Party that bear "la Grande Responsibilité" for the conflagration (3: 129). Riel, one infers, is the one person who is not at fault for the calamity that unfolded along the South Saskatchewan River. His response is classic Riel, for soon after arriving in Canada the previous summer, he boasted to his brother Joseph and to the husband of his sister Octavie, Louis Lavallée, how dramatically his circumstances had changed since leaving Montana. Whereas not long ago he was a "humble maître d'école" on the distant banks of the Missouri River and no one accepted him in Manitoba's "cercles politiques influents," now everybody wants him in the North-West. Even bankers invite him to their table and "applaudissent avec la foule" (3: 12). But despite exerting such enormous influence over both the masses and the speculating classes in the region, he is simply the victim of malicious forces.

Riel's blaming the Liberal opposition for the 1885 troubles is significant in that it points to his lasting sympathy toward Macdonald's ruling Conservative Party—under whose banner he ran for Parliament three times. His writings show that, even after his imprisonment, Riel anticipated becoming the supreme leader of Confederation. As we have seen, in some of his texts he accepts that he would be hanged for his actions, an event that would be followed by his resurrection. But in other texts, he asserts that he is predestined to be "a happy governor of 50 years—50, 60, 70, 80 years! I die at the age of 92 years" (*Collected Writings* 3: 324). Riel adds that "God revealed to me that I was the highest man in a government which was led by Fear. I was in front. I was the first. God revealed to me that a magnificent and grand career was still open for me. I am the first minister of a great government. I am at the head of the dominion" (3: 323). It is his conviction that he will become "premier Ministre de la Puissance" (3: 330) that leads the jailed prophet to appoint in advance the Commissioner of the Mounted Police, Acheson Gosford Irvine, "gouverneur" of British Columbia—or, as he calls it, "la Colombie Anglaise" (3: 329)—and to recommend that the Mounted Police's Superintendent Richard Burton Deane be chosen the Lieutenant-Governor of Manitoba

(3: 131; see also Deane 189). His belief in his future political success is not surprising, since God assures Riel that he owes his power to "only the influence of His son" and to Riel's own "attentive and constant prayer" (3: 324). But then, at least since 1875, Riel has been aware that it is impossible for him to succeed in his righteous undertakings without an "intervention manifeste du secours de Dieu" (3: 165), explaining his conduct during the North-West troubles.

Besides showing that Riel possesses a personality imbued with religiosity, his writings reveal that this is a religiosity that he at times moulds in unexpected ways. In a subsequent letter to his mother from the Regina jail, written on 1 November, one of the holiest days in the Catholic calendar, All Saints Day or "la Toussaint," Riel bemoans that his "prison est loin" and it is not easy for the two of them to see each other as they would like (*Collected Writings* 3: 220). He further relays to his mother that he cannot thank her enough for having raised him in "la connaissance et le service de Dieu" (3: 221). More fascinating, Riel then asks Julie Riel to bless him as her "fils aîné" (3: 220). But he does not wish to risk that his mother will send him any random benediction that she might think of. Instead, he dictates to her how she should bless him.

Riel's composition of his mother's blessing has at least one precedent. In the summer of 1884, Riel solicited that Saint Albert's Bishop Vital Grandin allow the Métis people to adopt Saint Joseph as their "principal" patron saint and Saint John the Baptist as their secondary one (Le Chevallier, "Aux Prises" 17). Grandin acceded to the request, and the occasion was marked with a "fête patriotique et religieuse," which closed with the bishop blessing and signing a special benediction that Riel "avait écrite de sa main" (17, 18). Riel's All Saints Day plea for his mother's benediction becomes even more compelling since the exchange was not restricted to the two of them. Considering that Julie Riel was illiterate, her letters to her oldest child were usually written by her daughter Henriette (Poitras). This is the case of the exchange regarding the blessing. In an addendum to the letter to his mother, Riel addressed Henriette directly and instructed her on how their mother should respond:

"Si notre Bien-aimée maman veut bien m'accorder la faveur que je lui demande, tu pourras copier les paroles de la bénédiction comme ce-ci: 'Mon fils, je vous bénis afin que Dieu vous exauce dans la prière. Je vous bénis afin que Dieu vous protège. Je vous bénis afin que Dieu soit avec vous dans votre affliction; qu'il vous en delivre; qu'il vous fasse jouir de son salut et qu'il vous accorde une longue suite de jours, si telle est sa volonté sainte'" (Collected Writings 3: 221). After another paragraph of similar content, Riel asked Henriette that she insert into his text the words that their mother "jugera à propos d'ajouter" (3: 222). The following day, he wrote a separate letter to Henriette reminding her to underscore to their mother the urgency with which he needed to obtain her benediction so that he could place it on the altar when Father André came to his cell to say Mass (3: 223). Yet, in his last letter to his mother on 15 November, the eve of his hanging, Riel acknowledged receiving the letter with her "sainte bénédiction" (3: 252), but he said nothing about his role in the composition of the "holy" text.

The extreme religiosity exhibited by Riel also sheds considerable light on his behaviour during the North-West War. Riel offers two explanations for travelling to Batoche in 1884. The first—which he strangely conveys in written English to Gabriel Dumont, who had little knowledge of the language and was illiterate—is that he is going to advise the Saskatchewan Valley Métis and their allies on the "various difficulties" they face dealing with Ottawa (Collected Writings 3: 4). The second is that he intends "to try and get from the Canadian government what they owe me," which is "two hundred and forty acres of land" and "five [other] lots" (3: 37, 4). His motivation for undertaking the northward trek is thus primarily financial and political. Yet the writings that Riel crafts in Saskatchewan, whether composed in the middle of a political-military campaign or a treason trial, are devoted overwhelmingly to mystical prophecies and other religious matters. In other words, there is a major disconnect between Riel's stated goals and his intellectual activities, impelling one to question the depth of his commitment to local issues. Granted, there are political ramifications to his religious views, above all the lack of support by the

Catholic clergy and some Métis, such as his childhood friend and Red River secretary Louis Schmidt. But even Riel could not pretend that the Saskatchewan conflict was at the core religious. He was not hanged for his religious ideas and actions but for his political ones.

One of the difficulties in tracing the evolution of Riel's self-image from his writings, as noted earlier, is the profusion of gaps in his story. Although it is probable that many of the texts he wrote have been lost, Riel could also be quite reticent about a variety of subjects. This is most apparent in his correspondence with his family. We have already seen that by the time he informed his mother he had wedded Marguerite Monet, he had been married for over a year. Then, after he returned to Canada in 1884, he seems to have written to Julie Riel only when he was in desperate need of financial assistance. For extensive periods throughout his life, Riel did not contact either his mother or any of his siblings, generating much anxiety for the whole family about his well-being and even his whereabouts. Riel's periodic non-engagement was most resented by his sister Sara during her missionary work in isolated Île-à-la-Crosse, northern Saskatchewan. As Sara closes a letter from her "land of exile," emphasizing her disappointment in him by writing in block letters: "BEFORE ENDING, LET ME TELL YOU, MY BROTHER, HOW CRUEL, YOUR SILENCE IS TO ME" (S. Riel 74, 75). Perhaps because of his lack of material success, or because of his failure to complete his Montréal studies and become the first Métis Catholic priest, Riel chose not to communicate with his family for long stretches of time. The result is that he did not leave behind texts documenting how he felt about key aspects of his life.

The challenge of understanding Riel through his textual production is further exacerbated by his ingrained ambivalence and his limitations as a writer. Riel is a poet who does not improve stylistically, as his early poems "are more worthy testimonies to his poetic virtues than is the later verse" (G. Campbell, "Introduction," Collected Writings 4: xlv). His defence lawyer, Charles Fitzpatrick, saw proof of Riel's megalomania in his "extraordinary love of power," as expected from "a man that is acting under the insane delusion that he is either a great poet or a god or a king or that he is in direct communication with the Holy Ghost" (*Queen* 296). Riel often avers that he is God's earthly messenger, but he makes no such claims about being a great poet. His writings display rather little interest in aesthetic matters, despite Stephen Cain's sally that "Riel wasn't hung [sic] for treason. He was executed for being a poet and / D'Arcy McGee was jealous" (101). In light of his textual production, Riel is a prophet who writes poetry rather than a poet with prophetic powers. Still, what his self-construction in his writings also shows is that, both culturally and theologically, Riel is a more hybrid First Nations-European figure than many of his contemporary admirers either realize or are willing to accept.

Part of the appeal of Riel to Canadians since the mid-twentieth century is the belief that he embodies an Indigenous way of being in Canada, enabling non-Indigenous Canadians to Indigenize themselves by championing him. Compared to the Scottish-born Macdonald, to say nothing of Thomas Scott and the other Red River Canadian expansionists, Riel is much more grounded in what is now Canadian space, as befits someone among whose aims is "to write 'The New World'" (*Collected Writings* 3: 354). But this does not mean that he is able to escape European paradigms, be they political or religious. For some pundits, like the sociologist Douglas Daniels, the Riel that was hanged by the Canadian state in 1885 strove for nothing less than "to end all churches and have only a highly democratic Christian community on the prairies, without hierarchical structures" (457), a view promulgated by the novelist Rudy Wiebe. Yet, from a different perspective, Riel's revolutionary religion is really a variation of ultramontanism. In his ostensibly egalitarian commonwealth, not only does Riel get to appoint Archbishop Bourget and then Archbishop Taché as the Pope of the New World, but there is no evidence that he even asked either man if he would agree to serve. Regardless of his outward deference toward the Catholic hierarchy, and his insistence that he did not control the Batoche theocratic council, to which he predictably gives a Latin name, the Exovedate, or out of the flock (*Queen*

277–78), Riel is very much first among equals. Riel also argues that the Métis derive their title to the land from their First Nations ancestors. Yet he contends that, when the Hudson's Bay Company was granted the North-West by England, the territory "belonged to france as history shows it" (*Collected Writings* 3: 47). If this is the case, then land title in North America is not necessarily an Indigenous right. Riel's privileging of France's historical ownership of the North-West may simply reflect his well-known Francophilia, including his belief in the righteousness of France's "mission" of evangelizing the New World's Indigenous peoples. But his appreciation of European culture is not restricted to the French. Riel is such an admirer of Christopher Columbus that, in one of his Regina revelations, he relays God's disapproval of the current name of the American continent and God's desire to have it renamed "Belle Colombie," in honour of the "bon chrétien et du grand homme qui l'a découvert" and who has "planté la croix" on its soil (3: 489). Rather than questioning the impact of the Christianization of the Americas, Riel wants to ensure that the Genoese navigator is given credit for his feat. Similarly, in another of his Regina revelations Riel writes that God wants Lake Winnipeg to be renamed "le Lac Ambroise-Dydime," not just to honour his Red River military commander, Ambroise-Dydime Lépine, but to forever efface the lake's "nom profane" (3: 328–29), troubling the notion that Riel personifies an "anti-colonial" alternative to the Canadian nation-state (Bruyneel 727).

In the end, his writings reveal that Riel is an immensely complex but contradictory figure, someone who often articulated conflicting views on a variety of subjects. Even an indefatigable defender of Métis rights like Thomas Berger concedes that, until his last days, "Riel remained maddeningly ambiguous" (52). This is something that is glaring in his attitude toward the British connection, both praising "Dieu qui glorifie / Le règne de Victoria!" (*Collected Writings* 4: 416) and attesting that he "renounce[s] forever all allegiance and fidelity to...Victoria Queen, of...whom I am subject" (*Collected Writings* 2: 220–21). Flanagan, who deems the Métis leader "a poet of considerable ability" ("Introduction," *Diaries* 19), asserts that the key to understanding him is to recognize that his "life was founded on systematic self-deception" (17). Flanagan writes that Riel was driven by the desire to be a leader, "whether in church or state...Yet he could not openly admit his consuming ambition, for his theologically well-trained mind knew that pride was the worst of all sins" (17–18). Without fundamentally disagreeing with Flanagan, I do not believe that Riel's great flaw is always so much self-deception as a lack of self-knowledge. As his poetry and prose demonstrate, Riel could advocate radical breaks with the status quo, yet he frequently needed the validation of authority figures. Robert Kroetsch hints at the nature of this paradox when he remarks that Riel "could imagine unseating the Pope, but hesitated to kill his battlefield enemies" ("Waiting" 3). Not only that, but Riel could also envisage himself as the Prophet of the New World—who ruled over princes of the church like Bourget and Taché—yet he lacked the fortitude or grace to convey to his fiancée Évelina Barnabé why he could not wed her or to apprise his family and spiritual advisors why he acquired the name David. That is, Riel is a David who will stand up to some Goliaths but who can be intimated into a paralyzing silence by the people closest to him.

In terms of Riel's lofty place in the Canadian and Métis pantheons, his self-construction in his writings creates two conundrums. Regarding Canada, it is hard not to notice that Riel has little positive to say about the country that now claims him as a national hero. Even when he identifies as a North American British subject, he is so threatened by the rising Dominion that he keeps beseeching the United States to shelter his people from it. As for the Métis, the dilemma posed by Riel is not a paucity of social identification but the reawakening of a collective past that many contemporary Métis would rather keep buried. With his passionate Catholicism and Eurocentrism, Riel is a constant reminder of the post-contact origins of the Métis people, their being products of the commercial, sociocultural, and sexual intercourse between the First Nations and the invading Europeans. For both Canada and the Métis, the Riel he fashions in his writings constitutes a problem, which is why the two groups usually prefer to imagine a Riel that does not take into account his voluminous poetry and prose, his voice.

The Precursors
John Coulter, Joseph Kinsey Howard, and the New Riel

2

Sachez que Washington est plus proche de nous
Que Londres. Vos voisins sont plus nobles que vous.
—LOUIS RIEL, *Collected Writings* 4

THE YEAR 1967 was a turning point in the memorialization of Riel. Counterintuitively, the one-hundredth anniversary of Canada's Confederation became the impetus for reassessing the role in the country's life of one of its earliest menaces. The most famous work produced that year was the opera *Louis Riel*, with music by the composer Harry Somers and a libretto by the playwrights Mavor Moore and Jacques Languirand. The Centennial was also the catalyst for campaigns to erect statues of the Métis leader in two provincial capitals, Regina and Winnipeg. Moreover, interest in Riel has not waned since. This was most evident when a federal cultural and scholarly funding agency and several universities joined forces to publish his *Collected Writings* in 1985. By 1992, his official rehabilitation appeared complete as the governments of both Canada and Manitoba recognized Riel as a founder of Manitoba. To crown his posthumous triumph, in 2008, Manitoba declared the third Monday in February Louis Riel Day, an honour that no province has bestowed on any prime minister, including John A. Macdonald.

Although the Canadianization of Riel may seem surprising in light of his conviction as "a false traitor" to Canada (*Queen* 3), it did not happen in a void. George Stanley traces the transformation of Riel's image from a heinous agitator to a potential Canadian hero back to the 1930s. He asserts that the publication of his book *The Birth of Western Canada: A History of the Riel Rebellions* (1936), A.S. Morton's *A History of the Canadian West to 1870–71* (1939), and Marcel Giraud's *Le métis canadien: son rôle dans l'histoire des provinces de l'Ouest* (1945)—translated into English as *The Métis in the Canadian West* in 1986—pointed to a more positive conception of Riel. But Stanley readily admits that none of those learned tomes "made much impact upon the general book-buying, or even book-reading public" ("Last Word" 50). This could also be said of Auguste-Henri de Trémaudan's *Histoire de la nation métisse dans l'Ouest canadien* (1936)—translated into English as *Hold High Your Heads (History of the Metis Nation in Western Canada)* in 1982—a Métis-commissioned chronicle that Stanley does not mention. The revival of interest in Riel would not occur until the early 1950s, with the staging of the play *Riel* by John Coulter in 1950 and the publication of Joseph Kinsey Howard's popular history *Strange Empire: A Narrative of the Northwest* in 1952. As pointed out by another leading Riel scholar, Thomas Flanagan, it was probably not an accident that neither author was born in Canada ("Icon" 20).

Canada's "Mythical" Hero: John Coulter's Discovery of Riel

Coulter's entanglement in the Riel story was serendipitous. Born in Belfast in 1888, John Coulter was already an established playwright, magazine editor, and journalist by the time he moved from London to Toronto in 1936. The reason for his relocation was his marriage to the aspiring Canadian poet and short-story writer Olive Clare Primrose, the daughter of the former dean of medicine at the University of Toronto, Alexander Primrose. Coulter was forty-eight years old when he came to Canada, and he did not believe that "anyone can emigrate successfully after their mid-20s" (qtd. in Abley 10). Yet he became determined to contribute to his new land's cultural life, particularly its theatre. Coulter states in his memoir *In My Day* that he desperately "wanted, and repeatedly tried, to write a contemporary Canadian play; but had always been foiled because the dialogue I wrote on one day, thinking it truly imagined in Canadian speech of current idiom, invariably seemed to me the next day to be concocted and false" (260). To circumvent the problem, he decided to focus on some memorable figure from the Canadian past. The idea gained momentum in 1947 when the celebrated British actor-manager Donald Wolfit appeared in Toronto in a touring production of Ben Jonson's seventeenth-century satirical comedy *Volpone*. At a luncheon with other theatre personages, Wolfit approached Coulter about writing "a new Canadian play in which Wolfit would star" in a projected Canadian tour the following year (237). Wolfit was interested in the fur trader Peter Pond, but Coulter persuaded the Englishman to let him search for a more satisfactory candidate. Coulter considered individuals as varied as the one-time Governor of Québec James Murray, the explorer Alexander Mackenzie, and the dogsledder and boxer "Klondike Mike" Mahoney (Garay 285–86), but eventually settled on Riel. Since Wolfit was "manifestly ill-suited" for the role, Coulter never submitted his outline of the play to him (Coulter, *In My Day* 238).

When Coulter arrived in Canada, all he knew about Riel was that he was "a western halfbreed" who "had been hanged as a rebel" (Coulter, *In My Day* 261), but he soon became convinced that the Métis leader was the very embodiment of a "Myth for Canada" (256). Despite the fact that Wolfit would not headline the project, Coulter still resolved to structure the play as an epic drama. Written in the Elizabethan style, Coulter's *Riel* has thirty scenes and over forty speaking parts, "all but three of them men" (258, see also 263). Yet the play was not destined to premiere at some prestigious venue in London, New York, or Dublin, possibly starring a matinée idol like José Ferrer or Anthony Quinn as the author had at times anticipated (254). Instead, it opened on 17 February 1950 on what Coulter describes as the "totally inadequate stage" of the basement theatre of Toronto's Royal Ontario Museum (258). *Riel* was produced by the New Play Society, the first professional theatre company in English-speaking Canada that included domestic plays (Sperdakos 150, 154). The company had been founded in 1946 by Mavor Moore and his mother, the theatre pioneer Dora Mavor

Moore, after whom Canada's most prestigious performing arts awards are named. An advantage of having the play staged in a Canadian city was that Dora Mavor Moore was able to fill the front row with "bemedaled veterans" of the North-West War. One of those former combatants told Coulter afterwards that while he had gone through the conflict, that evening was the first time he ever learned "a goddamn thing about that bastard!" (Coulter, *In My Day* 263), which must have confirmed to the playwright that his subject remained very much alive in Canada.

Riel is divided into two parts, the first dealing with the Red River Resistance of 1869–1870 and the second with the North-West War of 1885—misidentified in the text as having taken place in 1885-1886. The two segments are quite distinct, and the only characters who appear in both are Riel, his "white" mother, and Macdonald. Coulter, who grew up in a pious Protestant family in Belfast during that city's religious riots, vouched that "he was beaten by the Catholics for being a Protestant, and by the Protestants who thought him a Catholic" (Anthony 22). His Northern Ireland background perhaps explains his focus on the religious dimension of the Riel story, which is not exactly unwarranted, given the sectarian divide in Canada at the time between Catholics and Protestants, as well as between English and French speakers. The play opens with a group of Riel supporters waiting at his mother's house for the protagonist to return from one of his "solitary pow-wows with the Almighty" on the plains, something his mother says he does whenever he has an important decision to make (Coulter, *Riel* 1)—a curious observation to make considering that the twenty-something Riel has just returned to Red River after being away for over a decade. During Riel's absence, an anonymous Priest asks an Irish-born member of the Red River Council named (William) O'Donoghue to "help...restrain this madness" of trying to stop a Canadian survey party, but O'Donoghue replies that "I'm the maddest of the mad myself—if any of us *are* mad!" (*Riel* 2). He adds that he is far more radical than Riel and wants to ensure that they "won't let Canada do to us what England did to Ireland," which is "what any big over-blown nation in history does to a small neighbour—grab it! Gobble it up!" (3). From the outset, it is established that the conflict at Red River is a colonial one, and that Canada is the oppressive power.

Canada's expansionist ambitions become apparent the moment Riel arrives and openly ignores the Priest's advice for moderation, since he knows that "God will give us the victory" against what a Scottish supporter of his terms the "grabbers! Land grabbers!" (Coulter, *Riel* 6, 10). The most obnoxious of the rapacious Canadians is the Irish-born Orangeman Thomas Scott, who has recently arrived from Ontario but refuses to abide by the local regulations, "takin' no orders from a pack o' mongrel Papishes" (12). Scott and the other Canadians insist on mapping the land, but Riel will not allow them to do so. When the leader of the surveyors presses that they are "British subjects. Canadian citizens," Riel responds in no uncertain terms that "Canadians have no rights whatever in these Territories" (14, 15). The Canadians may think that the federal government has acquired the Red River Settlement and the rest of Rupert's Land from the Hudson's Bay Company, but Riel refuses to accept the legitimacy of the transaction.

In his exchanges with the Canadian surveyors, Riel articulates an incipient theory of nationhood, one that his antagonists either fail to grasp or reject. According to him, the HBC "traded or tried to trade these Territories and us that live on them to Canada—without consulting us. But we will not be bought and sold" (Coulter, *Riel* 16). Riel contends that the inhabitants of "a country... can not be taken over and incorporated into some other country without their own consent" (17). For him, it is a matter of "principle" to stand up to such an injustice, and he and his supporters will defend their birthright against any and all interlopers. Besides, he says, "God has directed" him to do so (17), demonstrating how inextricably linked politics and religion are in the world portrayed in the play. Another reason Riel feels confident about his ability to resist Canada is that he sees the people of Red River, including the Métis, as British subjects. So when the firebrand O'Donoghue lowers the Union Jack after the provisional government takes over the Settlement's commercial and administrative hub at Fort Garry,

Riel promptly forces him to raise it back up, arguing that they owe their loyalty to the British Empire in order that "three million British will have the honour of protecting us when we cannot protect ourselves" (25). Whether or not O'Donoghue appreciates it, accentuates Riel, the denizens of Red River "are not yet strong enough to stand on our own legs" without England's help (26). To highlight his point, he commands everyone to join him in a boisterous rendition of "God Save the Queen" (27).

O'Donoghue is never persuaded by Riel's trust in British institutions, such as the notion that England would stand by Red River against intrusions by "Anglo-Saxon" countries like Canada or the United States, and events prove him right. The central crisis in the play occurs when Riel comes to feel that the Canadian expansionists do not respect him and his government. This is especially true of the "evil" Scott, whom he sends "across the border, but he comes back" (Coulter, Riel 29). After the Ontarian is arrested a second time, Riel decides to subject him to a court martial. The official charge against Scott is that he is culpable of "having broken an oath not to take arms against...Provisional Government"—an oath he is not shown taking—and of "having struck his guards" (30). But Coulter's text suggests that there are other factors at play, a suspicion reinforced by Riel's justification for the trial: "Whatever Orange Ontario or Ottawa may do, later, now it is necessary to have acceptance here of our authority. It is my duty as President to compel this, first, before everything. I will not have all we stand for put in jeopardy by endless plotting against us...The prisoner, Scott, may bring our trouble-makers to their senses. He has been found guilty by Court Martial. The majority was for death. And he must die. If he did not, something of much importance—more than his life—might perish—our Government and all we hope from it" (36). Scott is thus executed not so much because of any grievous transgressions he may have committed as for reasons of state, to safeguard the authority of Riel and his provisional government.

Riel's desire to make an example of a peripheral figure like the labourer Scott leads one to ponder both his political motivation and his judgment. Throughout Coulter's play, there are hints that Riel may possess an authoritarian streak. When O'Donoghue questions his views on flying the Union Jack at Fort Garry since the Council has not yet deliberated the matter, a furious Riel retorts: "It is decided. I am the Council" (Coulter, *Riel* 26). More disconcerting, he not only tends to denounce as "traitors" all those who dare to oppose him but also threatens to "strike them down—without warning or mercy." As he rages during one of his paroxysms of verbal violence, "I will seize their homes and fields and stock and arms and stores. I will batter them down...sweep them from this soil they desecrate" (19). Even ecclesiastic authorities, like the Priest who counsels restraint toward the incoming Canadians, are reminded that they may believe "God speaks through Holy Church," but Riel has direct access to the divine and knows "God's will" (6, 5). As far as he is concerned, he is the sole authority, at least temporally.

Intriguingly, one person who is not disturbed by Riel's outbursts is Macdonald. While a mob outside his Ottawa chambers bellows the emblematic Orange song that dominates the play after Scott's execution, "We'll Hang Him up the River," the Prime Minister mounts an unexpected defence of "this—allegedly mad, but actually very astute—creature Riel" (Coulter, *Riel* 44), echoing the sentiments of his historical model (Pope 408). Meeting with his Québec confederate George-Étienne Cartier, the Bishop of St. Boniface Alexandre-Antonin Taché, and Colonel Garnet Wolseley, the English commander of the soon-to-be departing Canadian Expeditionary Force, Macdonald observes that Riel is still "master" in the North-West and that what the federal cabinet is "considering is whether we've any right to enter the territory of Riel's government without their consent. At present I think we have none whatever—no more than we have to enter the U.S.A. at Buffalo or any other port without the U.S.A.'s consent" (Coulter, *Riel* 42, 44; see also Macdonald, "Letter to McDougall" 408). Macdonald adds that he believes "Riel has fathered this new Province. He has proposed to name it—Manitoba" (Coulter, *Riel* 45, see also 60)—a name already used in early 1868 for the embryonic Republic of Manitobah, centred at Portage la Prairie (Bowsfield, "Republic"). In an attempt to soothe passions at Red River, Macdonald even rationalizes granting "a general amnesty" to Riel and his supporters for their actions during the disturbances (Coulter, *Riel* 45).

Of Macdonald's interlocutors, the only one who challenges his reasoning is Wolseley. For the much-decorated British Army officer, Riel is not the rightful leader of the people of Red River but "the scoundrel who murdered Thomas Scott." So Wolseley pledges that he will keep order in the Settlement until the new governor arrives, under anyone except "this criminal blackguard Riel" (Coulter, *Riel* 46). Even before the Canadian troops reach Red River, the local inhabitants learn that Wolseley is intent on avenging Scott and "spring his steel trap" on Riel (53) as he prepares to welcome them. O'Donoghue chastises his leader for falling for British perfidy, calling him "a fool," and Riel at last concurs. Realizing that the Expeditionary Force is not being sent to Red River to maintain the peace but to make way for waves of Ontario Protestant settlers, he has a revelation and declares: "I am not now a—loyal subject of Her Majesty" (53, 59).

Part I of Coulter's *Riel* could be interpreted as a dramatization of the protagonist's conversion from a British subject to a non-British subject. This is a political identity that he will retain for the rest of his life. By the time Part II opens, fourteen years later, Riel is living with his wife Marguerite in Montana Territory. They sit on *"rickety chairs"* and his *"clothes are shabbier"* than they were at Red River. His material condition has declined markedly, and he discloses to Marguerite that every day he thinks, "it is a long time I am an exile" (Coulter, *Riel* 67). But his fortunes are about to change. Riel is reading two letters, one of which informs him that his compatriots in the Saskatchewan country are suffering like they did in 1869–1870. The correspondent, the Oblate missionary priest Alexis André, also informs Riel that he is "the most popular man with all the people here" and "absolutely must come" to assist them in their struggle against the Canadian government (68). Marguerite fervidly attempts to prevent Riel from leaving their Montana home, telling him: "You will not go again to the North-West. You will not. It is trouble for you there—bad trouble" (69).

But with the arrival of a Saskatchewan delegation led by Gabriel Dumont, who does not step on stage for the whole play, there is never much doubt about what the decision will be. Soon Riel, Marguerite, and their two young children, along with their visitors, head north for another military-political confrontation between the Métis and Canada.

Since the first production of *Riel*, critics like Herbert Whittaker of the *Globe and Mail* have judged the second part of the play both "more pedantic" and "less rewarding" than the first, principally because of its cursory treatment of the North-West War (Karr et al. 22, 23). Almost the moment Riel reaches the Batoche area, he exhorts his followers to achieve the impossible. On the one hand, announces Riel, "Justice commands us to take up arms. Seize all stores. Stop the police and take their arms." But, on the other hand, they are to "not molest or ill-treat anyone" (Coulter, *Riel* 71), as if people would voluntarily surrender their possessions and armaments to the enemy. Also, instead of preparing his supporters to face the Canadian Army and the North-West Mounted Police, Riel turns against the local church representatives, including the priest who (in the play only) invites him to come north to help draft the petitions to send to Ottawa (Le Chevallier, *Batoche* 282–84). Coulter portrays the decisive military clash between the Métis and the Canadian forces at Batoche in a puny two-page scene, in which Marguerite largely presages that her husband "will be taken" by his adversaries (*Riel* 79). Most of the rest of the action is devoted to Riel's trial in Regina, where he is "found guilty of high treason" (122). Coulter's focus on the legal case against Riel, at the cost of everything else, gives credence to Chris Johnson's thesis that "the best Riel playwright is Riel" (175). But this may be less because he is such a theatrical figure than because the novelists, poets, and dramatists who write about his trial tend to rely so much on his words during his defence.

After the English-speaking and Protestant jury renders its verdict, the main suspense is whether Riel will hang or be spared by Macdonald. In a hallucinatory scene in his cell in the Mounted Police barracks, Riel vacillates wildly between affirmations of hope about his future and paralyzing confessions of despair. One moment he imagines himself interrogating the judge, "Can all the people be guilty? A whole people guilty of treason?" The Métis "own this land!" But the next moment, he is assailed by the ghostly voice of Scott, "You'll hang for this!" (Coulter, *Riel* 125), an eventuality that is foregrounded from early in the play (20, 37 ff.). The materialization of Scott in Regina's makeshift jail may be simply the product of a condemned man's tormented mind, but the Orangeman's return is very real to Macdonald as he assesses the consequences of his decision with one of his cabinet ministers. Both men know that it is not only the life of Riel that is at stake but also that of the Conservative Party, and perhaps of Canada. "If [Riel] hangs," the minister encapsulates the situation, "Quebec revolts." But if he does not hang, "Ontario revolts" (128, 129). Either way, Confederation could be imperilled, and the two politicians wish the British Colonial Office would make the decision for them. But Whitehall judiciously refuses to intervene, impelling Canada to take charge of its affairs. Macdonald is aware of the irony of the development and appreciates Riel's inadvertent contribution to the country's political emancipation. As the Prime Minister points out, "this wretch Riel is actually forcing us to take responsibility and govern Canada. How odd! The outlaw once more shapes the law. Henceforth, Louis Riel's name is scribbled across a chapter of our Constitutional Law!" (130–31). What Macdonald does not foresee is that his own role in one of Canada's earliest displays of nationhood, his assenting to Riel's hanging, would one day be deplored even by a growing number of his successors.

Coulter often boasted that, with the staging of *Riel*, he "initiated what has become the Canadian Riel Industry" (*In My Day* 268, 238; see also Anthony 61; Abley 10), and there is no denying his impact. Much of his play's influence is due to the reception of the original production. Although the cast of *Riel* was all white and all Anglophone, and operated in exceedingly precarious conditions, it was composed of an extraordinary number of reigning and rising stars of the Canadian stage, radio, and television. The production was directed by Don Harron, who also played Scott. Margot Christie played Riel's mother, Julie Lagimodière Riel. Robert Christie produced what Whittaker called a "superb and witty Sir John A. Macdonald" but which the *Toronto Star*'s Jack Karr protested was a Macdonald who was "a trifle more wily and unctuous than many of us like to regard the Father of Confederation" (Karr et al. 23, 21). Most important, the Anglo-Scottish Mavor Moore gave what Karr characterized as "a remarkably good performance" as Riel (Karr et al. 21). The following year, *Riel* was adapted for radio, under Moore's direction, and broadcast in the CBC's popular drama series *Wednesday Night*. Then, in 1961, it was turned into a two-part television film, with Bruno Gerussi as Riel. It was shown not only in Canada, the United States, and Great Britain, but also across continental Europe (Anthony 62, 104–05).

Still, the success of Coulter's *Riel* must be qualified. For all the accolades it received after its premiere, the play would not get "the major production" the playwright craved until its "triumphant" revival at the National Arts Centre in Ottawa in 1975 (Anthony 62, 104; see also Coulter, *In My Day* 272). There are several possible explanations for this state of affairs, besides the enormous size of the (almost all-male) cast. One of the play's limitations is its failure to probe the protagonist's inner life. With the shift from Red River to Montana occurring offstage between Parts I and II, Coulter misses Riel's mental breakdowns, the protracted amnesty saga, and his transformative epiphany in Washington, DC. Also, while Coulter emphasizes the religious component at the core of the Red River and North-West conflicts, he is not very interested in Riel's religious ideas. Thus, when Riel casually reminds his wife at the beginning of Part II that "I have a mission, I am the Prophet of the New World. God has spoken to me and I must obey" (Coulter, *Riel* 69), the audience has no idea of what to make of such a revelation, since his prophetic visions have not been broached before.

Nevertheless, the charge that Coulter's focus on "sectarian conflict" demonstrates that he does not see the Riel story on "North American" terms (Johnson 187) is not persuasive. A quick perusal of Canadian history would suggest that, whether religious or linguistic, sectarianism is as Canadian as maple syrup. One just has to think of Québec's relations with the rest of the country. But the strife is hardly limited to La Belle Province, as events in next-door Ontario illustrate. In the mid-nineteenth century, the Orange vigilantes Cavan Blazers became notorious for roaming through Peterborough County, burning down the farms of Catholic settlers (Winslow; see also Braz, "United"). Furthermore, such feelings were far from being restricted to rural areas. Now that Toronto has become the emblem of worldly multiculturalism, it is easy to forget that it was once known as the "Eden de l'Orangisme," as one of Riel's closest allies labelled it (J. Dubuc 627). It was not for nothing that Ontario's capital bore the moniker of North America's Belfast, "the WASP city of Canada, where Masons and Orangemen ruled," well into the twentieth century (Steele 43). The Catholic social justice activist priest Harvey Steele, aka Padre Pablo, writes that when he moved from Cape Breton to Toronto to attend university in the early 1930s, he was shocked by the overt "bigotry against Catholics" he encountered (46). Not surprisingly, Riel's birthplace is no exception. In 1884, just fourteen years after the signing of the Manitoba Act that brought the province into Confederation as a bilingual jurisdiction, the government of Manitoba passed An Act Restricting Public Printing, vouching that from then on "none of the public documents shall be printed in the French language except the statutes of the province" (qtd. in Russell 151). English-speaking Canada's determination not to allow a second Québec to arise in the West evidently had already borne fruit.

More pertinent is the critique that, as Vincent Tovell writes in his review of the opening production for the *University of Toronto Quarterly*, the playwright documents Riel exhaustively but "does not interpret him. In the end Mr. Coulter leaves us with the questions that stimulated him, the puzzle of Riel's personality and the problem of placing and evaluating him in history, but without the author's own opinions" (Karr et al. 25). While generally agreeing with Tovell's assessment, I would argue that a case could be made for Coulter's ambivalence toward Riel. The fact is that by the time the newcomer decided to write a play about the Métis leader, he could not help but discern that Canadians, including reputable scholars, were deeply divided about his subject. When Coulter told the University of Toronto librarian and historian William Stewart Wallace about his plans, the reaction was quick and unmistakable: "What! Louis Riel! You don't seriously mean to tell me you mean to stir up trouble again by writing about that—that infamous scoundrel" (qtd. in Coulter, *In My Day* 261). Likewise, when Coulter wrote to the influential historian of the Prairie West, W.L. Morton, for information about Riel, he was cautioned that the Métis leader was "a strange, unbalanced creature" (qtd. in Garay 291). This response foreshadows Morton's later admission that when he was an undergraduate student at the University of Manitoba in the late 1920s, he published an article in which he alleged that "Riel was 'a twisted and pathetic prophet of the old West which died with him'" ("Review" 162). No wonder that Coulter might have equivocated about celebrating Canada through such a polarizing individual, a quandary on which his other works on Riel may shed some light.

After the Canada Council for the Arts awarded Coulter a grant in the mid-1960s to complete a trilogy of plays on Canadian historical figures, he could not find anyone with "anything like the dramatic potential" of "my half-mythical, rebel half-breed, my John Brown of the North" (Coulter, *In My Day* 271). Therefore, Coulter decided to write two new plays about the Métis leader, *The Crime of Louis Riel* (1966) and *The Trial of Louis Riel* (1967), both of which are really adaptations of his epic drama. *The Trial of Louis Riel* is an edited transcription of the court proceedings, in which the dramatist's main task was to reduce "a five-day trial without loss of essentials to the two hours of playing-time on stage" (Coulter, *In My Day* 271). One notable addition is the inclusion of a large portion of text in French, thanks to the translation by Raynald Desmeules, to indicate when witnesses provide evidence "through an interpreter" (Coulter, *Trial* 28). The extent to which Riel's image had changed between 1950 and the Centennial year becomes apparent when one learns it was Regina's Chamber of Commerce that commissioned Coulter to write *The Trial of Louis Riel*, "frankly as a tourist attraction" (Coulter, *In My Day* 271). Also, the play has been so successful at attracting audiences that, except during the

COVID-19 pandemic of 2020–2023, it has been staged annually ever since (Ackerman).

Though *The Crime of Louis Riel* is basically a condensed version of *Riel*, it does include a prologue, likely based on the preamble that Coulter wrote for his epic play but then disregarded (Coulter, *In My Day* 261). Intended to be delivered to the audience by a member of the cast before the performance proper begins, the prologue summarizes the playwright's view of the importance of Riel as "one of the strangest and most theatrical characters in our strange and so theatrical North American story." More specifically, the play attempts to provide answers to the ever timely "question: when a man's people—his tribe—his nation—are menaced, is it a criminal act punishable by death to organize resistance, armed resistance, and fight? As did Riel" (*Crime* 1). This is the gist of the dilemma faced by Coulter in *Riel*, as in his two later plays. If Riel is justified in his opposition to Canada's expansion into Red River and the North-West as a whole, what does that say about Canada as a country? There is no way of evading the fact that it is Canada that fails to consult the Métis about their desire to be part of Confederation and then takes possession of their lands. It may be tempting to follow Coulter's lead and hold Wolseley responsible for the worst violence at Red River, but that would be too transparent a subterfuge. Canadians know only too well that it was not Wolseley who dreamed of a transcontinental country, connected from the Atlantic to the Pacific, but individuals like Riel's storied antagonist Macdonald and Riel's purported "new father," Cartier (Sweeny 188). Even as recently as 1968, at the aforementioned unveiling of the statue of Riel in Regina, Pierre Trudeau could assert that "Riel's battle is not yet won" (110). At the same time, the self-declared champion of human rights stated matter-of-factly that both he and his audience could "agree that Riel's dream of a vast, autonomous Metis nation-state in the middle of North America could never have been realized," for Canada and the United States would not "permit further fragmentation" in the continent (110). If after the late 1860s, Canada and the United States would not countenance the emergence of any other polity in North America, how can Riel be celebrated as a Canadian forerunner of the architects of the national resistance movements of the 1950s and 60s? What sort of "Canadian myth" can be embodied by the leader of a people that Canada does not allow to flourish?

Naturally, there are dramatic and historical shortcomings in Coulter's quest to present Riel as a Canadian hero. Not the least of these is that Coulter wrote three plays about the Métis leader, and in not one of them does he portray his 1885 military commander Dumont (Osachoff 134). Another weakness is that he fails to consider the Indigenous dimension of Riel's Métis nationalism, however problematic it may be at times. Yet another is that Coulter must have been deeply torn about his protagonist's politics. Astonishingly, one of the figures that Coulter contemplated having as the subject of his first Canadian historical play was John Beverley Robinson (Garay 286), the Crown prosecutor at the Ancaster treason trials (Bloody Assize) of 1814—and the father of the lead Crown counsel at Riel's own trial, Christopher Robinson. Still, the most critical of the political contradictions in Coulter's construction of Riel as a Canadian icon are hardly of his own making. Rather, they are inherent in a country's adoption as a national hero of someone who deemed it a threat to the survival of his own people, a reality that Howard revels in exposing.

The Continentalist Classic: Joseph Kinsey Howard's *Strange Empire*

Riel sometimes seems to be less a hero of a thousand faces than of a thousand ironies. One of those ironies is that the most influential book written about him is not by a Canadian, to say nothing of a Métis, but by an American. Joseph Kinsey Howard's *Strange Empire: A Narrative of the Northwest* (1952), also known as *Strange Empire: Louis Riel and the Métis People* or just *Louis Riel*, is often identified by Canadian writers and visual artists as the text that most shaped their conception of the Métis leader. The embrace of *Strange Empire* by Canadians is baffling, to say the least, given its unapologetic continentalism. Howard makes little effort to camouflage his support of U.S. expansion into North America's northern plains and north. But in the process of mocking the artificiality of the international border between Canada and the United States, he perhaps inadvertently also reveals that the sociopolitical differences between the two countries are not nearly as consequential as those between both of them and Indigenous peoples. Indeed, the main significance of *Strange Empire* is that it reminds readers that the real "War for the West" was not between Canada and the United States but between the two states and Indigenous peoples, including the Métis.

By the time Howard died of a heart attack in 1951, at the age of forty-five, he was one of the most respected writers in the western United States. The essayist and historian Bernard DeVoto considered Howard one of the "only two writers of national importance" in the interior West—the other being the Colorado poet Thomas Hornsby Ferril ("Remainder Shelf" 67). Howard was born in 1906 in the coal-mining town of Oskaloosa, Iowa, to Josephine Kinsey Howard and John Riggen Howard. When he was five, the family moved to southern Alberta, after his father became the manager of a coal mine in Taber. Howard would spend the next eight years in Canada, living in Taber as well as in Lethbridge, where his mother worked as a proofreader and the women's page editor for the *Lethbridge Herald*. In 1919, following his father's desertion of the family, his mother and he relocated to Great Falls, Montana, the city where he would spend the rest of his life and with which he is most closely associated (Hoyt 1–4).

Howard, whose formal education ended at high school, was a journalist, historian, short-story writer, and public intellectual. He joined the *Great Falls Leader* as a reporter at the age of seventeen and three years later became the newspaper's news editor. In addition, he served as "a correspondent for *Time* and *Life*" as well as the *St. Louis Post-Dispatch* (Roeder 5), and his fiction and nonfiction appeared in such diverse publications as *American Mercury, Collier's, Esquire, Mademoiselle, Nation, Progressive, Saturday Evening Post, Survey Graphic*, and *Yale Review* (Sestak 45–47). Today, his reputation as a writer rests on two books, a history of his adopted state called *Montana: High, Wide, and Handsome* (1943), which at the time was dubbed "the most brilliant interpretation of the contemporary West" (DeVoto, "Joseph" 3) and remains "the most popular book ever written about Montana" (Lehman 212), and *Strange Empire*, described variously as "his life's work" (Fox 43), "the most stirring of all the writing about Riel" (Bowsfield, "Foreword" 6), and "the best account of the Metis people" (Dobbin 255; see also Stegner, *Wolf Willow* 60; Dusenberry 135). *Strange Empire* was well received from its launch, particularly because it was the first comprehensive study to place the stories of Riel and the Métis in a North American context, as opposed to just a Canadian one. But there has always been considerable uncertainty about its genre—whether it is history or historical fiction.

Strange Empire's generic indeterminacy is partly due to the fact that it started out as a work of fiction. Howard planned to write a novel, tentatively titled "Falcon's Song," but he abandoned the idea after producing some 200 pages (Hoyt 147; see also Fox 43). Convinced that he was "not a novelist" (qtd. in Devine 64), he switched to nonfiction. Another contributing factor is that while Howard completed the manuscript before dying, he "had not [yet] begun to prepare it for the press" (DeVoto, "Joseph" 4). That task was carried out by his friend DeVoto, who spent several weeks near the end of Howard's life working with the author on the text and then tried to capture its internal logic. DeVoto had maps drawn and, acting on the advice of Howard's editor at the William Morrow publishing company, "arranged the opening paragraphs of three chapters in a different order" and wrote the "opening page" of another chapter (5; see also Stegner, *Uneasy Chair* 410-11). Howard's literary co-executor, Rosalea Fox, compiled a bibliography (J. Howard, *Strange Empire* 567-88). Of his own accord, DeVoto also decided not to add footnotes to the manuscript, reasoning that "no one can satisfactorily annotate someone else's book" and, besides, the text would "not suffer from omitting one of the conventions" (DeVoto, "Joseph" 5). DeVoto's decision may have been influenced by his awareness that Howard's hugely successful *Montana* does not bear footnotes, only acknowledgements and a bibliography (J. Howard, *Montana* 330–39). Still, this proved to be a serious miscalculation, judging by the reactions of most academic historians on the northern side of the border.

The main objections to *Strange Empire* as a work of history were articulated by George Stanley in his 1953 appraisal of the book for the *Canadian Historical Review*. Stanley, who had authored *The Birth of Western Canada* in the mid-1930s and who would go on to publish an authoritative biography of Riel in 1963 and serve as the general editor of his *Collected Writings* in the 1970s and 80s, claims that there are "two kinds of historians [who] write history, university professors and journalist-novelists," the first who are "usually historically precise" and the second who are "often wilfully emotional" ("Review" 65). Stanley, who does not cite *Strange Empire* in his life of Riel, consigns Howard to "the class of journalist-novelists." He contends that Howard is "a journalist-historian" who may have been able to produce a captivating book, but one that is "too idyllic and too naïve" to count as bona fide history (65). Stanley's evaluation of *Strange Empire* has been challenged but not nullified by later scholars. Thomas Flanagan describes Howard's text as "unreliable in fact and interpretation" ("Introduction," *Birth* xxi). Yet he not only deems it "the most gripping account of Riel's life" (*Louis "David" Riel* xii), but states that if he "were asked to recommend *one* book to read on Riel," it would be *Strange Empire* ("Review of *Strange Empire*" 739). Heather Devine, who finds Stanley's review "patronizing" (71), also admires Howard's text. She is impressed by his vast research on the Métis and sees his transnational approach as "a precursor to the cross-border studies of ethnic and racial collectivities that are now an integral part of the New Western History" (57). But Devine concludes that Howard "did not demonstrate the detachment and circumspection required of the professional historian of the post-war period" and that his book might best be classified as a work of "creative nonfiction" (72). Whatever else it may be, *Strange Empire* is not an orthodox history.

Although most academic historians judge *Strange Empire* a "splendid historical fiction" (D. Morton, "Reflections" 52), in which Riel is "Americanized" as the northern Patrick Henry or John Brown

(Owram, "Myth" 19–20), there is no avoiding its influence. The Calgary-born Stanley concedes that Howard "knew the West" and says that what is most valuable about his book is the "account of Riel's wanderings" between 1874 and 1884 ("Review" 65), a decisive period that the Métis leader spent largely in a series of locations across the United States, before settling down in Montana. Among the achievements of *Strange Empire* is that it establishes that it is impossible to understand Riel without exploring his complex relations to the United States. Howard's central thesis is that if the Métis had beaten Canada at Red River "in 1870, their country would have become an organized native state," a development that "would have vastly changed the history of the West, Canadian and American" (*Strange Empire* 251). The new polity would likely have led to the formation of "a native alliance" (251), which would have been critical after Sitting Bull's "Sioux...annihilated Custer's command" in 1876 and faced "a native state north of the forty-ninth parallel" (14, 15). For Howard, the Métis defeats at Red River and Batoche constitute "lost opportunities" when the destiny of the North American West could have been radically different (14). Instead, Canada emerged victorious, and the result was "*genocide*, destruction of a race, treason against the human spirit" (16). "There were no gas chambers then," he elaborates, "but there was malevolent intention" (17). The conflicts between Canada and the Métis, like those between the United States and First Nations, were really race wars.

Howard's interest in Riel and the Métis is usually attributed to his childhood years in Alberta, including by Howard himself. In the introduction to *Strange Empire*, he writes that the conception of his book can be traced to games of "Cops and Robbers" that he played with "a group of boys on the prairie of Western Canada" around the time of the First World War (11). From his playmates, he learned about the "older" and "simpler war" between Canada and the Métis (12). Howard also became semi-conscious of his U.S. nationalism. As "the only 'foreigner'" in the group, he avidly shared his coveted Mountie suit with one of the Canadian boys, for he was "ashamed of the red coat" and badly wanted "to adopt the role of traitor" (13)—

even if the Saskatchewan-raised U.S. novelist Wallace Stegner calls him an "Alberta boy transplanted to Montana" (*Uneasy Chair* 410). Howard remarks that, as "an American," he had developed "a skeptical attitude toward our approved Canadian history texts." He further discloses that he "discovered Manifest Destiny on the Northwestern frontier and read, with a thrill of recognition, about the Yankee dream: a State of Minnesota, or Territories of Dakota and Montana, reaching from the Great Lakes and the Missouri River to Alaska" (*Strange Empire* 13). The failure of a Métis state to materialize in 1869–1870 or 1885 is clearly not the only "lost opportunity" that Howard regrets. His book is very much a lament for the greater United States of America that might have been, a polity comprising a contiguous continental landmass not just from the Atlantic to the Pacific but also to the Arctic.

Critics often commend Howard for the gracefulness of his writing style, hailing him as "an uncommonly good writer" (Roeder 8), a popular historian who "seems to write the way a poet writes" (Gutteridge, "Riel" 12; see also Kittredge viii). Part of the resistance to his historical works by academic historians actually betrays the impression that his books are too eloquent to constitute proper history. That said, even his champions admit that Howard was prone "to rhetorical excess" (Kittredge x). But it is possible that his stylistic exuberance provides a key to the worldview that informs his work. Howard writes that one of the reasons he admires the Métis is that they are a transnational people who completely disregard the Canada-United States border. He finds such a spirit of independence admirable, since the forty-ninth parallel is "a wholly artificial boundary" (*Strange Empire* 49). Howard maintains that the international line was devised by politicians and "could not arrest the movement of men and ideas any more effectively than it could that of the buffalo herds," and so "made very little sense to anybody on either side of it" (14). Yet his experience of growing up in Canada hints otherwise. Judging by his words, the border is real. The only explanation for the inexorable political differences between him and his Canadian childhood mates is that the two have been shaped by distinct national narratives, or mythologies. Howard leaves little doubt of this, proudly stating that he later discerns he "had not been the first citizen of the United States to identify with the Dominion's enemies" (13). This also intimates that his animus toward Canada colours the way he envisages the continent and its peoples, raising the question of whether he prizes the Métis because of who they are or because of who battles them.

There are sundry indications throughout *Strange Empire* that Howard misreads the way the Métis, especially Riel, perceive other borders. As noted, Howard emphasizes the pan-Indigeneity of the Métis and claims that if they had triumphed at Red River, they would have created an Indigenous state north of the international boundary. Yet, while tracing the evolution of the Métis national consciousness, Howard discusses the impact of the Métis defeat of the Scottish Selkirk settlers at Seven Oaks in 1816. But he has nothing to say about their equally pivotal victory over the Yanktonai Dakota at the Battle of the Grand Coteau in 1851, regarded as their "most remarkable military feat" (W. Morton, "Battle" 46), the watershed event after which "the Sioux acknowledged the Métis as 'Masters of the Plains' and would fight them no more" (Teillet, *North-West* 126). His silence about the second conflict is intriguing, given that Howard is familiar with his subject's prolific writings (*Strange Empire* 355), and Riel is anything but reticent about extolling the Métis hegemony over the First Nations. In one of his best-known poems, the ode "Le peuple Métis-Canadien-français," Riel writes that he loves and cherishes the Métis nation boundlessly because, despite being a new collectivity, it has already distinguished itself militarily over a multitude of enemies. Significantly, the foes he identifies are not European but Indigenous. As Riel praises the Métis people:

> Il a fait connaître sa gloire
> Aux indiens du Minnesota.
> Il a toujours gagné victoire
> Sur les tribus du Dakota. (*Collected Writings* 4: 319)

In contrast, as he stresses later in the poem, produced during his Montana sojourn in the early 1880s, the main cause of the success of the "nation manitobaine" of the French Canadian Métis (4: 325) is that it has always been "bien guidé" by the Catholic Church (4: 320) and inspired by its "Esprit français" (4: 323). For him, the source of the remarkable achievement of the Métis is less their Indigeneity than their Europeanness.

His writings suggest that Riel is much less invested in pan-Indigenous alliances than in the eventual absorption of the First Nations by the Métis. It is true that Riel presents the Métis as "the natural mediators" between their First Nations and European ancestors (Braz, *False Traitor* 92), stating that many Métis have always paid "the most conciliatory role between their white parents and their indian relatives" (Riel, *Collected Writings* 2: 374). But he goes beyond that and avers that the level of cultural sophistication the Métis have attained because of "their constant communication with the whites" renders them incompatible to coexist with the First Nations. "Too civilized for the Indians," he underlines, the Métis "cannot stay nor live with them" (2: 272). The most concrete evidence that Riel is not overly concerned about the future of the First Nations, whom he believes are destined to "disparaître" (2: 409), is conveyed by his plan to divide the North-West. Even though Riel sets aside territory for the Métis incarnations of several European nations like the New Bavaria, New Belgium, New Italy, and so on, he only allocates "un septième" of those lands to the First Nations (*Collected Writings* 3: 318), when he mentions them at all (3: 312-13; *Queen* 355-56). The main alliances he anticipates are with other ethnonational groups, giving support to the allegation that he pictures the First Nations as little more than his "foot soldiers—the means by which he would realize his mission and deliver his people" (Stonechild and Waiser 77).

To be fair, Riel's stance was not unique among leading Métis or Halfbreeds at the time. For instance, the University of Toronto-educated journalist and lawyer James Ross (1835-1871), Riel's Halfbreed "counterpart" at Red River (Remis 6, 176), did not appreciate it whenever the Halfbreeds were conflated with the First

Nations. As he reminded his Franco-Métis challengers during
the Convention of the French and English parishes in early 1870:
"The fact is we must take one side or the other—we must either
be Indians and claim the privilege of Indians—Certain reserves of
land and annual compensation of blankets, powder and tobacco
(laughter)—or else we must take the position of civilized men and
claim rights accordingly. We cannot expect to enjoy the rights and
privileges of both the Indian and white Man" (qtd. in Remis 152;
see also Macdonald, "Half-Breed Claims" 125). The offspring of the
Scottish fur trader and historian Alexander Ross and his Okanagan
wife Sarah, James Ross left no doubt that the Halfbreeds belonged
among the civilized peoples of the world. This was a view shared
by his older brother, William. Despite having succeeded their
father as Red River's Sheriff, as James would subsequently, William
Ross blamed the "incubus" of the HBC's "monopoly—the peculiar government under which we *vegetate*"—for the Settlement's
economic and political stagnation, which had left it "half a century
behind the age." As he pointed to James in 1856, the only way to
reawaken the colony would be "to have a flood of new immigration
to infuse new life, new ideas, and destroy all our old associations
with the past" (qtd. in Van Kirk, "What" 210). Earlier, in the 1840s,
the Halfbreed fur trader, educator, and lawyer Alexander Kennedy
Isbister accused the HBC of having failed to live up to one of the
conditions of its incorporation, which was to facilitate "the introduction of Christianity amongst the Indians and the securing a
due provision for their moral, religious, and social improvement"
so that they could escape "the darkest heathenism" (Isbister et al.
4). In other words, for those individuals, the salvation of Red River
would come from the outside world.

    Howard, though, tends to downplay the ramifications of such
cultural divides on pan-Indigenous relations. His contention that
Riel would automatically welcome Sitting Bull into his "native
state" is particularly unconvincing. During the Sioux leader's
exile in Canada following the Battle of the Greasy Grass / Little
Bighorn in 1876, Riel worked closely with the United States military to persuade Sitting Bull and other "refugee Sioux leaders to

surrender to American authorities" (McCrady 224). In his letters to the commander of Montana's Fort Assiniboine, Lieutenant-Colonel Henry Moore Black, Riel trumpets how local Métis hunters "have exerted themselves during the whole winter to pacify the hostile Sioux" and help them "to change and to become friendly" (Letters to Black 228; see also Riel, *Collected Writings* 2: 218–19). Riel even advances that the reason Sitting Bull had not returned to the United States and "made peace long ago" was that he was "under the false and jealous influence of the Northwest Mounted Police" (Letters to Black 231). Rather than join forces with Sitting Bull, Riel assisted the Sioux leader's political foes (McCrady 224–25), the United States.

Riel's attempt to influence Sitting Bull on behalf of the U.S. military illustrates why his engagement in any continental pan-Indigenous confederacy is unlikely—his marked affinities with the United States preclude it. This unusually congenial relationship is something of which Howard fully approves, and which he details. One of the areas where *Strange Empire* excels is in the way it traces the extent of the involvement by the United States in the two political-military conflicts between the Métis and Canada. Howard's account of how the Métis nearly established a state of their own is always commingled with his mournful rendition of how Canada's victory "cost the United States its chance to acquire half a continent" (*Strange Empire* 28), a failure that was partly due to U.S. overconfidence. As Howard quotes a popular song with which "rapacious Yankees...long had been scaring the daylights" out of the feebler Canadians: "No pent up Utica contracts our powers; / The whole unbounded continent is ours!" (132). History proved otherwise, but it was not because of the lack of effort by the many stalwart promoters of the Great Republic.

Howard is apt at capturing the breadth of the "annexation fever" (*Strange Empire* 131) that took hold in parts of the United States in the second half of the nineteenth century with his fascinating portraits of what by then were mostly forgotten personages. Among these is Enos Stutsman, a frontier lawyer and journalist whose intelligence gathering could have made him "an American hero if Washington had been less timid" (81). Although born without legs, Stutsman became so closely involved with Riel's inner circle at Red River that he purportedly "had a hand in preparing" the Métis provisional government's Bill of Rights (131) and turned Canada's first appointed lieutenant-governor, William McDougall, into "the laughingstock of a continent" (83). Also gripping is the sketch that Howard draws of James Wickes Taylor. Another lawyer and journalist, Taylor was "a secret agent of the United States in Canada—to all intents and purposes a spy—[but] Canada knew him as a wise counselor and considerate friend" (76). In passing, Taylor was among the U.S. operatives who overestimated the appeal of U.S. expansionism to the inhabitants of Red River, being convinced that it was "irresistible. We have only to deposit an 'open basket'...under the tree, and the ripe fruit will speedily fall" (J. Taylor, *Correspondence* 51–52). Howard characterizes Taylor as the "finest expression" of the "dual citizenship of the Western frontier" (*Strange Empire* 66), but whatever his exploits, his long political-diplomatic career testifies to the depth of the involvement by the United States in what became the Canadian Prairies.

The reason U.S. annexationism proved to be such a formidable force of course was that there were people north of the border who were receptive to the idea, none of them more crucial than Riel—even if one of Cartier's biographers makes the unsubstantiated claim that the Québec politician in the late 1860s may have hired Riel as "an active intelligence gatherer" to spy on U.S. "expansionist forces" (Sweeny 189, see also 203). Howard recounts Riel's various sojourns in the United States, including the last one in Montana, during which Riel obtained U.S. citizenship (*Strange Empire* 349; see also Riel, *Collected Writings* 3: 267). He also shows how his wanderings across the United States enabled Riel to make extremely valuable friendships, like the one with Major Edmond Mallet, described by the Nebraska judge and writer Wilbur F. Bryant as Riel's "*alter ego*" (65). A Québec-born veteran of the U.S. Civil War who became a Washington bureaucrat, Mallet introduced Riel to President Ulysses S. Grant and other prominent politicians, such as the Indiana Republican senator Oliver P. Morton, to whom

Riel soon "presented a plan for taking Manitoba away from the Dominion" (J. Howard, *Strange Empire* 321; see also Riel, *Collected Writings* 1: 473-74 and *Collected Writings* 2: 6-17). It was also Mallet who, in 1885, pleaded with President Grover Cleveland to persuade Canada to show clemency toward Riel and not execute him. But Cleveland, whose "government represented Riel's last hope," chose not to intervene, perhaps for the same motives he "never officially acknowledged that...Riel was an American citizen" (Bumsted, "United States" 17, 36; see also Mumford 247-62). Even if one does not agree with the outraged Bryant that Cleveland's non-intercession made him "the murderer of Louis Riel" (qtd. in Richard 716, see also 715), it does call into question the value of Riel's vaunted U.S. citizenship.

Howard's chronicle of the transnational race for the northern plains is striking for several reasons. In the first place, Howard exposes the belatedness of Canada's interest in the region. Even a supporter of Canadian jingoistic expansionism like Stanley (Wade, Rev. 154) accepts that it was "American expansion [that] led to the vision of a greater Canada extending 'A mari usque ad mare'" (Stanley, *Birth* 25, see also 23). During the Province of Canada period (1841-1867), the government received a number of petitions from inhabitants of Rupert's Land expressing the desire to join the United Canadas, but with little effect. Dissatisfaction with the Hudson's Bay Company and its "fictitious charter" was pervasive among the English-speaking leadership, including the Halfbreed brothers Roderick and William Kennedy, who in 1857 gathered nearly 600 signatures in their petition to Parliament to "extend to us the protection of the Canadian Government, laws and institutions" (Kennedy et al. 59, 61; see also Shaw; Van Kirk, "What" 212). By then, the image of the North-West was being transformed from "a semi-arctic wilderness to a fertile garden well adapted to agricultural purposes" (Owram, *Promise of Eden* 3, see also 38-58). But what really sparked Canadian expansionism was the frenzied race to build railroads to the Pacific and the realization that, unless Canada acted soon, the United States would annex the territory, underscoring the extent to which Canadian politics can be driven by U.S. developments.

What Howard also accomplishes by detailing Riel's admiration of the United States and its institutions is to muddle the current Canadianization of the Métis leader (Braz, *False Traitor* 191–204), in which some established writers have gone as far as to present Riel as "a saint" and Macdonald as "a conniving bastard" (Wiebe, "In the West" 211; see also *Scorched-Wood* 323). Perhaps it could be argued that Riel is being politically strategic when he warns Canadians, as he does in the couplet that serves as the epigraph to this chapter, to beware that Washington is closer to the North-West than London and your "voisins sont plus nobles que vous" (*Collected Writings* 4: 248). But those lines appear in a long poetic diatribe against Macdonald that Howard himself characterizes as an "envenomed denunciation" of the Canadian prime minister (*Strange Empire* 355). Riel goes as far as to accuse his rival of having devoured him physically:

> Je ne souhaite pas, Sir John, que votre mort
> Soit pleine de tourments. Mais ce que je désire
> C'est que vous connaissiez et souffriez le remord:
> Parce que vous m'avez mangé, comme un vampire.
> (*Collected Writings* 4: 239)

Besides, Riel's attack on Macdonald and his national project is not an anomaly but typical of his discourse, as evidenced by his frequent appeals to U.S. politicians to protect the Métis from Confederation. In order to shield the Métis from nefarious Canada, Riel is willing to have his people live under U.S. rule.

Considering Howard's transparent favouritism of the United States over Canada in his depiction of the Riel story, the mystery is why the Canadian cultural intelligentsia responds so favourably to his continentalist tract. Numerous Canadian writers and visual artists have testified to the power of *Strange Empire*, as the Métis art historian and curator Catherine Mattes shows in her studies of the representations of Riel in contemporary art. Mattes writes that Howard's book has served as "an inspiration" to such varied figures as the sculptors Marcien Lemay and John Nugent, the painter John Boyle, and the graphic artist Jeff Funnell ("Whose Hero?" 16, 17, 55, 85, and 87). She attributes the impact of Howard's text to the fact that its pro-Riel (and pro-Métis) "interpretation was a change from the history that was traditionally taught in school and university classes across the land" ("Rielisms" 14, see also 16 and 17). Similarly, in the acknowledgements to his one-person inquiry into Riel's political career, the former Saskatchewan educator David Doyle thanks Howard for producing the book that "directed my generation of prairie youth to follow our prophet of the New World: Louis Riel" (Doyle). But the most forceful explanation for Howard's influence in Canada is offered by the Ontario poet Don Gutteridge, who too was "inspired" by *Strange Empire* to write his 1968 book *Riel: A Poem for Voices* (Gutteridge, "Riel" 12). For Gutteridge, Howard's triumph is that he "caught the essence of the Riel tragedy: the clash of cultures. He saw the nature of the conflict between Indian and American, between Metis and would-be Canadian, as a tragic encounter between two fundamentally different peoples" (13). Gutteridge adds that "Howard makes the white man feel ashamed, and fills the sensitive reader with a feeling of tragic loss" (13). Presumably, what Howard also does is convey the possibility of a connection between the self and the other, more precisely, between Indigenous and non-Indigenous North Americans, at least the tactful ones.

It is plausible that it is the very continentalism of *Strange Empire*, which has not been reprinted in Canada in decades, that renders it so attractive to Canadian artists and intellectuals. Continentalism has been characterized as a "specifically Canadian version of pro-Americanism" (Bélanger 32). The concept entails "some form of continental integration," its most "radical expression" being the annexation of Canada by the United States (32, 33). Still, continentalism has had considerable appeal in Canada across the ideological spectrum, as the reception of *Strange Empire* attests. For many Canadians, there is something salutary about someone from the United States writing so glowingly about what is deemed to be a Canadian subject. This is reflected in Gutteridge's contrasting responses to the portrayals of Riel by Howard and Coulter. Gutteridge writes that he was "totally unmoved" by Coulter's play *Riel* because "Coulter was not a native Canadian" and "had missed what Riel really was in Canadian terms." Gutteridge adds that when he says Coulter was not a Canadian, he means Coulter "was not only not born here, but more seriously does not think or feel Canadian" ("Riel" 11). The question of whether Riel can be unproblematically claimed as a Canadian is a fraught one, given that he saw much of the Canadian project "as oppositional to his interests" (Gaudry, "Métis-ization" 66). But without fully addressing the issue, it is clear that, for Gutteridge, the equally foreign-born Howard faces no such obstacles to understanding the Canadian mind, a feat that many Canadians have not accomplished. In *Riel*, Gutteridge vehemently distances himself from the nineteenth-century Canadian expansionists who battled the Métis leader and who tried to impose their alien ways on a landscape that saw them as "intruders" (29). In a single stanza, he has Macdonald present three of Canada's most vocal champions at Red River as "that idiot [John Stoughton] Dennis," "the sly [John Christian] Schultz," and "the insufferable [Charles] Mair" (15); the last is a poet that Gutteridge abhors with a passion (7–10, 19, and 26), even though Mair went on to author the standard account of the signing of Treaty No. 8 in 1899, *Through the Mackenzie Basin* (Leonard xxxvii). At the same time, Gutteridge salutes Howard for discerning that the Métis possess a "mystical, humane, constructive, and socially harmonizing" land ethos, a mindset "so powerful that it dissolved racial and language barriers" ("Riel" 13). But if an individual born in the United States like Howard is able to develop such insights about Riel and the Métis, one has to query what differentiates Canadians from Americans and whether the international boundary is a real border at all.

The irony is that, while Howard derides the forty-ninth parallel as one of the continent's great "political fictions" (*Strange Empire* 28), he keeps erecting the border between Canada and the United

States throughout *Strange Empire*. Most flagrantly, Riel's "native state" is limited to the northern side of the supposedly mythical medicine line. This geographical restriction is unusual not only because of the transnationalism of the Métis that Howard exalts but also because of their emotional attachment to their "first capital," Pembina, which since 1818 has been located in the United States (28). Howard also favourably compares the U.S. political system to the Canadian one, asserting that "the American way" was "one in which the people elected their leaders at regular intervals" and "were permitted even to choose their own judges" (114). Conveniently, he never defines what constitutes "the people," and if it would include the Métis, both individually and collectively, beyond noting that the Métis bilingual demands "would take some finagling" (131). Yet in light of the vicious wars between the United States and First Nations, some of whose members fled to Canada, it is difficult to imagine that the Métis would not have been dealt with in a similar fashion, especially given that "most Americans" perceived them as "exotic and distinctively Canadian figures" (Mumford 254). Stegner ventures that the Métis "might have developed into a people and a nation, with a life and land of their own" (*Wolf Willow* 57). But "if American annexationists had had their way," they could also "have become a vast northern extension of the United States" (57–58). The historian Jennifer S.H. Brown also points out that, "in contrast to Canada," in the United States "people of mixed descent never attained political or social recognition as a distinct group" (151; see also Mayer, "Negotiating" 98–100). So what remains a puzzle to the end is why Howard believes that an alliance with the United States would be so beneficial to the Métis.

There are other paradoxes, if not outright contradictions, in *Strange Empire*. In her article on the writing of Howard's book, Devine states that "the version...published after Howard's death was *not* the work envisioned by Howard himself" (57). She remarks that the last iteration of *Strange Empire* was subjected to major structural changes not only by DeVoto but also by editors at William Morrow (58). Devine, however, shows that one of the people most torn about the form the manuscript should take was its author. She quotes Howard in a 1945 letter of introduction to a New York literary agent, in which he confesses that part of his reluctance to write a traditional history of Riel and the Métis was that as "history alone the book would not do so well, because Canadian stuff doesn't do well [in the United States] and there's no use denying it. But it's more than history, because it has striking modern parallels" (qtd. in Devine 63–64). No less important, Howard is extremely equivocal about both Riel and the Métis. As mentioned earlier, the initial title of *Strange Empire* was "Falcon's Song," which survives as the name of the first part of the book (J. Howard, *Strange Empire* 21–105). This was an allusion to "La chanson de la Grenouillère," Pierre Falcon's poetic celebration of the Métis victory over the Selkirk settlers at the Battle of Seven Oaks. Yet in his brief discussion of the ballad, Howard is scornful of what has become the Métis national anthem. He writes that the composition "was not a very good song: the images were crude and the sentiment not at all elevating; it was a hymn of hate and thus like some other national anthems" (*Strange Empire* 31). It is not hard to see why he changed the title of his book, which he was reputedly led to do so by a dream (Devine 96).

Howard's portrayal of Riel is even more baffling. Regardless of its original subtitle as *A Narrative of the Northwest*, *Strange Empire* is generally interpreted as a biography of the historical Métis leader, with many critics ranking it as "perhaps the best book on Louis Riel" (Woodcock, *Gabriel Dumont* 230–31; see also Bowsfield, "Foreword" 5; Robin 5). A similar impression is conveyed by Howard through much of his text, such as when he describes Riel as "the greatest leader of the Métis" and the true "symbol and spokesman of the oppressed but gallant minority; revolutionist, leader, and lord" (*Strange Empire* 44, 48). Howard calls Riel "the brain" of the Métis people as well as "their voice: the only man they had ever produced who could fashion a philosophy from the crude materials of their semiprimitive way of life" (148). But perhaps one should have sensed that these might be only some of the facets of Howard's Riel. As early as the introduction, Howard presents his ostensible protagonist as a "dictator, who adored God and feared and hated bloodshed, defied his priests to lead the people he loved into a suicidal crusade" (16). Later, he notes that a "modern psychiatrist, studying the case record and Riel's own writings...would probably find him insane" (323). More alarming for someone who extols all things Western, Howard suspects that Riel may not be Western at all:

> Most Métis matured early, but Louis had had little experience on the hunt, where men were made, and had known few hardships. He was a mediocre horseman. He was clumsy and his hands were undexterous; many men of his race caught in prairie blizzards with no tool save a knife could survive, but he would have committed his soul to God and died. He could not shoot straight: he knew nothing of firearms and he dreaded and shunned them all his life. Living among people who drank to excess whenever they could, he used liquor sparingly; he had enemies who claimed they had seen him drunk, but as many friends swore he was a teetotaler. (147)

Worst of all, adds Howard, Riel was "a bit of a prig. Cursing, for instance, distressed him; he did not like to hear his Lord's name—or his own—taken in vain. He was, consequently, often distressed, because the West then as now was a cursing country" (182). Whatever may have been his motivation for writing a book about Riel, Howard chose someone about whom he was deeply divided.

The reality is that, before the end of his book, Howard disowns Riel. For Howard, Riel not only was not a true Westerner he may not have been much of a Métis, "being more white than red" (*Strange Empire* 337). The Montréal-educated poet and mystic definitely does not measure up to "a practical man" like Gabriel Dumont, who "simply liked to fight" (16). It is not Riel but Dumont who emerges as the hero of *Strange Empire*, which may be why a Dumont fan like George Woodcock is such an admirer of the monograph. Howard charges that the main reason the Métis were defeated at Batoche in 1885 was that Riel was their "supreme

leader" rather than the "much more militant Gabriel Dumont."
He elaborates that, "If Riel had not frightened the Anglo-Saxon
settlers, alienated the priests, and, above all, if he had not interfered with Dumont's aggressive military program"—that is, if he
had been an altogether different person—"the War for the West
might have ended differently and certainly would have been
much bloodier than it was" (375). The tragedy of the Métis is that
they did not follow "their only military strategist" but "their only
prophet of nationalism" (501), fatally favouring the mystical intellectual over the man of action.

By elevating the *"muy hombre"* Dumont (Woodcock, *Gabriel Dumont* 64) over the mystical Riel, Howard inaugurated a trend that persists to this day, in which writers and scholars who profess to champion Riel often end up dismissing him as either delusional or ineffectual. This is not an unproblematic development. For one, the lionization of Dumont requires the denigration of another Métis, Riel. More perplexing, the pragmatic Dumont "sabotages himself" by choosing "to follow someone he knows is far less knowledgeable of the world in which they live" (Braz, "Prairie Adam" 50), failing to recognize "the veering in Riel's mind away from rationality" (Woodcock, *Gabriel Dumont* 13). Yet Howard leaves no doubt that he prefers Dumont to Riel, for it is not the "cardboard prophet" (*Strange Empire* 483) but the buffalo hunter that he acclaims as the "'prince of the prairies'" (358). Granted, Howard complicates his apotheosis of Dumont by alleging that both Riel and his military commander believed the Métis were destined to lose a confrontation with Canada, no matter who led them. Even under the "far more bloodthirsty (or realistic)" Dumont, writes Howard, it was evident to the two "men...that if it came to a full-scale war the Métis could not win" (386, see also 459 and 474). The most they could hope to achieve was "to make a stand" that would help the Métis to have their collective rights respected (490). From Howard's perspective, it was preordained that the northern plains would belong to either Canada or, as he would much prefer, the United States. So one cannot help but conjecture if it is not Howard's focus on the Canada-U.S.

dimension of the conflict that explains the appeal of his book to Canadians. As depicted in *Strange Empire*, the Métis wars were a continental contest in which a popular U.S. writer admits that Canada somehow triumphed over its mighty neighbour. No wonder that Canadians have turned the book into a classic, despite (or perhaps because of) its continentalist politics.

Singing *Louis Riel*
The Centennial Quest for Representative Canadian Heroes

3

If Riel is executed, mark me! the children of his executors [sic], in the not-distant future, will erect monuments to his memory.
—EDMOND MALLET, 24 Aug. 1885

THE 1967 OPERA *Louis Riel* is a pivotal work in the Métis leader's metamorphosis from an enemy of Canada into the quintessential Canadian hero. Composed by Harry Somers, with a libretto by Mavor Moore in collaboration with Jacques Languirand, the opera was a Canadian Centennial project designed to celebrate the one-hundredth anniversary of the country that twice had clashed militarily with Riel and that was responsible for his death. The desire to articulate a more inclusive vision of Canadian citizenship is apparent in the number of cultures and languages included in the work, as well as in the various types of music. Needless to say, it is not possible for a country to convert a former enemy into a national hero without effacing its earlier defenders, or at least lampooning them for their failure to anticipate contemporary Canada's adoption of "manifest diversity" (Hutcheon and Hutcheon 18). Also, some of those individuals and groups that one claims as kin may resist the embrace, as the controversial 2017 remount of the opera has highlighted. While the focus of this chapter is on the original version of *Louis Riel*, toward the end, I will discuss the 2017 revival, since in many ways it constitutes a repudiation of the first iteration.

Riel's post-Second World War rediscovery coincides with a shift in English-Canadian historiography from a narrative of empire to one of nation (Perry 123, 129, 139; see also Stanley, "Last Word" 42–44). This identity transformation culminated in what has been called the Other Quiet Revolution of the 1960s, when "English Canada shed its definition of itself as British and adopted a new stance as a civic nation" (Igartua 1), most graphically exemplified by Parliament's approval of a new flag bearing no reminders of the country's colonial past or religious symbols, and later of the Multiculturalism Act. Although necessarily partial, the "'de-ethnicization' of English Canada" (1, 226) made possible the retroactive embrace of Indigenous leaders as keystone figures of Confederation. But the reconfiguration of the national body politic did not just create space for new ancestors, such as Riel. It also necessitated that Canadians renounce some of their earlier heroes, notably those individuals who opposed Riel on behalf of Canada.

No less a figure than Margaret Atwood has found it difficult to reconcile Riel's new place in the Canadian pantheon with his historical role. In her bestselling 1972 manifesto *Survival: A Thematic Guide to Canadian Literature*, she exposes some of the contradictions in the Canadian recovery of Riel. Atwood rightly notes that in works like Don Gutteridge's long poem on the Métis leader, "Riel stands for the authentic life of the land, Sir John A. Macdonald for the attempt to impose on the land an artificial structure alien to it" (200). At the same time, echoing Pierre Trudeau, she contends that Riel's dream of an autonomous Métis state in the middle of the Prairies was doomed to fail against "Sir John's monolithic vision," being destined to collapse "before an almost faceless authority like an old city block before a highrise developer" (201). Most apropos, Atwood remarks that in post-war representations of Riel, the "sympathies" of both authors and audiences "are with the rebels; but if the rebels had won, what then? Canadians—and not only Canadian Prime Ministers—are terrified of having authority undermined, monolithic federalism shaken...If the railroad hadn't gone through, the Americans would have got the West; if the country falls apart, who will inherit the pieces?" (204). Had Riel succeeded, cogitates Atwood, there might have been no transcontinental Canada, a national anxiety already detectable in the Centennial opera.

Like any other opera, *Louis Riel* was a collaborative work, but it is primarily associated with Somers, Moore, and, to a lesser degree, Languirand. All three were already well-known figures in Canadian cultural circles, with Somers being considered "Canada's leading composer" (Schafer 17) and Moore and Languirand being rising stars in the Toronto and Montréal theatre scenes. Curiously, the venture was not initiated by any of them. Rather, the catalyst was the publishing executive and philanthropist Floyd Chalmers, perhaps best known as the publisher of *Maclean's* magazine. In the early 1960s, Chalmers and his family established a foundation to support the performing arts in Canada. One of their main objectives, along with helping build the infrastructure of Ontario's fledgling Stratford Festival, was to commission "an opera for Canada's centennial year, a project [they] put in gear in 1963" (Chalmers 239). When Chalmers approached the director general of the Canadian Opera Company (COC), Herman Geiger-Torel, the latter was enthusiastic about the endeavour and suggested a number of potential subjects, beginning with Brian Moore's *The Luck of Ginger Coffey*. But Chalmers rejected the idea outright, since the novel deals with a recent Irish immigrant to Canada, and he "wanted an opera that was Canadian through and through" (239), a yardstick that led him to Riel.

Chalmers writes that he had been reading George Stanley's "heroic biography" of Riel, a dramatic story that not only had "all the dimensions of grand opera" but was "a capsule history" of Canada (239; see also M. Moore, *Reinventing* 313). Two of the facets of Riel that appealed to Chalmers were his bilingualism and his biculturalism, attributes that English-speaking Canadians had opposed so forcefully in the late nineteenth century, including in Riel's home province of Manitoba (Russell 143–86). Chalmers was never able to master French, despite his repeated efforts to learn the language, but he accepted "the premise that Canada, whether everyone likes it or not, is a bilingual country," and indeed that

Canadians should "turn bilingualism into a national asset rather than the divisive force" it was at the time (Chalmers 233). Chalmers discussed the idea of the Riel opera with a variety of people but concluded that Mavor Moore "was obviously the man to write the libretto," for the "sensitive writer and playwright...had been thinking along the same lines about Riel" (239). Chalmers and Moore decided that Somers should compose the score and, once he saw the libretto, Somers was so impressed that "from there on it was just a matter of accepting" (Somers, "Harry Somers" 26), even if privately he expressed "reservations...with the possibility of interference by the backer" (*Secret Agent* 60). Chalmers and Moore also agreed to invite Languirand to be the "co-librettist in French" (Chalmers 240), assembling the individuals most responsible for the "outstanding achievement" (Feldbrill 31) that would be *Louis Riel*.

Chalmers's choice of Mavor Moore as the architect of his opera was nothing short of inspired. If anything, the polymath actor, dramatist, theatre director, television producer, and cultural mandarin was even more fascinated by Riel. As we saw in the previous chapter, in 1946, Moore and his mother, Dora Mavor Moore, founded the New Play Society. One of the company's most successful productions was the 1950 staging of John Coulter's *Riel*, which Mavor Moore says "sparked the revival of Rieliana that swept across the country" (*Reinventing* 177), and in which he played the Métis leader. This would mark the first of his many encounters with Riel. Moore subsequently adapted Coulter's epic play for both radio and television. He also contemplated producing an operatic treatment of Riel for Prince Edward Island's Charlottetown Festival, of which he became the founding artistic director in 1964. Although Moore "longed to marry Riel and Somers" in musical theatre, he realized that such a creation "would fit neither Charlottetown's budget nor its merry image" (312). So he committed himself wholeheartedly to Chalmers's enterprise.

Louis Riel is divided into three parts. Acts I and II deal with the Red River Resistance of 1869–1870 and Act III with the North-West War of 1885. Most of the action fluctuates between either Red River or Batoche and Ottawa and revolves around two triangles.

The first triumvirate consists of Riel, Prime Minister Macdonald, and Thomas Scott, the Ontario Orangeman who defied Red River's provisional government and was executed after a polemical court martial in what is widely deemed Riel's great error in his political career. The second trio is composed of Riel, Macdonald, and Alexandre-Antonin Taché, the Catholic Bishop of St. Boniface who served as the intermediary between the Canadian government and the Métis during the Red River troubles and who became enmeshed in the controversial negotiations for an amnesty for Riel and his supporters. These triangles, in turn, are linked to two central issues in the work, and to the conflict between Riel and Macdonald and, by extension, between the Métis and Canada: the ownership of the North-West and whether an amnesty was ever promised by the federal government.

There are several key features in *Louis Riel*, particularly in relation to aesthetic Canadian representations of the Métis leader prior to the Second World War. The first of these is the way the text caricatures—and thereby distances itself from or even repudiates— the most boisterous opponents of Riel on behalf of Canada, or what members of the Métis National Committee term "le Canada d'Ottawa!" (Moore and Languirand 4). This bias is apparent from the outset, when the arrival of the new Canadian Lieutenant-Governor William McDougall at the United States-Red River border is heralded by "A SERIES OF CRASHING POMPOSITIES," something the self-important Ontarian proceeds to reinforce by declaring that he is determined to show the Métis "who is master here" and to "teach them to be civilized" (2). But the work's partiality is most conspicuous in the characterization of Scott, who is othered by his own allies. As the leader of Red River's Canadian Party, John Christian Schultz, confides as he travels across Ontario to raise funds to build a statue of the Orange martyr: "Thomas Scott alive / was a pain in every ass / but his corpse'll be a hero by and by" (25). Schultz demonstrates that he is not just a cultural and religious chauvinist but also a hypocrite who detests Scott, proving the Métis' assessment of both men. Yet one wonders if there is not some truth to Scott's cry, as he is being "shot...down in cold blood" by the Métis, that "'I die for Canada!'" (24). No matter how questionable his politics may be judged today, the main reason the Orangeman is eliminated by Riel, besides the latter believing that Scott is "rien" (8), is his zealous championing of (Anglo) Canada.

Another notable feature of the opera is its downplaying of the considerable Canadian anxieties about the plans by the United States to annex the North-West, and Riel's ambiguous overtures to leading U.S. political figures. In the decade before the conflagration at Red River, while the historical Riel was preparing for the priesthood in Montréal, "Americans were talking openly of annexing" Rupert's Land (Stanley, *Louis Riel* 38). One of their best-known operatives was the "secret agent" James Wickes Taylor, Canada's reputed friend whose "life-long ambition was to bring about the peaceful annexation of British territory to the United States" (Stanley, *Birth* 36; see also J. Howard, *Strange Empire* 76–77). After Taylor became the United States consul in Winnipeg in 1870, the historical Riel wrote to him complaining about the treatment he and the Métis had received at the hands of the Canadian government. More crucially, he sent petitions to two U.S. presidents, Ulysses S. Grant and Grover Cleveland, requesting protection from Canada. In his 1885 letter to Cleveland, Riel not only asked that he "blot out" the international boundary west of Lake Superior (*Collected Writings* 3: 187) but also that he appoint Taylor "governor General of these vast territories" and designate Riel "First Minister and secretary of the Northwest under Honorable James W. Taylor" (3: 187–88; see also *Collected Writings* 2: 6–17). If the United States had intervened and succeeded, Macdonald's "crazy dream" of a transcontinental country (Osler 23) would have vanished inexorably. Yet none of these issues is addressed in any depth in the opera, certainly not at Red River—even though the provisional government's Treasurer, William O'Donoghue, was a strident U.S. expansionist (Stanley, *Birth* 164) and Macdonald feared that Riel might be "in the pay of the U.S." (qtd. in Pope 418). Instead, the librettists have Riel assert that he and his people "are not rebels against the Queen / only against the [Hudson's Bay] Company /

that sells us off like cattle." Or as he tells his Canadian adversaries, he is not "starting a prairie fire" but "stopping one from breaking out" (Moore and Languirand 6). If the hostilities at Red River are the result of either irrationality or bad faith, it is hard to imagine that Riel and the Métis could possibly be the guilty party.

Similarly, the opera conveys the impression that Riel is not merely the leader of the Métis but of what has been branded a "myth[ical]" pan-Indigenous alliance (Stonechild and Waiser 239). Thus the Saskatchewan Valley delegation that travels to Montana Territory in 1884 to invite Riel to help them prepare their grievances against Ottawa included not just French-speaking Métis and English-speaking Halfbreed leaders but also the Cree Chief Poundmaker (Moore and Languirand 35), when the archival record shows that there was no First Nations representation (Riel, *Collected Writings* 3: 1–9; Stanley, *Louis Riel* 250). As well, just before Riel announces that he is breaking with the Catholic Church and starting a new religion, the Cree martial chief Wandering Spirit enters a little church near Batoche in "FULL WAR REGALIA" (Moore and Languirand 39), making the way for the Prophet of the New World. Finally, Riel's wife Marguerite is not a "Métisse canadienne française" (Riel, Letter to J. Riel 279) but an "INDIAN" (Moore and Languirand 34), once more implying that Riel appeals to various Indigenous ethnonational groups.

In contrast, Moore and Languirand accentuate the Britishness of English Canada—something that is even more glaring in the TV adaptation of the opera (*Louis Riel*), but which is already noticeable in the libretto. To begin with, mirroring history, in both conflicts the Canadian forces are led by British commanders: Colonel Garnet Wolseley at Red River and General Frederick Middleton in what is now Saskatchewan. So these are not quite "Canadian" military expeditions but more like colonial ventures, reflecting the ideological orientation of most of the Canadian participants. Typically, the opera opens with McDougall thanking God, not for enabling him to take possession of Rupert's Land for Canada, but for being "back on British soil" (Moore and Languirand 2). Even Confederation's great champion, Macdonald, at times seems unsure whether he is fighting for Canada or for the British Empire. As he banters with Taché, "Bishop, we are men of the world: / horse-traders—you for God and I for Queen" (11). Riel himself expresses immense pride in being a British subject. One of the most symbolically loaded incidents in the opera involves the confrontation over the flying of the Union Jack at Fort Garry. After the Irish-born O'Donoghue (spelled O'Donaghue in the libretto) not only lowers the British flag but "STAMPS ON IT," Riel forces him to pick it up before commending his followers "for having faith / in the crown of England" (28, 29). But then, as he stresses early on, he and the Métis "only fight for our British rights" (6). While the Red River combatants may not consider themselves kin, they are all British subjects.

Moore and Languirand are more subtle in their depiction of Macdonald than of the Red River Canadian expansionists, but the Prime Minister still comes across as ethically challenged. Macdonald's overriding aim is to safeguard Confederation. As he responds to the news of Riel's seizure of Fort Garry:

> Nothing can stop this country now.
> There may be local obstacles,
> jealousy and hate and pride:
> but the wheel, my friends, is turning and
> we are only flies upon the wheel.
> Nothing can stop us. Nothing will.
> If we unite from sea to sea
> we shall become a mighty power:
> if we do not, we'll all be naught!...
> shouting unheard in French and English both. (11)

Even so, Macdonald promptly asks the HBC officer Donald A. Smith to head west to persuade Riel to abandon his opposition to Canada, trying "the sugar first," which is "the oil for political machines," followed by some kind of "booty" (11). He may have founded a country, but he remains a consummate politician whose solution to any crisis is to bribe his opponents.

Granted, Macdonald's behaviour is likely affected by the fact that Canada confronts major challenges both externally and internally, as his cabinet is helplessly divided. His long-time ally George-Étienne Cartier reminds the Prime Minister that if he sends an army to Red River, "Quebec will start a war—right here!" Conversely, counters Wolseley, if he gives an amnesty to Riel and the Métis, "Ontario will start your war" (Moore and Languirand 26). There is no easy way to satisfy the conflicting interests of his different constituencies, and Macdonald knows it. So he prevaricates, living up to his moniker of Old Tomorrow. Macdonald readily agrees to Taché's demand that he will serve as Ottawa's commissioner to the Métis on the condition that a general "amnesty" be awarded to Riel and his followers for their roles at Red River (10; see also Macdonald, Letter to Taché 751), but never delivers it. After making endless requests for a copy of the document, Taché at last realizes that Macdonald will not produce the pardon. Almost against his will, Taché has to concede that he has been "made a tool" by the Prime Minister, a deception that will have devastating repercussions for his relations with his Métis parishioners. He bemoans that he has been lied to so often that "now my own flock thinks I lied!" (32). Or as the Chorus underlines, "Un prêtre nous a trompés!" (31). Yet Macdonald is untouched by the consequences of his actions for such a steadfast ally. Right after assuring Taché that "all the past will be erased" by his reprieve, he instructs Cartier that they "mustn't touch" the amnesty during the coming election, since "what shall it profit a man if he gain / the whole world, and lose his seat?" (17). For the Prime Minister, political expediency always trumps ethics or personal loyalty.

The caustic portrayal of Macdonald and other Canadian nationalists in *Louis Riel* has led some commentators to assert that, paradoxically for a Canadian work, the opera presents Canada as "the villain" (Hutcheon and Hutcheon 22)—but without really questioning the legitimacy of Confederation. As the Métis musicologist Colette Simonot-Maiello observes, "*Louis Riel* deconstructs the nationalism it suggests" (73; see also Giroux, "Goddamn"). Early in the opera, Riel reminds the Ontario poet Charles Mair and his expansionist associates that Canadians have no claim to Red River: "This land was ours before you came: / It is not yours to sell" (Moore and Languirand 6)—or, more correctly, to buy. In an attempt to help Macdonald understand the concerns of Riel and the Métis, Taché tells the Prime Minister that before there was a Confederation, "the people of the West were free; / to roam their land, to sell their furs." But now "the giant Canada" is imposing its alien ways on them, "taking their homes without their leave" (9). Macdonald cavalierly dismisses Taché's plea as a "sermon," not only failing to allay the Métis fears that the "damn Canadians are moving west" (9, 35) but also showing that Canada can be simultaneously a colonial and an imperial entity.

Moore and Languirand confuse matters, however, by drawing an implicit equivalency between the roles played by Riel and Macdonald in the deaths of Scott and Riel, respectively. Midway through Act II, Riel apprises Smith that he is unable to pardon Scott because "I cannot let one foolish man / stand in the way of a whole nation!" (21). This is a retort that Riel has already voiced a few pages earlier when he says basically the same thing in French: "Je ne peux pas laisser un imbecile / Compromettre les plans de toute une nation!" (19). Then, at the end of the opera, Macdonald ventriloquizes Riel when he tells Taché why he will not pardon the Métis leader: "I cannot let one foolish man / stand in the way of a whole nation!" (52). The articulation of the same political rationale by Riel and Macdonald suggests a parity between the two executions, a premise that critics like Jean Teillet, "one of the Métis Nation's legal warriors" (Teillet, *North-West* xvi), find "deeply flawed" ("Sermon" 31). Yet the historical Riel agreed with this interpretation. Just before he was hanged in 1885, he was quoted telling Father Alexis André that "Sir John Macdonald is now committing me to death for the same reason I committed Scott, because it is necessary for the country's good" (Riel, *Collected Writings* 3: 583). The real-life Riel also had a propensity to bully his opponents and censor the press, to say nothing of forcibly seizing the property of others (Bumsted, *Reporting* 182–83, 191–92). During the Red River Convention of English and French delegates in 1870, he branded his most vocal adversaries "traitors" and vowed that their "influence as public men [was] finished in this country" ("Proceedings" 23, 24), sometimes allegedly "enforc[ing] his arguments...pistol in hand" (J. Taylor, "Letters" 55). Even before the Convention, James Ross, who was determined at all costs to avoid "a civil war" between the Halfbreeds and their "French brethren" (J. Ross 437), took the rumours of Riel's threats against him seriously enough that he moved his wife and children to a relative's house and awaited arrest (439–43). In terms of the press, Riel not only closed down the Canadian-founded *Nor'-Wester* but even forced the editor of the more friendly *The New Nation* to remove "any mention of the execution" of Scott from the copies of the issue following his death destined for distribution outside Red River (Begg 331, 316, 332, 334), revealing that he was aware of the act's potential repercussions. Nevertheless, by imputing that the two antagonists share a similar moral code, Moore and Languirand insinuate that there is no discernible ethical difference between Riel and Macdonald.

The librettists also imply that Riel's and Macdonald's involvement in the deaths of their adversaries may have been the result of mental illness. Riel decides not to stop Scott's execution after he experiences "THE FIRST OF HIS 'BRAIN-STORMS'" and becomes convinced that he is the Christian "David!" (Moore and Languirand 13, 14). Macdonald is later shown passing over a bottle of medicine for a flask of liquor, the ingestion of whose contents sets him "COUGHING LIKE A CONSUMPTIVE" (15, see also 36). Macdonald's alcoholism could be seen as much of a "disability" as Riel's struggles with mental illness, even if most of his biographers have been reluctant to draw such a conclusion (Reaume 280, 288–91). The Prime Minister's behaviour may be interpreted to mean that he is no more responsible for his actions than the Métis leader is for his. But since the opera closes with Macdonald using Riel's words against him, it appears to be justifying the hanging of Riel. After all, the very last line is Schultz's exultation: "The God damn son-of-a-bitch is dead!" (32; see also Giroux, "Goddamn"), raising the question of who the central character is.

Moore and Languirand's equation of the behaviour of Riel and Macdonald is surprising for several reasons, starting with the substantial difference in age between the two opponents. When Riel elects not to grant clemency to Scott, he is in his mid-twenties and has had little experience of the world, having spent almost half of his life sheltered in a religious boys' school. But when Macdonald determines that Riel "shall hang, though every dog / in all Quebec bark in his favour" (Moore and Languirand 51), he is a seasoned seventy-year-old who is reaching the end of an eventful political career and life. Also, throughout the opera, Macdonald is portrayed in a much more negative manner than Riel, an effect that is accentuated by Somers's music. While Riel is usually accompanied by dramatic modernist sounds, Macdonald tends to sing to an off-kilter waltz, implying that Somers envisages Riel as the true protagonist and pokes fun at Macdonald. It is worth noting that when the director Franz Kraemer adapted the opera for television in 1969, the one major change in characterization he felt compelled to undertake was to make Macdonald seem "a little less farcical" (qtd. in Schafer 24, see also 19). Still, what remains most unexpected about *Louis Riel* is that a predominantly English-Canadian production would even consider presenting the Métis leader as a hero. As the historian Doug Owram observes, for English-speaking Canadians, until the 1930s, "Riel was simply not thought to symbolize anything positive" ("Myth" 12, see also 14). The country's transcontinental ambitions precluded the possibility that an individual "who stood in the way of...expansion, even if with some reason," could emerge as "a Canadian folk hero" (15). Yet the fact remains that the opera is not named after Macdonald but Riel, making one wonder what might be the political and cultural factors that account for such a transformation.

Owram traces the genesis of "the mythification of Riel for English Canadians" to the 1952 publication of Joseph Kinsey Howard's *Strange Empire* ("Myth" 18), something that Macdonald's biographer Richard Gwyn says "would have rattled" the Prime Minister because Howard was an American (493). As we saw in the previous chapter, Howard's hybrid history has become the

single most important book on Riel, shaping the conception of
the Métis leader of numerous Canadian writers and visual artists.
Moore, too, is an admirer of Howard's "marvelous" and "evocative novel" (M. Moore, "Riel" 7; Reinventing 312). But *Strange Empire*
could not have served as a model for a work even tentatively celebrating Confederation, given its continentalism. Howard does not
just vilify the Canadian expansionists but all Canadian nationalists, presenting the Canadian campaign against the Métis as a
form of ethnic cleansing (17). There can be little doubt that the
opera's main influences lie elsewhere, from Canadian biographies
of Riel to histories of the relations between the Métis and Canada.
In particular, I would argue, it is deeply affected by John Coulter's
Riel, the 1950 play in which Moore gave "a memorable" performance as the title character (Sperdakos 190) and which predates
Strange Empire by two years.

The theatre scholar Allan Boss, who has written extensively
on Moore, scoffs at "the misconception that the *Louis Riel* opera
was adapted from Coulter's play," insisting that the two works
"have nothing in common besides their subject matter" (49).
Moore is more generous toward Coulter. While maintaining that
Coulter's *Riel* "lacked the incandescence to serve as a metaphor
for Canada" (*Reinventing* 12), he writes that it was his "introduction" to Riel ("Theme" 29) and that it has played a crucial role in
Canadian culture, "inspiring, among other works, the opera *Louis
Riel*" (*Reinventing* 177). Moore goes as far as stating that it was the
Ulster-born playwright who "hit upon the irony that makes Louis
Riel's life into superb drama" by having Riel sacrifice Scott's life on
national grounds, a scheme Macdonald then employs against him
("Theme" 29). It is hardly by accident that the TV adaptation of
Louis Riel closes with "grateful acknowledgments" to Coulter's play
(*Louis Riel*), giving credence to Coulter's contention that the opera
"resembled" his script (*In My Day* 267).

Notwithstanding the protestations by Boss, Moore and
Languirand's debts to Coulter are too vast to ignore, even excluding
the outright borrowing of the anti-Riel Orange song "We'll Hang
Him up the River" (Moore and Languirand 25, 49; Coulter, *Riel* 56,

141). The notion that Scott is not just a xenophobe but "the devil," which has become a common trope in the literature on Riel (Braz, "Orange Devil"), is already articulated by Coulter (*Riel* 15). Likewise, Coulter dramatizes the showdown between Riel and O'Donoghue over the flying of the Union Jack at Fort Garry (23-25). Again anticipating Moore and Languirand (34), in his Dramatis Personae, Coulter erroneously describes Riel's wife as "*Indian*" (*Riel*), as opposed to Métis, although he later presents her as "*a half-breed Indian*" (67); in fairness to both writers, the historical Riel was cited in an 1885 newspaper interview as saying that he "married... a Cree woman" (*Collected Writings* 3: 565), information repeated by one of his defence lawyers at Regina (*Queen* 291). Most critically, Coulter implies that Riel may be a Canadian hero in the end when he has Macdonald remark that "this wretch Riel is actually forcing us to take responsibility and govern Canada" (130-31). So rather than being fallacious, the claim that *Louis Riel* is "somehow structurally linked to Coulter's play" (Boss 50) is a just representation of the relation between the two works (Elliott 12; Simonot-Maiello 74). Coulter, for one, failed to perceive the opera as "a tribute" to him (Moore, *Reinventing* 354) and "felt abused" for his involuntary contribution to Chalmers's venture (Chalmers 240).

That said, there are crucial differences between Coulter's play and the Centennial opera. The most important of these are the latter's bilingualism and biculturalism, which almost certainly are the result of the input by Languirand as the "coauteur aux dialogues français" (Paquette 163)—a role frequently erased in the recent scholarship on *Louis Riel*, which reputedly was "written by two white, English-Canadian men, from the cultural elite of the day" (Danckert 41; see also Segato 16). *Louis Riel* is not a truly bilingual work. This is underscored by the fact that the capacious exchanges between Taché and Macdonald about Riel's amnesty all take place in English, as the cleric pragmatically accepts that English is "the language of court" (Moore and Languirand 9). It is not too outlandish to extrapolate that one of the reasons Taché is so categorically outfoxed by Macdonald is not that the Prime

Minister is shrewder but that, unlike Taché, he is operating in his native tongue. Still, one should not minimize the amount of French in a work aimed primarily at an English-speaking audience.

French appears throughout *Louis Riel*, often as a sign of Métis resistance to the Canadian expansion into the North-West. But it is pervasive in articulations of Métis religious identity, which is not always easy to differentiate from Métis political identity. Thus Julie Riel discloses to both Bishop Taché and her oldest child that she only acceded to her parents' pressure to marry, instead of following her dream of becoming a nun, after she heard a divine voice. She then adds:

C'était la voix de Dieu
qui me dit aussi:
Ton premier-né sera le chef de sa nation...
Louis, mon petit,
choisi par Dieu... (Moore and Languirand 13)

Like his mother, Riel is guided by God, who does not just counsel but empower him, placing the would-be priest "à la tête des nations" (14). It is because of the intercession of his heavenly "libérateur," says Riel, that a people he did not know has become "mon sujet / Il s'est soumis au premier mot que j'ait dit" (14). However, even after Riel undergoes his transformation into the David of the New World, he continues to derive much of his authority from eminent ecclesiastic figures, notably Bishop Ignace Bourget. Riel states that he only takes possession of Father André's church upon gleaning that God has "abandonné le Pape," giving him licence to perform "les sacrements" (41). But the reason he is positive about the truth of his cause is that Bourget has sent him a letter informing him that he has a "mission," even if Bourget does not specify what the mission entails, beyond Riel having to carry it out to the end (41, 35). Also, whether from God or Bourget, most of these mystical communications are transmitted in French, which the historical Riel considered not just a beautiful and sophisticated language but a unifying force for the Métis (*Collected Writings* 1: 390), and which might explain its centrality in his cultural and political universe.

The uniqueness of the Moore-Languirand libretto's English-French bilingualism becomes obvious when one compares it to other well-known aesthetic representations of Riel produced around the Centennial year and beyond. In his poem *Riel*, Gutteridge fulminates against Scott for the narrowness of his vision as a "Canadian, Orangeman, bigot, blasphemer," but he then suggests that Riel hears the "voice of God calling through wilderness" in English (26, 37). Contrarily, in his monumental documentary play *Bois-Brûlés*, the Québec actor, director, and playwright Jean-Louis Roux has Riel and Scott discussing the latter's culpability in the death of what the Ontario chauvinist calls an "espion métis" (63)—en français! Judging by either text, it would be difficult to discern that Red River was a heterogeneous community and that linguistic polyphony was one of its great chasms. Even a more recent work, such as Chester Brown's *Louis Riel: A Comic-Strip Biography*, analyzed in chapter 7, does not adequately reproduce the discourse of characters when they express themselves in languages other than English, although the author attempts to develop a method to do so. Brown indicates that a character is speaking in French (or another language) by placing the text in the speech bubbles in brackets (9). Yet the result is that the writing still appears in English, meaning that Anglophone readers do not have to risk being alienated by communication in a tongue they may not understand. Those individuals never face the utter sense of disorientation that Moore and Languirand show the unilingual English-speaker Scott experiencing when the Métis court martial tries him exclusively in French. As an anguished Scott bellows, "Will someone tell me what the hell / is going on?" (19). Like the Orangeman's foes, the librettists sometimes choose not to translate.

Furthermore, other languages appear in *Louis Riel* besides English and French. After Riel refuses to pardon Scott, his sister Sara implores God to have mercy on her whole family in Latin:

"Deus miseratur" (Moore and Languirand 21, see also 7). Similarly, Father André is saying Mass in Latin when his church is invaded first by Wandering Spirit and then Riel (39-40). In addition, Act III opens with Marguerite Riel singing what has become both the opera's most famous and most contentious aria, "Kuyas," in Cree (*Louis Riel*). Early critics like the composer R. Murray Schafer deemed "Kuyas" "very beautiful" (19), but recently it has generated immense controversy because the Cree lullaby is based on a (West Coast) Nisga'a mourning dirge called "Song of Skateen." The musicologist Dylan Robinson has shown that this is not just a case of cultural appropriation but a "serious infraction of Nisga'a law" (qtd. in Communications Staff), since the song was reproduced without the permission of the family that owns the hereditary rights to it. Ironically, the last statement that Somers made before he died in 1999, which he dictated to his wife as he was no longer able to write, was the command: "No one can mess with *Riel* without consulting Victor [Feldbrill, the original production's conductor]—should only be performed in its entirety as in its last performances with COC" (Somers, *Secret Agent* 342). This has turned out not to be the case. In light of Robinson's intervention, in 2020, the Moore and Somers estates acknowledged that the unauthorized usage of "Kuyas" constitutes "an egregious breach" and agreed to have it replaced with a new aria by the Métis composer Ian Cusson, "Dodo, mon tout petit," based on an early draft that Moore had written for the aria but was not used (COC Staff). It is also worth mentioning that in the published libretto, unlike the opera, "Kuyas" appears in French, not Cree (Moore and Languirand 34-35).

The handling of the aria "Kuyas" underlines the import as well as the limitations of the bilingualism of *Louis Riel*, evincing its hegemonic Canadianness. Canada, as the comparative literature scholar and poet E.D. Blodgett has argued, is "a federation that refuses to consider the usefulness and value of the federation" (*Five* 18). This is most noticeable in literary studies, in which members of one of the two dominant cultural groups seldom engage systematically with the literary production of the other—a trend that

Blodgett contends solidified after the War Measures Act of 1970 ("Comparative" 5). By accepting that he needed to collaborate with Languirand to capture Riel's complexity, Moore demonstrates that he does not share this myopia. Yet what is also uncontestable is that Moore and Languirand still subscribe to a narrow vision of Canada, a Canada dominated by the so-called "charter" cultures, English and French. The complication is that, as the twentieth-century Métis political activist Harry Daniels points out in "The Myth of the Two Founding Peoples," it is not possible to capture the real Canada unless one realizes that "national identity" requires a vision that "has respect for and embraces all cultures" in the country (We Are 3; see also Blodgett, Five 207). More precisely, it is no longer possible to fashion a Canada that does not consider the contributions of Indigenous peoples.

Something similar happens in the opera musically. Somers's music contributes to the overall vision of *Louis Riel* in different ways. As there is a multiplicity of languages in the work, so there are many types of music. While favouring the modernist mode, Somers includes a number of folksongs. Unfortunately, most of them are not Métis but from random Indigenous sources. If the composer had wanted to use music as a marker of Métis identity, fiddling would have been the most obvious choice. But, as Simonot-Maiello shows, "Somers incorporated very little music of the Métis people into his opera," marking Riel with "a pan-Indigeneity" that overshadows his national specificity (76; see also Giroux, "Goddamn").

The musicologist Robin Elliott has encapsulated what contemporaneous critics identified as the main flaws in *Louis Riel*: "there were too many characters and not enough character development and only Riel emerged as a multi-sided and complex personality, while Macdonald was a caricature rather than a worthy opponent of Riel" (16). Some of the work's weaknesses are blatant, both historically and dramatically. When Riel goes into a "MYSTICAL TRANCE" at the church outside Batoche and tells the congregants that God spoke to him during the night and that "je prophétise / qu'une armée viendra de l'Est," the librettists have Gabriel Dumont translate Riel's words into English: "He said an army comes, from the East" (Moore and Languirand 42). This is a startling twist. Although illiterate, the historical Dumont was renowned for his facility for languages—except English, of which "he never learnt more than a few words" (Woodcock, *Gabriel Dumont* 45, see also 237)—and which was one of the reasons he decided to invite the formally-educated Riel to help prepare the petitions to send to the federal government. More debilitating structurally, the opera's creators could never determine who their protagonist is. It could be argued that if there is one tragic figure in the work, it is neither Riel nor Macdonald but Taché. There is no more poignant scene in the opera than at the end of Act I when, upon discerning that Ottawa will not be delivering the much-promised amnesty to Riel and his supporters, Taché cries out: "They've made me a traitor to my people..." (Moore and Languirand 32). Taché's lament reveals the sort of self-knowledge, and self-responsibility, of which both Macdonald and Riel appear incapable. In Riel's case, he publicly berates Taché for failing to deliver the pardon (31), as if his own actions had nothing to do with it. The reality is that the historical Taché had been promised by Macdonald that if "the insurgents" returned Fort Garry to the HBC, the Canadian government would pay for "any stores or goods" consumed, and there would be "a general amnesty granted" (Letter to Taché 751). But the reprieve was not meant to cover the taking of human life, such as the summary execution of Thomas Scott. Also, the St. Boniface prelate is able to attain such grandeur despite the fact the opera does not include the episode when the historical Taché returns from Rome to Red River early in 1870, only to be greeted by a "guard of 20 men" placed around his residence and orders from his protégé that "he is not allowed to see anyone" (Begg 332). Taché falls victim to the machinations of Macdonald and Riel, who turn out to be both mere politicians, not exactly the most promising material with which to create operatic heroes.

Regardless of the dissension it has elicited in the twenty-first century, *Louis Riel* remains a milestone, both politically and musically. Opera is considered the most elite genre in Western art music. It is an expensive art form that tends to be inaccessible to the general public because of its frequent use of unfamiliar languages and esoteric musical styles. This is particularly true of "grand opera," full-length and artistically ambitious works designed for a major national company. Before 1967, the Canadian opera scene was a poor copy of the European one, marking Canada as a backwater, what the editor of the German magazine *Opernwelt* characterized as "a blank on the cultural map" (qtd. in Chalmers 242). In that context, *Louis Riel* has usually been seen as the first serious, truly Canadian opera, signalling that Canada had come into its own from a cultural perspective and was no longer just the colonial cultural offspring of England and France. The work's modernist musical style, with its angular melodies and electronic sounds, put Somers (and Canada) in the company of an international group of composers active in the style of Western art music. Furthermore, it did so with a story about an Indigenous figure.

That said, the idea of presenting Riel as a Canadian hero was always bound to face major obstacles, possibly insurmountable ones. Riel, as the Centennial opera demonstrates, is "either a victim of Canadian expansionism or an enemy of Canada" (Braz, *False Traitor* 101), or perhaps both. It may be true that the historical Riel was "a champion of fundamental values and principles that Canadians hold dear today, including equality and social justice," as the Minister of Crown-Indigenous Relations, Carolyn Bennett, stated on 16 November 2018 (Bennett)—so long as those values encompass a tendency to silence the press and to threaten to arrest one's opponents (Begg 159, 296; see also Peel, *Early Printing* 19–37). But it is patently true that a member of Riel's counsel at his 1885 treason trial, the future minister of justice and chief justice of the Supreme Court of Canada Charles Fitzpatrick, described Riel to the jury as "a foreigner and an alien at least in language to us" and as "an alien in race and an alien in religion, so far as you and I are concerned" (*Queen* 302, 310). The latter is a detail that Moore, Languirand, Somers, and Chalmers had to forget before they could contemplate turning Riel into the national hero that Canadians ought to honour during the Centennial. The Canadianization of

Riel is thus not nearly as positive as it seems at first glance, since it requires the effacement of his national specificity as a Métis, the collective identity that led him to clash with Canada, and which cannot yet be fully recognized. Whatever else it may accomplish, Louis Riel dramatizes the difficulties of accommodating, even discursively, the various nations that exist within the nation-state called Canada.

Afterword: Louis Riel in the New Millennium

Many of the contradictions in Louis Riel arise from the fact it is the work of (at least cultural) descendants of the people who condemned the Métis leader to death. Less than three months before Riel was hanged for treason, his Franco-American friend Edmond Mallet foretold that, before long, "the children of his executors" would "erect monuments to his memory" ("Appendix F" 164). Mallet's prediction has come to pass, and the Centennial opera is just one of the better known of those monuments. Also, Mallet's apparent slip of the tongue may not have been so since the progeny of those who "executed" Riel have also become his "executors," largely controlling his posthumous image (Braz, False Traitor 4–5, 197–204). Still, some of the difficulties of representing Riel in the twenty-first century are due not only to his conflicted relationship with Canada but also with the First Nations and even with the Métis. This is evident in the 2017 revival of the opera, which transmutes his Métis nationalism into a pan-Indigenous sentiment. The individuals behind the new production conveniently neglect the specificity of the Métis, who, as a post-contact Indigenous people, are "disconnected from the legal and policy realities of the Indian Act" (Gaudry, "Building" 214). As the future Prime Minister Wilfrid Laurier pointed out in the mid-1880s, the Métis were "treated as a special class…participating in the rights of both the whites and the Indians" (217). Also, because of the ethnoreligious configuration of their nationalism, the Métis often failed to garner the support of both neighbouring First Nations and their Anglo-Protestant Halfbreed cousins (Riel, Collected Writings 1: 246–47; see also Prince 107–09; Stonechild and Waiser 77).

The Canadian Opera Company's remount of *Louis Riel* was part of the sesquicentennial of Confederation, and implicitly of Riel's contribution to it. The production, which premiered in Toronto in April 2017 and then toured Ottawa and Québec City, was managed by Peter Hinton, a respected theatre director with less experience in opera. Working in the aftermath of the release of the reports by the Truth and Reconciliation Commission, Hinton faced a series of challenges as he attempted to reimagine the opera, given the call by the Commission for Canadians to support "Aboriginal peoples' cultural revitalization and integrat[e] Indigenous knowledge systems, oral histories, laws, protocols, and connections to the land into the reconciliation process" (Truth and Reconciliation, *What* 4). Hinton's most topical response was to insert into the opera a Land Assembly, a chorus of Indigenous performers who silently appraise the performance, reflecting his conviction that "history is not linear but a circle; a circle that is inclusive and expanding" ("Director's Notes" 38). While voiceless, the Land Assembly does not merely judge the narrative being staged but shapes it, as Hinton concedes. He has explained that when Riel experiences his first mystical vision at the end of Act I, a female member of the Land Assembly "throws tobacco on his fire and he sees her and he begins a dialogue with God and the idea is that Riel sees a modern Indigenous women [sic], that is his vision, he sees today" (qtd. in Danckert 46), rousing the Indigenous chorus and, by extension, Indigenous people as a whole. Hinton adds that the interaction between the Land Assembly and Riel is "a double kind of thing, it's telling yes, people are awoken by Riel's prophecy but that Riel is seeing the country, like he is seeing the actual people, so, who is inspiring what, is the dialogue...he is such a symbol in that opera, a symbol for the reconciliation that hasn't existed" (46). Hinton's Riel, one infers, is not just a religious visionary but one who is inspired by Indigenous spirituality and is impelled to bring together the Indigenous and non-Indigenous peoples in Canada.

It may seem capricious to be critical of any promotion of the reconciliation of peoples, but there is something suspect about Hinton's interpretation of Riel. To begin with, one cannot help but notice that in the libretto, Riel's communion with God is not mediated by an Indigenous woman but by Bishop Bourget. It is because the Montréal ultramontane cleric informs him he has a "mission" that Riel becomes convinced not only that he is the David of the Christian era but that he is not "fou" (Moore and Languirand 35). Moreover, the librettists are reiterating claims made by the historical Riel (*Collected Writings* 2: 35), something that cannot be said of Hinton's exegesis. In his defence, Hinton asserts that a distinctive feature of the 2017 revival of *Louis Riel* is that it was shaped by "the counsel of those who have reminded us to listen," as he and his team sought and followed the "advice and guidance" of members of the Indigenous community ("Director's Notes" 38). Interestingly, one foundational Indigenous resource that Hinton and his associates appear not to have consulted is Riel's own writings. Evidence suggests that they did not even familiarize themselves much with biographies of Riel. To phrase it differently, they meant to pay homage to Riel without acquainting themselves with his ideas; perhaps through telepathy of the heart.

In his program notes for the performances of the opera at the National Arts Centre in June 2017, "Honouring Indigeneity in *Louis Riel* / Honorer l'indigénéité de *Louis Riel*," the COC's Adult Programs Manager Gianmarco Segato writes that Hinton made a conscious effort to counter the work's "cultural baggage" (16). Segato states that the remount corrected historical errors made by its 1967 predecessor. He offers the example that, according to the libretto, the Saskatchewan Valley delegation that travelled to Montana to meet with Riel was composed of three men: the Métis Gabriel Dumont, the Halfbreed James Isbister, and the Cree Poundmaker. "In actual fact," elucidates Segato, "a fourth man was part of the group, the European settler Louis Schmidt." So Hinton decided to emend the historical inaccuracy by re-including Schmidt in the production and have him "sing lines originally given to Poundmaker" (17).

This is an intriguing, if retrograde, approach, as the "European" Schmidt gets to sing lines that in the Centennial version belonged to Poundmaker, replacing an Indigenous voice with a white one. Also, it is true that the historical Saskatchewan delegation sent to Montana had four members: Dumont, Isbister, and two other Métis, Michel Dumas and Moïse Ouellette. Schmidt (like Poundmaker), though, was not part of the group, as the historical Riel's response to the invitation to travel north testifies (*Collected Writings* 3: 1–9). More puzzling, rather than being a European settler, Schmidt was Métis. Actually, he was a close friend of Riel since childhood, being one of the three Métis boys (along with Riel and Daniel McDougall) that Bishop Taché sent to Québec in 1858 to train for the Catholic priesthood. Schmidt is, therefore, an important figure in the Riel story, but for reasons that Hinton and his team appear to be oblivious. Along with Riel (and McDougall), Schmidt did not complete his studies, returning to Red River after three years because of poor health and other undisclosed factors (Huel, "Louis Schmidt" 88; see also Schmidt 458). When Riel came back home in 1868, the two young men renewed their friendship. Schmidt eventually became the secretary of the Red River provisional government, a position that rendered him both a participant and a witness to the Resistance; he may even have been one of the Métis loyalists secretly entrusted with the disposal of Scott's body (Dubé 39–41). In the "Memoirs" that he published serially in a Saskatchewan newspaper in 1912, Schmidt describes Riel as "a born orator," being naturally "enthusiastic and a little exalted," which is why "his speeches made a great impression on crowds" (465). After serving in the Manitoba Legislative Assembly in the 1870s, Schmidt joined the Métis exodus to the Saskatchewan Valley and became involved in local politics. He was asked to be part of the Montana delegation but could not go since he recently had been appointed to a position with the federal government's Lands Office in Prince Albert. However, after Riel arrived in Batoche, Schmidt offered his services to his friend, who advised him to stay at the Lands Office, "where he could do more good for the Métis cause" (Huel, "Louis Schmidt" 89). Riel later expressed his appreciation for the "very good service" that Schmidt rendered to the Saskatchewan Métis, being one of the few people who publicized their efforts to assert their rights (Riel, *Collected Writings* 3: 20).

But Schmidt must have come to regret his role in Riel's return to Canada. An orthodox Catholic, he grew progressively troubled by Riel's religious ideas, concerns he conveyed in a series of notes that he sent to their old mentor, Taché. So distraught was Schmidt by what he deemed Riel's heresies that he was grateful "Riel had been crushed just in time because more Métis were about to follow him into the horrible abyss of apostasy" (Huel, "Louis Schmidt" 92).

Thus there may be some logic to the Hinton production's transformation of the Métis Louis Schmidt into a "European settler." The historical Schmidt epitomizes some of the existential ideological divisions among the Métis themselves, to say nothing of those between the Métis and the Halfbreeds or the First Nations. Like Riel's military commander at Red River, Ambroise Lépine, Schmidt in time felt that he could not support Riel in 1885. This was not because Schmidt had changed, but because Riel had. Schmidt concluded that his friend's new vision would be catastrophic for their people, not only politically and economically but also spiritually, and Schmidt was far from being the only Métis who felt this way (Stonechild and Waiser 148, 162).

In an interview with the magazine *Opera Canada* before the 2017 premiere of *Louis Riel*, Hinton says that the Métis leader is "a great social activist. He is Martin Luther King a hundred years before Martin Luther King" (Hinton and *Opera Canada* 33). Yet it is not at all clear that Hinton's interventions in the opera are motivated by a desire to understand Riel, much less to honour him, as reflected in his lack of interest in Riel's writings. By foregrounding the work's "colonial biases rather than trying to minimize them," Hinton may have "intended to indicate that the opera itself was on trial" (Simonot-Maiello 75)—perhaps even that, as written, "the goddamn opera is dead" (Giroux, "Goddamn"). But despite his affirmations of inclusivity, and his avowed belief that history is an ever-expanding circle, there is no sense that we get a deeper insight into Riel in his remount of the opera than we do in the 1967 version. Riel remains a symbol, unencumbered by an awareness of his prolix self-representations, calling into question the motivation for restaging an opera bearing his name.

The Bard's Apocryphal Song

4

Rudy Wiebe, Pierre Falcon, and Riel

> we are not a part of your mosaic
> we are the mortar that glues you together
> —KATHERENA VERMETTE, *river woman*

IN A STUDY of the Canadianization of Riel, there are several questions that are extremely difficult to answer. The most glaring of these is the nature of his extraordinary appeal to contemporary Canadians: why are we so invested in Riel? In light of the mid-twentieth-century turn to the nation, and away from empire, it is not surprising that Canadians would search for heroes deeply grounded in the national space. But this could include almost any Indigenous historical figure. Moreover, most First Nations leaders would be much more indelibly shaped by strictly Canadian cultural, political, and spiritual forces than would the priest-educated Riel. So perhaps, as has been argued, Riel's allure resides precisely in his combining within himself both Indigenous and non-Indigenous elements, potentially serving as a bridge between Canada's two real solitudes (Stanley, "Last Word" 54). However, Riel also embodies some of the country's great divides—French and English, East and West, and Indigenous and non-Indigenous—making one wonder what sort of Canada he symbolizes. No matter from which angle one scans his story, it is hard to avoid the conclusion that he was a casualty of Confederation. Thomas Flanagan actually argues that what has given Riel his "immortality in the collective Canadian self-consciousness" is his death at the hands of the Canadian state (*Riel* 9), a misdeed that is complicated by his analogous treatment of Thomas Scott.

The individuals responsible for the creation of the best-known cultural representations of Riel have not been very helpful as to why they have chosen to memorialize him. Floyd Chalmers, for example, blazons that he rejected the request to finance an opera based on *The Luck of Ginger Coffey* because Brian Moore's protagonist was a recently arrived immigrant who "didn't relate much to Canadian history and traditions" (239). Coffey certainly does not evoke the nation-building tradition, being surrounded by people who tell him that the "greatest mistake" Canada "ever made was not joining the United States" (B. Moore 73) and that "nobody wants to talk about Canada, not even us Canadians. You're right, Paddy. Canada is a bore" (214). For Chalmers, what makes the Riel story so captivating, besides involving "colossal misunderstanding, mixed with death and destruction," is that it demands to "be sung in the two official languages" (Chalmers 239). But French-English bilingualism and biculturalism do not always seem to be integral to Chalmers's vision of Canada, nor does a focus on Canadian issues. Following the euphoric reception of *Louis Riel* as a modern operatic "masterpiece" (241), Chalmers was prompted to commission another opera. Some composers and writers he approached favoured Big Bear, the Plains Cree chief who resisted signing a treaty with Canada around the period of the North-West War, but Chalmers insisted that Sitting Bull was a more worthy subject for a grand opera. "I stuck to Sitting Bull," he stressed, "for one particular reason: he would have an equal appeal in the United States and in Canada. I do not want this opera to be perceived as only interesting to Canadians" (244). That is, some historical figures, like Big Bear, can be too domestic to warrant being memorialized in Canada, which may explain why Canadian writers, musicians, visual artists, and scholars keep returning to Riel.

Because of Riel's cultural and national liminality, there are other questions that pose a challenge. One is, what is the earliest representation of him as an unequivocal Canadian hero? Another is, what are the aesthetically significant portrayals of Riel, either as Canadian, Métis, or something else? Much easier to establish is, what is the most ambitious single volume of fiction ever written about Riel? That is undoubtedly Rudy Wiebe's 1977 novel *The Scorched-Wood People*. To a great degree, Wiebe would appear to have been the ideal writer to capture Riel in all his complexity. Deeply religious, he is not ill-disposed to many of Riel's spiritual beliefs, including those about the afterlife. As Wiebe stated during a 1980 joint interview with his close friend Robert Kroetsch, "death is change, just an entrance into something else that we're not aware of now. It's not the end of anything. It's impossible for me to conceive that death on earth ends anything" (Wiebe, Kroetsch, and Neuman 235). Wiebe also has long been concerned about the place of Indigenous peoples in Canada, and what it reveals about his homeland. By the early 1970s, in the heyday of Canadian cultural nationalism, other writers were penning panegyrics about Canada being "a collective victim" of successive imperial powers (Atwood, *Survival* 45). Wiebe, instead, was arguing that the previous two decades had "destroyed the myth that Canada is a classless, non-racist society" and that the situation would not improve until Canadians transformed the "Indian" into "our central, not our fringe figure" ("Western Canada" 29). Still, there is little agreement regarding Wiebe's achievement in his portrayal of Riel. For the literary scholar Sam Solecki, *The Scorched-Wood People* is not just "magnificent" but "the great novel about Riel that we all knew would eventually be written" (Bilan and Solecki 174, 178). Part of the reason Solecki is enamoured with the book is that he finds it "a brilliant fictionalizing upon an infrastructure of events drawn from history" (175). Yet the historian Donald Swainson calls *The Scorched-Wood People* "bad history, bad allegory and, at least to this ingrate, a singularly unsuccessful novel" (38). This chapter will attempt to show both why Wiebe's text has generated such antithetical responses and which is more persuasive.

Rudy Wiebe was born in 1934 in north-central Saskatchewan. The son of Mennonite immigrants who had recently arrived in

Canada from Soviet Russia, Wiebe spent the first twelve years of his life in a remote German-speaking community near Turtle Lake, halfway between North Battleford and Meadow Lake (Wiebe, *Of This Earth* 5-34). In 1947, his family moved to the small southern Alberta town of Coaldale, outside Lethbridge, where he would spend the rest of his youth. Upon completing high school, Wiebe travelled north to Edmonton to attend the University of Alberta. He had intended to pursue the "usual Mennonite boy's dream of making plenty of money" by, in his case, studying to "be a doctor." But he changed his plans after taking a creative writing course with a professor of English named F.M. Salter, who encouraged his students to write about their lived experiences and who would become a major influence in his career (Wiebe, Reimer, and Steiner 126; see also Wiebe, "Skull" 258–59). Wiebe earned a Bachelor of Arts in English in 1956 and then studied literature and theology at the University of Tübingen, in what was at the time West Germany (Kertzer, "Biocritical Essay" xiv). Following his European sojourn, he returned to the University of Alberta, where in 1960, he obtained a Master of Arts in creative writing for a thesis that he wrote under Salter's supervision and which would become his first novel, *Peace Shall Destroy Many*. Married and with three children, he relocated with his family to Winnipeg. In Manitoba's capital, he studied education and "for a while taught high school" before getting a BA in theology from the Mennonite Brethren Bible College (Kertzer, "Biocritical Essay" xvi), now part of the Canadian Mennonite University. Between 1962 and 1963, he served as the editor of the *Mennonite Brethren Herald*, "the largest Mennonite English paper in Canada" (Wiebe, "Skull" 263). Wiebe resigned from the position because of the controversy elicited within the Mennonite community by the publication of *Peace Shall Destroy Many* and, for the next four years, taught English at Goshen College in Indiana. Then, in 1967, the Centennial year, he joined the University of Alberta, where he taught English and creative writing until his retirement as a professor emeritus in 1992.

There are two overarching concerns in Wiebe's writings, the Mennonite condition and Canadian social history, particularly that of the Prairies and the North. Both interests are already evident in *Peace Shall Destroy Many* (1962), a text that I will revisit later in this chapter. Set in 1944 in a community very much like the one where Wiebe was born, the novel dramatizes how the pious residents of Wapiti may be able to avoid external wars but cannot evade internal ones. Although there are Indigenous people in the periphery of the settlement, the main focus is on what it means to lead a righteous Mennonite life, dominated by pacifism and a literal reading of the Bible. In his next two novels, *First and Vital Candle* (1966) and *The Blue Mountains of China* (1970), Wiebe continued to investigate the challenges of living a Christian existence in an increasingly secular age. Unlike his first novel, they also required a considerable amount of investigation.

First and Vital Candle depicts an agnostic's collision with "the ghastly emptiness of the modern world" and, as Jonathan Kertzer notes, features "the first of Wiebe's heroes to seek sanctuary in the far north" ("Biocritical Essay" xx). Symbolically, the protagonist heads to the Arctic only after making a pilgrimage to the St. Boniface tomb of the idealistic Riel, sacrificed by the Canadian state for being "so foolish as to try to realize" his dreams (Wiebe, *First* 40). *The Blue Mountains of China* is an epic chronicle of Mennonite history. It traces the Mennonite odyssey from its beginnings in sixteenth-century Netherlands and Switzerland, through the attempts to escape persecution by fleeing to northern Germany and Eastern Europe, to the subsequent migration to North and South America. One of the places to which Wiebe travelled to conduct research for the novel was the semi-arid Chaco region of western Paraguay, which has become home for several Mennonite colonies. It was his experience in South America that enabled Wiebe "to see much more clearly" the true nature of the relations between Canada and Indigenous peoples (Wiebe, Kroetsch, and Neuman 239). The consequence of this interchange was the writing of his novel *The Temptations of Big Bear* (1973), his historical meditation on the implications of the Cree chief's resistance to the settlement of what became the Canadian Prairies.

The Temptations of Big Bear, a text that Riel haunts, is a landmark in Wiebe's career. Besides being the recipient of the 1973 Governor General's Award for Fiction, it was the work that first gained Wiebe acclaim among both critics and the general Canadian reading public. Equally important, and perhaps not accidentally, the novel signals "an expansion" of Wiebe's sphere of interest "from the history of his own people to the history of his land" (Keith, *Epic Fiction* 13). Since Wiebe is not Indigenous, such a shift inevitably raises questions about cultural appropriation as well as perspective. These are issues that Wiebe examines at length in his much-anthologized short story "Where Is the Voice Coming From?" (1971), an exploration of the difficulties of capturing the essence of an individual like the young Saskatchewan Cree warrior Almighty Voice when the author does not "understand the Cree" ("Where" 40). The matter of perspective becomes even more pronounced in Wiebe's fifth novel, *The Scorched-Wood People* (1977), his fictionalization of the rise and fall of the Métis nation as a political entity, concentrating mainly on Louis Riel and Gabriel Dumont.

The most unusual feature of *The Scorched-Wood People* is that it is narrated by the Métis bard Pierre Falcon. Born in 1793 in what is now the west-central Manitoba town of Swan River, Falcon is recognized as the first denizen of Red River who "put the life of the country into verse" (M. MacLeod 1). Although most of his compositions were never written down and have been lost, they are believed to have been "carried by the voyageurs from the Saint Lawrence [River] to the Mackenzie" (Peel, "Falcon"). Falcon's surviving songs deal almost exclusively with Métis political events, and none is more influential than the one celebrating the Métis victory over the Selkirk settlers at Seven Oaks on 19 June 1816, which marked their genesis as a people. Known under a variety of titles, such as "La victoire des Bois-Brûlés," "La bataille des Sept-Chênes," and, most commonly, "La chanson de la Grenouillère," or "The Song of Frog Plain" (Braz, "Duelling Authors" 162), Falcon's "chanson de vérité" immortalized the day when brave Métis, under the leadership of Falcon's brother-in-law Cuthbert Grant, repulsed the attempt by a group of Scottish interlopers to "piller not' pays" (Falcon,

"Bataille" 6). As Katherine Durnin has perceptively remarked, the power of Falcon's Seven Oaks song lies in the fact that it is at once an "expression of a pre-existing national sentiment" and "a *performance* of nationhood aimed at building national consciousness through its rhetorical effects" (62). It is no wonder that contemporary Métis have adopted it as their national anthem (Chartrand, *Pierriche Falcon* 4–5), or that Wiebe would present his novel through the creator of such a canonical Métis work.

One complication with having Falcon narrate a Métis political history is the time frame. The then septuagenarian Falcon did not participate in the 1869–1870 events at Red River, even if he allegedly expressed the desire to be allowed to distract the incoming Canadian lieutenant-governor William McDougall at the international border so that his younger comrades could "strike hard and get in many good blows" (qtd. in Peel, "Falcon"). Since Falcon died in 1876, he could not have taken part in the disturbances along the South Saskatchewan River in 1885. For critics like George Woodcock, Wiebe's reliance on Falcon as a "spectral narrator strains one's credence to the wrenching point" (Woodcock, "Riel" 99). While sympathetic to Woodcock's reading, I am not persuaded that the most crippling feature of *The Scorched-Wood People* is its having a deceased narrator. Texts such as Machado de Assis's 1881 classic *The Posthumous Memoirs of Brás Cubas*, whose narrator nostalgically dedicates the manuscript to the worm that first "Gnawed the Cold Flesh of My Body" (Machado de Assis), suggest that post-death narration does not have to be fatal to a novel. What is much more damaging than Wiebe having a defunct narrator is that he does not always respect his narrator's integrity.

Wiebe's Falcon does not just narrate *The Scorched-Wood People* but writes it. According to the epigraph to the first edition of the novel, the text was composed by the Métis bard himself:

And who has made this song?
Who else but good Pierre Falcon.
He made the song, and it was sung
To mark the victory we had won;

> He made this song that very day,
>
> So sing the glory of the Bois-brûlés. (Wiebe, *Scorched-Wood*)

The epigraph, which is an English translation of the last stanza of Falcon's Seven Oaks song (Falcon, "Bataille" 7), has not appeared in later editions of the novel (Braz, *False Traitor* 178). But as one reads Wiebe's text, one cannot help but sense that it is designed to convey the impression that it emanates from within the Métis community.

The ostensible Métisness of *The Scorched-Wood People* is emphasized from the outset. Wiebe's novel is divided into four asymmetrical parts: 1) Riel's Province; 2) Wilderness; 3) Gabriel's Army; and 4) Riel and Gabriel, a five-page, epilogue-like conclusion. The text begins with an extended and somewhat ponderous description of Riel getting attired in front of a mirror for some official occasion. We gradually learn that it is 8 December 1869, and Riel is about to declare to the inhabitants of Red River that he and the rest of the Métis National Council have seized Fort Garry and will form "the Provisional Government of the North-West for the maintenance of law and order and the protection of its people" (30). The as-yet unidentified narrator, who states that he "know[s]" intimately both Riel's mind and the inner goings-on of his government, also reveals that sixteen years later, "Riel would be dressing himself again, just as carefully," before being "hanged by his neck until he is at last, perfectly, dead" (10). By the end of the first paragraph, we are made privy to the narrative's tragic denouement and to the fact the protagonist is doomed.

Falcon is of course the narrator and, as he often points out, he is a Métis insider. He is such a respected elder figure that even Riel addresses him reverentially as "Grandfather" (Wiebe, *Scorched-Wood* 35 ff.). If one had any doubts about his exalted position in Métis society, they are dispelled when most members of the Red River provisional government enthusiastically assemble to listen to the new song that Falcon has composed to commemorate their ascent to power. Titled "The Sad Ballad of King Muck," the song derides the pretensions of the would-be lieutenant-governor McDougall, who "viewed our prairies" as his fiefdom (39) but whose "progress royal" was halted by a handful of intrepid Métis (41). Falcon refers to the Métis political leaders and soldiers as "our boys" and "my children" (18, 38), and credits them with having "given" him the McDougall song (36). He also affirms that he is someone who mulls over "the existence of lords and rulers" with Riel (11), just as he had with Grant back in 1816 (13, 55). In short, he is the embodiment of the Métis tradition.

Critics have long interpreted Wiebe's portrayal of Falcon as the narrator (and author) of *The Scorched-Wood People* as a way to give the novel ethnocultural authenticity. In his review, R.P. Bilan writes that Falcon's narration not only makes the story of Riel, Dumont, and their people "particularly vivid and compelling," but ensures that "history is seen completely from a Métis point of view" (Bilan and Solecki 171, 173; see also Grace 114, 116). Bilan does admit that at times, "Falcon seems less the voice of the Métis than the spokesman for Wiebe himself" (172), but I would argue that there are many instances in which Wiebe's impersonation of the Métis bard is far from seamless. Before all else, the historical Falcon was an oral poet. He composed narratives in verse that were intended to be shared with the general Métis populace, as one can discern even in James Reaney's English translation of the opening of his Seven Oaks song:

> Would you like to hear me sing
> Of a true and recent thing?
> It was June nineteen, the band of Bois-Brûlés
> Arrived that day,
> Oh the brave warriors they!
>
> We took three foreigners prisoners when
> We came to the place called Frog, Frog Plain.
> They were men who'd come from Orkney,
> Who'd come, you see,
> To rob our country. (Falcon, "Battle" 7)

Wiebe is wont to style himself as first and foremost "a storyteller" (Wiebe, Reimer, and Steiner 128), but it is hard to imagine *The Scorched-Wood People* being declaimed around a campfire, or anywhere else. In his essay "The Storyteller," the cultural critic and philosopher Walter Benjamin contends that what sets "the novel [apart] from all other forms of prose literature...is that it neither comes from oral tradition nor goes into it" (187). This is patently true of Wiebe's novels, which are renowned not for their accessibility but their denseness, including their nonlinear narratives and "idiosyncratic...punctuation" (Morison and Wiebe 22). Whatever else it may be, *The Scorched-Wood People* is not an oral text but a written one and not likely to be the creation of an oral poet.

Furthermore, Wiebe's portrayal of Falcon is problematic not only formally but also thematically. One of the most peculiar aspects of *The Scorched-Wood People* is that it depicts Dumont as being actively engaged during the Red River troubles. As we saw in chapter 2, John Coulter wrote three plays about Riel without presenting his 1885 military commander as a character in a single one of them. In an apparent case of Saskatchewan-centrism, Wiebe compensates for Coulter by inserting Dumont into the Red River conflict, where he is not known to have played any role at all. Wiebe introduces Dumont at the beginning of the novel, when he has the buffalo hunter arrive from the Saskatchewan country with three of his fellow "savages" just in time to join Ambroise-Dydime Lépine's patrol tasked with preventing McDougall from entering Red River and then to publicly salute "our chief, Louis Riel!" (Wiebe, *Scorched-Wood* 19, 33). In an earlier treatment he wrote for an aborted CBC Television film on Riel, Wiebe also places Dumont at Red River in 1869–1870, but he specifies that "Dumont must be seen in the background" ("Riel" 158). In the novel, however, Dumont's intervention at Red River is critical to the Métis success. As Wiebe's Falcon underlines in one of his proclamations, "That was what built our unity in 1869: the planning and ceremony of Riel, the emotion of Gabriel" (Wiebe, *Scorched-Wood* 33, see also 186). For Riel, Dumont is such "a great strength" (109) that he is unable to think of ways to express the breadth of his gratitude.

Falcon's assessment of Dumont's contribution to the Red River Resistance is perplexing. Woodcock, the author of a much-lauded biography of Dumont, was not amused by the liberties Wiebe takes with the subject, whom Woodcock contends is portrayed as "a muscular oaf" ("Riel" 100), in line with his traditional image as "a kind of bluff, sturdy Sancho Panza to the Canadian Don Quixote" (*Gabriel Dumont* 8). Wiebe himself has never persuasively explained what justifies having Dumont at Red River, either historically or dramatically. In a 1981 interview with the editor of the *Riel Project* BULLETIN *du Projet Riel*, during the editing of Riel's *Collected Writings*, Wiebe says his "point is not that Dumont actually was at Red River dancing on a buffalo robe, but that this is what he would have done" (Wiebe and Rocan 4). His reasoning sounds circular, especially for someone who deems "names...very important" and "would not ascribe words or actions to historical people which are out of character for those people" (4; see also Wiebe and Wyile 72, 75). If the "true" Dumont would have gone to Red River, one is prompted to ask, who or what stopped him?

Another reason that the characterization of Dumont is dubious is that it is anything but innocent. Wiebe is not satisfied with lionizing Dumont because, as he remarks in the just-mentioned interview, "Dumont...represents the wild and passionate part of the Métis" (Wiebe and Rocan 4). He also uses Falcon to disparage Riel's Red River commander, Lépine, who is found wanting in relation to the Saskatchewan force of nature. Falcon imparts to the reader, as he listens to Dumont and Lépine discuss Riel's leadership qualities, that "Lépine is very big and has a general's looks and good voice but when Riel chose him I told him Lépine had no words" (Wiebe, *Scorched-Wood* 13). Lépine, insinuates Falcon, is no Cuthbert Grant, who, despite his relative youth "in 1816, already had the words that could persuade us of anything, that made us feel we could gallop over the world before we rode out to face [Robert] Semple at Seven Oaks" (13). Falcon adds that he ascertains other Métis "men laughed but Lépine didn't. That's what I told Riel too: Lépine never laughs either" (13–14, see also 23). Given that Riel attained his greatest political triumph, not in partnership with Dumont but with Lépine, it is bewildering that the treasured Métis bard would be so determined to malign him.

The Red River historian and Presbyterian minister R.G. MacBeth, for example, had a very different conception of the historical Lépine, describing him as a "striking figure...a man of magnificent physique, standing fully six feet three and built in splendid proportion" (43). MacBeth, who was in his early teens during the Resistance, writes that Lépine "had great influence amongst his compatriots" and that it was doubtlessly because of "his physical prowess and striking military appearance" he "soon obtained control of their armed movements" (44). Without excusing Lépine's "complicity" in the Thomas Scott affair, MacBeth contends that "of all the leaders of the rebellion he was the only one who manifested anything like manliness after it was over, by refusing to stay abroad and by submitting to arrest, saying that the law could take its course with him seeing he had only done what he thought was his duty" (44). This appraisal is echoed by Riel's Red River secretary Louis Schmidt, who defines Lépine as "bravery itself...Like all superior men, he was mild with the smaller ones. But he did not spare the big and strong," although noting that he was not "the idol of the soldiers" (465, 466). Most important, the historical Riel did not share Falcon's view of Lépine, whom he considered one of his "dévoués amis" who worked tirelessly to help him achieve his political aims (Riel, Collected Writings 1: 403)—and who, it has been asserted, was "put in the dock" for the death of Scott as a stand in for his exiled leader (Bumsted, Louis Riel 7). Riel was devastated when he learned that his first commander was found criminally guilty by the court, a verdict he repudiated, pronouncing Lépine "pas du tout coupable" (Riel, Collected Writings 1: 403). Also, his admiration for Lépine never wavered. In one of the revelations he received in the Regina jail in 1885, Riel writes that God informed him he wished to reward Lépine for having risked his life in defence of the "droits saints de l'église et de la patrie" (Collected Writings 3: 328), by renaming Lake Winnipeg after him (3: 329).

Granted, the historical Lépine will forever be negatively associated with Riel because of their imbrication in what is almost universally judged to be Riel's fatal error, his condoning the execution of Scott. Contemporary writers on Riel, such as Wiebe, often denounce the Canadian government for the political tenor of Riel's trial and for its slowness in acceding to "Riel's last request" to be buried alongside his father in St. Boniface (Wiebe, *Scorched-Wood* 348). But the reality is that, as Wiebe shows, Riel is defended by a brilliant team of lawyers and the federal government not only transports his body by train to Winnipeg but allows a public funeral to be held at St. Boniface Cathedral, what Wiebe's Falcon elegiacally characterizes as "the last great procession of our people behind the last of our chiefs" (349). In contrast, besides not being provided with a lawyer, Scott is not permitted to speak at his own trial, presided by Lépine, since his presence is "not necessary in a hunters' court" (79, see also 83). This is a peculiar rationale, given that the proceedings do not take place in the middle of the plains but at Fort Garry and under the jurisdiction, not of a hunting party, but of the supposedly duly constituted provisional government. No less troubling is that, according to testimony at the historical Lépine's trial, members of the squad that executed Scott "appeared to be excited by liquor," failed to kill him with their first rifle volley, and one of them had to finish Scott off by shooting "him in the head with a pistol" (*Preliminary Investigation* 58, 63). Most damning, something glossed over by Wiebe, the historical Riel did not intercede when Lépine authorized "the spiriting away" of Scott's body after the execution (38; see also Bumsted, "Trial" 16). Riel's inaction later led the Secretary of State J.A. Chapleau to advise Macdonald to allow the burial of Riel "to prevent the avengers of Scott's death from doing with Riel's body what was done with Scott's remains" (Chapleau 366)—a detail that becomes even more absorbing when one realizes that Chapleau had defended Lépine at his own trial. As depicted in Wiebe's novel, a priest tells Riel that he is "the leader here" and he "alone will be remembered for this" (*Scorched-Wood* 85). Yet Riel chooses to not intervene, which suggests that, even in his mid-twenties, he does not have to learn how to conduct realpolitik—or perhaps better "riel-politique" (Dubé 223-26)—from his older Canadian adversaries.

The historical Lépine is a controversial figure, as evident in the fact that, after refusing to give up Scott's body for proper burial, he allowed his lawyers to argue that there was no proof the Ontarian was dead as there was no corpse (*Preliminary Investigation* 8–9; see also Bumsted, "Trial" 12, 17). But then, to this day, no Métis has expressed "quelque regret" for Scott's execution (Dubé 227). As well, Wiebe's text hints that it is not Lépine's involvement in the death of Scott that renders him suspect but his close association with the Catholic clergy. Later in the novel, Falcon remarks that, like Grant, Dumont was not subservient to the Church and maybe "that was one reason they were our great generals: the priests had no hold over them" (Wiebe, *Scorched-Wood* 234). The insinuation is that this is not the case with Lépine. Presumably, it is because of his Catholic piety that Lépine who, earlier than most other Métis, "believed...Riel could hold the North-West for us," became deeply perturbed whenever "Riel left his body" during his religious ecstasies (21). It is true that when the North-West troubles erupted in 1885, the historical Lépine was conspicuous by his absence (Ens and Sawchuk 548). But it is also the case that during the 1849 Sayer affair, the ecclesiastically unfettered Grant served as one of the magistrates who upheld "the HBC's monopoly" that groups of Métis were challenging (Woodcock, "Grant"). So Lépine's real transgression seems to be his failure to accept Riel's fast-evolving religiosity.

Like Coulter, Wiebe emphasizes the religious dimension of both Métis-Canada conflicts, though at Red River, Riel's concerns were explicitly political, and he had not yet begun to see himself as a prophet. The focus on spiritual matters leads Wiebe to highlight the divide between Riel and the Catholic hierarchy, particularly Bishop (later Archbishop) Alexandre-Antonin Taché. Wiebe has Falcon inform the reader in the opening section of the novel that "I can tell you Bishop Taché was never Riel's mentor, not after he returned from Montreal and Chicago and St. Paul grown and cassockless" (*Scorched-Wood* 23, see also 98). Falcon adds that "Riel's confidant and guide" was Father Noël-Joseph Ritchot (23), the long-bearded Québec-born parish priest that the historical

Riel sent to Ottawa early in 1870 as the head of the delegation that negotiated the terms of Red River's relationship with Canada (Mailhot). Falcon further asserts that while Taché "loved us," unlike Ritchot, he "never learned: prayer in a language we could all understand but still kept in that path of holiness" (Wiebe, *Scorched-Wood* 24). Taché, Wiebe implies, preached down to his Métis flock, lacking the humility to learn their ways of being spiritual.

It is no secret that there was a rift between the historical Riel and Taché, primarily regarding the latter's failure to deliver the general amnesty that Prime Minister Macdonald had promised to all those involved in the Red River disturbances. This is emphasized by Riel's mordant response in Wiebe's novel when Taché returns to Red River from Rome in the middle of the Resistance, following a stopover in Ottawa: "It is not Bishop Taché who is passing, it is Canada" (*Scorched-Wood* 105; see also Stanley, *Louis Riel* 118–19). Yet even a casual acquaintance with Riel's writings would demonstrate that Taché remained a key figure for Riel his entire life. The most notable testament of Riel's esteem for Taché is his long poem "Alexandre-le-grand," written during his internment in the Beauport Asylum in the late 1870s. After declaring that he is nothing but the cleric's "Zouave," his ever-loyal foot soldier, Riel begs Taché to help him leave the hospital and reach the United States: "Soyez mon libérateur" (Riel, *Collected Writings* 4: 159, 162). As late as the summer of 1885, after the fall of Batoche, Riel describes himself to Taché as "votre petit protégé" and the Archbishop as "mon protecteur" (*Collected Writings* 3: 143, 144). In a letter to his brother Joseph, believed to have been written in 1884, Riel states that he is considering travelling from Montana to Manitoba because he has completed a (lost) book and would like to show it to Taché before publishing it as a form of "déférence et de respect" (*Collected Writings* 2: 328), underlining that he will only publish the manuscript if Taché approves it. Then in one of his Regina revelations, in which Riel is in the federal cabinet, he says to a Manitoba representative: "His Grace must rule matters here" and everyone must consult Taché before doing anything, for: "Nothing can go right without the approval of His Grace" (*Collected*

Writings 3: 218). Even more pertinent, one of the reasons Riel lambastes Macdonald in his poetic diatribe against him is that the Prime Minister attempted to "disgrâce" Taché (*Collected Writings* 4: 234), by not delivering the general amnesty to the Red River combatants. In addition, in his Regina "Journals," Riel writes that the "hommes puissants" who plotted to discredit Taché, Ritchot, and other clergy will themselves be discredited (*Collected Writings* 3: 440) and that God has informed him the decision by Pope Leo XIII that most pleased the Saviour was the selection of Taché as "Pontife-Majeur" of the Americas (3: 492). If Taché was not a transformative figure in his life, Riel has an odd tendency to copiously proclaim otherwise.

Perhaps for the same reasons that he has Falcon minimize Taché's impact on Riel, Wiebe writes that there are many affinities between Riel's religious beliefs and Mennonite theology, "which is totally anti-Catholic" (Wiebe and Bergman 167). He contends that Riel "hits the Catholic Church on exactly the same point that the Anabaptists did: that is, the Church putting form and structure over and above justice to the poor—the kind of human justice that everyone should expect" (167). Yet *The Scorched-Wood* shows that Riel is not quite free of Catholicism. Unlike Martin Luther or Menno Simons, the Riel portrayed in Wiebe's novel—mirroring his historical model—is less intent on eviscerating Catholicism than in controlling it. Thus Riel appoints Bishop Ignace Bourget Pope of the New World, because "he was our pope, not Leo XIII" (Wiebe, *Scorched-Wood* 326). Following Bourget's death in June 1885, Riel has the papal sceptre "passed" on to Taché (326) without any explanation as to why he would entrust such a hallowed office to someone he reputedly does not trust. To further confound matters, the historical Bourget and Taché were both committed ultramontanes who, in the former's words, were adamant that every Catholic should not deviate from the Church's dogma, starting with the lowliest parish priest: "I hear my *curé*, my *curé* hears the bishop, the bishop hears the Pope, and the Pope hears Our Lord Jesus Christ" (qtd. in Wade, *French Canadians* 360). As well, after his Washington epiphany, the historical Riel presented himself not only as a prophet but also as the Infallible Pontiff and Priest-King (Riel, *Collected Writings* 2: 73). At times, he even claimed that God had consecrated him the "successeur" of Pius IX, the Pope who instituted the doctrine of Papal Infallibility in 1870, and whom Riel calls "l'Immortel" (2: 96). Such was Riel's reliance on the authority of the Catholic hierarchy that, as discussed earlier, he had to have his divine visions corroborated by Church leaders. Wiebe writes that the reason the Biblical prophets "had such great voices" is that "they felt they spoke directly from God" (Wiebe and Mandel 155). But this tends not to be the case with Riel, as Wiebe demonstrates in his novel. Riel's revelations are usually mediated by Bourget, whose 14 July 1875 letter to Riel confirms the truth of his "mission," a letter which he always carries with him (Wiebe, *Scorched-Wood* 138–39, 214, 315). In other words, Wiebe's Riel may be the result of exhaustive archival research, but he is not always someone that the historical Riel would recognize (Martel, Rev. 321).

The same could be said of Wiebe's Falcon. Throughout *The Scorched-Wood People*, Wiebe has Falcon lavish much praise on Riel. A few pages into the novel, while outlining the composition of "The Sad Ballad of King Muck," Falcon divulges to the reader: "Let me tell you immediately, Louis Riel was a giant. If God had willed it, he could have ruled the world" (36). The fact Riel does not end up running the world might lead one to deduce that perhaps God does not favour him, but this is an avenue that Falcon does not explore. For the bard, if Riel is not one of God's chosen, he ought to have been, as behooves someone whose vision is a veritable earthly paradise. As Falcon has Riel say, "Why don't we make a heaven here in the North-West, where we can have peace between all people, no killing..." (53). Or as Falcon quotes Dumont as he attempts to impress upon Riel why he should not return to Montana since the Saskatchewan Valley Métis still need him to inspire them to imagine what they are capable of achieving: "You have a vision here bigger than at Red River. Heaven and earth—show us, help us to see!" (215). Riel, one surmises, is not just a political leader but a spiritual one, a redeemer of his people, if not all people.

Wiebe's Falcon also offers a provocative explanation of why Dumont follows Riel in 1885. After Riel and his family arrive in the Batoche area, Dumont tells a superintendent of the North-West Mounted Police, "I am still chief here. We asked him to come, all French and English, to be our political advisor" (Wiebe, *Scorched-Wood* 196). Dumont's need to persuade others that he is in charge hints that his power may no longer be self-evident, perhaps even to himself. Anyhow, Falcon maintains that what galvanizes Riel during the North-West conflict is that, for the first time, he has a true disciple, Dumont. "Riel had never known anyone," says Falcon, "who had the faith to find him in his godless reaches of silence and he did not yet grasp that this man had given him his commitment of fealty before an altar and he would never retract it even after the name Riel meant at best madman, at worst pathetic child; such evidenceless faith was still too much for Riel to believe he could inspire" (216). When the local Catholic priests refuse to bless the Métis combatants as they prepare to face the Canadian forces, it is Dumont who assures Riel: "You are our priest" (231). In the same way that it was possibly "Riel who made Gabriel Dumont a greater general than Cuthbert Grant," writes Wiebe (235), it is Dumont who gives Riel the confidence to inspire the badly outnumbered Métis to confront their Canadian foes.

Where Wiebe becomes much less convincing is when he has Falcon depict Riel as a champion of today's Prairie West, leading his narrator to conflate Ontario and Québec. Late in the novel, Falcon quotes Riel as saying that the Spirit of God told him "Macdonald has to hang me...Then the people can make me a saint" (Wiebe, *Scorched-Wood* 337). On the very last page, Dumont says the reason Riel had to die was not that he was insane, which "he wasn't," but that "no white country can hold a man with a vision like Riel, with people like us who would understand it and believe it, and follow. Canada couldn't handle that, not Ontario, and not Quebec, they're just using him against the English. They all think he was cracked, mad" (351). The notion that Central Canada is unified against the Métis is articulated by Falcon from the beginning. It is he who describes the chief objectives of

Confederation as "burn the flag and nail down a railroad, cinch the North-West tight against Ontario and Quebec, forever. What piddling difference does it make, Ontario or Quebec—strangers all, laughing and fixed upon our potential" (44). Falcon's hostility toward Ontario is understandable, and in character. Early on, he explains that of the four main ethnonational groups at Red River, it is the English-speaking Canadians "who almost destroyed us all." With Confederation, says Falcon, there was a surge in conceitedness among "the Upper Canadians—they were so *upper*—somewhere got the notion that Red River must be their proper colony" (25-26). He quotes Riel to the effect that the only reason Macdonald wants the North-West is to "raise money from it! Don't you know Ontario?" (61), a charge that is corroborated by the (Upper) Canadian expansionists themselves (92). What is puzzling is that Falcon would also portray the people of Québec as "strangers," like those from Ontario. Falcon himself tells the reader as he watches the recently arrived Riel, "I too once went to school in Montreal, long ago, and I saw all the great men there" (35). Later, he notes that "Riel like I decades before was supported by some kind, charitable French Canadian" (135). Falcon could even have expanded that his model was taken as a child to Lower Canada, where he was baptized and "apparently lived with relatives," and did not return west until the age of fifteen (Peel, "Falcon"). For the historical Falcon, as for the historical Riel, the people of Québec are kin. The fact that Wiebe has his narrator downplay such a vital connection makes one wonder for whom he speaks. Or to put it in Wiebean terms, where does Falcon's voice come from?

Admittedly, Wiebe is far from being the only contemporary Western Canadian who has attempted to claim Riel as a cultural and political forebear by turning him into someone "who twice rebelled against the claim of Protestant Ontario and Sir John A. Macdonald to control the West as a territory of central Canada" (Kaye, *Hiding* 186). George Stanley asserts that Riel has been transformed, even by "some historians and would-be historians," into "the first of a long line of prairie political patriots, extending from John Norquay to Peter Lougheed," in an attempt "to give coherence to western political identity" ("Last Word" 52). But Stanley, who considers Wiebe "unquestionably the most accomplished novelist" to fictionalize the Red River and Saskatchewan Valley conflicts, finds it "an oddity to see Riel, the man who contested elections as a Conservative and who envisioned a theocratic state for western Canada, so readily welcomed to the ranks of left-wing Socialists" (52, 53). Also, the fact the Halfbreed Norquay was instrumental in dismantling some of the language rights that Riel had fought to enshrine in the Manitoba Act (Russell 155–56; Friesen, *River Road* 25) suggests that the two leaders did not have the same conception of the Prairies. As Stanley points out, Norquay was among Macdonald's friends who impressed upon the Prime Minister that "any clemency shown Riel would lose the Conservative party the votes of English-speaking Canada" (*Louis Riel* 366; see also Friesen, "Political Thought" 64–65), underscoring how party (and cultural) politics could trump regional identity.

Another prominent Western Canadian who is skeptical about the connection between Riel and Prairie regionalism is Thomas Berger. For the former justice of the Supreme Court of British Columbia, "The Metis are no more the progenitors of the Progressives, the CCF, and Social Credit than they are of those powerful interests in the west today who say they are alienated; it is the Metis who have become strangers in their own land" (46). Despite being a staunch defender of Métis collective rights, Berger has serious reservations about Riel's politics, contending that his "administration bore many aspects of a military dictatorship" (37), something that one would not sense from Wiebe's novel, except perhaps for Riel's tendency to label anyone who opposes him a "traitor" (Wiebe, *Scorched-Wood*, 64–66, 227). Yet Berger insists that, since Seven Oaks, the "Metis were trying to impede agricultural settlement of their territory" (31), at least by Anglo-Protestants. Implicit in Berger's statement is the whole question of Métis sovereignty, which in Saskatchewan is further complicated by the fact local First Nations perceived the Métis as "recent arrivals in the region" who were threatening to displace them (Stonechild and Waiser 73). In any case, the territorial claims by the Métis placed them on a collision course not only with an expansionist Canadian government, but with most would-be Prairie settlers.

It is this very conflict between Prairie agricultural settlers and Indigenous peoples, particularly the Métis, that Wiebe fictionalizes in *Peace Shall Destroy Many*. As mentioned earlier, Wiebe's first novel is an exploration of the Mennonite experience. It dissects some paradoxes in three pillars of Mennonite life: pacifism, brethrenism, and land relation. One central character, the school teacher Joseph Dueck, articulates the conundrum of pacifism in a time of war when he states that "we Mennonites can practise our belief in Canada only because other Canadians are kind enough to fight for our right to our belief. The godless man then dies for the belief of the Christian!" (Wiebe, *Peace* 60). The matter of who constitutes the Mennonite family, or Brethren, is no less complex. Wapiti residents travel as far afield as India in their attempt to disseminate their faith, yet they show little inclination to spread the Gospel to their Indigenous neighbours, such as the Métis. The reasons for this incongruity soon become apparent. For most denizens of Wapiti, the people they call the *breeds* or *half-breeds*, "lived as they lived" because "they were part of unchangeable Canada" (31)—a statement that likely would be challenged by many of today's Métis activists and academics, as well as by Riel—and "you can't change a breed" (74). In the words of Pete Block, the son and namesake of the community's founder and supreme leader, Deacon Peter Block, the Métis "can't join our church...They don't live like us... They're just not like us" (194). Deacon Block is even more blunt, expounding that their "moral and spiritual discipline" demands that Mennonites "remain apart from the world. And that includes the breeds, who are culturally and morally backward" (202). Thus when Deacon Block discovers that his unwed daughter Elizabeth has become pregnant by a Métis named Louis Moosomin, whom he hired as a labourer during the war, he not only calls Elizabeth a "whore of a daughter," but pronounces her "dead" to him (144, 146), a decision that threatens to rend the community asunder.

An additional factor that probably accounts for the people of Wapiti's lack of interest in proselytizing among their neighbours is their consciousness that they are displacing the Métis and other Indigenous peoples. Early in the novel, we learn that Wapiti has existed for nine years, and that since then "the breeds [have] settled back farther into the wilderness" (Wiebe, *Peace* 17). The Métis have not moved out of the area naturally, though. Deacon Block's vision of "a district of Mennonites" is contingent on their buying out the Métis, just as they "bought out all the English settlers" when they first arrived (21). This is an aim that seems eminently feasible as there are "only four breed families left" in the area (22). After he learns of his daughter's sexual entanglement with Moosomin, Deacon Block becomes obsessed with dislodging the Métis even from "the edge of the settlement, where their dark wolfish faces could betray weak women" (153). His response is ironic since Moosomin swears that it was Elizabeth who came to him one night and cried at his bed that "she had to have a man— she could not live—she had to have a man" (184). Still, as the text underlines, Block vows to "buy [the Métis] out personally, every one of them, and send them all to wherever their animal natures could destroy themselves without involving others" (153–54). The social cohesion of the community requires that the Métis vanish from the immediate surroundings. Late in the novel, the protagonist Thom Wiens observes ruefully that "the half-breeds don't exist in Wapiti any longer. They never have" (234), suggesting that even the memory of their presence has been erased.

One peculiar way in which the Wapiti settlers rationalize their exclusion of the Métis from the community is their own relation to the land. The settlers are inordinately proud of being farmers. Even the outward-looking Wiens does not escape the spell of cultivating the soil, sensing "within himself the strength of his forefathers who had plowed and subdued the earth before him. He, like them, was working out God's promise that man would eat his bread in the sweat of his face, not pushing a button to watch a divine creation blaze to earth" (Wiebe, *Peace* 12). Farming requires back-breaking labour from all members of a group, doubly so when trying to hack a settlement out of the bush. But this is an ethos that the Métis purportedly lack, having "no concept of planned farming" (31), which explains why they could never be at home in Wapiti.

The notion that the Métis do not cultivate the land would be severely questioned by the historical Riel who, in a text like "Les Métis du Nord-Ouest," writes of the lands occupied by the Métis, which belong to them not only through their Indigenous title and for having defended them in war but for "les avoir bâties, cultivées, clôturées, travaillées et habitées" (*Collected Writings* 3: 288). Moreover, the idea that the recently arrived Mennonite settlers in *Peace Shall Destroy Many* have a deeper relation to the land they inhabit than do the Métis is undercut by their own actions, which prove they have little sense of the history of that land. This truth is dramatized in an episode that has become iconic in the whole of Wiebe's oeuvre. When Wiens prepares to cut hay with a team of horses along the edge of a marsh, he stumbles on something. At first, he thinks it is a rock or the roots of a tree. But it turns out to be the skull of a buffalo, which baffles him since buffalo are not supposed to have been in the area for "at least fifty years" (Wiebe, *Peace* 82). The incident leads Wiens to reflect on Canadian history, starting with the question: "Why was Canada called a 'young' country?" (82). He deduces that the only reason Canadians can believe their country has no past is their failure to consider Indigenous history, as evident in the fact that First Nations have "lived here for thousands of years, and we don't know a single thing that happened to them except some old legend muddled in the memory of an old crone" (83). What also seems to become apparent to Wiens is that a collectivity's lack of knowledge of the history of the land it inhabits undermines its claim to it.

Near the end of *The Scorched-Wood People*, Wiebe has Riel state that individuals or groups "who wrest from its people a country commit sacrilege!" and that the "Government of Ottawa is guilty of conscienceless sacrilege towards the Métis" (335). But if the seizure of a territory by outsiders constitutes sacrilege, then it is not just the federal government that is guilty of that sin—all non-Indigenous

Canadians are. In "Louis Riel: The Man They Couldn't Hang," his keynote address to the 1985 Guelph conference on Riel's image in Canadian culture, Wiebe intimates that the victory of the agricultural settlers over the Métis may have been culturally preordained. Alluding to the parallel conflict in the Book of Genesis, he observes that "Cain the agrarian kills his brother Abel the herdsman/hunter. It is in the very bones of human existence that the literate agrarian always destroys the oral hunter: how could it be otherwise?" (199). The historical Riel was not exactly an oral hunter. As he writes in one of his Keeseville poems, what he loves the most is "la culture des champs" and he prays to God that, after he regains his health, his agricultural endeavours will bring about his "prospérité" (*Collected Writings* 4: 196, 198). Yet it is hard to imagine that Canadians living in the Prairies are any less implicated in this conflict than their compatriots across the country, including those in the distant provinces of Ontario and Québec. The English Mountie John Donkin, who guarded Riel in Regina, remarks that the reason the federal "Government was on the horns of a dilemma" regarding the Métis leader in 1885 was that while "the Catholics of Lower Canada enshrined him as a martyr," the "people of Ontario and the North-West clamoured for his execution" (183). The Superintendent of the Mounted Police, Richard Burton Deane, goes further and asserts that "the Rebellion saved the country" by providing well-remunerated employment to any "farmer who owned, or could provide himself with a team of horses and a wagon" (183). Those views are bolstered by the Prairie novelist and women's rights activist Nellie McClung, who states in her autobiography that when it was announced that "the North West rebellion was over and Riel captured a great wave of thanksgiving swept over Western Canada" (192), reflecting the region's anxieties during the conflict and its loud calls for retribution against Riel and other "insurgents" afterwards (Stonechild and Waiser 127–226). The behaviour of the principal characters in *Peace Shall Destroy Many* surely gives little support to the idea that Western Canadian settlers did not share the dominant ethos of the day.

Wiebe often contends that he does not have to invent stories; he just discovers texts in archives and then transmutes them into historically-informed fictions. As he says of his handling of the Riel material that he incorporated into *The Scorched-Wood People*, "why should I...rewrite Riel's marvellous speech? Why should I rewrite those documents, those diary entries?" (Wiebe, Kroetsch, and Neuman 237). The Saskatchewan poet Eli Mandel was not persuaded that a writer's reshaping of found texts into fiction is as straightforward as Wiebe hints, insisting that, even if Wiebe is not an "inventor" of narratives, "you're a shaper. You give that story shape and form" (Wiebe and Mandel 153). Kroetsch, similarly, tells Wiebe that he inevitably transforms Riel's archival documents by fictionalizing them: "you rewrite them by putting them in the context of that novel. You have rewritten them endlessly" (Wiebe, Kroetsch, and Neuman 237). Wiebe does not refute the points made by Mandel and Kroetsch, but he also does not elucidate why he is so invested in creating the illusion that some of his historical fictions are not written from his perspective but from that of his characters, specifically his Indigenous narrators.

I have no desire to minimize Wiebe's contribution to Canadian literary culture, which is considerable. Wiebe was one of the first mainstream Canadian writers who attempted to (re)introduce Indigenous people into Canadian life. As Mandel notes, since the early 1970s, Wiebe has been "recreating a history" of the Indigenous peoples of the Prairies, "bringing them back into the land" (Wiebe and Mandel 151). In the process, Wiebe has demonstrated that Canada can be simultaneously colonized and colonizer and that Canadians are not haunted "by our lack of ghosts," as Earle Birney famously proposed (49), but "by our ignorance of our ghosts" (Tefs 157). Not surprisingly, the fashioning of a national genealogy that includes both Indigenous peoples and latecomers is not unproblematic, especially for someone whose family "acquired" its homestead from the much-maligned CPR and who remains deeply grateful to the rail company for bringing his kin to Canada (Wiebe, *Of This Earth* 7, 188, 193). Wiebe recognizes that, even more than elsewhere in the country, in the Canadian West "there isn't much white tradition. It's awfully short. What we have to do is dig up the whole tradition, not just the white one" (Wiebe and Melnyk 206). The incorporation of Indigenous peoples into the "Canadian" tradition could be construed as a way to address a perceived deficiency. To put it more bluntly, it could be seen as a way to legitimize the settler presence in Canada by implying that settlers belong to the same national family as Indigenous peoples. This is a function that Indigenous peoples may not wish to perform for, as the Métis fiction writer and poet Katherena Vermette expresses in the couplet that serves as the epigraph to this chapter: Indigenous peoples are not part of the settler "mosaic," they are merely "the mortar that glues you together" (*river woman* 66).

In his rumination on the hybrid nature of Canadian civilization, *A Fair Country: Telling Truths about Canada*, the political philosopher and novelist John Ralston Saul posits that the reason non-Indigenous Canadians find it difficult to accept that Indigenous peoples have played a fundamental role in Canada is that it is "the least palatable part of the settler story. We wanted the land. It belonged to someone else. We took it" (27). Saul adds that this awareness of the initial theft of the land has engendered a persistent dilemma. On the one hand, settlers perceived "First Nations civilization as inferior [to theirs] and therefore destined to disappear." But, on the other hand, they viewed themselves as "successors" to the First Nations, fated to "inherit their natural relationship to this place—the mythological aspect of what we call ownership" (30). To further trouble the situation, continues Saul, settlers never fully believed that they could vanquish the First Nations, no matter how oppressive the measures they instituted, which he interprets as "the expression of a deep and growing Euro-Canadian anger at the refusal of the noble ancestor to reach for his full apotheosis by disappearing" (32).

Notwithstanding his professed sympathies toward Indigenous peoples, Wiebe has not escaped this syndrome, as reflected in his characterization of Falcon—someone, incidentally, that the historical Riel never mentions in his *Collected Writings* (Ens, Intervention).

One of the most surprising aspects of *The Scorched-Wood People*, a text ostensibly narrated by a Métis, is its elegiac tone. Wiebe's Falcon devotes his life (and afterlife) to composing oral poems about the political feats of the "French Métis—Bois-brûlés, my song name for us" (Wiebe, *Scorched-Wood* 25). From the victory over the Selkirk settlers in 1816 to stopping William McDougall at the United States-Red River border in 1869, Falcon has always risen to the occasion to celebrate major Métis events. Or more precisely, time and again, he has "received songs" about "the violent and silly acts of our people" (140). Falcon confides that he prayed for years "to the Good Father" for the Riel song but did not receive it "until I lay on my deathbed" (140, see also 36). Perhaps the reason the song has such a protracted gestation is that it documents not just "our greatest vision and commitment to a hard road" (140–41), but the "last act of our people" (284, see also 328). Wiebe's Falcon is even more definite about the end of the Métis as an ethnonational entity in the novel's conclusion, when he summarizes their history: "Our New Nation blossomed and faded for a few short months in Manitoba in 1869–70, it blazed up in 1885 and in less than two months died in Saskatchewan" (348). Even the author of what has become the Métis national anthem accepts that the collectivity he has so often extolled in song is dead and buried, interred alongside Riel. But is it plausible that Falcon would share this sense of national finality? The historical Riel did not. In one of the prophecies he wrote in his Regina "Journal" of October 1885, only weeks before his hanging, Riel predicted that Manitoba would become "tout Métis-Canadien-français" and, in five hundred years, would have a population of forty million people (*Collected Writings* 3: 490). Prior to that, during the military campaign against Canada, he kept reassuring his followers that they would prevail because God favoured them. Wiebe does not appear to believe that this is true. Judging by the way they are portrayed in *The Scorched-Wood People*, the Métis have been vanquished and will vanish, to be replaced by newcomers such as the Mennonites of Wapiti settlement and other members of what a U.S. Indian agent called "the peaceful army of the plow" (qtd. in Dusenberry 132). If God has any chosen peoples in the Americas, it is fair to say, it is not the Métis. More than anything else, it is this fatalistic acceptance by Wiebe's Falcon of the predestined disappearance of his people that leads one to question the authenticity of his song. Given the way it clashes with the historical Métis bard's compositions, one must conclude this is an apocryphal Falcon specimen.

Consecrating Canada's Icon   5
The Projet Riel Project

> We [Canadians] are a métis civilization.
> —JOHN RALSTON SAUL, *A Fair Country*

A COUNTRY'S NATIONALIZATION of a former enemy is an inherently paradoxical act. Since there is bound to be evidence of the particular country being defended by people who battled the individual now deemed a patriot, as well as of that individual opposing the country, the process of consecration necessarily entails much forgetting. However, in 1985, Canada chose a radically different strategy to mark the centenary of the death of Louis Riel, whom it had hanged for high treason. Instead of trying to mask the more inopportune statements made by the Métis leader, it decided to gather and disseminate his extant writings. The result was the publication of a five-volume critical edition called *The Collected Writings of Louis Riel / Les écrits complets de Louis Riel*, under the general editorship of the prominent historian and Riel biographer George F.G. Stanley, also known as the designer of Canada's Maple Leaf flag (Foot and McIntosh). The singularity of the event is reflected in the fact that at the time no such honour had been bestowed on any (other) Canadian public figure, including Riel's archfoe, Prime Minister John A. Macdonald. Given that Riel is not considered a major writer, there was always suspicion that the project was a political enterprise. Still, there was hope that the assembling of the whole of his textual production might help to finally unravel the enigma that is Riel. Neither issue, though, has been conclusively resolved. By tracing and analyzing the evolution of the publication of Riel's poetry and prose, including its reception, this chapter attempts to answer why someone so prodigiously self-documented remains so elusive.

The release of *The Collected Writings of Louis Riel* in 1985 was the culmination of the Projet Riel Project, whose trajectory was surprisingly haphazard—laying to rest some of the potential conspiracy theories about its political nature. Centred at the University of Alberta in Edmonton, the Riel Project lasted between 1977 and 1984 (Stanley, "General Editor's Remarks" 3, 6). Besides Stanley, who was a professor emeritus of Canadian Studies at Mount Allison University and soon would be appointed Lieutenant-Governor of New Brunswick, the other editors were the University of Calgary political scientist Thomas Flanagan, who served as the Deputy Editor and edited volume 3; the University of Lethbridge historian Raymond Huel, who edited volume 1; the Université de Sherbrooke sociologist of religion Gilles Martel, who edited volume 2; the University of Calgary French professor Glen Campbell, who edited volume 4; and the political scientist and Administrative Officer Claude Rocan, who, along with Stanley and Flanagan, edited volume 5. Interestingly, none of those individuals initiated the project, which at first was not supposed to focus exclusively on Riel. Rather, the catalysts were two University of Alberta English professors, Noël Parker-Jervis and David Jackel, and their primary objective was to acquire funds "to publish significant works to do with Western Canada in reliable editions so as to preserve, bring forward, and enliven the traditions of the region" (Parker-Jervis, "Western" 49). Parker-Jervis writes that as early as 1970, he "organized a petition...to the National Library urging it to produce under its auspices a Canadiana reprint programme" (49). The National Library declined to support the initiative, but the idea continued to germinate and later developed into what became the Western Canadiana Publications Project, still aimed at publishing both original texts and reprints dealing with Western Canada. To

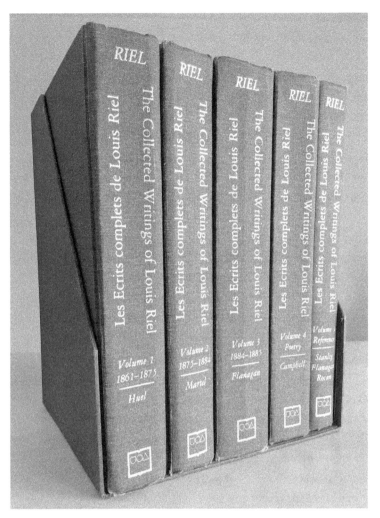

The University of Alberta Press five-volume edition of *The Collected Writings of Louis Riel / Les écrits complets de Louis Riel*. (Photo by Carolyn Kapron, used with permission.)

determine what were the most relevant undertakings, Parker-Jervis and his colleagues conducted an exhaustive survey of Canadianists around the world, receiving some "143 replies, [with] 204 reprint titles and 62 original titles suggested, and 64 offers to edit" the volumes (49; see also "Complete Edition" 1). Based on the enthusiastic response, they elected to proceed with an application for funding.

First of all, the Western Canadiana promoters assembled an advisory board composed of eminent scholars working at universities across Western Canada, "weighty names" that they "could drop on funding agencies," such as the bibliographical librarian Bruce Peel, the novelist, literary scholar, and university administrator Henry Kreisel, and George Woodcock, the anarchist thinker and founder of the scholarly journal *Canadian Literature* (Parker-Jervis, "Western" 50). By May 1976, after receiving approval as a president's committee at the University of Alberta, they informed the Canada Council (later the Social Sciences and Humanities Council of Canada) of their intention to apply for a major editorial grant. The notification prompted "a most useful letter of support" from the head of the Committee on Bibliographical Services for Canada, Margaret Williams, followed by an equally profitable visit to campus by one of the Council's negotiating officers. This officer, whom the organizers suspected of being sent "to test the firmness of [their] purpose," apprised them that "an application for a major editorial grant, in order to succeed, had to have 'a narrow and homogeneous corpus' and had to exercise one particular kind of scholarship" (Parker-Jervis, "Western" 50). It was only at this stage that the Western Canadiana committee members shifted their attention to Riel the writer. Their survey of Canadianists had identified three main areas of interest: "Riel and attendant circumstances, the roots of prairie fiction, and the documents and propaganda of settlement" (50). In light of the inside knowledge shared with them by the unidentified Ottawa cultural bureaucrat, they decided to concentrate solely on a critical edition of Riel's writings. This turned out to be a wise choice. Working in conjunction with most of the collection's eventual editors, as well as the historian John E. Foster, they prepared a 115-page application titled "The Collected Papers of Louis Riel" (Western Canadiana, Application). They submitted it to Ottawa in June 1977 and, by the following April, learned that they were the recipients of "the first major editorial grant to be awarded a western [Canadian] university, one of the few on a Canadian subject, and the first to publish the complete papers of a noted figure in Canadian history" ("Complete Edition" 1). Often called the "million-dollar grant" (Owram, "Riel Project" 207; Friesen, "Review" 92), the award would be more accurately labelled "the half-million dollar" grant (D. Morton, "Reflections" 53)—which more closely approximates the contribution made by the Canada Council, $580,000, with the remaining sum provided by the supporting universities of Calgary and Sherbrooke and, especially, the sponsoring University of Alberta (Owram, "Riel Project" 207; see also Western Canadiana, Revised Submission).

The success of the Riel Project application underlines the extent to which funding agencies, with their at times nebulous criteria for what constitutes useful knowledge, determine the types of scholarship that are pursued and produced. Parker-Jervis writes that he and his colleagues "chose Riel for several reasons: there was a defined corpus; the task exercised one particular kind of scholarship—historical; the subject was an important one, for Western Canada particularly; and we had at hand two noted Riel scholars," Stanley and Flanagan, who "were keen to work on Riel" ("Western" 50). Parker-Jervis made the same point in a 1976 letter to Stanley, explaining that the committee members selected "Riel first because of the importance of the subject and because scholars of note, like yourself, were engaged in it" (Letter 1). Stanley and Flanagan were established figures in Riel and Métis studies. In addition to *The Birth of Western Canada: A History of the Riel Rebellions* (1936), Stanley was the author of an authoritative biography of Riel (1963) and several short works on him. Flanagan, whose popular *Louis "David" Riel: "Prophet of the New World"* would appear in 1979, had already published a series of key articles on Riel, as well as edited *The Diaries of Louis Riel* (1977) and, with Martel and Campbell, coedited his *Poésies de jeunesse* (1977). Yet, despite the fact that a considerable body of both cultural work and historical scholarship was growing around Riel, it is not clear why the individual once vilified by a North-West War veteran as "the serpent" in the Canadian garden (Needler 80), and long perceived as an enemy of Confederation (Braz, *False Traitor* 43–67), had come to merit having the publication of his writings heavily subsidized by the taxpayers of the country that fought him.

Stanley himself had expressed serious reservations about Riel, undermining the claim that he "almost single-handedly created the myth of a blameless Louis Riel" (D. Morton, "History" 681). In *The Birth of Western Canada*, Stanley describes the Métis leader as an "ardent patriot of his people" who "was destined to become one of the stormy characters upon the Western Canadian scene" (67). But he also contends that the conviction "Riel was insane would not, at the present time, be seriously contested...One cannot read his political and religious writings, even prior to his return from the United States [in 1884], without realizing that they were the work of an unbalanced mind" (384). No less forcefully, in his 1954 booklet *Louis Riel: Patriot or Rebel?* Stanley argues that "Louis Riel was not a great man; he was not even what [Thomas] Carlyle would call a near great" (24). But, by 1963, his position was changing. As he indicates in the preface to his biography, "When I wrote a pamphlet on Riel several years ago...I thought I knew all the answers: now that I know more about Riel, I am less certain what the answers are" (*Louis Riel* v). However, even then, Stanley reveals doubts about Riel's character, writing that the reason Riel jeopardizes his achievement at Red River is that his "feeling of insecurity" toward Canadians leads him to clamour that his government carry out the execution of Thomas Scott, which is not just "a political act" but a "political blunder" (116). Stanley further states that Riel is prone to "petulance" and "even as a schoolboy had been noted for an inability to brook opposition" (95, 112). This hardly seems to be a candidate for the publication of a rare Canadian collected writings.

Similar misgivings about Riel were voiced by the assessors of the original application submitted to the Canada Council. The applicants tried to present Riel as a focal personage in Canadian life, insisting that his "papers deserve publication because of his undisputed historical significance. He is a figure of central importance in the early history of the Canadian West, and a figure, as well of national importance" (Western Canadiana, Application 1). But the anonymous reviewers were not convinced. Assessor B, for example, writes that "the publication of the J.A. Macdonald Papers or the Wilfrid Laurier Papers would have a more significant impact among scholars and the public than the publication of the Louis Riel Papers." Nevertheless, the person asserts that the project "would be of tremendous importance...With the emphasis placed by governments and the press on minority groups such as Indians and the French, Louis Riel, as a defender of minority rights has increased in status in the eyes of the public" (1). Along the same lines, Assessor E remarks that the application does not "indicate what kind of Riel will emerge from this, the first, scholarly examination of Riel material in all aspects," since that would demand that one "define the place and role of Riel in Canadian history," something the application does not do (1). The referee elaborates that Riel is neither "a major writer" nor "a major historical figure. Why, then, this proposal? The answer offered to that question is that Riel had, in his own lifetime, and still more in history since, a major symbolic quality...It has for some time been my own belief that part of understanding Canada since 1867 is to understand Riel, why he was what he was, and why he did what he did" (1–2). The person, then, goes on to add that it "would be a major scholarly achievement" to fathom Riel's mindset and concludes that "I am moved to support the project thus strongly because, while not a Riel scholar myself, I have always been fascinated by him and his career" (2). Whether they realized it or not, the assessors were partly accepting the logic that informs the application's promotion of Riel, which is that his writings should be published because of what he has come to represent rather than what he accomplished. To quote the application, "no one person better epitomises the conflicts which have marked Canadian history: English-French, Catholic-Protestant, native-white, East-West, British-American" (Western Canadiana, Application 1). Riel's value is not only primarily symbolic, the application's sponsors suggest, but of a negative kind of symbolism. More than any other figure, he embodies the great cleavages in Canadian life and culture.

All the referees ultimately approve the application, but they are divided about both the high cost of the project and the competence of the editorial team. Some are impressed by the multidisciplinary backgrounds of the editors and their bilingualism. "The publication of Louis Riel's writings," writes Assessor B, "will have a significant impact on the field of Canadian History...Seldom does one find such reputable scholars from the two major cultures in Canada working together on a project of such magnitude and of such importance" (1). But other referees have concerns about the project, not the least its proposed budget, which initially was $1,541,160, with $678,105 to be contributed by the Canada Council (Western Canadiana, Revised Submission). Appréciateur C deems the venture "valable, susceptible d'intéresser plusieurs groupes de lecteurs" (2). But the person argues that the budget could be reduced "au moins 50%" (5), a verdict echoed by Assessor F (1). While wholly supporting the application, Assessor F questions the qualifications of most of the editors, being "profoundly disturbed" by the poorly-defined role of the general editor and his location in far-off New Brunswick; wonders if Flanagan is "the best man to be editing the correspondence. I disagree, as do many others, with the conclusion he drew and published in his edition of the [Riel] diaries"; and characterizes Campbell as "basically a linguist," who may not have "the historical background to deal with the political poetry" (1). Likewise, Assessor E is "somewhat dismayed" that only one editor is Francophone, Martel, feeling that "editorial difficulties will arise that would be dealt with more readily and to better effect if the team included a French Canadian scholar of the second half of the last century to throw light on Church history—not religious—in Quebec, 1864-1885, or Riel's background in Quebec, his friends, patrons and critics, and on the real nature of the reaction in Quebec to his trial and execution" (4). Assessor E's apprehensions must have had an impact, since when they revised the proposal, the applicants acknowledge that the "lack of Western Francophone participation is a particularly serious problem" (Western Canadiana, Revised Submission 2)—which is presumably why they approached the University of Winnipeg historian Robert

Painchaud and, after his death in a plane crash, Huel. Yet no one raised the lack of Métis representation, although the applicants note that they had contacted Stan Cuthand of Brandon University, because of his expertise in "the Cree language and Métis culture" (Western Canadiana, Revised Submission 2).

The editors started to work on the collection at the beginning of October 1978. Their first task was to gather texts by Riel, which they succeeded in locating in "over forty different repositories" in Canada and the United States (Stanley, "General Editor's Remarks" 5). Even excluding volume 5, which is allotted to reference, the collection amounts to about 2,200 pages of material by Riel. The editors had planned to organize the edition by genre, with volumes devoted to correspondence, religious writings, poetry, and miscellaneous prose. But they soon realized that there was too much "overlapping" between categories and decided to structure the collection chronologically, only separating the poetry from the prose (Western Canadiana, Revised Submission 4). Volume 1 spans from 29 December 1861 to 7 December 1875, that is from what was then Riel's first known letter—to his Québec benefactor Sophie Masson (Riel, Collected Writings 1:1)—to the eve of his mystical experience in Washington, DC, when God anoints him the Prophet of the New World. Volume 2 covers from 8 December 1875 to 4 June 1884, or from the blessed day when "le Saint Esprit" took full possession of his being at St. Patrick's Church (Collected Writings 2: 49) to the arrival of the Saskatchewan Valley delegation in Montana Territory to invite him to help prepare their grievances against Ottawa. Volume 3 spans from 5 June 1884 to 16 November 1885, beginning with the school teacher Riel pondering the "invitation" by the northern visitors to return to Canada (Collected Writings 3: 1) and closing with the Regina "Journals" that the prisoner Riel writes as he awaits his fate in 1885, and every word of which is "inspiré" (3: 417). Volume 4, devoted to poetry, documents Riel's evolution as a poet, from his earliest known literary exercises at the Collège de Montréal (Collected Writings 4: 1) to his mystical meditations in the Mounted Police barracks (4: 445). Lastly, Volume 5, Reference / Référence, includes the "General Editor's Remarks," in which Stanley details the history and methodology of the Riel Project; an article in French by Roger Motut on the relation between Riel's written language and the language spoken by the Métis; entries on genealogy and chronology; photographs of the Riel family; maps; a bibliography of works on Riel; and an index to the whole collection.

The mandate given to the editors was "to publish all of Louis Riel's extant writings" (Stanley, "General Editor's Remarks" 6). In the process, they were to make his poetry and prose "more readily available to students...and, in this way, to encourage further research in the field of Western Canadian history" (2, see also 8). Or as the *Riel Project* BULLETIN *du Projet Riel* elucidated in its opening issue of April 1979, the "critical edition" would "present a printed version faithful to what Riel himself wrote, being 'critical' in the sense that errors will be noted, variants recorded, and annotations furnished" ("Welcome" 1). The collection often includes not just the final draft of a document but several drafts of it. Thus the first version of the letter in which Riel responds to the invitation by the Saskatchewan delegation is ten-lines long and barely mentions that the visitors have crossed the international boundary to seek his advice regarding the circumstances that have rendered the inhabitants of "the British northwest...unhappy under the ottawa government" (Riel, *Collected Writings* 3: 1). But the fourth (and last) draft is nearly two pages long and not only discusses the transnational dimension of the trip but also discloses that Riel sees the northward trek as having "the proportions of a remarkable fact" (3: 4), that he is now an "American citizen," and that his "intention is to come back [to Montana] early this fall" (3: 5). Also, at the end of each of the first four volumes, the editors include an appendix with texts pertaining to Riel but not authored by him, such as the certification of his election to the House of Commons in 1873 (*Collected Writings* 1: 489) or the 1875 letter by Bishop Ignace Bourget, informing Riel of his God-given "mission" (1: 492), as well as textual notes about Riel's documents. Partly because the Canada Council demanded that the introductions to the volumes "be kept short" (Flanagan, *Riel* viii), the editors restricted their commentary to bibliographical matters, eschewing contextual analysis.

Stanley and his coeditors also had to face "the linguistic dilemma" posed by the fact Riel wrote in French and English, and "sometimes he used both languages in the same document" (Stanley, "General Editor's Remarks" 18). The first application to the Canada Council stated that *"The Collected Papers of Louis Riel"* would be published by the University of Alberta Press in "ten hardbound volumes," which would be "fully bilingual in French and English, matched entry for entry" (Western Canadiana, Application 17–18). Needless to say, this is not what transpired. The editors considered "presenting all material in both languages," but they had to reject the idea "because the funds provided by the Council did not cover the cost of translation" (Stanley, "General Editor's Remarks" 18). Their compromise was to publish each text in the language in which Riel produced it, with commentary by the volume's editor in the same language. One of the people who initially opposed this option was Stanley, who outlined his objections in some detail in a letter to Parker-Jervis in May 1976:

> I would prefer to see these documents translated into English. The fact is that relatively few Canadians interested in western Canadian history are really fluent in French and need translations. I know that when I wrote the *Birth of Western Canada*, I was tiff-necked about this, and left the French quotations in French. Now I realize that this was an error and cut down the value of the book to undergraduate students. When I wrote the biography of Louis Riel, some years later, I translated the French quotations. I prefer to see an all-French or an all-English book. (Stanley 1)

It is fair to say that the language question was never satisfactorily resolved, and perhaps could not be. This is evident even in the divergence in the collection's title, which promises to be Riel's *"écrits complets"* in French but only his *"Collected Writings"* in English. Stanley himself sometimes used both terms interchangeably, even in English, announcing at a conference on Riel in 1978 that the project would publish the subject's "complete writings" in an edition called his "*Collected Papers*" ("Riel Project" 15).

The reviews of *The Collected Writings* were generally positive, some of them glowing. The most laudatory were those by the Québec historians Andrée Désilets and Nive Voisine and the geographer Jean Morisset. Désilets describes the collection as an "oeuvre monumentale" and says that the federal government's grant was well-spent (429). A great-granddaughter of Riel's 1885 defence lawyer François-Xavier Lemieux (Noël), Désilets is fascinated by the complexity of the mind that is revealed in the compilation of the subject's poetry and prose. Unlike most other reviewers, she quotes extensively (and judiciously) from Riel's writings to illustrate the difference between his political texts and his religious ones. She observes that some of his works lead one to conclude that the person who wrote them could not possibly be an "aliéné mental," yet others suggest that he at times must have succumbed to "le délire" (431). This is one of the reasons that Désilets compliments the editors for having the foresight to organize Riel's writings in chronological order, which is the only way that readers can discern the variations among his texts.

Voisine is also effusive, exalting the edition as "le meilleur monument" erected in Riel's honour during the centenary of his death. "Rien n'égale ni ne surpasse cette oeuvre hautement scientifique" (174). He touches on what would emerge as the dominant issues raised by reviewers: the language in which Riel's texts are reproduced; the extent of the contextual commentary provided by the editors; and the notion that Riel's unstructured documents comprise a form of autobiography (177), a view promulgated by Stanley ("General Editor's Remarks" 2). Voisine commends the collection for its rigorous and at times nimble methodology and states that one should underline "l'effort fait pour présenter une édition totalement bilingue" (175, 176). Without judging Riel a classic author, say like the French Catholic priest and political theorist Félicité de Lamennais, he thinks highly of his writings, asserting that each of Riel's poems constitutes "une fenêtre qu'il ouvre sur son 'moi' intérieur" and, often, his verse is a veritable "monologue intérieur où le subconscient de l'auteur remonte à la surface" (176). Voisine does suggest that Stanley's "General Editor's Remarks," which appears in the last volume, should be read first—ideally alongside Motut's article on Riel's written language and Métis orature (Riel, *Collected Writings* 5: 47–60). This is a view shared by Stanley. In a letter to Flanagan at the end of 1983, he writes: "Since the General Introduction to the Edition will appear in Volume 5, I wonder if the Volumes should be renumbered? That is, should Volume 5 be numbered (1), with the previous volumes renumbered" (Letter to Flanagan 2: 1). Yet, so impressed is Voisine by the collection and the light it sheds not only on Riel and the Métis but also on French Canada's "histoire religieuse et culturelle" at the end of the nineteenth century (177) that he closes by stressing that he cannot imagine how Canadian libraries, and even individual readers, can afford not to acquire it.

Morisset's review is unique in its trans-American focus. A geographer, poet, and traveller who has crisscrossed the continent from the far north to the extreme south, Morisset has come to identify métissage as "le principe constitutif" of New World nations ("Louis Riel" 59). He places Riel among the great exponents of pan-American solidarity, alongside such figures as Simón Bolívar and Toussaint Louverture, and judges his writings "documents capitaux" in the history of both Canada and the United States (60). For Morisset, the reason Riel has been underappreciated is that he was born in British America, one of the few corners of the New World "fondée officiellement sur la prohibition du métissage" (59). However, he claims that it is not only English-speaking Canada that is threatened by Riel's biocultural hybridity. So is Québec, whose systematic exclusion of the "métis-québécois" thinker from its literary patrimony is really a rejection of its "rapport à l'américanité," its relation to its true origins (60). But Morisset ventures that Riel cannot be silenced, thanks to his prolific textual production. He submits that Riel's most insidious transgression was of surviving his hanging by over "2 000 pages de textes," and adds that the publication of his *Collected Writings* will enable Riel to take his rightful place in the "panthéon" of the Americas (63), as befits one of the continent's great liberators.

J.M. Bumsted's appraisal is less encomiastic than those by the Québec scholars but, in some ways, it is more representative of the reception accorded to *The Collected Writings*. Bumsted begins by pointing to the irony that "the nation's most famous traitor" has become "the only major Canadian whose papers have been collected and published with the full panoply and scholarly apparatus" usually devoted to world-historical figures ("Mahdi" 47). He finds the publication of Riel's correspondence during his banishment in the United States most "useful" (50) and advances that "Riel's prophetic messianism probably makes more sense seen in the context of nineteenth-century American Protestant millennialism than Catholic supranaturalism, and comparisons with spiritual leaders like Joseph Smith and Brigham Young are hardly farfetched" (51). At the same time, Bumsted is critical of the failure of the editors to provide sociocultural context, which makes it extremely difficult for the non-specialist reader to understand Riel's actions. Given that "the texts are not self-narrating," he writes, "a good deal of context is often necessary to make sense of them" (54). Bumsted expresses similar concerns to those articulated privately by Stanley about reproducing Riel's texts in the language in which he wrote them. Upon noting that the decision is "certainly intellectually and even politically justifiable," he states that "a considerable gap does exist between the official Canadian language policy and the realities of everyday life. Louis Riel wrote mainly in French, and the absence of translations means, one suspects, that the effective audience for his papers, particularly in Western Canada, is both small and converted already" (54). Regardless of its laudable erudite organization, the collection is unlikely to be able to meet the language needs of most of its target readers.

Like Bumsted, Gerald Friesen is skeptical about the editors' decision to publish texts in the language in which Riel crafted them, given that, with "a ratio of perhaps three French pages to one in English," this "may cause problems for English-speaking students" ("Review" 92)—and, one might add, English-speaking academics.

But Friesen is much more ebullient in his appraisal of *The Collected Writings*, which he twice characterizes as a "remarkable collection" (89, 91) and once as "an extraordinarily rich and valuable set of documents and a remarkable feat of editing" that "will stand the test of time and will influence our perception of Canada, especially our appreciation of the native role in Canadian life" (92). His estimation of the collection reflects his uncommon admiration of Riel as a writer. Friesen does not go as far as Rudy Wiebe, who rhapsodizes that to read the Métis leader's "writings is to wander into world history from the beginnings of creation to the eschatological resolutions of time beyond eternity and the archetypal relations of the godhead considering only itself" ("Louis Riel" 203). Still, for Friesen, Riel is "a great native writer and political philosopher" ("Review" 93, see also 91), even if he later tempers his evaluation, calling Riel "a powerful political essayist" and "a serious writer" (*River Road* 18). Friesen expands that the substantial library of secondary literature on Riel does not fully prepare the reader "for the man who appears in these pages" and that the essay "Les Métis du Nord-Ouest" is "one of the finest statements of native claims in Canadian history and should receive attention in today's classrooms, meeting halls, and constitutional debates" ("Review" 89; see also Riel, *Collected Writings* 3: 278–94). Friesen does regret "the segregation of the poems" into a separate volume, which he deems "an unwelcome complication" for historians ("Review" 92), conceding that literary scholars may appreciate it.

Contrary to Friesen, to say nothing of Désilets, Voisine, or Morisset, Bennett McCardle is in awe of neither the collection nor its subject. McCardle judges *The Collected Writings* an "impressive production" and "one of the basic works of reference on the history of western Canada" (140, 144). But he sounds irritated by the "persistent note of self-congratulation in the editors' introductions," which "suggests that even they are somewhat surprised at having survived the experience, and are eager to exact due recognition for it" (140). As might be expected of an archivist, McCardle pays close scrutiny to the location of the materials and how they were accessed. He is not persuaded that the editors can be certain that the "collection

[is] really complete" and regrets the absence of "*a simple list of archival collections consulted*" (142). McCardle raises questions about the language in which the texts appear, describing the edition as "quasi-bilingual...Anyone lacking a working knowledge of both French and English will probably not find this work of general use" (141). He also has reservations about the literary value of Riel's "'little scrips'" (139–40; Riel, *Collected Writings* 4: 431) and of their appeal to non-academic readers. As McCardle asks, "If Riel's writings do not sell reasonably well (for example, if they cannot appear as moderately-priced paperbacks) will other publishers be discouraged from similar ventures and fall back to sagas, on the level of [Peter C. Newman's] *Company of Adventurers*?" (144). This is obviously an issue that cannot be easily separated from the bilingualism of Riel's texts.

More than any other reviewer, the historian of religion Michael Gauvreau chastises the editors for failing to underscore, and perhaps realize, that Riel's context is not easily accessible to most contemporary readers, even educated ones. Gauvreau rejects the "widespread but erroneous belief" that just because the mindsets of the late nineteenth century seem familiar, they are "somehow immediately accessible and comprehensible to the modern mind." Therefore, the approach that the editors present as "ostensibly value-neutral" is, in "fact highly charged." Gauvreau writes that "the dominant theme that emerges from this remarkable collection is the extent to which, for Riel, religion, politics, journalism, and poetry were bound up with one another, in a manner which can be only dimly comprehended by the modern reader." By neglecting to provide the sociocultural context in which their subject operated, the editors ensure that "Riel remains...accessible only to the initiated specialist," for Riel must be placed in the context of his time not only in Western Canada but in the world.

The critiques of *The Collected Writings* indicate a degree of dissatisfaction with the collection, primarily regarding the minimalist editorial intervention. But the matter is not as simple as some might like it to be, as the conflicted response by Frits Pannekoek reveals. Pannekoek, who doubts the project will make a major "contribution to a new understanding of either Riel or the prairie West," feels that the introductions to the volumes "are unfortunately limited, although intentionally so" ("Review" 121, 122). He thus voices the hope that the other editors will emulate the prolific Flanagan and "attempt similar insights no matter how controversial." Yet Pannekoek immediately adds that, in light of "the highly volatile state of emotions on the Riel question, the editorial decision to minimize the introductions was probably wise" (122). That is, in an ideal world, the editors ought to be sharing with the general public what they have gleaned from preparing the edition. But in 1985, it may not have been advisable—or permissible—to do so.

Whatever its ramifications for the collection, the paucity of editorial commentary was not accidental. Stanley relates in his "General Editor's Remarks" that, from the beginning, the aim of the compilers was to allow Riel to speak for himself and "it was agreed that no Project editor would seek to impose his own interpretation of Riel upon the readers of the Project's publication" (5). Or as he writes elsewhere, "The Riel Project is not...an academic effort to exorcise the haunting phantom of Riel" ("Last Word" 57). Granted, this decision, too, may have been influenced by the referees. Assessor D was adamant that "the style and tone of the 'extended' scholarly essays prefacing each group of volumes" should "be tolerably uniform and pitched at a conservative, objective level of commentary." The person alleges that hyperbolical "rhetoric has often spoiled the tone of such publications," in both French and English, since "regional studies have a tendency to use inflated styles stemming from excessive local chauvinism which bring Canadian scholarship as a whole into disrepute" (2). If the editors had forgotten the "regional" image of their project, such a "minor note of caution" (Assessor D 2) could not help but make them acutely aware of their geographical location. In his review of the collection, Friesen notes that at a Royal Society of Canada symposium in 1986, the distinguished Toronto-based editor "Francess Halpenny stated that [the University of] Alberta's success with the Riel proposal was cause for celebration at the

University of Toronto Press because charges of regional favouritism were affecting the latter's Disraeli, Erasmus, and Dictionary of Canadian Biography projects" ("Review" 92). Moreover, the wisdom of their editorial policy would become apparent to the editors even before the edition was released, following the 1983 publication of Flanagan's *Riel and the Rebellion: 1885 Reconsidered*—which he had published in book form because he was unable to produce his "version of events as an introduction to [his] volume" of *The Collected Writings* as the funding agency "wished such introductions to be kept short" (Flanagan, Riel viii). The research for *Riel and the Rebellion*, as Flanagan acknowledges, was "supported financially by the Louis Riel Project" (Riel ix). In the aftermath of the controversy precipitated by his contention that "Riel's resort to arms [at Batoche] could not be explained by the failure of constitutional agitation" and that he opposed a "free pardon" for the Métis leader (viii, 150), a concerted campaign was mounted to have him expelled from the Riel Project.

The magnitude of the opposition to Flanagan is captured in a letter to the president of the University of Calgary, Norman Wagner, by the vice-president of the Metis Association of Alberta. Speaking on behalf of the organization, Jo-Ann Daniels accuses Flanagan of having "breached a trust of using documents supposed to be used for historical research...to deliberately build a case against the Metis. This case is politically and historically incorrect and [is] being used to promote the 1969 Government [of Canada's] White Paper of assimilation of Aboriginal people" (J. Daniels 1). Consequently, she and her association feel that "Dr. Flanagan should be removed from the Louis Riel Project and should not be given funds through the University of Calgary or any other such special funding for research because of the breach of trust and Dr. Flanagan's racist promotion. Canadian people do not tolerate racist policies or statements" (1). Having begun by asking Wagner to confirm whether Flanagan's views "are the policies of the University of Calgary," Daniels closes her letter by demanding that the university "promote a policy of not allowing Professors to use entrusted research resources to make personal public statements that interfere with a nation's right to exist and that interfere with a nation's legal, political, and cultural identity" (1). While she does not specify how Flanagan has hindered the Métis nation's right to exist, the implication is that he has, and that organizations like hers should serve as the arbiters of such transgressions.

In response to the attacks on Flanagan, his fellow "Full Professors of Political Science" at the University of Calgary came to his defence. They wrote to Wagner that "Louis Riel is a controversial subject" and any attempt to prevent him from being rigorously examined would not do "much good for the causes of research, Riel, the Métis, or Canada. If Louis Riel's place in history, or that of anyone else, cannot stand scholarly analysis, or can be defended only by preventing such analysis, then his status will be neither convincing nor respected" (Full Professors 1). The dispute was so charged that Flanagan became "not only controversial...in Métis circles" but, as he phrases it, "almost radioactive" (*Persona* 17; see also Mayer, "Survival" 353–54). Matters were inflamed by a seven-page article in the 5 December 1983 issue of the magazine *Alberta Report* (Weatherbe), whose cover read "THE RIEL PARDON: Why his biographer says it endangers Canada," and showed Riel standing behind a noose. Fearing that the polemic might threaten the completion of *The Collected Writings*, Stanley felt compelled to intervene publicly, by outlining the project's editorial framework. As he explained in a press release in early December 1983, which is worth reproducing in full:

> Owing to the controversy following the recent publication of Professor Thomas Flanagan's *Riel and the Rebellion* and Professor Flanagan's association with the "Projet Riel Project", some clarification of the author's relationship with the Project is necessary. Let it be clear from the outset that whatever views Professor Flanagan has expressed about Riel in his book are entirely his own and in no way represent the collective opinion of the members of the Project. The task of the Project is, and has been, to collect and publish all the known writings of Louis Riel, correspondence, speeches, poems, diaries, prayers, pamphlets.

Our responsibility is to ensure the accuracy of these documents, not to offer an interpretation of them, or to write a biography of Louis Riel.

In all fairness to Professor Flanagan, I wish to point out that he has worked diligently for the Project and has carried out the duties I have assigned him, without, in any way attempting to impose his interpretations or opinions of Riel upon the other members of the Project. Neither has any of the other members of the Project team, which includes Raymond Huel, Gilles Martel, Glen Campbell and Claude Rocan. Neither have I, for that matter. The resulting publication will embody only the views of Louis Riel, as stated in his private writings and his public statements.

It would be most unfortunate for those, who seek the truth about Riel, were the present controversy in any way to discourage, delay or prevent the completion of the Project's plans to publish a five volume edition of Riel's writings in 1985. The only voice that would be silenced, should this happen, would be that of Riel. And I cannot believe that any Métis, White or Indian people would wish that to happen. (*Statement* 1)

In private, Stanley was equally supportive of Flanagan, assuring him: "Your views are your own business. I would never challenge that. You are quite within your rights to publish whatever conclusions your researches may lead to" (Letter 1: 1). Yet Stanley makes it clear his primary "concern is for the future of the Project" and that he is worried some people might withdraw their "permission to publish documents." He writes Flanagan that "I rather wish you had held off a little longer" and urges him "to keep cool and avoid making any further statements that would exacerbate the native peoples and add bitterness to the controversy...Please avoid further controversy and leave the issue to me" (1). Stanley's apprehensions were warranted. The Riel Project's Administrative Officer, Claude Rocan, informed him that "our relations with the Métis right now are not as sweet as we might like. The low-point in all this" occurred when the Alberta Métis leader Elmer Ghostkeeper told Rocan "by telephone, using a rather 'Riel-esque' turn of phrase, that 'the bullets of the Métis nation will strike down the Flanagan corpse'" (Letter 1). To make the situation even more titillating, Ghostkeeper had studied with Flanagan at the University of Calgary and publicly accused "his ex-mentor of advocating assimilation of ethnic groups" (Weatherbe 37). Regardless of what one may think of the Flanagan affair, it is evident that the editing of Riel's textual production was never just a scholarly endeavour.

The political reverberations of the Riel Project were perhaps inescapable given its subject. It may be true that, as the editor of the *Western Canadiana Publications Project Newsletter* wrote in 1978, "Every mature culture as a matter of course produces complete papers and works of its statesmen and authors" ("Complete Edition" 1). Thus the publication of *The Collected Writings of Louis Riel*, the same individual opined seven years later, is a momentous event, since "it is the first complete works of any Canadian personage, literary or political, to come into being." Yet, "Isn't it ironic that they are of a man our laws condemned and our government executed?" ("Louis Riel" 1). This is the great paradox embodied by the collection. The editors presume that Riel is a Canadian political and cultural figure, but his poetry and prose repeatedly reveal how little he identifies with the country. The rest of this chapter explores how Riel's national identity cannot be evaded in a compilation of his writings. As it does so, it also queries whether the relative failure of *The Collected Writings* to influence post-1985 views of Riel stems from the extent to which his own words often refute the ways he is being portrayed.

The question of Riel's national affiliation would seem to have become moot by 2010, when John Ralston Saul pronounced Canada "a métis civilization," or "métis nation" (*Fair Country* 1, 106), concurring with the novelist Guy Vanderhaeghe that Canadians "have a subconscious Métis mind" (qtd. in Saul, *Fair Country* 9). Saul further argues that it was Riel who fashioned the "brilliant conceptualizations of what contemporary Canada wishes to be" (20). This is a view shared by the religion scholar Jennifer Reid, who writes that "the Riel myth speaks to the possibility of *métissage* being a foundational factor in Canadian identity" (182). For Reid, Riel's idea of métissage is potentially "a primordial source for the Canadian state (and perhaps by association, other postcolonial states), since it refers to the creation of radically new individual and social bodies" (185). If Canadians are fundamentally a Métis (or métis) people, then it follows that Riel could be one of our national heroes, possibly even the national hero. But to the chagrin of both Saul and Reid, history reminds us that this has not always been the case and may not yet be for a sizable portion of the populace. As well, Saul subverted his thesis when he organized his Extraordinary Canadians book series and only devoted one title to Métis individuals, Joseph Boyden's *Louis Riel and Gabriel Dumont*; to add insult to injury, he forced the two Métis leaders to share a single volume, unlike most other subjects (Marchand). The reality is that the Métisness of Canadian society is far from being universally accepted by Canadians in general, or by today's Métis, raising the question of how a fervent Métis nationalist like Riel can be transformed into a Canadian icon.

What renders the Canadianization of Riel most vexing is that contemporary Métis artists and scholars keep stressing that his struggle was not on behalf of Confederation but against it. As early as the 1990s, in her thesis on the images of Riel in art, Catherine Mattes observes that "often the new respect for Riel in mainstream Canadian society has little to do with the Métis" and that, if his "motives helped in the creation of Canada, it was not necessarily intentional" ("Whose Hero?" 1, 77). Writing more recently, the political scientist Adam Gaudry is more blatant. After stating that the historical Métis leader was executed "much to the jubilation of the Anglo-Canadian citizenry," Gaudry asserts that the "Canadian identification with Louis Riel has created a mythological cult around the man who was, at his core, antithetical to the emerging Canadian project, and who fought for Métis political independence from an expanding Canadian colonialism until his death at Canadian hands" ("Métis-ization" 64, 66). Gaudry's assessment clashes with that of the mid-twentieth-century Métis activist James Brady, who contended that Riel was one of Canada's "finest sons" and that he "shall yet be enshrined as one of the founders of Canadian democracy" ("Hero" 1; see also "Trial and Execution"). Still, even the Marxist Brady does not deny that, instead of championing Confederation, Riel opposed it, for which he paid the ultimate price.

Strangely, most recent reclamations of Riel rely little on his words as gathered in *The Collected Writings*, the greatest repository of his archival imprint. In the first substantial analysis of the Riel Project, published right after the collection's release, Doug Owram concludes that "Riel has now been researched over and over. His complete writings are now available and presented according to the highest standards of scholarship. The controversy, however, remains" ("Riel Project" 217; see also Bumsted, *Louis Riel* 7). I generally agree with Owram's appraisal, but I would counter that one of the reasons the controversy about Riel persists is that so many commentators on him and his ideas do not engage with his writings. In fact, this is a trend that was inaugurated by Owram, who examines the significance of the publication of Riel's poetry and prose without citing a single text by him. The sole reference to *The Collected Writings* in Owram's article is not to a text by Riel but to Huel's introduction to volume 1 ("Riel Project" 215).

The most flagrant example of a pundit who judges Riel's literary achievement without providing evidence of having read much of his textual production is the Métis literary scholar Emma LaRocque. In her book *When the Other Is Me: Native Resistance Discourse, 1850–1990*, LaRocque praises Riel as a trailblazer who "today would be understood as a liberation resistance fighter," even if "he was in many ways deeply colonized" (23, 83). LaRocque comments on his "style" and his "spiritual poetics" (83) but she refers to a single fragment of Riel's writings, taken from an anthology. She also gives no indication that most of his work is not in English but French—which may explain why all the poems that Glen Campbell includes in his edition of Riel's *Selected Poetry* were "originally composed...in French" ("Introduction," *Selected Poetry* 9). Similarly, Boyden manages to write his *Louis Riel and Gabriel Dumont* without apparently having perused Riel's *Collected Writings*

(187–88). In her book *The North-West Is Our Mother: The Story of Louis Riel's People, the Métis Nation*, Jean Teillet remarks that she has "tried to present this history from the perspective of the Métis Nation" (xvii). But, despite judging Riel the "best and brightest [Métis] voice" (5), she cites him very selectively, never alluding to his *Collected Writings*. Finally, in his introduction to a 2021 special issue of the *Canadian Historical Review*'s coverage of Riel over the previous hundred years, M. Max Hamon's bewails the lack of "Métis views" in Canadian history ("Re-presenting Riel" S5). Yet, while selecting reviews of books on Riel, he fails to include Gerald Friesen's "glowing" assessment of Riel's collection (S23; see also Hamon, *CHR Presents*), which seems a curious method for making space for more Métis voices.

Given the wide accessibility of *The Collected Writings of Louis Riel*, it is puzzling that people who claim to value him so often refrain from engaging with his work. Riel himself thought highly of his writings, as befits texts composed under "la dictée du Saint Esprit" (Riel, *Collected Writings* 2: 86). At his 1885 treason trial, he stated that he had "written not books but many things" and that he had delivered his papers to a trusted associate in the hope that they would "be published, if they were worth publishing, after [his] death" (*Queen* 313). Riel's admission that he did not write any books clashes with the widespread belief that he devoted much time in the early 1880s to composing a huge manuscript titled *Massinahican*, Cree for the Book, or Bible (Riel, *Collected Writings* 2: 229). *Massinahican* has been variously described as Riel's "new revelation" (Flanagan, "On the Trail" 89), his "roman" (Morisset, "Louis Riel" 61, "Postface" 97) or "étrange roman" (Toussaint, *Bison* 84), and a rewriting of the Bible according to the Métis "culte...pour la nature" (Toussaint, "Présentation" 23-24). But since the longest surviving fragment of this "ouvrage fondateur" of Métis culture (Toussaint, "Présentation" 24) is a mere two pages long (Riel, *Collected Writings* 2: 230-31), we will never be able to determine if it was truly his magnum opus. In any case, in a letter to the Commissioner of the North-West Mounted Police, Riel sounds extremely confident about the value of his texts. He informs Acheson Irvine that when he was living in

Montana, he "had a vision" in which "the Angel of Keysville" appeared to him and told him, "Publish: God will choose the one of your writings which he will please, in french it was: / 'Publiez: Dieu choisira celui de vos écrits qu'il voudra'" (*Collected Writings* 3: 217, see also 417). Riel elaborates that he has long believed the publication of his writings would "accomplish a miracle or something wonderfull," which was to enable people to "see for themselves and be satisfied that I have indeed a mission given to me by the one whom we all adore and unto whom we all pray" (3: 217). For Riel, a critical dimension of his poetry and prose is that they will demonstrate the veracity of his prophetic visions. He avers that he is the "joyeux téléphone" that transmits God's messages and songs to the world (*Collected Writings* 4: 146), but he knows that not everyone will accept his claims at face value, a task that must be facilitated by his texts.

There was yet another function that Riel hoped his writings would perform: a monetary one. Starting midway through 1885, as he began to realize that no pardon might be forthcoming, he appealed to the prison officials to listen to his lonely voice and allow him to use his writing to support his family. As he implores the Acting Commissioner of the Mounted Police during his incarceration after the fall of Batoche:

My wife, my children
are poor, have no bread.
Could I use my pen
In Jail, for their aid? (*Collected Writings* 4: 400)

This was something that he had already tried to do during his Montana sojourn. At a time when he was facing crippling litigation over his attempts to curtail the indiscriminate sale of alcohol to the Métis community, Riel offered to "sing" in his poetry about anything from "the big trains" of the Northern Pacific Railway and "the fair amazone / With her long dress on the saddle" (4: 279) to "our military" and "our Judiciary" (4: 280). Still, in a poem written to one of his "good" jail guards, asking him that when he goes to church to leave his prayers behind and return with the Gospels, Riel expresses the certainty that sometime in the future "the Boys / Will gather all my little scrips" and publish them "To celebrate / A true Prophet: Louis 'D[avid]' Riel" (4: 431; see also McCardle 139-40). It is as if he anticipated the venture that resulted in the editing and dissemination of his voluminous poetry and prose.

Although *The Collected Writings of Louis Riel / Les écrits complets de Louis Riel* is a tribute to the Métis leader, a recurring motif throughout the collection is the literary status of Riel's textual production. Even the editors and the other promoters of the Riel Project were not too sanguine about the aesthetic merit of their subject's writings. In the revised version of their application for funding, they disclose that they "feel that the English word 'Papers' and the French word 'Ecrits' are better than 'Works' and 'Oeuvres' to designate Riel's compositions. Our choice of terms emphasizes that Riel's writings are not so much literary works as historical documents" (Western Canadiana, Revised Submission 1). However, I suspect that the reason writers and scholars who work on Riel tend to avoid his writings is not because his worldview is too alien for contemporary readers, as Gauvreau asserts, but because his writings often conflict overtly with the dominant images of him in both popular and scholarly discourse. In her omnibus review of *The Collected Writings*, the historian Jennifer S.H. Brown hints at why Riel's words might trouble some of the narratives about him. Brown states that the collection "put[s] us more in touch with Riel and his circle than do any other sources," supporting the "thesis that the Metisism of Riel was resolutely Catholic and French in orientation" (152). More crucially, she underscores that the Métis-First Nations relationship, "though acknowledged and cherished as a maternal gift, was muted in Riel's thinking and writing...For the most part, Indians did not figure in Riel's intellectual universe as persons and groups whom he understood deeply and about whom he could write with knowledge" (153; see also Stonechild and Waiser 77-78). Or as McCardle phrases it, Riel has an "interestingly ambivalent attitude towards the Indian tribes" (141), ambivalent meaning questionable.

In his "General Editor's Remarks," Stanley partly justifies the time and resources that enabled the publication of *The Collected Writings* by venturing that any individual's "private or official correspondence, diaries, speeches, prayers, poems, and written comments will reveal more of what is on his mind, of his real motivations than the conjectures of other people, however astute or observant they may be" (2). Stanley's reasoning seems uncontestable, suggesting that it is impossible to understand Riel without knowing how he envisaged himself and the world. It also underlines how unique an enterprise the collection is. Whatever may have been Canada's motivation for memorializing someone it had hanged as an enemy, there is something commendable about a polity that is willing to finance the compilation of every single known word by an oppositional figure, someone who by definition is not always going to say adulatory things about it. Yet, in the end, the collection is a qualified triumph. The fact that a team of respected scholars has made available the bulk of Riel's textual production does not mean people will read it, and not merely because of the hurdle of translation. Thus, the collection has attained a peculiar status, simultaneously existing and not existing. Like the monument it is, it is largely unread—or at the least unacknowledged. No wonder that its prolix author remains as enigmatic as ever.

The Naked Martyr
Sculpture and the Shifting Image of Riel

6

A portrait is all the more pleasing if the warts are removed.
—GEORGE F.G. STANLEY, "The Last Word on Louis Riel"

THE POLITICAL REHABILITATION of Louis Riel is one of the most fascinating developments in recent Canadian history, but what is even more striking is that it has elicited so little resistance, both in cultural and political circles. While his absolution is not yet official, the general impression is that "Riel is now acknowledged as a Father of Confederation and the Founder of Manitoba" (Teillet, "Louis Riel" 56). So widely accepted is his image as "the living embodiment of all that is Canadian" (Dimaline 55) that it has become impossible for political figures of any stripe to question Riel's contribution to Confederation, as illustrated by the opprobrium elicited by the the former Edmonton Conservative MP Peter Goldring's opposition to the campaign to "'unhang' Riel" (Goldring 2-3; see also Puxley). A similar consensus prevails among writers and visual artists. Since the early 1960s, there have been remarkably few negative aesthetic representations of the man that nineteenth-century Canadians tended to perceive as either a "heartless rebel" (Cleomati 64) or a "faux prophète" (Grandin et al. 20). Predictably, given their high level of approbation, these works have not generated much controversy. Along with the 2017 remount of the Centennial opera, the exceptions are three sculptures, two of which were deemed so incendiary that they had to be removed from their original locations on the grounds of two provincial legislatures. In this chapter, I will argue that the main reason the sculptures of Riel have engendered such discord, when other works about him were silently accepted by the Canadian citizenry, is that sculpture is the most public of art forms. At the same time, I will examine how the critics of the sculptures have raised serious concerns about who is entitled to speak for Riel, including Riel himself through his own writings.

Although I just asserted that sculpture is the ultimate public art form, I realize that the statement is not self-evident. In fact, the term public is no less contested than art itself. As Harriet Senie asks in her book *Contemporary Public Sculpture*, "Who is the public? What defines art or sculpture today, for that matter? What makes it public—its essence, its patron, or its location?" Senie even suggests that it might be wise to jettison altogether the idea of "'public art'" in favour of "'art in public spaces,'" in which the site would be the sole determining factor in establishing the publicness of the art form (3). Senie's observations are germane, but the three sculptures of Riel that I discuss—John Nugent's *Louis Riel Memorial* (1968); Étienne Gaboury and Marcien Lemay's *Louis Riel* (1971); and Miguel Joyal's *Louis Riel* (1996)—all seem to constitute public artworks. To begin with, they have been "seen by a mass audience," which is one of the criteria that makes an art work public (Kaye, "Any" 107). Also, they were designed to engage with the general populace. Most important, the three sculptures were first located not just in public spaces but on the grounds of legislatures and were themselves commissioned by members of those political bodies. Thus, many of the viewers probably felt entitled to voice their opinions of the sculptures not merely because they were art spectators but because, as taxpayers, they had knowingly or not subsidized those works.

The controversy over the Riel sculptures mirrors the great transformation in modern art in general and sculpture in particular. The rise of modern art, which is usually traced to the end of the Second World War, coincides, "roughly, with the general erosion of the lexicon of high-minded allusions—literary, religious, and social—once shared by the audience for public sculpture." Consequently, modern audiences have been alienated from today's art because of its extensive reliance on "private mythology, self-reference, and the language of mass culture" (Wilkin 10). But there is one specific reason why sculptures of Riel are bound to be polemical: his dominant collective or national identity. Regardless of his image today, the fact is that, in the second half of the nineteenth century, Riel twice clashed militarily with Canada. The literary scholar Frances W. Kaye sums up this conundrum when she writes that the "problem with the Riel monuments is in making the hero of one group serve as the representative of another larger group which he in some measure opposed" ("Any" 109). Some contemporary Métis writers and scholars are anything but enthusiastic about the Canadianization of their historical hero. Adam Gaudry states that it is "quite ironic that Riel himself has been so thoroughly Canadianized when he was opposed to Canadian control over Métis lands, language, and lives, even sacrificing his life for this end" ("Métis-ization" 71). Rather than being a foundational figure in Canadian nation-building, asserts Gaudry, "Riel led two armed movements against Canadian imperialism" ("Métis Night"). The Canadianization of Riel is therefore not just about absorbing the former enemy into the national family but also about camouflaging the true nature of the relationship between the Canadian state and the Métis, in the past as much as today, explaining the avoidance of this astounding shift in the national narrative.

The pitfalls of commemorating Canada through Riel are manifest in the saga of the Nugent sculpture. In the mid-1960s, the Saskatchewan Arts Board decided that one of its contributions to Canada's approaching Centennial would be a public sculpture. The board held a competition and the winner was the submission by the Saskatchewan modernist sculptor John Nugent, an abstract rendition of Riel comprising two rectangular steel plates enveloping a long spike. The Regina arts reporter Will Chabun writes that "it takes only a little imagination to see in it two hands reaching out and one other element reaching out to the sky." But one person who was not dazzled by the maquette was Saskatchewan's socially conservative Liberal Premier Ross Thatcher, who was determined to have not only a realistic representation of Riel but a "'manly'" one (L. Mitchell 2). The Mountie-turned-sculptor Nugent and Thatcher wrangled over the design for three years. At one point, the premier even convened an extraordinary meeting of his cabinet to discuss the form of the monument (Chabun). Nugent remained steadfast that Riel still had relevance at the time and "had to be expressed in contemporary terms" (qtd. in L. Mitchell 2), but he had a large family to support and could not afford to forego the commission. So he reluctantly agreed to produce a figurative sculpture, which Thatcher barely tolerated. Modelled on his initial concept, it shows Riel with his right arm stretched high above his head as if reaching out to the heavens. He is barefooted and, except for an unbuttoned cloak draped over his body, naked.

Nugent's *Louis Riel Memorial* was unveiled on 2 October 1968 in front of the Saskatchewan Legislature in Regina, ironically the city where the Métis leader had been hanged for treason nearly eighty-three years earlier. The ceremony was attended by Thatcher and other Saskatchewan dignitaries as well as by Prime Minister Pierre Trudeau, who delivered an eloquent speech about the difficulty of understanding an individual like Riel and the "forces [that] motivated" him. Trudeau pondered how many modern Riels might "exist in Canada, beyond the fringe of accepted conduct, driven to believe that this country offers no answer to their needs and no solutions to their problems" (109). This was a view that must have resonated with Saskatchewan university students, a thousand of whom took advantage of the Prime Minister's presence at the Legislature to organize a massive demonstration against Thatcher's threatened cuts to higher education (Eisler 218), turning a carefully staged media event into a public relations nightmare.

While Nugent was not invited to the unveiling of his sculpture, he initially appeared to have emerged victorious in his clash with the aesthetically challenged Thatcher. Yet, in many ways, his triumph was a Pyrrhic one—as reflected in the fact that Trudeau did not mention the artist's name in his address, even if he "kept

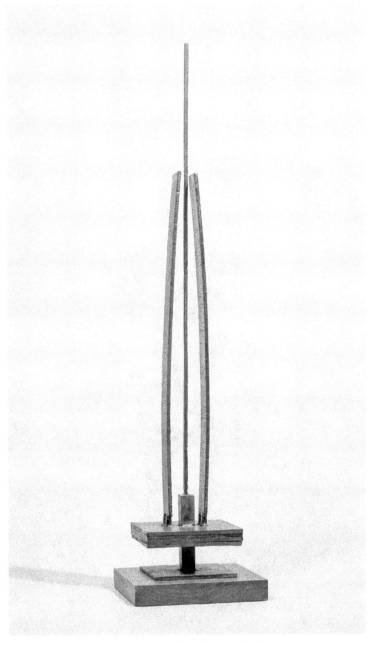

Maquette of John Nugent's proposed sculpture of Riel. (Steel and wool, 1968, 99 × 24.2 × 24.2 cm. Photo by Don Hall, used with permission of Karen Nugent and the MacKenzie Art Gallery.)

John Nugent's figurative sculpture of Riel. (*Louis Riel Memorial*, 1968, bronze, 238.1 × 84.1 × 71.4 cm. Photo by Don Hall, used with permission of Karen Nugent and the MacKenzie Art Gallery.)

the maquette...on his desk" for years (Osborne 313). It is true that the monument became a tourist attraction. However, this was not because it captured the inner Riel but because of the subject's nudity. Nugent described his intentions for his composition by jesting that Thatcher and his government "wanted a real *man*. They've got one" (qtd. in L. Mitchell 2). His Riel was not only partly clothed but, under his short vestment, his genitals were visible to anyone who cared to look. As well, Thatcher's misgivings about Nugent's figurative Riel were shared by a cross-section of the Saskatchewan Métis community, who resented both its nudity and not having been consulted about how they would like to see their historical leader memorialized. Thatcher was defeated by Allan Blakeney's New Democratic Party (NDP) in the 1971 provincial election, and would die soon after, but opposition to the sculpture continued to grow over the years. On 31 May 1991, it was removed to the vaults of the nearby MacKenzie Art Gallery, where it has been stored ever since—or, as prominent art historian phrases it, "incarcerated" (Tippett 160).

The fate of the Gaboury-Lemay monument was no less ignominious than that of the Nugent one. In May 1970, Manitoba's Minister of Cultural Affairs, Philip Petursson, announced that the province had awarded the architect Étienne Gaboury and the sculptor Marcien Lemay $35,000 to build a statue of Riel. The work, to be coordinated by Gaboury, would consist of two parts. Gaboury would produce "an outer shell, 30 feet in height, in the shape of a hollow cylinder split in two from top to bottom." Lemay would create "a humanoid figure some 15 feet in height" to be placed inside the shell (Manitoba Government, "Riel...Chosen" 1). Gaboury and Lemay's monument was meant to celebrate the centenary of Manitoba's entry into Confederation. This was an event in which Riel played a central role, as the bilingual inscription on the outer shell reminded viewers: "I know that through the grace of God I am the founder of Manitoba. / Je sais que, par la grâce de Dieu, je suis le fondateur du Manitoba" (Dorge 12; see also Manitoba Government, "Riel... Unveiled" 2). The surprise is that it had taken so long to build a sculpture of Riel in Manitoba, to the point that Saskatchewan would beat the Keystone Province to it.

On Christmas Eve 1948, a Winnipeg high school history teacher and administrator named H.C. Knox published a letter in the *Winnipeg Tribune* suggesting that the most appropriate way to mark the city's upcoming seventy-fifth anniversary was by erecting a monument to Riel, who had been "far too long the forgotten and neglected man in Manitoba history" (7). Knox asserted that Riel should be honoured not only for bringing "truly representative" government to Red River and for being "responsible for the formation of our province" but as "the first man to fight for the recognition of the West and the rights of all Westerners." He also specified that the monument should be installed on the rear grounds of the Manitoba Legislature, overlooking the Assiniboine River. In addition, Knox expressed the desire that it be unveiled by Prime Minister Louis St. Laurent, "the leading man of [Riel's] race in Canada today" (7). Writing for a Québec historical journal in 1964, following the publication of his biography of Riel, George Stanley forecasted that one day we would see a statue of the Métis leader "devant le parlement du Manitoba à Winnipeg!" ("Louis Riel" 25). Later that decade, the Manitoba Communist leader William Kardash made a request to the premier at the time, Douglas Campbell, to ensure such an eventuality would take place (Doug Smith 47), but Kardash does not seem to have had a preference for whether the statue would sit in front or behind the Legislature.

More critically, in the 1920s, the Union nationale métisse Saint-Joseph du Manitoba initiated a campaign to erect a monument to Riel in Winnipeg (Bocquel 228–29). The Union nationale métisse, then known as the Union métisse Saint-Joseph de Manitoba, is the oldest active Métis organization in Canada, having been founded in 1887. Its initiative was part of a sustained attempt by Manitoba Métis to rehabilitate the image of their much-abused historical leader. To that end, they formed a group called "Amis de Riel," whose task was to persuade Manitobans of the rightfulness of their cause. The group was aware of the magnitude of the challenge ahead, noting in a communiqué to the *Winnipeg Free Press* announcing its founding that it had to do "*a great deal of necessary educative work to* 'clear up the historical data on the times of Riel'" (qtd. in Bocquel 229). This would prove to be an understatement, as evident in the response by another *Free Press* reader, who demanded that as long as "*the memory of our Winnipeg boys, now sleeping in Flanders fields, has not been immortalized by a permanent memorial, it is no time to consider a monument to Louis Riel, the rebel*" (qtd. in Bocquel 229). Privately, the "Amis de Riel" probably already knew that it would take more than an educational campaign to rehabilitate Riel, but this would not deter them.

The key difference between the history of the commissioning of the Nugent monument and the Gaboury-Lemay one is that the latter had considerable Métis input, notably by the NDP Member of the Manitoba Legislative Assembly Jean Allard. As Petursson outlined in his press release, the Gaboury-Lemay design had been selected as "the most distinctive among the eight submissions" by the Louis Riel Statue Committee (Manitoba Government, "Riel... Chosen" 1). The committee was chaired by the Chief Justice of Manitoba, C. Rhodes Smith, and included such luminaries as the directors of the Manitoba Museum of Man and Nature and of the Winnipeg Art Gallery, but it was the brainchild of Allard, who at the time was also the president of the Union nationale métisse. Allard had spent years trying to garner support from the province's political and social elites for the creation of a public work of art honouring Riel in his cherished Red River. As he explained in a 1966 interview with CBC Television, "We need a statue of Riel because Riel was the father...the founder of Manitoba" (Allard and Holting). Once the Gaboury-Lemay monument was approved, Allard became its most boisterous champion. Yet, in the end, that would not be enough to save it.

Gaboury and Lemay's *Louis Riel* was unveiled on 30 December 1971 on the Assiniboine River grounds of the Manitoba Legislature, as first envisaged by Knox. It was a "brief" ceremony attended by NDP Premier Edward Schreyer, the secretary of the Union nationale métisse, Ida Carrière, and other leading political and civic figures (Manitoba Government, "Riel...Unveiled" 1). Likely because of its awareness of the Nugent controversy in neighbouring Saskatchewan, prior to the unveiling, the Manitoba Centennial Commission had engaged the Franco-Manitoban historian Lionel Dorge to write a bilingual educational pamphlet to help viewers understand the work's context. Titled *Louis Riel, Manitoban, 1844–1885*, the tract bears a stylized rendition of the monument on its cover. In the text Dorge explains that, with his spheres, Gaboury had "attempted to achieve a feeling of both unity and separateness to create a tension appropriate to the conflicts and dichotomy of Riel's life" and that, by placing "Riel within the shells," Lemay was striving "to convey the mood and suffering of a man sacrificing himself for his beliefs" (Dorge 1). Dorge's interpretation is supported by the architectural historian W.P. Thompson, who states that Gaboury's split outer shell "gave the sculpture a greater visual presence from a distance and, up close, an enhanced and dramatic statement of imprisonment" (11). But notwithstanding the information provided to the public, the response was overwhelmingly negative. Even Schreyer could not conceal his disappointment, writing in a personal note that the "statue looks terrible. Poor Riel" (qtd. in Bower 32).

The reaction to the Gaboury-Lemay monument was visceral among the leaders of the recently-created Manitoba Metis Federation (MMF), specifically the Lemay component; in fact, since the controversy revolves almost exclusively around the humanoid figure, for the rest of this chapter I will focus chiefly on Lemay's sculpture. Founded in 1967, the MMF has long had an adversarial relationship with the Union nationale métisse, a conflict that reflects the demographic transformation of the Red River Métis from a predominantly Francophone group to a mainly Anglophone one. While the Union nationale métisse prides itself on being "the only Métis organization started by the Métis for the Métis and funded by themselves" (qtd. in Morrison 109), the MMF has the advantage of getting substantial government funding, both provincial and federal, as well as of the perception that it represents a larger segment of Manitoba's Métis populace. In any case, most MMF leaders objected to the portrayal of Riel not only as tormented but also naked and helpless, captive, with his hands held behind his back. Before long they started to pressure the Manitoba government to remove the

Bronze sculpture by Marcien Lemay of the "tormented" and naked Riel, surrounded by concrete walls by Étienne Gaboury, at the Université de Saint-Boniface. (*Louis Riel*, 1971, bronze/concrete, 3 m/6 m. Photo by Carolyn Kapron, used with permission.)

monument from the site and replace it with a "statesman-like" one (Mattes, "Whose Hero?" 19). The matter seemed to be resolved when Lemay accepted a commission by the MMF to produce "a more lifelike rendering" of Riel, whose maquette was exhibited at Winnipeg's Franco-Manitoban Cultural Centre (Manitoba Government, "Assiniboine" 2; see also Manitoba Government, "New"). But there was no way of bridging the divide between Gaboury and Lemay's supporters and their opponents. After the Manitoba government announced that it had donated the original monument to what is now the Université de Saint-Boniface, in response to a request by the latter's student association (Dubé 179; O'Toole 69), Allard and others camped by the work to prevent its removal, with Allard at one point chaining himself to the structure. But their protests were to no avail, and the monument was transported across the Red River and relocated to the grounds of Riel's alma mater. After the outer shells were shortened and the gap between them widened to give more prominence to the sculpture (Sickert 11), the work was rededicated on 30 November 1995.

Lemay's realistic Riel, though, never got to stand outside Manitoba's Legislature. As late as the end of May 1993, the secretary of the MMF, Billyjo Delaronde, praised Lemay's new design for its depiction of a conventional Riel. Delaronde stated that among the "highlights" of the proposed sculpture were "the scroll representing the Manitoba Act: the moccasins and frock coat representing the nature of the Metis (Riel)," and "the clenched fist [which] shows Riel negotiated from a position of strength." Delaronde emphasized that Lemay "created both statues and has given his blessing to replacing the present 'monstrosity' with this new work" (A7). But allegedly because of Lemay's "participation in the protest" against the removal of his and Gaboury's monument from the Legislature's grounds, Delaronde and the MMF awarded the commission of the new sculpture to another Winnipeg artist, Miguel Joyal (Krueger B1). It was Joyal's version that was unveiled on 12 May 1996, Manitoba Day. Also titled *Louis Riel*, it not only shows Riel fully clothed, but is almost indistinguishable from the subject of any other memorial to a political figure. Without addressing its similarity to Lemay's realistic Riel (Krueger B1; Dumontet 108), one cannot help but notice how little ambiguity it possesses, which may have been precisely the aim of both Manitoba provincial politicians and Métis civic leaders.

Despite the animus they have generated, both of Nugent's sculptures and Lemay's so-called "tormented" Riel have seldom been criticized on aesthetic grounds. On the contrary, the works are usually extolled by critics, who rue the impact they were not allowed to have on the Canadian arts scene and on Canadian society.

Sculpture by Miguel Joyal of the "statesman" Riel at the Manitoba Legislature. (*Louis Riel*, 1996, bronze, 3.5 m. Photo by Carolyn Kapron, used with permission).

Nugent's *Design* for his abstract rendering of Riel has come to be especially prized by art curators and critics. In her history of Canadian sculpture, Maria Tippett describes Nugent's maquette as "reminiscent" of Vladimir Tatlin's ground-breaking Constructivist *Monument to the Third International* (157). Tippett writes that had Nugent had the opportunity to transform his concept into "a finished work, it would have been the only modernist sculpture in the country to embrace the ideas of...Tatlin," who "sought to bring art and technology into accord" (159). Similarly, the Regina curator Timothy Long, who studied with Nugent, argues that the Saskatchewan sculptor's original model was "something people could have related to—if it was built." Long stresses that if Nugent's vision had been "realized...[w]e'd still be admiring this sculpture" (qtd. in Chabun), and he may well have a point. At the least, we would have avoided all the controversy over Riel's nudity or objectionable political symbolism.

Nugent's figurative Riel has also received accolades from critics because of its creator's evident attempt to convey the complexity of his subject. The same is true of Lemay's agonized Riel. The fact is that both sculptors have strong affinities with Riel and, whatever one may feel about their works, it is hard to deny that they take the man and his ideas seriously, including his religious convictions. Nugent was not only a devout Catholic but a fervent believer in the power of religious art, as behooves someone who "supported his family for years" by "making...beeswax candles for liturgical use" (Pincus-Witten 18). Lemay, too, was sensitive to the spiritual. Michael Gauvreau finds "uncanny" parallels between his encounter with Lemay's sculpture and with Riel's writings. For Gauvreau, like Riel's poetry and prose, Lemay's sculpture "immediately and insistently assaults" viewers with "the realization that they stand in the presence of a man who can be comprehended only with great difficulty." Gauvreau adds that the Métis leader's "twisted and tortured body, reminiscent of the Christs of Latin American liberation theology, sustains a head upon which is written an expression at once suffering, quizzical, and ironic, one which defies a facile evaluation of Riel's inner constitution and his achievements" (Gauvreau). Rather than being flippant or blasphemous, Lemay's sculpture can be seen as a work of reverence.

Granted, both Nugent's figurative *Louis Riel Memorial* and Gaboury and Lemay's *Louis Riel* were subjected to extensive acts of vandalism, which some commentators have interpreted as political or cultural rejections of the monuments. In "Canadian Culture: Another Riel Poem," Tom Wayman writes that there is "nothing indecisive" about someone taking a hammer to Lemay's Riel to rip his exposed genitals (30), affirming that the "mutilation" was "conducted in secret / by the powerless" (31). However, the motives that drive people to damage a public sculpture are much more indeterminate than Wayman supposes. For one, we live in what has been called "an age of vandalism" (Thompson 12). As well, the Legislature's Assiniboine grounds had long been known as a gay cruising site. There were even suggestions that the Gaboury-Lemay monument "be renamed 'The Spirit of Gay Liberation'" (Dafoe 6). But the more gruesome reality is that, less than six years after the unveiling of the Riel monument, "a man was brutally beaten to death within [its] shadow" in an apparent case of gay-bashing (Mullin 2; see also Osborne 317). While the defacement of Gaboury and Lemay's *Louis Riel* is regrettable, it is hardly unique. Besides homophobia, people desecrate works of art for all sorts of reasons, not only cultural and political, but even financial, as conveyed by the term "profit vandalism" (Doss 406). Again, the motivation for defiling works of art is seldom transparent.

Public art becomes most "vulnerable to acts of symbolic vandalism" when it is perceived as an emblem of "disputed narratives of identity, ownership, legitimacy, belonging, or control" (Doss 409). In such instances, physical attacks on works of art ought to be considered less "wanton acts of destruction" than "sociopolitical challenges to the standard or sanctioned stories that public art often tells" (410). But, contrary to Wayman's view, it should not be assumed that those acts are necessarily committed by the powerless. In the case of the Lemay work, it was not just Métis who objected to it. In her study of the sculpture controversy at the Manitoba Legislature, Shannon Bower shows that among the most vitriolic letters Premier Schreyer received were not from people who were outraged that Riel had been portrayed in an undignified manner, but that he had been memorialized at all. Some of those correspondents even insisted that "a statue to Thomas Scott should instead be erected" (qtd. in Bower 35). A "former Manitoban" was so incensed upon learning the province had approved the making of "a statue of that madman Louis Riel" that the person hoped if the project ever came to fruition, "someone [would] have a good supply of red or green paint handy." The unidentified individual boasted that they would be "delighted to come home for the 'paint-in'." It would be the person's Manitoba "Centennial project" (qtd. in Bower 35). Moreover, it was not merely everyday Manitobans who held such views of Riel. In 1968, when Allard invited the Conservative cabinet minister Sterling Lyon to join what became the Louis Riel Statue Committee, the future premier told him in no uncertain terms that "Riel was a traitor who deserved to hang and he received what he had coming" (qtd. in Allard A9), underscoring the extent of the opposition to the new hero.

Any public aesthetic representation of Riel is bound to be polemical not only because Canadians appear to remain divided about him but also because the cultural landscape itself often serves as a reminder of the conflicts that he still embodies. It should not come as a shock that when the Métis visual artist David Garneau first staged his performance piece *Dear John; Louis David Riel* in 2014, he did so in front of a statue of Prime Minister Macdonald in downtown Regina, a few metres from where Riel was tried and sentenced to hang in 1885. The Edmonton-born Garneau, who became a professor of visual arts at the University of Regina in the late 1990s, writes that when he moved to the city, he was astounded "to see a larger-than-life-sized sculpture of Macdonald in the main civic square." To Garneau, the monument was not just "in bad taste but an obvious provocation," which helps to understand why he later created "an itinerant performance in which the spirit of Louis Riel," wearing a hood over his head and a noose around his neck, "confronts statues of John A. Macdonald across Canada" (D. Garneau, "Extra-Rational" 73). If Garneau could find ghostly aesthetic incarnations of Riel's antagonists in Regina, this would have been a much easier task in Winnipeg. As a journalist remarked about the unveiling of the Gaboury-Lemay monument, not the least of its achievements was that "Riel ha[d] finally made it to the English side of the Red River" (Maunder 1), a crossing of no little political and cultural significance.

Winnipeg, like Manitoba as a whole, now likes to call Riel one of its favourite children, but this has not always been the case. Quite the opposite, historically, Winnipeg has been much more closely identified with Riel's enemies, such as his millstone Scott. From 1902 to 2017, the city was home to the Scott Memorial Orange Hall, an "impressive three-storey building" in the downtown area occupied by a "fraternal" society that entertained anything but brotherly feelings toward Riel or the Métis (Manitoba Historical Society, "Scott"). Equally telling, less than a year after Riel's hanging, "Winnipeg proclaimed a civic holiday to unveil a monument," not to the Métis leader, but to the Canadian volunteer soldiers who gave up their lives battling him, "the heroic War Dead" (Osborne 309–10; see also Gibbons 28–29). Also, such sentiments are not restricted to the distant past. In 1970, about the same time that the Manitoba government commissioned Gaboury and Lemay to build their statue to the man Premier Schreyer later called the visionary who "dared to expect, politically, representative government" (qtd. in Maunder 1), the city of Winnipeg felt that there would be no more appropriate adornment to its new Centennial Concert Hall than the old and "imposing monument to some half dozen young men of the Winnipeg Rifles who died fighting Riel in the North-West Rebellion" (Harrison 293; see also Welch). This is a regiment whose predecessor, the 90th Battalion, in 1885 earned the nickname of the Little Black Devils for its feats against the Métis. The literary scholar Dick Harrison terms the relocation of the *Volunteer Monument* (Manitoba Historical Society, "Volunteer") "historically and culturally ludicrous," even after conceding that "Riel remained a villain in the [Canadian] West for generations" following his death (Harrison 293). But what the act also reveals is that, as late as the 1970s, the good burghers of Winnipeg were not certain of whom they were more proud: the soon-to-be declared founder of Manitoba or the Canadian soldiers who fought him. More importantly, there are indications that not all of those attitudes have died out. In 2020, a well-known Manitoba historian took Winnipeg Mayor Brian Bowman to task for suggesting that the memorial to the Winnipeg Rifles is not inclusive enough, since it "commemorates the loss of life in the Battle of Batoche…for everybody but the Métis" (qtd. in Bowler). Gerry Bowler retorted that the flaw in the argument by Bowman, the city's first Métis mayor, is that "the Riel of 1885 was not the brilliant young man of 15 years earlier—Riel had become an unhinged messianic who fancied himself God's prophet for the New World," and who led his followers in a catastrophic war against Canada. Statues to the Canadian "army's dead in Winnipeg," added Bowler, "should no more mention the rebels than the D-Day memorial on Juno Beach should honour the Wehrmacht" (Bowler). Evidently, not all Canadians are quite ready to see Riel exalted as a national hero.

The one group with whom Riel has consistently been identified is the Métis, some of whose leaders now claim the exclusive right to determine how he should be memorialized. Curiously, most commentators, Métis or otherwise, agree that those individuals are entitled to such a prerogative. In her 1998 MA thesis, "Whose Hero? Images of Louis Riel in Contemporary Art and Métis Nationhood," Catherine Mattes justifies the removal of both the Nugent and Lemay sculptures because they are "disrespectful to Louis Riel and the Métis nation" (14–15 ff.). Similar claims are made by Frances Kaye and Shannon Bower in their respective studies of the controversy. Bower contends that "it is ultimately only the Métis who are fundamentally entwined with Riel," and so any portrayal of "Riel must be understood as a representation of the Métis people" (31). Kaye is no less categorical, writing that "[a]ny group clearly has the right to define its own national hero" ("Any" 127). The conflation of Riel and the Métis is perplexing, considering how often the same individuals insist that the lettered Riel is an atypical Métis, being a "thoroughly assimilated man, far more European than Indian" (Kaye, "Any" 121). Also, one cannot help but wonder how they would react if the federal government, or any provincial government, attempted to dictate how artists should represent the historical figures they are commissioned to portray.

One central issue that the critics of Nugent and Lemay tend not to raise is what makes a given Métis person an authority on Riel, or who truly represents the Métis. Mattes herself points out the irony that the MMF-linked figures complained about "the exclusion of the Métis [from the process of selecting the Gaboury-Lemay monument] when Jean Allard, President of the Union Nationale Métisse Saint-Joseph du Manitoba, lobbied for the sculpture" ("Whose Hero?" 48). The controversy over Gaboury and Lemay's *Louis Riel* actually could be seen as an intra-Métis organizational coup, in which one group (the Union nationale métisse) lobbies for decades to have a monument erected to Riel and another group (the MMF) later assumes control of the issue, simplifying what may not be simple at all. For instance, the founding president of the MMF, Angus Spence, was extremely critical of the Gaboury-Lemay monument. He felt that it did a service "neither to Louis Riel nor the Metis people of Manitoba," and wished that Riel had been "depicted as a man of dignity." At the same time, Spence was grateful that "the government ha[d] at last done something to honor Riel's contribution to Manitoba" (qtd. in "Metis Head" 53). Nugent's *Louis Riel Memorial* illustrates another discrepancy. The Saskatchewan Métis community is supposed to have been universally opposed to Nugent's work. Yet, in its 1979 publication *Louis Riel: Justice Must Be Done*, the Association of Métis and Non-Status Indians of Saskatchewan not only includes a page-size photograph of the sculpture (Association 1) but even uses the work's existence to challenge the notion that Riel rebelled against Canada. As the authors write, "If political leaders and the public of today recognize him as a just man fighting for a just cause, why does the blot of a criminal conviction continue to stain his reputation? Why erect statues to a criminal?" (5). That is, some Métis figures approved of the monuments, at least when it was expedient to do so.

What is most mystifying about the censure of Nugent and Lemay is how calculating it is. Commentators do not usually condemn either sculptor for misinterpreting Riel, but for providing politically inconvenient portraits of him. For almost every Métis civic leader, the main source of discomfort about the Nugent and Lemay sculptures is their nudity. It is the subject's lack of clothes that is identified as disrespectful and that precipitated the demand for the respective work's replacement with a "statesman-like" portrayal. One can understand that today's Métis are uncomfortable with having their nineteenth-century leader depicted in partial nudity, either because of contemporary prurience or, more likely, because of the frequent association of nudity with both poverty and mental illness. Yet the question that none of Nugent's or Lemay's critics has cared to ask, even those who emphasize the fundamental need to be aware of "the social and historical contexts" that inform the works (Bower 32), is how Riel perceived nudity, something that is easy to ascertain by consulting his writings.

The reality is that Riel had a quite different view of nudity than do most contemporary Métis activists, such as the MMF leaders. Rather than seeing nudity as a manifestation of mental instability, much less as a form of male "emasculation" (Bruyneel 723, 726), Riel judged it a sign of divine election. He writes that the reason he at times sheds his clothes is that God orders him to do so, being "content de ton dépouillement" (*Collected Writings* 2: 57; see also Flanagan, *Louis "David" Riel* 63, 70). As he elucidates his behaviour during his internment at the Longue-Pointe Asylum in 1876:

> Pendant que je me promenais dans le corridor, aux yeux de tous, Dieu me disait: "quand l'homme se dépouille de lui-même, je ne suis pas 24 heures sans achever en lui l'oeuvre de la rédemption et sans le mettre en ma présence comme étaient Adam et Eve avant le péché, dans la jouissance des délices de l'innocence." L'Esprit de charité m'a dit: Celui qui est bon doit se montrer tout nu. Car il est beau. Celui qui désobéit, c'est celui-là qui doit se cacher. Car il est laid. Ensuite le bon Seigneur me disait: en vérité, en vérité, le jour vient que les hommes se lèveront tout nus du sein de la terre. (2: 58; see also Flanagan, *Louis "David" Riel* 70)

Because of Bishop Bourget's negative response to his views on nudity, Riel accepted the cleric's advice that is it imperative to be always "bien habillé" (2: 59). Yet he immediately added that vain men and women believe they are "admirables" because of the beautiful clothes they wear, when Satan is using those vestments to mask their shame (2: 60). By portraying Riel naked, or partly naked, Nugent and Lemay thus were not being impudent but striving to capture the way Riel saw himself and the universe.

It is not difficult to fathom why people like to be memorialized, or have their heroes memorialized, in an adulatory manner, whether those heroes happen to be human or divine. This is a view held by Riel. Nearly half a century before the consecration of Rio de Janeiro's colossal *Christ the Redeemer* (*Cristo Redentado*), Riel writes that "God reveals me that he wants to have for his beloved son a statue which will stand sixteen feet high from the ground up to the waist" and "eighteen feet high from the waist to the top of the head," noting that God divulges that "Christian cities are disagreeable to Him because they have not yet erected such a statue to His beloved and only Son for the ornament of their public spaces" (*Collected Writings* 3: 324). More recently, in her sequel to *The Handmaid's Tale*, Margaret Atwood has her character Aunt Lydia observe that, like other statues, hers is "larger than life" and shows her "as younger, slimmer, and in better shape than [she has] been for some time" (*Testaments* 3). Yet Aunt Lydia is cognizant that idealization is just one of the conventions of public statuary, particularly of political figures. As George Stanley quips in the passage that serves as the epigraph to this chapter, "A portrait is all the more pleasing if the warts are removed" ("Last Word" 51). But the individuals mainly responsible for the hauling of the Nugent and Lemay sculptures from the grounds of the Saskatchewan and Manitoba legislatures seemed unaware of the difference between a convention and the truth. While claiming that their historical leader was an extraordinary figure, they demanded that he be represented like a humdrum politician. Their actions led the *Winnipeg Free Press* editorial writer Terence Moore to infer that the MMF did not wish to see a monument erected to the real Riel. What they wanted was "a self-portrait of the politically active

Metis people of Manitoba today," one that would "express what they want to express about Riel and about themselves" (A6). In the case of the MMF, given its long record of mismanagement, to put it politely (Morrison 91–92), perhaps what its leaders wanted was a truthful portrait of anyone but a contemporary political activist. All indications are that they got their wish with the irony-free Joyal sculpture.

One redeeming feature of Joyal's *Louis Riel* is that it may empower young Métis by enabling them to see themselves as being linked to "the founder of Manitoba" (Farrell Racette 50). But perhaps pundits, such as Jean Teillet, ought to temper their triumphalist rhetoric that the Joyal monument is significant because "[n]o one is trying to tear [it] down" ("Louis Riel" 57). Whatever else it may have been intended to achieve, the official approval of "the more communally beneficial" (Dumontet 104) Joyal sculpture over Lemay's, and by extension over Nugent's, marks a flight from complexity in the aesthetic representations of Riel. Although he was hanged for his political actions, Riel was not just a politician. He was also a prolific writer who, among other things, envisaged himself as the Prophet of the New World. This is the reason that a political scientist like Thomas Flanagan is flabbergasted by Riel's Batoche and Regina writings of 1884 and 1885. As Flanagan observes, "the reader will quickly be struck by how little attention Riel devoted in his diaries to what historians regard as the major issues." Instead, he focused mainly on his "'conversations with God,' that is, prayers and answering revelations" ("Introduction," *Diaries* 16)—what another scholar calls his "rambling spiritual confessions" (Cook, "Confessions" 76). Flanagan's analysis is reinforced by Glen Campbell. The main editor of Riel's poetry, Campbell notes that the I in Riel's "verse is more often than not, a tormented being, one who is deeply troubled by events in which he plays a major role" ("Tormented Soul" 354), elaborating that the reader of Riel's poetry "senses a man not at peace with himself, a man with unattained goals" (363–64). Like Gauvreau, Campbell contrasts Riel's verse with Lemay's sculpture, both of which "reveal the anguish of a man caught in his destiny, a man who has been unable to reconcile his utopian idealism with the surrounding hostile reality" (364). For undisclosed reasons, most promoters of Riel's monuments dread any evocation of his at times harrowing relation to the world. So they have attempted to sanitize his image, and have largely succeeded, thanks in no little part to the complicity of critics, many of whom are also profoundly uncomfortable with Riel's multiplicity.

Kaye is a case in point. She makes the provocative allegation that "Nugent believe[d]" that Premier Ross "Thatcher would have hanged Riel again had he had the chance" ("Any" 110), a response that may not be exceptional among the political figures behind the memorialization of Riel. More predictably, Kaye lambastes Thatcher for his antediluvian aesthetic tastes, charging that he does "not know art" (112). Yet she demonstrates that Thatcher favours the same kind of art as do most Métis civic leaders—conventional sculptures—which would suggest that they also do not know art. What Kaye fails to examine is her own contradictory feelings toward Riel, for she reveals that she too does not think much of him. Kaye contends that the reason Thatcher supported a figurative sculpture of Riel is that the Métis leader was "a symbol of exactly the kind of assimilated person he [Thatcher] wanted Native people to become" (114). Unlike other Indigenous leaders, such as Gabriel Dumont and the Cree chiefs Big Bear and Poundmaker, Riel was "a European man, European dressed, European educated, and European in his antecedents and in his hopes for his family." This is reputedly why current scholars and activists "are now looking at many issues that concern the community but have nothing to do with Louis Riel" (122, 121). Like so many other self-described defenders of Riel, Kaye ends up disowning him, making one wonder what to make of her condemnation of people like Thatcher for their anti-Riel biases.

The fates of the Nugent figurative sculpture and of the Gaboury-Lemay monument raise critical issues about the value of public art, whose publicness makes it extremely vulnerable to the vagaries of popular aesthetic tastes and to populist political influence. On the positive side, the controversies mark two of the rare instances

when we get a sense of how the general Canadian populace—
as opposed to the cultural, political, and academic elites—feels
about Riel. This is due to the fact that, as the arts critic Alison
Gillmor writes, public art has "the potential...to reach broad audiences, address big social questions, transform city spaces and
connect communities" in ways that art galleries and museums
do not (Gillmor). But on the negative side, the audiences for
public art tend to favour soporific representational sculpture, a
taste that they share with politicians and social activists. This is
a debilitating drawback, since the most iconic works of art often
encounter much resistance when they are first unveiled.

Partly in response to the Joyal sculpture's displacement of the
Gaboury-Lemay statue, the painter Cliff Eyland concludes that
public art is pointless. "Our official culture can only be uncontroversial," deplores Eyland, and is "not worth making" (122). Yet,
in a way, the battle of the Riel sculptures is a vindication of art—
autonomous art. As commentators like Bower have remarked, it
is "the ambiguity" of works such as Lemay's sculpture that most
disturbs critics. However, this is not because it allows for "drastic
misinterpretation," as she posits (34), but because it is open to a
variety of competing interpretations. After all, a work of art that
allows for only one interpretation is not really art. Most importantly, it is only complex works of art that engender vigorous
discussion, not just about their meaning but their potential implications. This is a truth that the MMF leader Guy Dumont has come
to accept. In a letter to the *Winnipeg Free Press* in 1994, just before
the Gaboury-Lemay monument was relocated to St. Boniface,
Dumont confesses that he had favoured the work's removal from
the moment he saw it, feeling "it was a grotesque representation
of our esteemed leader." But he gradually discerns that the "monument as it now stands has probably evoked more controversy and
brought more attention to the Metis people than even our most
eloquent leaders" (G. Dumont A9; see also Bower 318). If there is a
moral to be extracted from the saga of the Riel sculptures, it is that
it is the controversial ones that trigger debates, probably because
they are living works of art. The comfortable sculptures favoured by

political and civic leaders have little impact, being born dead like so many other museum pieces.

The Problematic Patriot

7

Chester Brown's Louis Riel *and Canadian Nationalism*

> Canadian national identity was born in opposition to First Nations and Metis people. To reconstruct an understanding of these conflicts is to deconstruct Canada.
>
> —SHERRY FARRELL RACETTE, "Metis Man or Canadian Icon"

THERE ARE MANY PARADOXES about the posthumous Canadianization of Louis Riel, as we have seen throughout this study. One of these is that almost every important cultural work that purports to portray Riel as a Canadian hero eventually betrays considerable reservations about either his Canadianness or his character. Another paradox is that fictional representations of Riel do not appear to possess the imaginative power of nonfictional ones. In a 1991 article on *The Scorched-Wood People*, Dennis Duffy contends that, excepting Rudy Wiebe's novel, literary works on Riel lack "the quality" of nonfictional texts like Joseph Kinsey Howard's *Strange Empire: A Narrative of the Northwest*, Thomas Flanagan's *Louis "David" Riel: "Prophet of the New World,"* and George Woodcock's *Gabriel Dumont: The Métis Chief and His Lost World* (207). Even if Woodcock's book is interested in Riel only in juxtaposition to his 1885 military commander, this assessment still holds true today. One exception to the rule is Chester Brown's *Louis Riel: A Comic-Strip Biography*. Yet, in the end, the 2003 bestseller too proves to be much less enthralled by its eponymous hero than it advertises, reflecting

Brown's conflicting and conflicted attitudes toward the Métis leader.

Born in Montréal in 1960 and raised in suburban Châteauguay, Chester William David Brown is the best-known comic strip writer in Canada, playing an "instrumental role in pushing Canadian graphic narrative well beyond adolescent fantasies of super-heroism" (Bell 16). One of his colleagues, Seth, deems Brown not just the country's most accomplished comics writer, but "without doubt one of the most important writers (or artists) in any of Canada's art forms" (10). Similarly, the novelist Joseph Boyden calls Brown a "brilliant comic strip author" and his Riel book "brilliant and beautiful and moving, a great example of how history can be told in a new and refreshing way" (62, 188). Brown owes his renown to a series of innovative comic strips and books that he began publishing in the early 1980s, works with titles such as *Yummy Fur* (1983), *Ed the Happy Clown* (1989), *The Playboy* (1992), *I Never Liked You* (1994), *The Little Man: Short Strips, 1980–1995* (1998), *Paying for It: A Comic-Strip Memoir about Being a John* (2011), and *Mary Wept over the Feet of Jesus* (2016). Thanks to his experimental strips, which are often both risky and risqué, Brown soon emerged as "an alternative-comics star" (Bell 148). But the turning point in his career occurred in 2003, when he published his graphic biography of Riel, which became "an instant classic" (Tousley 126). Brown had conceived the project as a book, but he agreed with his publisher to have it appear in a magazine-style "series before publication in book form" (Bell 165), which it did in ten issues between 1999 and 2003. Nevertheless, it was only with the work's publication as a single volume that general readers realized that *Louis Riel* is "a masterpiece of modern Canadian comic art and a major breakthrough in terms of the scope of comics" (Bell 165), taking Riel to a broad, international audience.

Brown's interest in Riel should not have come as a complete surprise, since Brown has striking affinities with the Métis leader. To begin with, he has always had a strong interest in history, as befits a grandson of the historian Chester William New, an ordained Baptist minister who became a much-admired professor at McMaster University and who is best known for his political biographies

(Brown and Epp; Bell 164). Also, for someone who grew up in Québec in the second half of the twentieth century, Brown was raised in a very strict family. He still considers himself "a religious person," which is the reason he has no difficulty accepting that Riel's "visions were in some sense true" and does not think Riel was "crazy or insane in the way that most people would understand those terms" (qtd. in Arnold). Religion is a pervasive theme in his work. Brown has composed sketches like "The Twin," which explores Gnostic theories about the duality of Jesus Christ (*Little Man* 38–41). In the 1980s and 90s, he also produced an extensive series of "comics adaptations of the Gospels," publishing over "twenty installments of the Gospel of Matthew" alone (Bell 158). His interest in the Bible is most evident in *Mary Wept over the Feet of Jesus*. A series of interlinked stories such as "Cain and Abel," "Tamar," "Rahab," "Bathsheba," "Mary, the Mother of Jesus," and "Mary of Bethany," the collection examines the prevalence of prostitution in Biblical times, including by the Virgin Mary (*Mary Wept* 115), as well as the notion the God favours disobedience over "subservience" (170).

Like Riel, Brown is guilt-ridden about both his carnal desires and his use of language, sometimes to the point of prudery. In his autobiographical graphic novel *The Playboy*, which depicts his discovery of sexual desire and pornography, he comes to the realization that he prefers "masturbating to actually having sex" (151). Then in *I Never Liked You*, a bildungsroman set largely in Châteauguay and documenting his coming of age, he relates how vulgar language is not tolerated in his family. After his mother overhears the grade-school Brown saying the word "shit," she picks him up by the shoulders and shakes him violently until he promises to never "**use that word again!**" (3). Possibly because he internalizes his mother's sentiment that "only crude and ignorant people" employ indecorous language (4), Brown becomes determined not to utter profanities. Thus, as late as high school, he is known as the "kid that won't swear" (22), and refuses to do so on principle, even after some of the other children tease him endlessly about it and rough him up (24). He is not just a proud individualist and rebel but that oddity, a late twentieth-century

Canadian teenager who refuses to swear because about everyone else does. Yet, in his later book *Paying for It*, Brown documents his experiences as a john. His memoir has been described as "a daring, courageous and gorgeous account of his adventures in the sex industry, paying for sex" (S. Lee 18), but Brown is not content to sing the joys and virtues of commercial sex. Instead, he feels compelled to condemn "the romantic love ideal" as being nothing less than "evil" (Brown, *Paying* 183). Whether dealing with the ethics of (not) swearing or of paying for sex, Brown tends to evince few doubts about the rectitude of his position.

Another parallel between Brown and Riel involves their attitudes toward the concept of madness. Throughout his work, Brown reveals much interest both in the question of insanity and the scientific treatment of mental illness. In *I Never Liked You*, he shows how his mother experiences "mental difficulties" (146) and later dies in a hospital after falling down a flight of stairs as she wanders through the complex, "apparently in a confused...state" (158). But it is in "My Mom Was a Schizophrenic," the closing strip in *The Little Man* and the early work that best "prefigures *Louis Riel*" (Langager 42), that Brown engages most methodically with what he labels the myth of insanity. Despite his mother's psychological struggles, Brown sees mental illness essentially as a discursive construct. He writes that early psychiatrists did not discover the diseases they linked to conditions like schizophrenia, "they invented them," and the symptoms have less to do with mental disorders than with a person's "socially unacceptable beliefs and behaviour" (*Little Man* 153, 154). "My Mom Was a Schizophrenic" consists of six pages of graphic text and six pages of notes, and Brown openly admits that he framed it as "a short introduction-to-anti-psychiatry type of strip" (171) in order to combat what he perceives as misleading information about what is really a social problem. Given his skepticism about the "science" behind mental illness, it is not unexpected that he would gravitate toward Riel, someone who was hospitalized in mental institutions after he declared himself a prophet, and a historical figure who calls into question the line between sanity and insanity.

Louis Riel is divided into four parts of unequal length, plus a one-page epilogue. Part I deals with the Red River Resistance of 1869–1870, which in many ways was Riel's golden moment, marred only by his sanctioning of the execution of Thomas Scott. Part II depicts Riel's first exile in the United States, after the fall of Red River; his main mental breakdown; and his religious epiphany, when he becomes convinced that God has anointed him the David of the New World. Part III portrays his exile in Montana Territory, where he works as a teacher; his return to Canada to lead the Saskatchewan Valley Métis during what John Ralston Saul terms "the Canadian internal war of 1885" ("Introduction" xiii), and his defeat at Batoche. Part IV examines his trial for high treason in Regina and subsequent hanging. Finally, the one-page epilogue recaps the aftermath of Riel's political life, focusing on the fate of those who survived him, from Dumont and other Métis combatants, through his own wife and children, to John A. Macdonald and the head of the Canadian Pacific Railway (CPR).

Brown's book on Riel, as other critics have pointed out, crystallizes many of the author's "themes of religion, anti-authoritarianism and madness" (Arnold). In his foreword, Brown writes that he has not produced "a full biographical treatment of Riel's story" but has "mostly concentrated on Riel's antagonistic relationship with the Canadian government, and even that has been simplified and distorted in order to make it fit into a 241-page comic-strip narrative" (Louis Riel). He also mentions that he has relied extensively on Maggie Siggins's Riel: A Life of Revolution (1994), a text he judges "the best, most comprehensive biography" of his subject and which "presents the Métis rebel as a heroic figure" (C. Brown, Louis Riel)—indeed, as "a kind of Che Guevara of the Métis people" (Siggins 293). If one accepts Brown's statements at face value, his graphic narrative is not just a life of Riel but a sympathetic one, mirroring his "belief that the Métis got a raw deal" (Conner C20). Yet for a biography of Riel, Brown's book does not begin with a sketch of his ostensible hero but of the latter's supreme foe, Macdonald. Perhaps this focus on Canada's founding prime minister could be seen as being meant to underscore the Métis people's subjection to the machinations of external forces, be they governmental or mercantile. From the opening panels, we discover that the Hudson's Bay Company is about "to sell Rupert's Land to the Canadian government for 300,000 pounds" (C. Brown, *Louis Riel* 7), even though there is a substantial population in the region. The local residents have not been consulted about the selling of the territory they call home, and they are not about to get much representation either. As Macdonald remarks, "we can't allow the people who live [in Rupert's Land] to elect their own representatives—not yet" (7; see also Macdonald, Letter to Taché 750). The Prime Minister is also clear that he does not want "another Quebec developing on the Red River" (8). In order to understand Riel's actions in 1869–1870, one would need to be aware of the forces he faced.

The idea that Brown's graphic narrative is designed to dramatize how vulnerable Riel and the Métis are to the Machiavellian schemes of their powerful enemies is accentuated by his visual representation of the two leaders. Brown paints a reverential portrait of Riel, presenting him almost always immaculately dressed and with no discernible physical flaws. In contrast, he draws a broad caricature of Macdonald, depicting him with a clownish nose and showing him to venerate no philosophical principle or deity more than a bottle of hard liquor. Brown also emphasizes that Macdonald possesses a conniving streak and will stop at nothing as he pursues his political and business ends, insinuating that Macdonald deliberately provokes the North-West War.

Brown actually shows in some detail that the reason the 1885 negotiations between Riel and the Canadian government fail is that Macdonald sabotages the process. At first, the Prime Minister thinks of bribing his adversary by giving him "some money" to return to the United States (*Louis Riel* 132). This is a proposition that Riel entertains so long as he receives enough cash to cover his losses in Manitoba, possibly as much as "100,000" dollars (137), a riposte that hints he has a price. However, Macdonald then has one of his drunken epiphanies and gleans that a war may not only be politically expedient, but may make a critical contribution to national unity. "Career's over if railway doesn't get built," he ponders while in the company of his inseparable bottle of alcohol. More importantly, "Canada's over." The only way that both Canada and the transcontinental rail project can be saved is if he manages "to get people excited about the railway" (133). The most promising option, it dawns on Macdonald, is to instigate a new war with Riel and the Métis, a conflagration that would have both political and economic benefits. He outlines his plans to rescue the railroad to the president of the CPR, George Stephen, in three consecutive panels:

> The half-breeds in the North-West are close to rebelling—Riel is leading them now, and I'm sure he'll get them to take over a fort or something soon.
>
> When they do that, we'll send soldiers out on your trains. The soldiers will easily defeat the half-breeds, and the whole nation will cheer.
>
> But the people won't just be cheering for the brave Canadian soldiers—they'll also be cheering for the railway that enables the Canadian government to bring law and order to a remote part of the country. (136)

Brown does not go as far as the twentieth-century novelist Howard O'Hagan, who writes that "Canada was made a dominion" so that the CPR "might be built and that men might gain money from its building" (11; see also A. Dubuc 114-15), giving voice to the common cynicism that Canada could be seen as "a railway in search of a state" (Lower 381). But he reveals an equally unsavoury vision of the origins of Confederation. As Brown has Stephen respond, with a mixture of repugnance and awe, "you devious bastard" (136), a feeling that seems to be shared by the author.

In light of Brown's rendering of his two central personages, one has to deduce that Macdonald orchestrates the North-West War, which as mentioned is why he loses all interest in bribing Riel (*Louis Riel* 137-38; see also McLean 116). Macdonald makes little attempt to conceal his duplicitous aims. "To be quite frank, I want the half-breeds to rebel," he tells the HBC factor Lawrence Clarke, who is visiting Ottawa from the North-West (140). This is a strategy that Clarke also supports, since "more police in the area would bring in more money" (141). Macdonald thus could be construed as the villain in Brown's narrative. He could be seen as a terrorist of sorts, or at least a nakedly devious politician who will stop at nothing to get his way, to the point of dragging the country into an unnecessary war. If this is the case, then there is not much for which Riel can be held responsible. As has been said of his historical model, he is "sentenced and hanged in order to serve the political purposes of the Macdonald government" (Teillet, "Putting History" A7; see also McLean 122 and Sprague 184). When Riel and the Métis get themselves embroiled in the second military conflict with Ottawa by "tak[ing] up arms" to form their own government (C. Brown, *Louis Riel* 143), they are just doing what the federal government hoped they would.

Brown's apparent sympathies toward Riel and the Métis are reinforced by his acerbic portrayal of Thomas Scott. If Macdonald is the historical Riel's nemesis, Scott is his albatross, the catalyst for what remains the most perplexing episode in his political career, Riel's countenance of the Orangeman's execution. This is an episode that even his most forgiving supporters have trouble rationalizing. Brown himself states in an interview that if Riel "hadn't had Thomas Scott killed, who knows how things would have played out after that...It kind of changes everything, or it *might* have changed everything" (Brown and Epp). Since his death in 1870, Scott has been transformed into "one of the few truly demonic personages in Canadian culture," becoming "the foremost symbol of Anglo-Canadian racism" (Braz, "Orange Devil" 41, 42). Some recent writers and scholars are not satisfied to characterize him as an "ignoramus" but bestialize him as "a rabid dog" (Boyden 33), a non-person who was "killed because he was a stranger with no kin ties" (Hamon, *Audacity* 198)—a peculiar accusation to make in a predominantly immigrant country, where newcomers often arrive alone. The complication with the dominant narrative about the nefariousness of Scott is that there is no proof that he committed any grievous crime, other than being "no more willing to temporize than his captor" (Stanley, *Birth* 105). There is not even archival evidence that he used "racial or religious slurs" against his opponents (Bumsted, *Thomas Scott's Body* 200). The historical Riel himself at first only claimed that Scott was "'a very bad man'" and that he had "'insulted'" his guards (qtd. in Stanley, *Louis Riel* 114). He also dismissed the execution as nothing more than "un détail" (Riel, *Collected Writings* 1: 362). Riel eventually conceded that Scott's killing was "a political mistake," but he continued to reiterate that "before God and my conscience I did not commit a crime" (*Collected Writings* 3: 583). Whatever may have been Riel's true motivation, history has interpreted his role in the death of Scott largely as "'a fatal blunder'" (Sprague 5). While there is no corroboration that the incident "haunt[ed] Riel for the rest of his years" (Boyden 33; see also Toussaint, *Bison* 57), there is little doubt that it did irreparable damage to his reputation.

 The conclusion reached by most scholars is that Scott was condemned to death because, as Riel reportedly declared at the time, "'we must make Canada respect us'" (qtd. in D.A. Smith 40). Brown, however, justifies the killing of Scott. Like other contemporary writers and visual artists, he depicts the Ontario expansionist, not merely as what Riel's nephew Auguste Vermette brands "un matamore, un 'troublemaker'" (Ferland 104), but as an irredeemable xenophobe, which is why Brown silences him "in the name of cultural diversity" (Braz, "Orange Devil" 51). So emphatically does he disapprove of Scott that often he does not even grant him his own voice. When Scott speaks, Brown tends to insert a series of Xs, which he explains in a footnote "indicate racist comments and profanity" (*Louis Riel* 61). In some of the captions, Scott makes indeterminate statements such as "**imprisoned by a bunch of xxxxxxx xxxx xxxxxx!**" or "**xxxx xxxxx xxxxx xxx!**" (61). His lack of humanity, as conveyed by his lack of intelligible speech, becomes most conspicuous when Brown contrasts him to the cultivated Riel. When the Métis leader goes to prison to warn Scott that his "non-stop insults are getting to t'e guards" and it is "no way to speak to a 'uman being," the latter replies that he is **"not scared of your xxxxx xxx guards!,"** who are **"too busy xxxx xxxxxxx each other to bother shooting me!"** (63). Most crucially, before Scott's imprisonment, Brown shows that he is a cold-blooded killer. He portrays the Orangeman chopping a "half-breed spy" as if he were a piece of wood, with blood dripping graphically from his axe. Scott seems possessed by hatred and does not stop attacking his helpless victim until he is ordered to do so by his leader, John Christian Schultz, since "you've killed him!" (53, 55). Brown completely others Scott as an inveterate racist, underlining the magnitude of the ethnoracial prejudice faced by Riel, and partly justifying his behaviour. Yet Scott's murder of the Métis "spy," who is not identified in the text but is based on the politically ambiguous Norbert Parisien, is not mentioned by any of his enemies afterward.

Brown's undisguised animosity toward Scott is startling in comparison to the depiction of the Ontarian in the two other best-known graphic narratives about Riel. In *Louis Riel, le père du Manitoba*, the Montréal cartoonists Zoran and Toufik treat Scott cursorily. They not only represent him in less than one page but also suggest that he is killed, not for murdering anyone, but for his intemperate language. Zoran and Toufik have Riel inform his perplexed enemy that a crime that is unforgivable for the Métis during the buffalo hunt is **"l'insubordination**, et tu en es **coupable!"** Riel adds that the reason Scott must be eliminated is political, to demonstrate who is "le maître ici" (Zoran and Toufik 19). The Manitoba painter and comics writer Robert Freynet is even more laconic in his treatment of Scott in *Louis Riel en bande dessinée*. In his fifty-eight-page book, Freynet allots the Orangeman a single panel, in a section pregnantly titled "**le martyre de Louis Riel.**" He notes his regret that Canadians are trying to kill Riel because he was the president of the provisional government that "fait exécuter un 'Canadian' rebelle, Thomas Scott" (39). Also, Freynet only alludes to Scott retroactively, after he has already shown the twenty-five-year-old founder of Manitoba being chased by Canadian soldiers like "un animal" (36). Freynet, of course, never acknowledges that the rabble-rouser Scott is known in some circles as "the 'Martyr of Red River'" (Bumsted, *Thomas Scott's Body* 3). Still, it is as if both Zoran and Toufik and Freynet are not positive that they will be able to make a convincing case of why the "grand idealist" Riel (Teillet, *North-West* 229) allows Scott to be executed, something Brown has no difficulty doing, since he pictorially implicates the Orangeman in a cold-blooded murder.

Yet there are many hints in *Louis Riel* that the fact Brown disapproves so categorically of Scott may not mean that he admires Riel. This becomes increasingly evident toward the end of the book. In his comprehensive analysis of Brown's development as an artist, the comics archivist and historian John Bell observes that "Brown's political views evolved over the course of the five-year Riel project" (166). Bell's analysis is persuasive because Brown is much more sympathetic toward Riel in the early part of his narrative than in the later stages, suggesting that his perspective of the conflict between Riel and Macdonald underwent a metamorphosis during the production of the manuscript. Brown has said that when he began planning a book on Riel, he was very interested in the "whole schizophrenia angle," explaining that when "I first started working on it, I thought I would play up that angle more than I ended up doing. The religious aspect of the story was also a draw" (qtd. in Arnold). But in the process of fashioning the text, his focus shifted to Riel's political life, a development that may have clashed with his initial conception of the Métis leader.

Brown's turn to the political probably reflects the influence of Thomas Flanagan. In his foreword to *Louis Riel*, Brown recommends not only Siggins's biography but also Flanagan's "less sympathetic judgement of the man," *Riel and the Rebellion: 1885 Reconsidered*, and his "fascinating study of the development of Riel's religious thinking," *Louis "David" Riel: "Prophet of the New World."* By the time Flanagan published *Riel and the Rebellion* in 1983, he had switched his focus from Riel's religious ideas to his political activities and had become deeply concerned about his new image as "Canada's own leader of national liberation, a home-grown Fidel Castro or Ho Chi Minh" (*Riel* 11). In the process, he also became much more supportive of the federal government's position in 1885, arguing that "the *Métis* grievances were at least partly of their own making." So perturbed was Flanagan about "the gathering movement to grant Riel a posthumous pardon" (*Riel* viii) that he felt it was incumbent on him to publicly oppose it, a view that finds echoes in the latter part of Brown's narrative.

In any case, Brown's political turn is not total, not the least because when it comes to Riel, it is not easy to separate the religious and the psychological from the political. Thus a psychiatrist who examines Riel questions his mental state, since "you murdered Thomas Scott" and "anyone who commits murder is insane" (*Louis Riel* 111; see also H. Howard 641). Riel defends himself by arguing that he was not part of the court martial that conducted the trial, even if he was the president of the provisional government, and it is not very plausible that such a momentous decision would be taken without his assent. As well, he stresses that he does not consider the jurors murderers, for "we were all acting to preserve order in our community" (C. Brown, *Louis Riel* 111). Yet the fact Brown links the execution of Scott to Riel's potential mental instability implies that the Métis leader may be guilty of more than the crime of having "**tant aimé la terre natale**," as Archbishop Alexandre-Antonin Taché would have it ("Lettre" 206). Perhaps he is also culpable of hubris, of confusing his personal predilections with the collective aims of his people.

In Brown's book, Riel is usually juxtaposed to Anglo-Canadian figures such as Scott, Macdonald, and the "**pseudo-gouverneur**" of Red River William McDougall (Ferland 84), all of whom are transparently dishonest, if not outright chauvinistic. Riel is supposed to be different from those he fights. Yet he is shown to be an autocrat who does not tolerate opposition. This aspect of his personality becomes most apparent when he scolds his cousin Charles Nolin, "you're either with us or you're against us. If you're against us, we'll have to try you for treason, and the punishment is death if you're found guilty" (C. Brown, *Louis Riel* 147; see also "Proceedings" 23–24). But the trait is discernible in his relations with several other people, including the clergy. When one priest inquires if Riel is planning to raise arms against Canada and then says that he will "refuse to give the sacrament to anyone who participates in a rebellion against the government!" Riel punches him, shouting, "Rome has fallen! Get out of my way!" (C. Brown, *Louis Riel* 143). Also, the priest is elderly, with snowy white hair. But when Riel strikes him, none of the Métis comes to the cleric's assistance, suggesting that they may feel intimidated by their leader. Similarly, when Riel breaks with the Vatican in the name of the Métis, declaring that "the Pope no longer has any authority over us!" and "I am God's prophet for the new world!" (144), there is no indication that this is the will of the community. Brown makes no effort to camouflage his condemnation of "un perturbateur invétéré" of the public order like Scott (Morice, "Louis Riel" 185), but this does not prevent him from presenting Riel as a demagogue, again hinting that the Ontarian may not be the only personage of whom the author does not approve.

The fact is that there is a major discrepancy in *Louis Riel* between what the text tells us about the title character and what it portrays him doing, which may be why some scholars argue that "Brown shows us a Riel whose symbology remains undecipherable, an impossible but necessary figure with...blank eyes" (T. MacDonald 60). The comics theoretician Scott McCloud has written that the space between the panels of a comic strip is called the gutter, and that it is "in the *limbo* of the gutter" that "the human imagination takes two separate images and *transforms* them into a single idea" (66). McCloud adds that "nothing is *seen* between the two panels, but the *experience* tells you something *must* be there!" (67). What one often detects in the gutters of Brown's book, and sometimes beyond those empty spaces, is a discordant representation of the Métis chief. Throughout the text, Riel is described as a benevolent leader, particularly next to the wily Macdonald, yet Brown frequently shows him engaging in overtly autocratic behaviour. The existence of this despotic streak in Riel cannot help but raise the question of whether he embodies a higher or nobler form of politics than do Macdonald and his underlings, and what sort of place he should occupy in Canada's national pantheon.

Riel is an extremely problematic figure in both Canadian culture and political history, challenging some of the dearest images that

Canadians have of the country. One of the most popular myths of Canada is as "a victim," a perpetual "colony...from which a profit is made, but *not by the people who live there*" (Atwood, *Survival* 45). As the Toronto poet Dennis Lee writes in his long meditative poem "Civil Elegies," "we are a conquered nation: sea to sea we bartered / everything that counts, till we have / nothing to lose but our forebears' will to lose" (56). Needless to say, Canadian writers who perceive their country as a colonized state are bound to find it difficult to imagine that it is also a colonizer. More precisely, they are unlikely to be able to consider Canada's own colonialism, an internal colonialism that reveals not all Canadians are victims in the same manner, many of them being victims of their more privileged co-citizens.

The discomfiture caused by the history of Indigenous and non-Indigenous relations in Canada was palpable in Prime Minister Justin Trudeau's 2017 address to the General Assembly of the United Nations. Trudeau began by stating that Canada is "a country built on different cultures, different religions, different languages all coming together" and that "diversity has become our great strength." However, he promptly clarified that this "is not and has not always been true for everyone who shares our land" ("Prime Minister"). Trudeau then continued that "Canada is built on the ancestral land of Indigenous Peoples—but regrettably, it's also a country that came into being without the meaningful participation of those who were there first." For the country's Indigenous populace, "those early colonial relationships were not about strength through diversity, or a celebration of our differences" but were rather mostly experiences of "humiliation, neglect, and abuse" ("Prime Minister"). Trudeau appeared to concede that since Confederation there have been at least two distinct Canadas, one Indigenous and one non-Indigenous, and the "official" Canada has not had much space for the descendants of the country's original inhabitants. On the contrary, it has often forged its collective identity by excluding them. As the Métis visual artist and scholar Sherry Farrell Racette states in the passage that serves as the epigraph to this chapter, "Canadian national identity was born in opposition to First Nations and Metis people" (46), and better than any other figure Riel reminds us that it is impossible to imagine Canada without addressing those antagonisms. That is, Riel remains culturally and politically alive for Canadians because, more than anyone else, he embodies the central conflicts at the heart of the Canadian polity.

Brown's increasing awareness that it may be difficult to reconcile his Canada with Riel's perhaps explains why he gradually distances himself from the Métis leader. But there may be other issues at play, especially the fact that Brown does not believe in critical aspects of Riel's cause. Along with his interest in religion and sex, Brown has become known for his libertarianism. It is because of his belief in the desirability of maximizing individual liberty and freedom that he has so zealously opposed mainstream psychiatry and the treatment of mental patients against their will. "My inclination is to let people hurt themselves," Brown sums up his position. "I know it's a controversial standpoint but I believe we should give people their freedom, and that includes the freedom to hurt themselves." He adds that "people should have the *legal* right to hurt themselves without fearing that they're going to get locked up for doing so" (Brown and Epp). Also, Brown's libertarianism is not restricted to the promotion of the individual rights of people believed to suffer from mental illness. It is because of his libertarianism that Brown is opposed to government programs such as "nationalized health care." When it is pointed out that his books are subsidized by the Canada Council for the Arts, he counters that "I'm against government giving money to artists, but I'm not against artists taking money. Just like I don't have a moral problem with people taking healthcare from the government, but I don't think government should give it" (Brown and Gilson). In particular, his libertarianism is manifested in his absolute championing of individual property rights, a position that puts Brown at odds with a promoter of collective rights like Riel.

In an extensive 2002 interview with the poet and cultural critic Darrell Epp, aka Two-Handed Man, Brown asserts that the basic difference between rich and poor societies is their legislation on property rights. His view is heavily indebted to the U.S. journalist

Tom Bethell's 1998 book *The Noblest Triumph: Property and Prosperity through the Ages*, which argues that "[t]he great explanatory hypothesis of history" is that when "property is privatized, and the rule of law is established in such a way that all including the rulers themselves are subject to the same law, economies will prosper and civilization will blossom" (Bethell 3). As Brown tells Epp:

> If you look at poor countries, their property rights are either weak or non-existent—look at rich countries and they have strong property rights. If you accept this premise (and if you don't, you should really read Bethell's book) then it should be obvious why Indians in North America are so poor: weak property rights. People on reserves aren't allowed to buy, sell, or own the land they live on. This comes from their traditional respect for the natural world—no one should be able to own the land. This was one of the fundamental differences (perhaps THE fundamental difference) between the natives of North America and the incoming Europeans. So, if they were to accept property rights they'd be giving up at least one thing that makes them culturally distinct. And it would go beyond that—reserves would cease to be reserves. If non-Indians could buy reserve land from Indians, then reserves would, over time, cease to be centres of cultural identity for Indians. This would mean assimilation. (Brown and Epp)

When Epp interjects that he cannot grasp why Indigenous people would favour assimilation, since it would amount to their "destruction", Brown replies that he is "not forcing anyone to do anything." He simply believes that Indigenous people "should understand the consequences of the way they organize their communities. They aren't going to be able to keep their culture AND enjoy the kind of economic growth that we see in the rest of the US and Canada. They can't have both—it's one or the other" (Brown and Epp). Brown may have a point in the sense that the First Nations were unable to exercise their collective property rights during the European invasion, an issue that he does not address. But his ideas on private property merit some attention, since they reflect the views of Macdonald's government (and, possibly, of millions of Canadians). For example, in the 1890s, the Methodist missionary John McDougall wrote that "Tribal communism has always been hurtful to individuality, and without this no race of men can progress" (70), and at least one contemporary observer claims that Macdonald's "National Policy required that the land in the West eventually be privately owned" (McLean 51). Yet Brown is unequivocal that for someone to believe in collective rights is to consign one's people to a future of indigence, that is, to doom them, which sheds some light on why the collectivist Riel becomes increasingly unappealing to him.

As one reflects on Brown's book, it becomes apparent that the portrayals of Riel and Macdonald could be interpreted very differently from the way they are described by the author. Even with his lampooning of the Prime Minister's physiognomy and values, Brown is much more emotionally engaged with Macdonald than with Riel. *Louis Riel* ends, as it begins, with Macdonald centre stage, and the text informing readers that the North-West War enabled the CPR, and Canada, to complete the first transcontinental railroad across the country, which it did on 7 November 1885 (241), only days before Riel's hanging. This is a peculiar way to finish a representation of the Métis leader, not by recapitulating the significance of his life, but by underscoring what Canada gained because of his defeat. The opening and closing frames of Brown's graphic narrative cannot help but make one wonder if the text does not have a dual focus—on Macdonald as much as on Riel. It is as if the book is designed to lead us to consider if Riel is merely one of the sacrifices that is required during the process of Canadian nation-building—and, perhaps, the individual acquisition of property rights. Time and again, Brown intimates that the clash between Riel and Macdonald is not a duel of equals. Distracted with obtuse theological disputations on whether the Métis are God's "new chosen people!" or whether he can "breathe the Holy Spirit" on his followers (144, 145), Brown's Riel never seems to stand a chance of being more than a victim of this highly uneven process. He is just another casualty of history.

The suspicion that *Louis Riel* is divided about its purported subject is reinforced by an unusual piece of paratextual information that the author appends to his text proper. Brown's narrative is billed as a work of historical fiction, but it bears over twenty pages of endnotes, as well as a bibliography and an index. Brown has written that he uses footnotes to show readers where he "deviated from historical truth, or maybe invented a thing or two, or combined characters" (Brown and Carter). He describes the device as the graphic writer's equivalent of a film "director's commentary" on a DVD, which is "the best way" to inform his readers of his authorial choices (Brown and Carter) and, one infers, his ideological predilections. In one of the notes to *Louis Riel*, Brown divulges that he portrays Macdonald as being responsible for the North-West War, not because he believes the theory, but because "it makes Macdonald seem more villainous—villains are fun in a story, and I'm trying to tell this tale in an engaging manner" (259). But then he makes an even more stunning disclosure about his views of the political visions of Riel and Macdonald: "Incidentally, even though I think that Macdonald was capable of abusing his power, I don't think that he actually was a villain. I disagree with much of what he did and stood for, but I recognize that he tried to do what *he* thought was best for the country. And, quite frankly, I'd rather have lived in a state run by John A. Macdonald than one run by Louis Riel" (259). This is an astonishing confession for the author of a life of Riel to make at the end of his book, a declaration that is bound to affect one's reading of the text. One would imagine that a writer who produces an avowedly partisan narrative about how Riel is victimized by the machinations of the unscrupulous Macdonald would favour the Métis leader over the Canadian prime minister. But this is not the case. Therefore, the reason "the Riel of *Louis Riel* might best be understood not as a comic book or nationalistic (super)hero but, rather, as anti-mythological and anti-heroic" (Lesk 80) is not that the author rejects unitary notions of history but that he is extremely ambivalent about his ostensible subject. Brown is explicit that he prefers the world symbolized by Macdonald to the one embodied by Riel. The Métis lost, he writes, and it is regrettable that Canadian politicians were so devious, even racist, but it is all for the better, since Canada represents a higher form of government, or perhaps even a higher form of civilization. Canada's victory over Riel and the Métis in 1885 thus becomes almost providential, an articulation of Canadian nationalism that not only explains the political contradictions in Brown's graphic narrative but also forces readers to reconsider who is the true protagonist of *Louis Riel: A Comic-Strip Biography*—Riel or Macdonald.

Confronting the Hero   8
Contemporary Métis Engagements with Riel

> *I want to scream. listen you idiots,*
> *Riel is dead! and I am alive!*
> —RITA BOUVIER, *papîyâhtak*

THE FLUIDITY OF THE IMAGE of Louis Riel in Canadian discourse is hardly a secret, but what is not so well known is that there is also no consensus about him among the Métis, who appear to be simultaneously mesmerized by their historical leader and threatened by him. The resistance to Riel by contemporary Métis is twofold. First, there is resentment that he has come to eclipse the collectivity he represented. As Emma LaRocque protests, "Riel overshadows his own people" (LaRocque and Enright 45). Or as the poet Rita Bouvier seethes with rage at a conference in which "strangers" debate whether Riel is a hero or insane, while ignoring living Indigenous voices: "I want to scream. listen you idiots, / Riel is dead! and I am alive!" (28; see also Mattes, "Rielisms" 21; Farrell Racette 50–51). Second, there is a feeling that Riel is not a typical Métis, being too European not only biologically but also culturally and spiritually. Riel's omnipresence in the discourse about settler-Indigenous relations in Canada has been attributed to Western civilization's infatuation with the Great Man concept of history (Miller 40–41). But some Métis, such as LaRocque, hold Riel partly responsible for this state of affairs, claiming that he was "different from the people" (LaRocque and Enright 45). If Riel "cared so much" for the

Métis, she asks, "why has he loomed so much larger than them?" (Walz, Payment, and LaRocque), blaming him for his posthumous image. The discomfort with Riel's Europeanness has led a number of today's Métis to find him wanting in comparison to his Saskatchewan military commander, Gabriel Dumont, who is deemed more authentically Métis. As an oral figure, Dumont has the enormous advantage of not having produced an extensive body of writing, and thus of possibly having some of his texts qualify if not contradict others. Still, what the recent Métis responses to Riel also reveal is that the New Nation has undergone fundamental changes since the late 1800s, both demographically and linguistically. In many ways, the Métis nation with which the historical Riel identified and today's Métis nation are not the same entity (Ens and Sawchuk 112). But this does not mean that the fates of Riel and of contemporary Métis do not remain intertwined, which is why the Métis appear unable to imagine themselves without him.

The first major attempt by Métis to control Riel's image—and Métis history—came to fruition in the mid-1930s. In 1909, an "eminent" group of Winnipeg-based Métis decided to organize a Historical Committee (Comité historique) "to set down a clear record" of the Red River Resistance and the North-West War (Historical Committee, "Foreword" xii). The members of the Committee all belonged to the Union métisse Saint-Joseph de Manitoba, which that year metamorphosed into the Union nationale métisse Saint-Joseph du Manitoba (Bocquel 125). The main objective of the Historical Committee, like that of the Union nationale métisse, was the rehabilitation of Riel and, through him, the Métis people. As the Committee declared, it was formed to promote Métis "history and use every occasion to answer attacks on the Métis—in short, to insist on a respect for the truth" ("Foreword" xiii). Meeting at the historical Riel home in St. Vital, then owned by Riel's brother Joseph, himself a member of the group, the Committee began its tasks by examining the copious documents owned by the Riel family and acquiring new ones. But it soon discovered that some individuals and institutions felt threatened by the idea that "the Métis had decided to write their history and defend themselves." Those unidentified groups "hastened to cast suspicion on this movement and even to use intimidation" (Historical Committee, "Foreword" xii), since they feared that the "scandalous" manuscript "would unveil secrets damaging to the reputation of certain noted persons now dead" (Trémaudan, *Hold* x). Sensing that public opinion at the time was not favourable to the project, the Committee decided to focus on reading and collecting documents on Riel and the Métis and to postpone the publication of its findings to a later date.

Another reason the Historical Committee did not pursue the publication of its chronicle more doggedly was that none of its members was an established writer. That problem was solved in 1926 when Auguste-Henri de Trémaudan assented "to write the [Committee's] history" (Historical Committee, "Foreword" xiii; see also Bocquel 256). Born in Québec in 1874 to French immigrants, Trémaudan grew up in France and then relocated with his family to Saskatchewan as a young adult (Verrette). Working variously as a school teacher, journalist, and lawyer, in both Saskatchewan and Manitoba, Trémaudan published widely on sundry facets of the French-speaking world. Around the beginning of the First World War, upon transferring to St. Boniface, Trémaudan became immersed in Riel and the Métis. This enthusiasm did not dissipate even after 1924, when he moved to Los Angeles for health reasons, a development that led him to sell his sizable library on the Métis and Prairiana to the Union nationale métisse (Bocquel 228; Trémaudan, *Hold* ix), of which he had become an "honorary" member (Trémaudan, "Louis Riel" 132). So when Trémaudan accepted to write the Métis history for the Historical Committee, part of the contract stipulated that the Committee would ship his old books to him in California. The Committee and Trémaudan agreed on the format of the manuscript, which would be "a simple story, as complete as possible, about the deeds of French-Canadian Métis in the West" (Historical Committee, "Foreword" xiv). Trémaudan worked on the book between January 1927 and May 1928, at which point he sent a draft to the Committee. Anticipating Joseph Kinsey Howard's *Strange Empire*, the manuscript was "carefully documented" but did not include references as the author did not wish to "burden the text with footnotes" (Trémaudan, Hold xi). This was an unexpected turn, since the articles and research notes that Trémaudan published on Riel in the *Canadian Historical Review* during this period are characterized by their heavy reliance on footnotes, which sometimes are longer than the main text (Trémaudan, "Louis Riel" 137-40; 222-34). Anyhow, Trémaudan died in 1929 and would not see the book through the press. *Histoire de la nation métisse dans l'Ouest canadien* would not be published until early in 1936—although it bears the copyright of 1935 (*Histoire*)—because of the editorial/authorial work performed by the Historical Committee.

When the Historical Committee commissioned Trémaudan to write its chronicle, the issue that concerned it the most was the portrayal of Riel during the North-West troubles. The events of 1885 were not only "the obscure point" in Métis history, but the majority of the documents about the conflict purportedly "had been written by enemies of the Métis with a single political aim—to vindicate the government of the day" (Historical Committee, "Foreword" xiii). According to the Committee, it was this "special chapter…about the most controversial part of the 1885 events" that Trémaudan had not managed to write before his untimely death (xv; see also "Appendix" 175). Yet, while stressing it approved of Trémaudan's "*history in its entirety*," the Committee notes that it felt there were "certain very important points which require[d] some comment" ("Foreword" xv). This meant that the members of the Committee had to provide the conclusion to the book, which would take the form of a lengthy—and combative—appendix. The Committee's intervention was precipitated not just by the need to "complete" Trémaudan's work but also by its overarching desire "to correct the generally accepted version" of the relations between Riel and Canada (Historical Committee, "Appendix" 175). Regardless of whose name appeared on the cover as the author of the monograph, the Committee would have the last word.

The Historical Committee's contribution to the *Histoire de la nation métisse* was even more extensive than it acknowledged.

In their study of the writing of the Métis chronicle, the historian Gerhard Ens and the anthropologist Joe Sawchuk state that, contrary to what the Committee asserts, Trémaudan finished "an entire revised draft of his manuscript prior to his death" (120). Their claim is supported by both the Oblate priest-scholar Adrien-Gabriel Morice and the journalist Bernard Bocquel, the author of an encyclopedic history of the Union nationale métisse. A linguist, ethnographer, and historian who wrote widely about Western Canada, as well as a friend of Trémaudan, the French-born Morice wrote that Trémaudan had told him years before he died that his Métis book had long been "fini" and the reason it had not been published was that he and his patrons could not agree on its contents, charging that they wanted to make him say things he knew "n'être pas vraies" (qtd. in Morice, *Race métisse* 8, see also 43–44). Bocquel relates that, following Trémaudan's death, his widow returned his old books on the Métis and Prairiana to the Historical Committee. But, for "raisons sentimentales," Madeleine de Trémaudan insisted on keeping her husband's final version of the chronicle. Hence, the Committee had one of its Los Angeles operatives use subterfuge to obtain the "original" from Trémaudan's widow and then informed her that, contractually, the text was the "propriété" of the Union nationale métisse (Bocquel 278; see also Ens and Sawchuk 553). It seems the issue facing the Committee was not that its author did not produce an account of Riel's role in 1885 but that the Committee did not accept its scribe's interpretation. As the Committee had underlined to Trémaudan, it was imperative that the book "not touch the questions of 'religion' and of 'madness'" ["ne pas toucher aux questions de 'religion' et de 'folie'"] (qtd. in Bocquel 268). The Committee also demanded such substantial revisions that Trémaudan threatened to abandon the project. In his last letter to his Manitoba confrères, which he dictated to his daughter in English since she was more comfortable in that language than in French, the gravely-ill Trémaudan even suggested that "*the book be published by the historical committee*," with a short description of his contribution (qtd. in Bocquel 278). This was an option that the

Committee could not entertain, not only because everyone knew that Trémaudan was "notre historien" but also because the group felt that the chronicle would be more effective if it were perceived to be authored by someone from *"outside of our ranks"* (qtd. in Bocquel 267, 366). In other words, the Committee was determined to fashion the monograph but without being given credit for it.

With Trémaudan no longer around to hold its reins, the Historical Committee proceeded to perform "radical surgery" on his manuscript (Ens and Sawchuk 120). It cut around "50,000 words" out of his last draft, reducing an approximately 145,000-word text to a 95,000-word one (123, 124). Granted, not all the excisions were instigated by the Committee. Trémaudan had hoped that the chronicle would be published in both French and English, with the French version produced by a Parisian press (Bocquel 252, 256, 266). But in the end, the book appeared under the imprint of Montréal's Éditions Albert Lévesque, which, in order to keep the retail price as low as possible, demanded further reductions (331–32, 350). Still, whatever the breadth of the cuts, it would not affect the length of the Committee's own supplements.

In the appendix, the Committee lists in point form ten charges that have been levelled against Riel and the Métis and which it intends to "refute." These vary from the allegations that the Métis campaign in 1885 was "senseless"; that "Riel and the Métis took over the church in Batoche and desecrated it"; that he held priests and nuns "prisoners" and "founded a new cult"; and that "Riel was insane" (Historical Committee, "Appendix" 175). Methodically, the Committee repudiates all the complaints not just as unfounded but preposterous. Rather than being rebels, Riel and his followers valiantly attempted "to defend the land of their birth: the Canadian West," which before long would "salute them as precursors and liberators" (177). Contrary to the accusations that the priests were incarcerated by the Métis, "the Fathers remained free in their rectory" (183). Most incendiary, instead of being a megalomaniac possessed by visions of grandeur, Riel was betrayed at Batoche by the priests, who became "informers to General [Frederick] Middleton, Commander of the Federal troops" (194). Indeed, thanks to the poise with which he withstood the endless tests he faced in 1885, "Riel became a saint and a martyr" (197), and it would be a matter of time before all fair-minded people recognized his unrivalled achievement.

For the Committee, which in 1932 renamed itself the Société historique métisse, Riel is less wrong than wronged. He is guilty of nothing more than uttering some "reckless words," and even that is perfectly understandable considering that he lived "under the sway of intense moral torture" (Historical Committee, "Appendix" 194). The Committee supports its conclusion that Riel neither committed heresy nor founded a new faith by the fact that, in their exhaustive investigations, its members had "never yet found a single adherent of Riel's so-called religion" (190). It further boasts that, despite "having cried to high Heaven that Riel apostatized, our adversaries now admit that they have no written proof" (193). The problem with this sweeping claim, for which the Committee provides no documentation, is that Riel himself supplies ample evidence that he broke with the Catholic Church. At his Regina trial, Riel was accused by former associates of having declared that "Rome had tumbled. *Rome est tombée*" (*Queen* 151). He was more circumspect during his own testimony, but he still affirmed that he believed he was the Prophet of the New World and "wish[ed] to leave Rome aside, inasmuch as it is the cause of division between Catholics and Protestants" (319, see also 322). He was even more explicit in his writings. In a March 1885 letter to his English-speaking "Dear Brothers in Jesus christ," asking them to join forces with the Métis, Riel writes that "The french Half-breed members of the Provisional Government of the Saskatchewan have separated from Rome" (*Collected Writings* 3: 70). Likewise, in a letter to the commander of the Regina jail, Richard Burton Deane, he states, "I respect the bishop of Rome and I pray for him: but I have nothing to do with him anymore," adding that he prays to God that the "catholic countries, nations and tribes of the New World may, in time, become separated from the Bishop of Rome" (3: 95, 96, see also 124). If that were not conclusive enough, Riel is unequivocal about his feelings toward the Vatican in a long 24 July 1885 letter to Archbishop Alexandre-Antonin Taché. While awaiting the official beginning of his trial, Riel informs his former mentor that he has "séparé de Rome" and has "prié" the Métis to do the same, if they wish to do so (3: 146). He also apprises Taché that, following the death of Montréal's Archbishop Ignace Bourget, Taché is next in line as the Pope of the New World, "*Pontifex Major totius Novi Mundi*" (3: 147). Typically, Riel makes those statements at the same time that he implores Taché to send priests to assist him in such a desperate period in his life.

The work of the Historical Committee has been interpreted as being part of an attempt by Winnipeg Métis to bridge the chasm that had opened between themselves and the Catholic hierarchy (Ens and Sawchuk 115). But the Committee's strategy was not nearly as deft as it anticipated. First of all, the Catholic clergy saw nothing conciliatory about the monograph. This is especially true of Morice, who became so incensed by the accusations made in *Histoire de la nation métisse* that he promptly wrote a book to counter them, *La race métisse: étude critique en marge d'un livre récent* (1938). Morice is quite forgiving toward his friend Trémaudan. He excuses lapses like the omission of Pierre Falcon and what he judges the fallacious portrait of the Métis as a nation—as opposed to a race—to the text being the labour of "un homme malade," who would have done a more professional job had he been healthy (Morice, *Race métisse* 7). His real target is the appendix, admitting that he probably would not have written his critique of the Trémaudan chronicle if the Committee had not "infliger" its supplement on it (6, see also 8), and to which he devotes more than half of his text. Morice, who envisaged himself as a champion of the Métis, took the Committee's intervention as a personal insult. He refers to the members of the Committee derisively as "soi-disant historiens" (44) and St. Vital "théologiens" (69) and describes their work, not merely as faulty, but as the most brazen ["éhonté"] attempt of which he is aware against "les droits de la vérité" (43). The appendix, he underscores, is not a work of scholarship but a fanciful cover-up, a "roman" (52).

Morice was a well-known "polemicist" (Huel, "Clergyman" 59), so one could dismiss his clash with the Historical Committee over its interpretation of Riel's role in 1885 as idiosyncratic, even if Joseph Riel had singled out his earlier historical work for its "impartialité" (qtd. in Bocquel 202) and he has been seen as "the leading Métis apologist" (J. Howard, *Strange Empire* 185). Yet it is hard to deny that many of Morice's points are legitimate. The fact is that the Committee is so determined to prove that Riel is both mentally stable and a good Catholic that it has to disregard much of what he writes and stands for. The Committee is also oblivious to the paradox that it is his supporters who tend to perceive Riel as mentally ill and that the people who are most intent on proving he is sane are his enemies—who do so in order to justify having him hanged. Since the members of the Committee are positive that Riel is rational as well as an orthodox Catholic, they cannot grasp why the priests might oppose him, or conversely why they agree to give him solace during his imprisonment. Their conflicting portrayal of Father Alexis André is a case in point. One moment, they castigate the veteran Oblate missionary, who had ministered to the Métis across the continent for two and a half decades, for testifying at Riel's trial and for not cutting relations with Métis who did not support Riel (188, 183). Yet the next moment, they shower extravagant praise on him for ultimately respecting Riel's faith and for condemning Ottawa's treatment of him (190, 197). What the Committee cannot explain is why Riel would beg Taché to have "Le Bon Père André" (Riel, *Collected Writings* 4: 429) give him spiritual sustenance as he awaits his execution, or why André would stand by him.

The Historical Committee may have had some misgivings about its depiction of the clergy. It is telling that while the Committee's focus in the appendix is on the North-West War, this is not what happens in the foreword, where the two central concerns involve events from 1870. The first is the execution of Thomas Scott, which the Committee argues "brought peace and accord back to the country" ("Foreword" xv). The Committee contends that if anyone was responsible for the Red River conflict, it was the main representative of the Hudson's Bay Company in Canada, Donald A. Smith, who "went about distributing money unstintingly to make the English Métis rise against the French Métis" but was "foiled in his plans by Riel's shrewdness and the disgust of those on whom Smith had counted" (xv). The second issue highlighted in the foreword was no less sensitive for the Métis, Riel's provocative reception of Bishop Taché upon his return to Red River from Rome. The members of the Committee assert that "Riel was never forgiven for placing guards at the Archbishop's [sic] residence" and, after the episode, "the attitude of the clergy completely changed towards Riel and his men" who "became objects of suspicion" (xv). They defend Riel by writing that if Taché had prevailed and gained "the upper hand," it is possible that "Riel would have stood alone" (xv). Yet they never address what it says about Riel that the moment he gains power, he feels compelled to show the whole of Red River that he does not trust the man to whom he owes his singular education and on whom he would be dependent for much of his life.

Regardless of its scholarly limitations, the Historical Committee's contribution to the *Histoire de la nation métisse dans l'Ouest canadien* remains significant for several reasons. Not the least of these is that the chronicle's publication occurred during the Forgotten Years, the period between 1885 and the 1960s when the Métis were almost reduced to voicelessness and invisibility. No less crucial, the book testifies to the major cultural and linguistic transformations that the Métis were undergoing. Throughout the foreword and the appendix, the Committee is clear that its chronicle is not a celebration of the Métis as such but of "the French-Canadian Métis Nation" (Historical Committee, "Foreword" xiii). As the authors state, the impetus for the Trémaudan history was the recognition that early twentieth-century "Métis owed to themselves, and to those who have gone before, a chronicle that will inspire in the new generation a pride in their ancestry and their past" (xvi). Besides being Indigenous, this past was primarily Catholic and French. For what differentiates the Métis from their neighbours is that, although numerically small, they have heroically "fulfilled [their] mission and carried on the best of French tradition in the West." The Committee closes the foreword with the statement that the French "race" should be "proud of this branch which in Western Canada was faithful to its civilizing mission" (xvii), words that accent the centrality of France to Riel and his people and which are bound to be interpreted very differently today than they were at the time.

The extent to which the Métis collective identity would change in the next few decades is vividly illustrated by the title of the text that has come to exemplify the revival of Métis culture, Maria Campbell's 1973 memoir *Halfbreed*. Born in 1940 in north-central Saskatchewan, approximately 200 km north of Batoche, Campbell is very much part of the Red River Métis diaspora, her paternal great-grandmother, Cheechum, being "a niece of Gabriel Dumont" (M. Campbell, *Halfbreed* 9, see also 10). Yet, starting with her first (and best-known) book, she identifies herself and her ancestors, not as Métis—much less French Canadian Métis—but Halfbreeds, a name historically associated with people of mixed First Nations and European ancestry who are English-speaking and Protestant, and which has become "odious" to some Métis intellectuals (Teillet, *North-West* 405). Campbell's choice of group nomenclature is not accidental. It mirrors a decisive cultural and linguistic change in Métis identity, one that is seldom acknowledged and which is not always appreciated by descendants of the historical Halfbreeds (Dahl 123–24, 127).

Campbell is profoundly ambivalent about Riel, who plays a minuscule role in *Halfbreed*. Written when she was still in her twenties (M. Campbell, "Strategies" 7), her memoir traces her journey from a childhood of poverty in rural Saskatchewan; early marriage to a white man she does not love and escape to the West Coast; descent into drugs and prostitution; and rebirth as an Indigenous social activist. Campbell's book has been applauded for bringing the "contemporary Métis experience to a national consciousness" in its attempt to "awaken Canadian society to the existence and harsh lived reality of many Métis, but also to awaken Métis people" (D. Garneau, "Métissage" 379). *Halfbreed*'s greatest achievement, however, is that it solidified a shift in Métis discourse from the male to the female (Tétreault, "Red River Poetics" 244), embodied in the author's Cheechum, and the author herself, which in her case also denotes a switch from privileging European to Indigenous ancestry. In the introduction, Campbell informs her readers that she wrote the manuscript "for all of you, to tell you what it is like to be a Halfbreed woman in our country" (*Halfbreed* 2). She then offers a brief overview of Métis political history, including the 1884 decision by Dumont and other Saskatchewan Valley leaders to travel to Montana Territory to invite Riel to come north to advise them. Campbell openly favours Dumont over Riel, as the fabled buffalo hunter was "ready to take up arms," having "no faith in the federal government" (4, 5). Yet even Dumont is problematic for her, since it was the Métis men who let their people down in 1885, "fail[ing] during the Rebellion to make a dream come true" (8). But this was not the case of Métis women, at least the traditional ones. "Cheechum never accepted defeat at Batoche," writes Campbell, "and she would always say, 'Because they killed Riel they think they have killed us too, but some day, my girl, it will be different'" (11). Or as Campbell expands near the end of her text, "My Cheechum never surrendered at Batoche: she only accepted what she considered a dishonourable truce" (183–84). More specifically, Cheechum is waiting for "a new generation" of politically committed Métis (184), such as her great-granddaughter, to save the Métis.

Given the prominence of men in the Métis tradition—as reflected in names like Cuthbert Grant, Pierre Falcon, Louis Riel, Ambroise Lépine, and Gabriel Dumont—Campbell's focus on female figures would be noteworthy by itself. But her turn is not just about gender; it is also about cultural identity, especially her distancing herself from her people's European heritage, including Christianity. Campbell says that "[a]ll our people were Roman Catholic" and that she and her siblings were "all baptized and [she] had to go to catechism" (*Halfbreed* 28, 29). The exception is her Cheechum, who not only believed with "heart and soul in the little people" of Indigenous folklore but also possessed "the gift of second sight" (18, 19). In a community where nobody ever criticized the Catholic Church, Cheechum "hated [priests] with a vengeance" (32) and did not think much of the Christian God either. Campbell says that she has held "the same attitude as Cheechum about Christians" since she turned ten (28) and has long been perplexed that her pious Catholic mother could not see through the hypocrisy of the clergy when even a child could (32). Her Cheechum, she emphasizes, is the only model she wishes to emulate.

The vision of the Métis embraced by Campbell's Cheechum, and Campbell herself, is one devoid of European influences, save for the irrefutable physiognomic ones. This becomes evident when Campbell is in her early teens and her father takes the family to a trappers' convention that he is attending. Most of the people at the assembly are First Nations who engage in traditional cultural practices. Campbell writes that after they watched a group playing a gambling game that included Indigenous drums and singing, her Cheechum told her that "we used to live in much the same way before the white man came" (*Halfbreed* 42). Considering that the Métis are a post-contact people, one wonders what sort of Métis society she imagines existed prior to the arrival of the Europeans in North America. But then Cheechum is the kind of Métis who pronounces that "nothing good ever comes from a mixed marriage" (121). Elsewhere, after mentioning that her ["treaty Indian" (*Halfbreed* 15)] maternal grandmother was "a happy, laughing person, a devout Catholic" (M. Campbell and Hillis 48), Campbell states that she rejects both cultural and religious syncretism. "You either follow The Old Way or you become a good Catholic," she tells an interviewer, "but don't play with the two of them. You can't take the Pipe Ceremony and the Catholic Mass" (M. Campbell and Hillis 58). Campbell has also confided that she has "always felt a kind of historical guilt" because the Métis were "the link between Indians and whites...We were children of two peoples who wanted something of each other. And when they started to hate each other, they focused their hate on us, their children, until we were just like a band of gypsies, landless" (Griffiths and M. Campbell 19-20). In *Halfbreed*, she notes that she has "green" eyes and that her elders attribute her forthrightness to "the white in her" (95, 26). Yet, for Campbell, the Métis cannot incorporate a mix of their two ancestral groups; they must embrace only one of them, and there is little doubt which choice she deems ethically correct.

Campbell titles one of her early books *Riel's People*, and there she calls today's Métis "the descendants of Riel's people" (46).

But her conception of the Métis differs dramatically from Riel's, or from that of the Union nationale métisse for that matter, even if she remarks that her grade-school teacher derided her activist father as Saskatchewan's "new Riel" (*Halfbreed* 74). Writing in the late 1870s, Riel asserts that the name Métis "signifie mélange." Although Métis initially served to designate "la race issue du sang mêlé des européens et des Sauvages," it is equally appropriate to designate a race of humans resulting from the "mélange de tous les sangs" (*Collected Writings* 2: 120). Riel also prizes dearly his French ancestry, stressing that it is in passing through the French Canadian mould that every new hybrid race in the North-West will preserve the memory of its "origine, en s'appellant métisse" (2: 120; see also Braz, "End of Hybridity" 67–68). For Riel, this heritage includes both Catholicism and the French language, which he considers a powerful means of "union morale" (*Collected Writings* 1: 390). Campbell, who is no less messianic than Riel, is as antagonistic toward the French language as she is toward Catholicism. She describes the usage of French by Saskatchewan Métis as a form of ethnocultural passing, achieved by "get[ting] rid of all of the Mitchif" (M. Campbell and Lutz 51)—the traditional Métis language, most commonly spelled Michif. Thus, when she revises her writing, "if there is too much French, I take it out and reword it into broken English" (51; see also Braz, "Western" 120), erasing the traces of common cultural practices of which she does not approve.

Campbell's equivocation about Riel is most apparent in *Stories of the Road Allowance People*, a 1995 collection of "old men's stories" (M. Campbell, *Stories* 2) that Campbell collected and then translated into English in free verse form. The tales deal with Métis history, including "da big fight at Batoche," in which Dumont "organize all da Halfbreeds an dey get Louis Riel" to come north (53). Particularly compelling is the sketch "Joseph's Justice," which is about a Métis man who "don take part in dat war" against "dah Anglais" (105). The storyteller observes that there were many other Métis like Joseph and that their choice did not mean they feared either the English or the government:

Dey jus wasen interest in fighting for land
or edjication
cause dey don believe dat Anglais government
hees gonna give dem anything.
So
Dey jus mine dere own business. (105)

The storyteller's approval of Joseph's decision not to get involved in the conflict is notable in that it points to the political schisms among the Métis. The best-known non-supporter of Riel and Dumont in 1885 was the veteran buffalo hunter and trader Norbert Welsh, who refused to take part in the military campaign against the federal government because he thought "Dumont was no kind of a leader" and "Riel...had more education than brains" (Weekes 74, 155). But, unlike Welsh, the storyteller admires the "spirit man" Riel, who was different from Dumont and everyone else and "give hisself to dah peoples" (M. Campbell, *Stories* 108). The teller of "Joseph's Justice" adds that, contrary to the claims made in Canadian history books, not only "dere was less den a hundred [Halfbreeds] at Batoche," but "mos of dem / dey was ole mans" (123), raising the question of what all the patriotic young Métis men were doing and why Riel and Dumont failed to persuade them to join in the defence of the homeland.

The dilemma at the core of Campbell's construction of the Métis in *Halfbreed* is one that permeates contemporary Métis discourse: writers evoke Riel as an ancestor but then often proceed to divorce themselves from pivotal aspects of the collectivity to which he devoted most of his adult life. Historians generally posit that two key factors in the ethnogenesis of the Métis as a people were Catholicism and Frenchness. Emerging in a region of North America that was supposed to be part of the Anglo-Protestant world, the Métis regarded themselves and were regarded by others as distinct from their neighbours. This sense of difference demonstrates why they developed a national consciousness when their Halfbreed cousins did not (Foster 80–81; Pannekoek, *Snug* 1–5), or later denied that their forebears had Indigenous ancestry (Friesen, *River Road* 11). It was also the Franco-Métis who instigated both the Red River Resistance and the North-West War, in order to protect themselves from the predominantly Anglo-Protestant Canadian forces that were assailing them, and who were most affected by the two conflicts. For instance, the Halfbreed civil servant and scholar Gregg Dahl writes that after 1870 "life for some Half-breeds seems to have continued pretty much as it had prior to the political actions taken by Louis Riel and his supporters" (98). Similarly, the first shots during the North-West War were fired by the Halfbreed interpreter "Gentleman Joe" McKay, not on the side of the Métis but of the Mounted Police (Stonechild and Waiser 86). As well, two sons of Manitoba Premier John Norquay fought with the Canadian forces in 1885, with the blessing of their father, who hoped the "insane movement" would come to a speedy end and that "the Rebels" would be routed (qtd. in Friesen, "Political Thought" 64; see also Teillet, "Louis Riel" 58). Yet many of the self-identified progeny of the Franco-Métis, like Campbell, are extremely uncomfortable with the very traits that set their people apart and gave them a sense of oneness, even if they continue to construe their collective foes as the English (M. Campbell, *Stories* 119–25). This unease manifests itself in their conflicted attitude toward Riel, whom they tend to place at the centre of their national tradition but either portray in ways that the historical Riel would not recognize or actually disown him.

Riel plays a more prominent role in what is considered the first important Métis novel, Beatrice Mosionier's *In Search of April Raintree* (1983), even if it too does not escape the prevailing ambiguity about the Métis leader. Published a decade after *Halfbreed*, and set mostly in and around Winnipeg between the mid-1950s and the early 1970s, Mosionier's book explores the impact of the disintegration of Métis society on one family, particularly the sisters April and Cheryl Raintree. April and Cheryl's parents, Henry and Alice Raintree, led a tolerable existence in the early part of their married life in the small northern Manitoba town of Norway House. But all that changes after Henry contracts tuberculosis and the family moves some 800 km south to Winnipeg. There, the world of the Raintrees soon begins to revolve around "welfare cheque days" and what they euphemistically term "medicine days" (Mosionier, *In Search* 10), an eventuality that results in the hospitalization of their new-born baby Anna and their surrendering of the pre-school April and Cheryl to Children's Aid. April and Cheryl are sent to separate foster homes, but they never lose track of each other. Yet the novel shows that the challenges they face growing up are compounded by their own attitudes toward their ethnoracial heritage, not the least the fact that the larger community always sees them generically as "Natives."

Mosionier, formerly known as Culleton, has stated that while *In Search of April Raintree* is a work of fiction, it was structured "parallel to [her] life" ("April" 140), which is why it has been characterized as a "fictional autobiography" (Suzack 10, 51). The novel is dedicated to the memory of her two older sisters, Vivian and Kathy, both of whom struggled with alcohol addiction before committing suicide (Mosionier, "April" 139–40). Mosionier also discloses that, in the process of writing the book, she came "to understand and acknowledge that [she] had a deep shame of being part Native" (140). Whatever may be the relation between the text and the author, one cannot help but sense that biocultural hybridity is an obstacle for the two main characters.

Despite its title, *In Search of April Raintree* is a bildungsroman about the intellectual formation of both April and Cheryl. This is a pedagogical journey that never escapes the impact of race, as manifested in skin colour. April, who is the narrator and is eighteen months older than her sister, has their mother's Irish-Anishinaabe "pale skin" (Mosionier, *In Search* 10); Cheryl has black hair and dark-brown eyes like their father, who is "a little bit of this, a little of that and a whole lot of Indian" (9). In a world in which skin pigmentation appears to be destiny, perhaps their cultural affinities are preordained. Cheryl identifies mainly with her First Nations ancestors, wishing that she and her sister were not "part Indian and part white" but "whole Indians" (45). April, in contrast, is determined to pass as white. This aspiration is a constant source of anxiety for her. April desires nothing more than to live with Cheryl. At the same time, she fears that the presence of her "Métis sister" (49) would reveal to others that she possesses Indigenous ancestry, a conflict that she is never able to overcome.

Ironically, it is the younger Cheryl who attempts to educate the older April about their culture. The first foster family to which Cheryl is sent is the middle-class MacAdamses, who have a large library, including a variety of books on the First Nations before European contact. Mrs. MacAdams, who is Métis, feels that "we should be proud of our heritage" (Mosionier, *In Search* 45). Thanks to her influence, Cheryl decides to give April a book about Riel for her birthday. But the gift does not have the desired effect. "I knew all about Riel," an irked April mutters to herself. "He was a rebel who had been hanged for treason. Worse, he had been a crazy half-breed. Also, I had read about the Indians and the various methods of torture they had put the missionaries through. No wonder they were known as savages. So, anything to do with Indians, I despised. And here I was supposed to be part-Indian" (44–45). April is just relieved that none of her classmates knows about her ethnonational background, and does not even open the book.

Still, over the years, Cheryl keeps sending April copies of the school papers she writes about Riel and the Métis. A scholastic high-achiever, Cheryl is committed to providing "the Métis side of things" (Mosionier, *In Search* 84–85), examining every major event from the buffalo hunts to the political uprisings. April, however, remains untouched by her sister's cultural activism. As she discloses after reading Cheryl's paper on Riel and the Red River conflict, "Knowing the other side, the Métis side, didn't make me feel any better. It just reinforced my belief that if I could assimilate myself into white society, I wouldn't have to live like this for the rest of my life" (85). Given her obsession with social status, no one is likely to be surprised when April marries an upper-crust white lawyer from Toronto and moves with him to his hometown, a development that Cheryl interprets as a spurning of herself. Equally predictable is that the marriage does not last, being sabotaged by a mother-in-law who broadcasts that "the trouble with mixed races" is that one never knows how their offspring are "going to turn out" (126), a view shared by April herself (189). Before long, she is back in Winnipeg.

Oblivious to her sister's feelings of rejection, April suggests that the only way Cheryl could attain peace is if she somehow forgets about their parents, "forget[s] that she was Métis" (Mosionier, *In Search* 71). Although this does not happen, something dies in Cheryl. Upon quitting her university studies, she becomes a social worker at Winnipeg's Indigenous Friendship Centre, but she gradually descends into alcoholism and a life in the street. When Cheryl at last succeeds in locating Henry Raintree, she is both *"horrified and repulsed"* by the broken man she encounters, the *"gutter-creature"* the knowledge of whose existence she needs to shelter April (217, 218). Cheryl has spent her life dreaming of finding her parents and building a new life together by returning to the old First Nations ways, and in a moment watches the dream evaporate. Her shock magnifies when her father tells her the reason Alice stopped visiting her and April during their scheduled meetings at the Children's Aid office was that *"your Mama did not want you girls to see the way she was"* and later jumped into the Red River from the Louise Bridge (220). Cheryl confides in one of her journals that she belongs with the city's *"other gutter-creatures. I'm my father's daughter"* (225). Soon after, in an attempt to join her mother, she leaps to her death from the same bridge from which Alice Raintree killed herself.

Like Cheryl, April undergoes a life-changing transformation, but hers occurs earlier. After the failure of her marriage, April persuades Cheryl to take her to her first powwow, a festivity being held at a First Nations reserve south of Winnipeg. While April watches the dancing competitions with interest, she does not join in during the breaks. But in the evening, as everyone sits around a bonfire and listens to the singers, April suddenly "felt alive...For the first time in my life, I felt as if all of that was part of me, as if I was part of it" (Mosionier, *In Search* 166). Following her sister's death, April discovers that Cheryl has a baby son named Henry Liberty (Lee) Raintree and that Cheryl wanted her to raise him. As April gazes at the infant, she is saddened that "it had taken Cheryl's death to bring me to accept my identity," to dedicate herself to "MY PEOPLE, OUR PEOPLE" (228). She then closes the novel with the declaration that "for Henry Lee and me, there would be a tomorrow. And it would be better. I would strive for it. For my sister and her son. For my parents. For my people" (228). Without questioning her sincerity, it is far from clear who her people are.

Less than halfway through Mosionier's novel, Cheryl becomes so incensed at the way Indigenous peoples are portrayed in an institutional history of Canada that she writes April, the textbook "makes me wish those whitemen had never come here. But then we would not have been born" (Mosionier, *In Search* 84). This, in essence, is the Métis conundrum: no matter how they may feel about their two sets of ancestors, they know they could not exist without either of them. It is also an admission that is striking because it is so rarely made in contemporary Métis literature, reflecting the acute awareness by Métis that First Nations people often perceive their European ancestry as a manifestation of their Indigenous inauthenticity. Thus the Cree scholar Janice Acoose praises Maria Campbell for "firmly rooting" her memoir in "her Halfbreed-Indigenous ideology" (93). But when Campbell emphasizes her Métis particularism, Acoose rebukes her for her "subtle conformity to the white-eurocanadian-patriarchy," which leads Campbell "to fragment Indigenous peoples" (99). Similarly, the Anishinaabe scholar Cheryl Suzack describes a real-life Manitoba case of child custody "involving a First Nations mother and Metis adoptive parents" and the parallel one in Mosionier's novel as instances of "'out-adoption'" (52), suggesting that the Métis are not quite Indigenous like the First Nations. Even April, who for most of her life does not want to have children, thinking "they might turn out looking a little native" (Mosionier, *In Search* 189), favours the pre-Métis Indigenous past over her people's less homogeneous condition. When the white lawyer with whom she is romantically involved at the end of the narrative remarks that he senses she is "not too proud" of being Métis, April agrees: "I'm not. It would be better to be a full-blooded Indian or a full-blooded Caucasian. But being a half-breed, well, there's just nothing there. You can admire Indian people for what they once were...But what have the Métis people got? Nothing. Being a half-breed, you feel only the short-comings of both sides" (156–57). Cheryl clearly privileges the First Nations over the Métis. She believes that in pre-contact days her father "*would have been a warrior if he had been all Indian*" and occasionally refers to "*we, the Indian people*" (218, 168). Even though Cheryl draws inspiration from Riel, she too betrays considerable doubts about the collectivity with whom he so passionately identified. It is perhaps to compensate for such apprehensions about the Métis that she comes to see Riel as a "leader to both" the Métis and First Nations (Mosionier, In Search 168). In truth, Cheryl seems to revere Riel because she regards him as a pan-Indigenous trailblazer.

As is most evident near the conclusion, In Search of April Raintree is an aesthetically uneven work. Mosionier is prone to the melodramatic and, as a consequence of the clash between the histrionic and the realistic in the text, her characters' actions at times appear to be psychologically unmotivated. In a short essay on her novel, Mosionier writes that "Cheryl had to have a downward spiral" and kill herself, not because of some event that transpires in her life, but "because, by this time in the story, she represented my sisters" ("April" 141). Cheryl is not so much a character as a symbol. This is also true of Mosionier's (and Cheryl's) Riel. Like many other contemporary Métis writers and visual artists who allude to Riel, Mosionier is less interested in understanding the historical figure than in using him as a means to establish her Métisness, or perhaps her Indigeneity. The result is that her Riel is often only loosely connected to his model's life and concerns.

The drafting of Riel to validate one's Métis identity is also pronounced in contemporary visual representations of him. Riel has inspired a variety of Métis artists, such as David Hannon, Sherry Farrell Racette, Rosalie Favell, and Jane Ash Poitras (Mattes, "Rielisms" 20–21). But the most important contribution to the iconography of Riel is by David Garneau, not only because of the breadth of his engagement with the historical Métis leader but also because he does not eschew the complexity of his subject. Garneau's achievement in his multifaceted explorations of the public and private Riel is probably linked to his cognizance of the inherent heterogeneity of the Métis experience, underlined by the fact that "Métis appearance is not always easy to read, even by Métis" (D. Garneau, "Prophetic Obligation" 107; see also "Métissage" 380). But it may also reflect his considerable affinities with Riel.

Like Riel, Garneau is not a typical Métis, his enviable Métis pedigree notwithstanding. Garneau is a great-great-grandson of Laurent Garneau, a founder of the city of Edmonton after whom the district where the University of Alberta campus sits is named—as well as James Brady's maternal grandfather (Dobbin 31). Garneau states that he grew up without any sense of being Métis, but not because of material or social oppression. He told the curator Catherine Mattes, with whom he has collaborated, that "he has basically lived the life of a privileged White man" (Mattes, "David Garneau"). Garneau's father, Richard, was an executive with Esso Resources Canada who later became deeply interested in Métis genealogy and history (R. Garneau). Yet Garneau attests that he does not recall ever hearing "the word 'Métis' from [his] father's lips" when he was growing up (D. Garneau, "Métissage" 381). This life path may elucidate why he was born in 1962 but only "became a Métis in the fall of 2001," or possibly in the 1990s (380–81). As he writes in the subtitle of an article about one of his exhibitions, he is "a Retroactive Métis Artist" ("Métissage" 396), and Riel has been a key part of his quest for a cultural identity.

Garneau's first involvement with Riel culminated in his 2003–2004 exhibition *Cowboys and Indians (and Métis?)*, which includes works he created as early as 1997. The show opened in Winnipeg and, after an uneventful stop in Windsor, Ontario, travelled to Fort McMurray, Alberta, and Brandon, Manitoba. Garneau relates that the "exhibition changed as [his] Métis consciousness evolved" while he toured across the Prairies ("Métissage" 377, see also 384–85). One of the most arresting pieces in the collection is the oil painting *Riel/Van Gogh*, which overtly evokes the Dutch master's iconic self-portraits. Psychiatrists who write on Riel have long remarked that his mental state is not unique as there is a continuing debate about the "psychiatric pathology and diagnosis" of such canonical cultural figures as the philosopher Friedrich Nietzsche, the playwright August

Painting by David Garneau of Riel à la Vincent van Gogh. (*Riel/Van Gogh*, 2002, oil on canvas, 153 × 122 cm, used with permission of David Garneau).

Strindberg, and the painter Vincent van Gogh (Littmann 449). By linking Riel to van Gogh, who was his near contemporary (1853–1890), Garneau demystifies the whole question of Riel's sanity. True, unlike those other individuals, Riel was not just an artist or thinker but a political leader, someone whose actions had tremendous ramifications for his followers. Still, by conjuring van Gogh in his portrayal of Riel, Garneau is bound to lessen some of the stigma attached to his name.

Much of the effectiveness of Garneau's work on Riel is due to its being simultaneously political and playful. Garneau manages to inject levity into even the most abysmal of situations, as evident in his extensive and adroit usage of the noose. He has written that his reliance on the noose as a Métis symbol is provisional, only until he finds "a more positive image" ("Métissage" 383). Yet when he employs it as defiantly as he does in his painting *Noose/Fist (Metis Flag)*, in which he seems to be giving the finger to the enemies of the Métis, it is less a sign of defeat than of resilience (D. Garneau, *Online Portfolio*). The effect is more sombre but equally poignant in his oil painting *Riel's Last Portraits (Mug Shots)*, which is composed of three panels (Left, Centre, Right), each bearing a police mugshot-like portrait of a hooded Riel with a noose around his neck. No matter from which angle one faces the figure, one is forcefully reminded of what the Canadian state did to Riel (*Online Portfolio*). The result is even more powerful in *Patrimony*, which shows a white shirt sporting a noose as a necktie. Garneau asserts that the oil painting is about his "father, an executive with an oil company, who nevertheless refused to wear a regular tie—he wore a bolo" ("Métissage" 383). However, it is hard not to see (the absent) Riel in the white shirt, an interpretation supported by the artist's statement that "the image stands for all the Métis who were silenced by the shadow of the noose" (383). Garneau may have grown up without knowing he was Métis, but through his work he demonstrates that Riel and his people are very much part of his heritage. By probing Riel's multiplicity, Garneau also shows that, while many Canadians now consider Riel a national hero, this has not always been the case and that at least some Métis have not forgotten it. Most importantly, he hints that perhaps Riel can only be claimed as a Canadian patriot if one excludes his head, what he believed in and fought for.

Other contemporary Métis artists have not been as successful as Garneau at reclaiming Riel without excising critical facets of him. The poet Gregory Scofield is one such case. Born in 1966 in Maple Ridge, British Columbia, Scofield used to be rather unenthusiastic about his Métis ancestry. In his 1999 memoir *Thunder through My Veins: Memories of a Métis Childhood*, Scofield details his discomfort

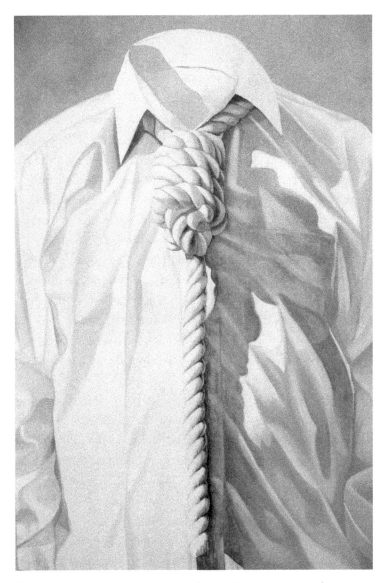

Painting by David Garneau of a dress shirt, with a noose as a necktie.
(*Patrimony*, 2003, oil on canvas. 92 × 61 cm, used with permission of David Garneau.)

about being part of a collectivity that other Indigenous peoples consider "sort-of-Indians," a band of "Frenchmen pretending to be Indians" (43, 64). He writes that when his family's Métis roots were confirmed, he was "disappointed that we weren't *pure* Indians" and started to "dissociate myself from anything white or mixed-blood" (107). This response was complicated by his own physiognomy, as reflected in his angst about wearing a powwow outfit or dancing in public, since "I didn't look right—I was too white" (68, see also 112). His antipathy toward the Métis only dissipated after a guidance counsellor at a community college in Saskatoon slyly took him to a Back to Batoche Days gathering. Scofield confesses that he would never have consented to travel to the historic site had the counsellor told him beforehand, but the trip turned out to be a turning point in his life. He underwent a collective awakening and discovered not only that he was "home at last," but that he had "new heroes—Louis Riel and Gabriel Dumont—the half-breed soldiers who had given their lives for *our* homeland, freedom and independence" (166). This was an ethnonational epiphany that has left a major imprint in his poetry.

Scofield writes that, during his grade-school days, he was "humiliated" when his social studies teacher presented Riel as "crazy and a traitor to the Canadian government." But following his unplanned pilgrimage to Batoche, he learned that the real Riel had "dreams of peace and equality" (*Thunder* 64, 8). Presumably, this is the Riel who inspired his 2011 collection *Louis: The Heretic Poems*. The volume is divided into four chronological sections: Le Garçon (The Boy); Le Président (The President); Le Porte-parole (The Spokesman); and L'Homme d'État (The Statesman). The foregrounding of the French headings, which appear in a larger font, is baffling in what is really an English work. The headings seem designed to suggest that the book is a translation, but what they accentuate instead is the absence of French—and Frenchness—in the text. They are also misleading, since the collection's focus is less on the public Riel than on the private one.

Louis devotes pieces to such topics as Macdonald, the European settlement of Canada, and the execution of Thomas Scott, to whom

Riel denies a grave because the obstreperous Orangeman would be turned into a martyr (Scofield, *Louis* 31–32), a sentiment voiced by numerous other writers on Riel (Trémaudan, "Execution" 233; Osler 111; Bumsted, *Louis Riel* 117; Dubé 41). But the core of the collection concentrates on Riel's role as a poet and his relationships with women, including his romantic interests. Scofield attributes the failure of his protagonist's liaison with the young Montréaler Marie-Julie Guernon, whom Riel calls "my nourishment" and vows to consume bodily, to her parents' objection to his "mixed heritage" (*Louis* 21, 22). Riel's romance with Évelina Barnabé, in turn, seems to collapse because of her sinful carnal desires, her being "heat-sick" for her beloved. But the transgression may also have to do with her being "the daughter," as opposed to the sister, of a Catholic priest (44).

More significant are Riel's relationships with his female relatives. Scofield opens his collection with a poem about his subject's paternal great-grandmother, Marie-Joseph (LeBlanc). Titled "Marie-Joseph's Recitation of Names," the piece is ostensibly "[t]ranslated from Chipewyan to English" and bears as an epigraph part of a poem by Riel in which he boasts that *"Indian Blood throbs in me"* and applauds his Indigenous forebears for teaching him the "Huron Carol" (Scofield, *Louis* 13; see also Riel, *Collected Writings* 4: 178, and Siggins 3). As portrayed by Scofield, Marie-Joseph displays little fervour about Christian education. Her overarching aim is to assure her great-grandson of his Indigenous ancestry, repeatedly telling him that he is "in the blood" (*Louis* 13–14). She also intimates to Riel—and the reader—that she likely follows another belief system, since she never truly embraced Christianity. Regardless of her devotion to her French Canadian voyageur husband, Louis Boucher, with whom she had the daughter who gave birth to Riel's father, Marguerite Boucher, Marie-Joseph stresses that she never did "spit on their cross" or "say their Jesus / Put spots on our faces." Never, that is, but "once" (13, 14). Since she still refers to "their" Jesus and "their" cross, that one time must have been conclusive.

Even without addressing the centrality that Scofield gives to Marie-Joseph LeBlanc, his portrayal of her is intriguing, if not convincing. Maggie Siggins hypothesizes that the historical LeBlanc and Boucher must have had a "loving" relationship, for when Boucher returned to Lower Canada, he took her with him and "they legitimized their marriage" (27). More germane, Riel's pride in his Indigenous heritage is seriously qualified in the next stanza of the poem that Scofield cites, as we can see in Paul Savoie's translation:

> The tribes have since disappeared
> From the banks of the river.
> A strong new breed has appeared
> He calls himself an explorer.
> The Indians who now remain
> Have a fondness for the settler:
> If success has a French name
> Why not support a winner?
> (Riel, *Selected Poetry* 59; see also *Collected Writings* 4: 178–79)

Also, there is no evidence in Riel's writings that LeBlanc had much influence—if any—on his life. The woman who shaped Riel the most was the individual that Scofield describes as his "dear sweet mother" (*Louis* 36, 37), but otherwise ignores. The real-life Julie Lagimodière Riel, of course, was a zealous Catholic who hesitated to marry because she was intent on becoming a nun. She was also one of the first white children "born in wedlock in what is now Manitoba" (Stanley, *Louis Riel* 1) and later would regale her offspring with stories about their "noble" French ancestry, professing to be descended from King Louis XI (Flanagan, *Louis "David" Riel* 5; see also Riel, *Collected Writings* 3: 209 and *Collected Writings* 4: 267). So one can understand why she would not be spotlighted in a poetic narrative designed to celebrate Indigenous pride and self-sufficiency, hinting at what the Métis literary scholar and fiction writer Matthew Tétreault terms the "dissonance" between Scofield's Riel and the historical one ("Reading Scofield" 45).

There are other false notes in *Louis*, none more flagrant than the protagonist's diction. Scofield's Riel is not just a revolutionary poet, a "lamb with a gun" (62), but one whose innate equitability leads him to swear like a sailor—or perhaps a buffalo hunter. Riel presents Scott not simply as a "snake," but as "a son of a bitch" (31). He responds to Macdonald's derogatory comments about the Métis by telling the Prime Minister: "va chier!," which Scofield translates as "*go fuck yourself*" (33). Although it is not clear which Métis soldier quotes Death as saying: "*I am Middleton's whore / his holy cunt full of grace*" (71), Scofield's Riel is the sort of poète maudit who has no qualms about blaspheming in order to produce a great work of art, or more likely to shock the bourgeoisie. The problem with this type of characterization is that it clashes frontally with the Riel that materializes in his writings. The historical Riel was renowned for his prudishness, a trait of which even his most sympathetic biographers do not always approve. However, his puritanism was not due only to his being "something of a prig and a momma's boy" (Siggins 32; see also J. Howard, *Strange Empire* 182), but to his debilitating fear of the afterlife. Riel wrote copiously about his desire for a "bonne mort" (*Collected Writings* 2: 354, 3: 457), an earthly demise that would lead to his eternal salvation, but possibly not before enduring thirty years in purgatory (2: 338). So it seems counterintuitive that he would risk being condemned to burn in the endless fires of hell (*Collected Writings* 3: 453) by repeatedly indulging in what he deems puerile behaviour like swearing. As Riel writes in one of his maxims: "Heureux celui qui ne blasphème pas et qui ne jure pas!" ["Fortunate is he who neither blasphemes nor swears!"] (3: 427), one of the many representative texts by his subject that Scofield either has not read or has failed to absorb.

Considering its title, *Louis: The Heretic Poems* conveys the impression that it is framed as a homage to the nonconformist Riel. Yet it is hard not to notice the lack of magnanimity in Scofield's portrayal of the Métis leader, most discernible in his insistence that a nineteenth-century figure see the world the way a twenty-first-century one does. In his desire to claim Riel as an ancestor, Scofield fails to grasp that the latter's Métis nationalism is always tempered by his privileging "la patrie céleste" over "la patrie ici-bas" (Riel, *Collected Writings* 3: 329)—even if he at times states that the heavenly homeland means

Manitoba and the earthly one Lower Canada (*Collected Writings* 2: 71). For Riel, our earthly existence is merely a preparation for our real life, which "begins / When we come to our end" (*Collected Writings* 4: 416). As he writes to a "Bon Canadien" Mountie during his Regina imprisonment:

> La terre
> N'est rien.
> L'affaire
> C'est votre salut éternel. (4: 427)

Or as Riel expresses in one of the meditations he produces in Montana just before heading to the Saskatchewan Valley, "Our home is not here" (*Diaries* 90; see also *Collected Writings* 2: 354), which he follows with a plea to the Virgin Mary to pray for everyone.

Scofield's slanted reading of Riel is exacerbated by his implicit belief that the current zeitgeist is more desirable than the one that prevailed during Riel's lifetime, when religious heresies were not tolerated. The reality is that we are the products of our time as much as Riel was of his, a truism underscored by the contemporary unease with his difference, notably his European cultural identity and his Christian spirituality—the fact Riel perceived Catholicism, not as alien faith for the Métis, but as "la religion de nos Pères, les Francs et les Canadiens" (*Collected Writings* 3: 24). In another collection, Scofield writes that in 2006 he became "the 389 thousand, 785th person / to name myself Metis," a momentous event that led to his becoming his "own resistance" (*Witness* 74, 75). But this defiance does not extend to striving to understand his titular protagonist in his own context. The result is that Scofield constructs a Riel that is unrecognizable to anyone who has even a basic familiarity with his life and times. The greatest heresy in *Louis: The Heretic Poems* is that there is so little of Riel in it.

There is much more generosity toward Riel in Marilyn Dumont's characterization of the Métis leader in her poetry. Dumont, who is a great-grandniece of Gabriel Dumont and who notes that she grew up in a small Alberta "town with fewer Indians / than ideas about Indians" (*Brown Girl* 20), has long been fascinated by Métis history and culture. This interest has led her to address the troubled, and often troubling, relations between the Métis and Canada, as well as the First Nations. In her first collection, *A Really Good Brown Girl* (1996), Dumont includes a poem titled "Leather and Naughahyde," which enacts an encounter over coffee between the text's Métis speaker and a First Nations man from "up north." While laughing at the peculiar ways of urban white people, the two strangers craftily attempt to discern each other's collective identity. The speaker eventually discloses that "I'm Metis like it's an apology," to which the northern man responds, "'mmh,' like he forgives me, like he's got a big heart and mine's pumping diluted blood" (58). After her admission of her Métisness, the speaker senses that her interlocutor begins to act as if he believes he is more culturally authentic, underlining how First Nations individuals can expose anxieties among Métis about their Indigeneity. This is an issue that not only permeates Métis writing, as we have seen with Campbell, Mosionier, and Scofield, but Métis life in general (Voth 67–68), even if First Nations people are not necessarily any less "mixed" biologically than the Métis (Andersen, "Métis" 5, 38).

A Really Good Brown Girl also contains a poem titled "Letter to Sir John A. Macdonald," in which the speaker defiantly informs Riel's implacable foe that "I'm still here and halfbreed, / after all these years" (52; see also *Pemmican Eaters* 9). But Dumont accentuates that it is not only the poet-speaker who has outlasted Canada's first prime minister, so have the Métis as a people, among them Riel, who is "dead / but he just keeps coming back" in all proud contemporary Indigenous leaders (*Brown Girl* 52). Macdonald's Confederation project, conversely, is not supposed to be faring so well, having been conceived around "steel tracks that didn't last" and "settlers who wouldn't settle" (52). For the poet, it is not yet clear who emerged victorious in the clash between Macdonald and Riel.

More recently, in her fourth collection, symbolically titled *The Pemmican Eaters* (2015), the words with which Macdonald disparaged the Métis, Dumont devotes several more poems to Riel and his relationship with Canada, such as "Requiem for Louis Riel" and "Our Prince." The first, which is written to the tune of Hank Williams, Sr.'s "Cold, Cold Heart," laments that Canada can neither acknowledge nor "see its unjust heart" (58). The poet tells Riel that she knows "you tried to make men see what they would not believe" and the reason he was executed was that "No other man before your time knew just what you knew then" (57). Dumont also states that "now we sing about those men that took the life from you," which is not convincing, as none of Riel's adversaries even approaches his centrality in Canadian culture. More persuasive is the poet's contention that "now they value our beliefs about this dying earth" (57), even if it is not self-evident what these holistic beliefs are. In his celebrated account of a Métis buffalo hunt, Alexander Ross writes how "hundreds of animals are sometimes abandoned, for even a thunder-storm, in one hour, will render the meat useless" and how the chase results in a "most profligate waste of animals" (258, 264). More apropos, in the epigraph to her poem "I Wanted to Treat Them as We Would Have Treated the Buffalo," Dumont writes that the title comes from a statement Gabriel Dumont made about General Frederick Middleton's soldiers in 1885. But what the utterance reveals is not just the great buffalo hunter's lack of kinship with the Canadian troops but also with the buffalo, the animals that provided the Métis "their marrow" (*Pemmican Eaters* 13), and which in another poem she calls "Notre Frères" (10). That said, in "Requiem for Louis Riel" there is no escaping the sundry grievances among the Métis that contemporary Canadians are appropriating their national culture, including their historical leader.

The Métis resentment of the Canadian treatment of Riel is even more pronounced in "Our Prince." Dumont presents Riel as both a sage and a seer, implying that his sagacity is what impelled the federal government to eliminate him. As she fulminates, like an ancient oracle, in the segment that provides the epigraph to this book:

> God curse them, Louis. They will regret this!
>
> Regret hanging you
>
> It will be the shadow side of Canada's story
> indelible as the iron stakes of ancestral memory
> on this grid map... (*Pemmican Eaters* 60)

Those responsible for the death of Riel, the poet forewarns, will come to rue their actions. Most ominously, Dumont closes the poem with the prophecy that "when their children ask" what the Métis leader did, "they will have to answer" (61). In light of the endless proliferation of clashing Canadian representations of Riel, that moment has come to pass.

Dumont's identification of Riel as a Métis hero is total in "Our Prince." Starting with the title, Riel is not just "*our* prince" but also "*our* prophet" and "*our* seer" (*Pemmican Eaters* 60, 61, my emphasis). Dumont writes that what makes Riel unique among Métis is his prophetic mysticism, his being "the one among us [who is] gifted" (61). Interestingly, she says nothing about the fact that Riel's emancipatory religion is infused with retrogressive ultramontane Catholicism, much less that his "New World" church is headed by two white men, first Archbishop Bourget and, following his death, Archbishop Taché. Instead, Dumont focuses on Riel the founder of Manitoba who "brokered pluralism / and language rights" (61), the Métis visionary whose political and social ideas Canadians have been arrogating for decades.

Whereas Dumont's strategic silence about Riel's fervent Catholicism may betray some uneasiness about his spirituality, there is no such ambiguity in Maia Caron's 2017 novel *Song of Batoche*. Caron, or at least her central character Josette Lavoie, leaves no doubt whatsoever that she deems Riel's religious ideas not just disturbing but utterly repugnant. *Song of Batoche* opens with the imminent arrival of Riel in the Saskatchewan Valley and ends with the reverberations of the North-West War, as Gabriel

Dumont escapes to the United States and then joins Buffalo Bill Cody's Wild West Show, along with such famed sharpshooters as Annie Oakley. Like many other historical novels, it is centred on a fictional figure, Josette Lavoie, who is both an insider and an outsider. A mother of five who is married to a brutish former buffalo hunter, Josette is young and exceptionally beautiful, having "a form slim as an unmarried woman" (Caron 12). She is also unusually well-educated, which is the reason she is able to see through the duplicitous Riel like no one else in the community.

Caron's animus toward Riel is most evident in her depiction of the Thomas Scott affair. In the literature on Riel, by Métis writers and scholars as well as others, Scott has been demonized as "an obnoxious bully boy" who triggered much of the violence during the Red River Resistance (Teillet, *North-West* 214; see also Braz, "Orange Devil"). Riel is simply the most prominent victim of the Ontario Orangeman's xenophobia. But this is not how the conflict between the two men is portrayed in *Song of Batoche*. Early in the novel, as the community eagerly awaits the arrival of the "saviour" Riel, a morose Josette tells Gabriel Dumont's wife Madeleine that Prime Minister Macdonald will learn about the development and "will punish us for Riel's sins at Red River" (Caron 10, 11). This is an admonition that she repeats throughout the text (15, 73, 86, 202). Josette holds Riel responsible for the fact that the execution of Scott led to the death of her father, Guillaume Desjarlais, and has considered Riel "a distant enemy" for the last fifteen years (19, see also 47). She assigns solely to Riel what is generally interpreted as a collective decision by the court martial headed by Ambroise Lépine. More critically, she portrays the death of Scott not as a mistake or an injustice but as a moral transgression, a misdeed by Riel with severe consequences for all Métis. Josette contends that rather than sacrificing himself for his people, as he and his supporters so often proclaim, Riel brings unnecessary pain upon the Métis, and becomes determined to stop him before he causes even more havoc.

Besides blaming Riel for the death of her father, Josette is unable to trust him because she believes he is insane. Josette is fixated on the question of Riel's mental state, not the least because the information about it has been withheld from the Saskatchewan Métis, a view held by many other members of the community (Caron 35, 124, 147, 178). When she sees Riel's long-time friend and Red River secretary Louis Schmidt being welcomed to Batoche by Riel and Gabriel Dumont, Josette becomes convinced that she must try again to persuade Dumont that "the man he followed, despite her warnings, was on a path to destruction." Without specifying why this is the case, she stresses that once the predominantly Protestant Halfbreeds and white settlers learn that Riel plans "to use his political authority to stage a holy war and throw down the Catholic religion," they will abandon the Métis combatants and so will many Métis (132). For her, the only way that such a catastrophe can be averted is if she proves to Dumont that Riel has "lost his mind" and that the two of them must join forces to stop him (204–05). Josette is both politically and sexually attracted to the much older Dumont, who does not blindly "have faith that God would protect" the Métis but believes in the power of "his gun and the need, one day, to fight the tyrant" (82). Naturally, she never manages to convince Dumont that he is following a misguided leader, even when it becomes apparent that the Métis cannot triumph. Part of the reason may have to do with Riel's Red River mystique. It is also possible that, perhaps against his will, Dumont half-believes that Riel is a prophet who will bring about a miraculous victory over the Canadian forces. But the most likely explanation is that Dumont has more in common with Riel than he does with Josette, who is far more alienated from the Métis community than she realizes.

While a work of fiction, Caron's novel has familial roots. In her author's note in *Song of Batoche*, Caron writes that she is a Red River Métis and that several members of her extended family, who were "among the founders of Batoche...fought with Louis Riel and Gabriel Dumont during the North-West Resistance of 1885" (Caron). Elsewhere, she has stated that she grew up on the British Columbia side of the Rocky Mountains and only discovered she was Métis when she was in her twenties. One of the most captivating ancestors unearthed by Caron is her paternal great-great-grandmother Marguerite Dumas

Caron, who confronted the historical Riel in Batoche (Caron and Gordon). Marguerite Caron reportedly lambasted Riel for not sending reinforcements to help Métis fighters trapped during one of the battles, telling him: "You were more eager to break into the stores and pillage than to go and help your people who are in danger there. If you do not want to go, tell me. I will go and see if they are alive or not" (qtd. in Payment, "'La vie'" 27, 36). Such gumption is also much evident in Josette. The complication is that other aspects of her personality set her apart from the other Métis, no matter how patriotic the latter may be.

Thanks to the education she received from nuns at Red River, the now fanatically anti-clerical Josette is not just a poet but an avid reader of philosophy. Her favourite book is Baruch [Benedict de] Spinoza's *Ethics*, a work that "transformed her, lifted her from brood mare to a woman of letters" (Caron 18). Josette's passion for the 1678 classic is not exactly anticipated. Spinoza's magnum opus is an extraordinarily dense text, as we can see from its first definition of God as "a being absolutely infinite, that is, a substance consisting of an infinity of attributes, of which each one expresses an eternal and infinite essence" (Spinoza 1). *Ethics* is also a masterpiece of Western rationalism. Thus Josette counters the pernicious effects of Riel's Eurocentric spiritualism by embracing another hegemonic Western philosophical and theological tradition, which she justifies by contending that Spinoza takes her to Indigenous ways of seeing.

"If Spinoza were here in Batoche," asserts Josette, "he would not follow Riel." This is a conclusion she reaches because the Red River Catholic priest who gave her the copy of the *Ethics* told her that "Spinoza believed God was like the Great Spirit and did not require a prophet or priest for explanation" (Caron 273). Without dwelling on the fact she relies on a priest to prove that people do not need priests to understand God—or at least Spinoza's God—Josette embraces the Dutch-Jewish philosopher because he has attained the same insights as Indigenous seers. This is critically important to Josette, since she believes that in order to be themselves, the

Métis must adopt an exclusively Indigenous spirituality, a stance that puts her at odds with other Métis, particularly the women. One of the reasons Josette feels superior to the other women at Batoche is that she is literate, ironically because she was "meant to be a nun" (127). As Madeleine Dumont remonstrates, "Why did Josette flaunt her learning? It was a slap in the face to any woman who could not read and write" (97). Josette's emphatic condemnation of female illiteracy is perplexing because, as the historian Diane Payment has shown, Métis women were better "educated than their male counterparts" ("'La vie'" 22). Also, Josette idolizes Gabriel Dumont, whose historical model was illiterate, unlike his wife Madeleine.

Another reason Josette condescends toward the other Métis women is that, whereas most of them have "half-breed mothers and grandmothers," her "mother was a Cree" (Caron 50). That is, she perceives herself as more "authentically" Indigenous than the other Métis women because she is less Métis, undermining the Indigenousness of the people with whom she purports to identify. This, indeed, is the central contradiction in Josette. She claims to love the Métis people, yet she is emotionally distant from almost everyone else in the community. It is striking that Josette keeps emphasizing her non-Métisness, including being the "granddaughter" of the Cree chief Big Bear, his "celebrated blood grandchild" (Caron 42, 109). The latter turns out not to be true, as her mother was a member of the Blackfoot Confederacy who was orphaned during a Cree "raid and adopted by Big Bear" (109). Still, one has to wonder why Caron implies that Josette is Cree through much of the narrative. Why would her Cree identity be favoured in a Métis community? In that sense, Josette is quite different from the historical Riel who, after the mid-1860s, identified primarily as a Métis, even if he had serious reservations about key features of Métis culture.

Caron's depiction of Riel in *Song of Batoche* is the most negative portrayal of the Métis leader by any contemporary artist, being approximated only by Jean-Pierre Dubé's *Évangile de Louis Riel*, which too sees the execution of Scott as one of the "gestes les plus regrettables" in Canadian history and a "grave erreur de jugement" (222). Josette Lavoie is so determined to renounce Riel that she dissociates herself from most other Métis, conducting what is essentially a one-person insurgency. While extreme, Caron's representation of Riel is not idiosyncratic. In a way, it is the logical consequence of Maria Campbell's reconfiguration of the Métis in *Halfbreed* and later works, with the privileging of their First Nations ancestors over the European ones. I would argue that the dominant Métis vision today is not that of Riel but of Campbell. It is not accidental that most contemporary English-speaking Métis writers and visual artists pay homage to Campbell. Beatrice Mosionier opens *In Search of April Raintree* with an excerpt of a letter in which Campbell avers that the novel is a "powerful" narrative, "the kind of writing that will begin the healing of our people and help a dominant society understand and feel the lives of a people it almost destroyed" (Mosionier, *In Search*). David Garneau praises Campbell for the "radical attitude" she exhibits in *Halfbreed*, a book designed to galvanize the Métis people "to end their silence and embark on the next stage of their cultural evolution" ("Métissage" 379). Then Gregory Scofield not only states that *Halfbreed* is "one of the most important books of [his] life" but that, over the years, its author "has become [his] friend, sister, and mother" (*Thunder* 116, 197). It is as if today's Métis need Campbell's imprimatur to vouch for their ethnonational authenticity.

The most obvious ramification of Campbell's influence on subsequent Métis writers and visual artists is that it makes it extremely difficult for those individuals to understand Riel and the nineteenth-century Métis—or Halfbreeds—as they conceived themselves. On Christmas Eve 1856, James Ross wrote an earnest plea to his siblings to honour their Indigenous ancestry, notably their mother. Ross had discerned that young people in his community had become ambivalent "toward their native mothers, which was in essence an ambivalence toward their own Indian blood and heritage" (Van Kirk, "What" 211). Since their influential white father had died recently, Ross feared that his brothers and sisters might embrace such views and start showing disrespect toward their mother just because she was Indigenous. So he admonished them, "What if mama is an Indian!...remember the personal qualities that ought to endear mama to us. Who more tender-hearted? Who more attached to her children & more desirous of their happiness?" (qtd. in Van Kirk, "Many" 236). As he underlined, "What avail those accomplishments in etiquette & fussy nonsense of which she happens to be destitute?... Better far give me my mama with her Christian meekness" (qtd. in Van Kirk, "Many" 236–37; see also Schultz 17, 21). While mounting a passionate defence of his mother's natural attributes, Ross reveals that he suspects his siblings (and perhaps himself) find her wanting when it comes to civilizational accoutrements like "writing & hairbrushing and gait and posture" (qtd. in Van Kirk, "Many" 237). Riel had similar apprehensions about the First Nations component of the Métis people, feeling that "les défauts de Notre Sang Indien" must be corrected by the "bonnes qualités canadiennes-françaises" (*Collected Writings* 4: 326; see also Braz, "Whitey" 157). For Riel and Ross, the problematic ancestor in the proverbial family "woodpile" (Cariou, "Epistemology" 909) was not the European but "the Indian" (Braz, "Whitey" 159). But today, the reverse is true. Because of the historical Riel's Eurocentric identity, writers like Campbell and Caron have such sweeping misgivings about him that it is bewildering why they feel compelled to write about him. Indeed, one cannot help but ponder, why do they need Riel? What does he offer them that other early Métis figures do not? The inevitable question that is elicited by these works is how much can contemporary Métis distance themselves from Riel and still call the collectivity with whom they identify Riel's people, the collectivity that was so irrevocably shaped by two historical events in 1869–1870 and 1885, both led by him?

Conclusion
Louis Riel in the Twenty-First Century

> *The Riel fever will I think die out. If not it will be the worse for those who keep the fever alive.*
> —SIR JOHN A. MACDONALD, 12 December 1885

LOUIS RIEL IS VERY MUCH ALIVE in the twenty-first century, both for the Métis and Canadians in general. After having been hanged for high treason in 1885, Riel has risen from the dead, and there is no indication that he will vanish from people's consciousness anytime soon. Unlike any other figure in Canadian history, Riel continues to capture the imagination of writers, visual artists, and scholars. Even politicians and bureaucrats do not seem immune to the appeal of the nineteenth-century Métis politician, poet, and mystic, often attempting to shape his place in history. Just in 2019, the Royal Canadian Mint marked the 175th anniversary of the birth of Riel by issuing a proof silver dollar, designed by David Garneau, celebrating him in Michif, English, and French ("Silver Coin"). Less than a month after Riel's death, Prime Minister John A. Macdonald predicted that the "Riel fever" would soon "die out" (qtd. in Martin 104). In contrast, a mere four days after Riel's hanging, his last confessor made a rather different prognostication. Writing to the defence lawyer François-Xavier Lemieux, Father Alexis André prophesied: "Riel is dead, but his name shall live in the North West when the name of Sir John, his mortal enemy[,] shall have long been forgotten" (139). Regardless of Macdonald's success and longevity as a politician, André has proven to be the far more accurate soothsayer. The fact is that Riel remains as popular today as he has ever been, not only in the Prairies but across Canada, and beyond. Yet it must be acknowledged that there is still considerable ambivalence about him, even by people who champion his cause, which probably contributes to his appeal.

The extent of Riel's current acclaim is evident in the creation of another opera about him. Produced by the Métis poet and librettist Suzanne Steele and the Winnipeg composer Neil Weisensel, and first workshopped in 2019, *Li Keur: Riel's Heart of the North* aims to give an insider's perspective of the Métis leader's life and political career, with seventy percent of its content being "in Indigenous tongues—including Michif and Saulteaux" ("New Louis Riel Opera"). Another Winnipeg composer, Andrew Balfour, has written an oratorio about Riel, *Empire Étrange* (2013), whose title hints at the continuing influence of Joseph Kinsey Howard's *Strange Empire*. Convinced that "Riel is a dramatic subject worthy of any Wagnerian libretto," the Cree Balfour focuses mainly on his death in order to explore the religious dimensions of this modern-day Elijah (Balfour; see also Simonot-Maiello 77–78). In addition to the recent works discussed in this study, Riel has also inspired several novels and collections of poetry. The most irreverent (and wittiest) contemporary representation of Riel, though, is Frances Koncan's 2020 play *Women of the Fur Trade*. Intended to recover the contribution of women to Manitoba's history, the satire cannot escape the allure of the Métis "Che Guevara" (Koncan 43). The Anishinaabe-Slovene Koncan has much fun with the relationship between "the heroic Monsieur Riel and the villainous Mr. Scott" (4), who are respectively "hot" but "also smart" and "[d]reamy and delightful" (9)—and best friends. Koncan, who dedicates her play to Riel, Manitoba's "Mr. Brightside" (Koncan), has an Anishinaabe central character protest that all she hears is "Louis Riel this, Louis Riel that," before dismissing him as "overrated" and "so...mediocre" (21, 26). But everyone else, including Thomas Scott, is captivated by the "Rebel! Poet! Leader! Hero! Prophet! Moustache!" (43). The main impression the play conveys is that it is hard to imagine the history of Manitoba without its almost mythical founder, a feeling relayed by many other works.

In the poem "when Louis Riel went crazy," the Winnipeg Métis poet and fiction writer Katherena Vermette notes how "our names are scattered / seeds all over" her hometown, which is really a Métis "graveyard" (*river woman* 87, 88). After listing a profusion of Métis surnames plastered across the city, from Ritchot, through Traverse, to Cote, she remarks:

and Riel
Riel
everywhere Riel (89)

Vermette could have added that she bears some responsibility for the ubiquity of Riel, since she is the co-creator of one of the most fascinating recent projects about him. Working with the illustrator Scott B. Henderson and the comic book colourist Donovan Yaciuk, Vermette is the writer of *A Girl Called Echo*, a young adult graphic series about Métis history whose eponymous protagonist travels back in time to interact with Métis historical figures. The second and third volumes, *Red River Resistance* and *Northwest Resistance*, highlight Riel's impact on the teenager's nascent national consciousness. This is most noticeable when Riel helps Echo ascertain that the two military clashes between the Métis and Canada were not rebellions but resistances. In the first case, Riel points out, the Métis could not have rebelled against Canada, since they were "not a part of the dominion yet" (*Red River* 20). In the second, the Métis were just defending themselves from the military and police contingents that Ottawa had sent "to take us" (*Northwest* 10), evoking Marilyn Dumont's observation that when non-Indigenous Canadians "say, *treason*," the Métis "say, *self-defence*" (*that* 6). In both conflicts, Riel is at the centre of Métis opposition to oppressive external forces, underscoring his centrality in the Métis tradition. So sympathetic is Vermette toward Riel that she has even provided a justification of why the Red River provisional government did not return Scott's body to his associates for burial. In her 2021 novel *The Strangers*, Vermette has a traditional storyteller explain that Scott may not have been killed because he was an Orange xenophobe but a wiindigoo, and "you bury [wiindigoos] where no one knows, so they can't go lure someone else to their grave and make them wiindigoo too" (149). Thus, what has been generally construed as a stony-hearted decision by Riel and his government was really a culturally-informed attempt to protect the community from further killings by a human-turned-cannibal.

Riel's popularity transcends Canada and the political. In the Métis leader's one-time home of Montana, the journalist Stephen Maly, a manager for Helena Civic Television, has spearheaded an effort to "capitalize" on Riel's notoriety to attract Canadian visitors to the state's capital city (Maly, "Helena"). Among his initiatives is the 46-minute television documentary *A Prophet in Exile: Louis Riel's Sojourn in Montana* (2011), which Maly wrote, produced, and videographed, and which presents Riel as one of the most colourful figures in Canadian as well as Montana history. More important, there is a campaign to get Riel canonized as a saint. The late Métis Oblate priest Guy Lavallée considered Riel not just a "prophet" (*Prayers* 18–22), but "un saint pour notre époque" (qtd. in Bahuaud, "Saint Riel?" 31)—a view supported by the historian Diane Payment, who contends that the reconciliation between the Catholic Church and the Métis requires that Riel be recognized both as a political leader and a "chef spirituel" ("Autre son" 5; see also Dubé 141–47). In 2011, Father Lavallée interceded with the Archbishop of St. Boniface, Albert LeGatt, to initiate the process of canonization. LeGatt was cordial, exalting Riel as a great Métis leader and statesman, but he drew attention to such obstacles as the fact that Riel advocated violence, was briefly excommunicated, and is believed to have struggled with mental health issues. LeGatt further stressed that no "culte populaire" has emerged around Riel since his death (qtd. in Bahuaud, "Saint Riel?" 31), leading Lavallée to ask believers to think of Riel in their prayers and presumably the matter will be revisited if any miracles are reported.

The most remarkable aspect of the afterlife of Riel is obviously his Canadianization, what has been termed "the great national opinion reversal" of the Métis leader (D. Morton, "History" 673). Granted, his metamorphosis from a foe of Canada into the epitome of Canadianness is not complete. The proclivity of those who promote Riel to caricature his political opponents and to overlook the more controversial aspects of his personality and ideas, indicates that there is some discomfort about him. Also, there has been scholarly resistance to the Canadianization of Riel, which sometimes manifests itself in silence. It is telling that between 1955 and 1982, during the explosion of cultural interest in Riel, the *Canadian Historical Review* did not publish any articles on him (Hamon, "Re-presenting Riel" S19). Some historians probably kept their views to themselves about Canada's embrace of the one-time rebel, but others have made no pretense of accepting the new paradigm. In 1971, Ramsay Cook pilloried Riel as "a pathetic and unbalanced man" (*Maple Leaf* 202). Then, at the turn of the century, in his bestseller *Who Killed Canadian History?* J.L. Granatstein was adamant that while Riel may be a hero to the Métis, "he has no credentials as a hero to all Canadians, and no school should teach his life that way" (xi). Most flagrant, Thomas Flanagan has been a polemical figure ever since the early 1980s when he vociferously opposed a "pardon" for Riel, due to his having tried "to overthrow constitutional government in a favor of a new power" (*Riel* viii, 151; see also Dummitt, "After Inclusiveness" 107). Still, there is no evading the magnitude of the political and cultural transformation that enabled the former enemy of a country to emerge as one of its great heroes. The breadth of the change in Canadian iconography from 1885 to the early decades of the twenty-first century becomes plain when one contrasts the posthumous image of Riel to that of his bête noire Macdonald. Except demographically, today's Canada does not differ radically from the polity envisaged in 1867. Yet, instead of producing statues, films, poems, plays, and operas in honour of the main architect of Confederation, contemporary Canadians are more intent on removing any monuments dedicated to him (Innes; Oosterom). As the journalist and biographer Richard Gwyn writes, Canada has never had enough room for both Macdonald and Riel and, today, "Riel has taken up all the oxygen in the room" (415, see also 413). Moreover, Macdonald's treatment by his heirs is far from being an anomaly.

In *What Is a Nation?* Ernest Renan states that the fashioning of political formations is always a violent process. Writing about France, he notes that the unification of the country's north and south "resulted from a continuous reign of extermination and terror throughout most of a century" (19). Upon praising the early French kings for achieving "the most perfect national unity possible," Renan asserts that their reputation became sullied once their compatriots had time to scrutinize their actions, and the French monarchs were "cursed by the very nation they had formed" (19). Something analogous is occurring to Macdonald. As Canadians ponder the Prime Minister's role in the creation of the country, they have become increasingly critical of him and the values he promulgated. In an apparent case of what the English philosopher Roger Scruton calls oikophobia, or "hatred of home," preferring other cultures to one's own (96; see also Dummitt, "In the Eye" 25), many non-Indigenous Canadians loudly project the impression that they have more in common with historical Indigenous leaders than with Macdonald. Conveniently, they do not repudiate Confederation, much less vow to return Canadian territory to its Indigenous owners, which may explain some of the antithetical responses to Riel.

In 2002, CBC Television broadcast *The Retrial of Louis Riel.* Produced in conjunction with the Dominion Institute, a national organization devoted to the promotion of Canadian history, the three-part show consisted of a documentary about Riel's political career; a dramatization of his trial; and a town-hall meeting with contemporary Métis representatives (Charland 9–10, 16–18). Although controversial among both Métis activists and conservative commentators, the mock trial rendered an unequivocal non-guilty verdict. The outcome was perhaps inevitable, given that Riel was defended by the celebrated trial lawyer Edward Greenspan, who lauded Riel not just as a Canadian "patriot" but "the symbol of the ethnic and cultural diversity inside a parliamentary framework" (Greenspan).

As the columnist Andrew Coyne quipped, the program was "comically one-sided." By excluding critical voices, including historians, the producers ensured that everyone "agreed Riel was not merely innocent, but a saint" (Coyne). Riel, however, would have a different fate on another CBC show just two years later. When the national broadcaster televised *The Greatest Canadian* contest in 2004, Riel was nowhere near the favourites. The winner was the former Saskatchewan premier and leader of the federal NDP, Tommy Douglas, the creator of Canada's national health care system (Dixon). Riel came in in eleventh place, behind Macdonald, at eight, who himself trailed the flamboyant hockey commentator Don Cherry, at seventh (Gwyn 102).

Like the controversy over the sculptures of Riel in Regina and Winnipeg, the results of *The Greatest Canadian* intimate that there may be a discrepancy between the way the Canadian cultural and political elites perceive Riel and the way the general populace does, evidenced by the "troubling" online comments that tend to follow pro-Riel interventions (Mailhot 27). Yet even among writers, there are misgivings about Riel. Recent novels such as Stephen Legault's *The Third Riel Conspiracy* (2013) and David D. Orr's *Encountering Riel* (2017), both dealing with the North-West War, are striking for their unabashed sympathy toward the Métis leader. Legault opens and closes his fast-paced historical murder mystery with Anglo-Canadian characters shouting, "Long live Riel" (3, 255). Orr, who is a former Saskatchewan judge, has the leading members of the Toronto Light Infantry deploring that their political leaders "lied to us" about the Métis posing a threat to Canada (289, 306). But one cannot help but notice that Riel is largely absent from two books that promise to be about him. It is as if both authors recognize that while some Canadian volunteers considered the Macdonald government "incompetent and criminally indolent," they thought even less of Riel, deeming him "the primary villain" (R. Macleod xlvii, see also xiii). Judging by their accounts, whatever reservations the volunteers may have had about the federal politicians who led them into a war they came to resent, they left little doubt that they belonged to the same tribe.

Furthermore, it is not only non-Indigenous Canadians who feel compelled to revise the past when it comes to Riel. Métis are also prone to indulge in the same sort of behaviour. As we saw in chapter 6, one of the more curious aspects of the sculptures polemic is that their opponents seldom charge that the works are historically inaccurate. Rather, the overriding objection is that the sculptures represent a negative vision of Riel, a Riel that does not reflect well on contemporary Métis, or at least their leaders. There are other examples of Métis individuals or organizations attempting to control the image of Riel, most brazenly by persuading the federal government to have the Royal Canadian Mounted Police remove parts of the rope purportedly used to hang Riel from the museum at its Regina academy (Cosh 33). E.D. Blodgett was dumbfounded by the episode, writing that, according to Renan, the suppression of inconvenient historical facts is only implemented by the dominant groups in society, not peripheral ones. "When both sides choose omission," Blodgett blasted, "it is no longer clear what purpose is served" (*Five* 294). But perhaps in Canada there is more than one centre when it comes to Riel. Or, possibly, the so-called margin can be as uncomfortable with his multiplicity as the centre.

Among the elements that make Riel unique in Canadian history is that he has had his extant poetry and prose published, another detail that raises the question of whether he is a marginal figure or a central—if oppositional—one. The release of Riel's *Collected Writings* in 1985 should have enabled scholars, if not to unravel the enigma that is the Prophet of the New World, at least to gain a better comprehension of his character. In her 2014 poetry collection *The Winter Count*, Dilys Leman uses a variety of archival documents to dramatize her familial connection to the Riel story, as befits a great-great-granddaughter of the North-West Mounted Police's senior surgeon Augustus Jukes, who provided expert testimony at the Regina trial. As Leman versifies Dr. Jukes's response to the issue of Riel's mental stability:

> That question might be set at rest
> by a critical examination
> of his writings. (107)

Contrarily, the historian Andrée Désilets suggests that, instead of solving the mystery of Riel, the publication of his *Collected Writings* could "alimenter...et de façon féconde" the investigations of many generations of scholars to come (432). The Riel Project's coordinator, Claude Rocan, too contends that since "Riel was such a complex and multifaceted individual, his writings can easily give sustenance to several points of view" ("Images" 123)—but not likely as a Canadian patriot, or a champion of the First Nations. Still, the assumption in all these cases is that artists and scholars would strive to grasp the essence of Riel by dissecting his poetry and prose, an essential step that is seldom taken. Time and again, one encounters works by people who profess to prize Riel and his ideas yet ignore his writings, despite increased accessibility (University of Calgary Archives recently acquired a collection of his writing, celebrated in the 2023 exhibition "Devotion: Louis Riel Writes Home" ["Devotion," Murray]). Paradoxically, the Riel that he fashioned in his voluminous diaries, letters, pamphlets, poems, and prophecies seems unable to match the power of the mythological Riel (Braz, "Louis Riel's Trial"), undermining Renan's thesis that the scholarly study of history "often poses a threat to nationality" (19).

The most concrete illustration of the limited impact of *The Collected Writings of Louis Riel / Les écrits complets de Louis Riel* is that the best-known quotation attributed to him does not appear there. Peter Hinton introduces his "Director's Notes" to the 2017 remount of the Centennial opera with an epigraph by Riel, ostensibly written in 1885: "My people will sleep for 100 years and when they wake, it will be the artists who give them back their souls" (37). Hinton is far from being the only person who has fallen under the spell of the "Riel" artistic prophecy, one of whose French versions is: "Mon peuple dormira pendant cent ans. Lorsqu'il s'éveillera, ce seront les artistes qui lui rendront son âme" (Bahuaud, "Cloche"; see also Lalonde). With variations, the text has been cited by individuals as diverse as the visual artists Joane Cardinal-Schubert (28), David Garneau ("Prophetic Obligation" 109; "Métissage" 377, 396), and Edward Poitras (117); scholars such as Janice Acoose (115), Monique Giroux ("Giving" 64), Sherrill Grace (110, 118), and Catherine Mattes ("Rielisms" 21);

Street mural by Ray Renooy with the "Riel" artistic prophecy. (*A Tribute to the Métis Community*, 2007. Mural, Moose Jaw, Saskatchewan. Photo by Carolyn Kapron, used with permission.)

and even by the former judge and senator Murray Sinclair. The much-respected chair of the Truth and Reconciliation Commission singles out the statement as "a creative pathway" to effecting reconciliation between Indigenous peoples and other Canadians through the arts (M. Sinclair). But what all these examples have in common is that none of the authors identifies the source of the text, something the Métis sociologist Chris Andersen gestures to when he writes that "Louis Riel *is said* to have written that '[o]ur people will sleep for 100 years, and when they awaken, it will be the artists who bring their spirits back'" ("*Métis*" xiii, my emphasis). Riel's putative artistic prophecy "has seeped into popular culture" (Crean), from a civic mural in Moose Jaw, Saskatchewan, by the graphic designer Ray Renooy; through a large sculpture by Val T. Vint in the shape of a bison, built out of steel replicas of books and articles, and situated at the Forks of the Red and Assiniboine rivers in Winnipeg (Winnipeg

Foundation, "Education," "Public art piece"); to Koncan's play, where it is cited twice (7, 88). Yet, despite all this discursive activity, the origin of the quotation remains clothed in mystery.

To his credit, Edward Poitras has conducted an extensive search for the source of the artistic prophecy. A Métis painter with a deep interest in Riel, conceiving "a dance and opera for chant" about one of his divinations regarding Manitoba's glorious future as a French-speaking Métis society (Lilburn 26), Poitras relates that he first came across the quotation in a 1985 editorial in the Indigenous magazine *New Breed*, where he worked at the time as a graphic artist. Whenever he had a chance, he looked for the passage in Riel's writings but was unable to find "the original" (Poitras 117). So he contacted the author of the editorial, Tim Low, an administrator with what was then the Association of Métis and Non-Status Indians of Saskatchewan. Unfortunately, Low was not very helpful. All he could tell Poitras about the phrase was that "he read it somewhere" (Poitras 117), and evidently was never able to recall the location. Low's editorial is titled "Metis to Regain Lost Spirit," and the main difference between his version and Hinton's is that in Low's text, artists do not give back Riel's people their souls, but "their spirit" (Low 5). Low also contends that Riel wrote the generative words in "the dying days of the [North-West] Resistance" (5), making one wonder why the learned editors of *The Collected Writings* failed to include the passage in their critical edition.

Maria Campbell, who vouches that "you won't find the artistic prophecy in Riel's letters and diaries," states that she first heard it from James Brady (who lived between 1908 and 1967). She adds that Brady's comrade-in-arms Malcolm Norris told her that the Métis political leadership "had made a mistake back then in not working with artists" (Crean). This is the message most frequently derived from the prophecy—that artists will play a crucial role in the reawakening of the Métis people. Sometimes the term artists is used loosely, such as when the novelist Carrie Bouvette Mason sees proof of Riel's "vision...for things to come" in the explosive growth in post-secondary education among Indigenous peoples in Canada since 1986, when registrations "soared to an all time increase of

800%, with the Metis Nation leading the pack!" (v). Other times it is asserted, as Niigaanwewidam James Sinclair and Warren Cariou do in the introduction to their anthology of Indigenous writings from Manitoba, *Manitowapow*, that Riel "was not only speaking of Métis artists but also of other Aboriginal artists of the past, the present, and to come" (6). In all instances, it is implied that Riel presaged that it was artists who would precipitate the Métis (or pan-Indigenous) renaissance, a view pointedly challenged by the iconoclastic Jean-Pierre Dubé, who maintains that the Métis have never needed to be saved by anyone, be it Riel or contemporary artists (229).

More than any other artist or scholar, David Garneau has explored the significance of the artistic prophecy ascribed to Riel, but not without succumbing to some contradictions. At the unveiling of the Riel silver dollar, Garneau declared that the sentiment conveyed by the quotation "motivates many Métis artists," such as himself. He elaborated that political activists were the catalysts for change in the second half of the twentieth century, but now it is the turn of "the painters, sculptors, poets, musicians, authors, filmmakers, beaders, and other cultural workers to awaken the Métis spirit and deepen the expression of contemporary Métis identity" (qtd. in "Silver Coin"). Elsewhere, Garneau writes that this "prophetic obligation [comes] from Louis Riel" and that "Riel mandates the artist to serve the community" ("Prophetic Obligation" 109). Garneau acknowledges that "the source of this familiar, even foundational quotation is unknown," yet he insists that "[t]he frequency of this sentence's reiteration is expressive of a broad desire that is worthy of attention, even if the words are apocryphal" (111; see also "Métissage" 396). Despite there being no evidence that the prophecy originates with Riel, it is imperative to accredit it to him. Or to phrase it differently, the rationalization for claiming that the words attributed to "Riel the prophet are true" (Loring) has less to do with him than with contemporary needs and desires. This is a conclusion that is strongly supported by the fact that most people who cite the artistic prophecy do not refer to any (other) text by Riel.

The reality is that, while possible, it is highly unlikely that the artistic prophecy is the work of Riel. Campbell, who says "she's read" all of Riel's letters and diaries, affirms that "she recognizes the words [of the artistic prophecy] as his" (Crean). But her claim is not persuasive. Anyone who has even a perfunctory acquaintance with his writings knows that Riel has virtually nothing to say about the role of art or the artist, unlike that of politics and, particularly, religion. Judging from his 1885 texts alone, he heralds that it is "la religion qui va sauver le peuple métis" (*Collected Writings* 3: 72), begs his brother Joseph to supply him with water from Our Lady of Lourdes shrine (3: 94), and avers that "l'église...parle en moi" (3: 205). The figure that Riel foresaw as the saviour of the Métis people, and himself, was not the Métis artist of the future but Jesus Christ, whom he calls not just "our King" and "our chief" (*Collected Writings* 4: 403) but also "the General" (4: 404). Consequently, as the day of his hanging approaches, it is the "sun of justice" that he implores to save him, in Latin no less: "Jesus! sol justitiae, salve me!" (*Collected Writings* 3: 463). Unsurprisingly, this pervasive dimension of Riel's thought does not have much appeal in the contemporary literature about him.

To further muddle the situation, Janice Acoose both promotes and undercuts Riel's authorship of the artistic prophecy. In her study of stereotypical images of Indigenous women in literature, Acoose calls *Halfbreed* a "story of survival and subsequent liberation" and praises Campbell for "following Louis Riel, who prophesied at the time of his execution in 1885 that one hundred years later his people would rise up, and the artists, musicians, and visionaries would lead the way" (115). But Acoose then goes on to state that, following a trip to northern Saskatchewan in 1995, she becomes exceedingly confident about the resurgence of Indigenous cultures, because "I [was] finally able to understand an Indigenous prophecy which I heard over and over again as I grew up. The prophecy foretells that future Indigenous cultures will flourish and that the artists, musicians, writers, and other visionaries will lead the way to a cultural renaissance" (117). Riel is therefore probably not the source of the artistic prophecy, whose unidentified origins appear to be lost in the mists of time.

Acoose's conflicting accounts notwithstanding, the saga of Riel's so-called artistic prophecy seems to be a singular case of what classical scholars term pseudepigrapha, or falsely attributing texts to authors (Metzger 3–4). The phenomenon suggests that historical figures can be simultaneously omnipresent and absent in the discourse about them. In the process, it also illustrates the peculiar ways in which collectivities forget—and remember. Renan asserts that "it is the essence of a nation that all individuals have a great deal in common and also that they have forgotten a great deal" (21). The Czech-French novelist Milan Kundera is less dualistic, insisting that the human "struggle…against power is the struggle of memory against forgetting" (4). But he adds that people "want to be masters of the future only for the power to change the past" (30–31), underlining the appeal of iconography, political or otherwise. The afterlife of Louis Riel hints that the act of remembering may be no less duplicitous than the act of forgetting. After all, groups can collectively remember what their heroes almost certainly did not say.

What I have been calling the "Riel problem" is ultimately inseparable from the gathering and publication of his extant poetry and prose. As one of his recent biographers bemoans, "Riel's writings have been disproportionately preserved, archived, and reprinted" (Hamon, *Audacity* 157), which perhaps explains why they are so strategically avoided. The same individual adds that Riel's textual production "offers an important way to 'speak back' to the power of empire" (Hamon, *Audacity* 19). But this is not always true of the U.S. Empire and the French Empire, and at times even of the British Empire. Riel is much more complex, if not outright contradictory, than many of his self-described contemporary admirers are willing to accept, especially when it comes to the relations between Indigenous and non-Indigenous peoples. The paradoxical dilemma facing those who wish to mythologize Riel either as a Canadian patriot or a strictly Indigenous hero is that they will often be resisted by his own writings. Since it is impossible to reclaim a figure while deliberately ignoring that person's voice, Riel is bound to remain a problem.

Appendix
Variations on the "Riel" Artistic Prophecy

THESE QUOTATIONS, which constitute a small sample of the material available, appear in a variety of sources: magazines and newspapers (Low, Crean, Bahuaud, Lalonde), scholarly publications (Acoose, Mattes, Dorion and Préfontaine, Andersen, Hinton), a documentary film (*Prophet in Exile*), and creative works (Renooy, Bouvette Mason, Koncan). Despite the discrepancies in phrasing, all of them attribute the vatic words to Louis Riel.

> "My people will sleep for a hundred years, but when they awake, it will be the artists who give them their spirit back."
> —TIM LOW (1985)

> "Louis Riel, who prophesied at the time of his execution in 1885 that one hundred years later his people would rise up, and the artists, musicians, and visionaries would lead the way."
> —JANICE ACOOSE (1995)

> "My people will sleep for 100 years, and when they awake it will be the artists who give them back their spirit."
> —CATHERINE MATTES (2001)

> "My people shall sleep for a hundred years and the artists shall then lead the way."
> —LEAH DORION AND DARREN R. PRÉFONTAINE (2003)

"OUR PEOPLE will sleep for a hundred years—but when they awake, it will be the artists who bring back their culture."

—RAY RENOOY (2007)

"My people will sleep for one hundred years. When they awake, it will be the artists that give them back their spirit."

—SUSAN CREAN (2008)

"My people will sleep for a hundred years, but when they awake, it will be artists, poets, and storytellers who bring back their culture."

—A Prophet in Exile: Louis Riel's Sojourn in Montana (2011)

"Mon peuple dormira pendant cent ans. Lorsqu'il s'éveillera, ce seront les artistes qui lui rendront son âme."

—DANIEL BAHUAUD (2013)

"Louis Riel is said to have written that '[o]ur people will sleep for 100 years, and when they awaken, it will be the artists who bring their spirits back.'"

—CHRIS ANDERSEN (2014)

"My people shall sleep for one hundred years at which time they shall be awakened through the Arts."

—CARRIE BOUVETTE MASON (2017)

"My people will sleep for 100 years and when they wake, it will be the artists who give them back their souls."

—PETER HINTON (2018)

"Pendant 100 ans, mon peuple va dormir; dans 100 ans, il se fera réveiller, par les artistes."

—CATHERINE LALONDE (2019)

"My people will sleep for one hundred years, but when they awake, it will be artists who give them their spirit back."

—FRANCES KONCAN (2020)

Works Cited

Abley, Mark. "CanLit's Anonymous Parent." *Maclean's*, vol. 92, no. 28, 9 July 1979, pp. 10–11.
Ackerman, Jennifer. "50th Anniversary of Production Reunites Riel Louis Actors from Years Past." *Regina Leader-Post*, 24 Sept. 2017, https://leaderpost.com/news/local-news/50th-anniversary-of-production-reunites-louis-riel-actors-from-years-past. Accessed 8 Jan. 2019.
Acoose, Janice. *Iskwewak-Kah' Ki Yaw Ni Wahkomakanak / Neither Indian Princesses nor Easy Squaws*. Women's Press, 1995.
Adese, Jennifer, and Chris Andersen, editors. *A People and a Nation: New Directions in Contemporary Métis Studies*. UBC Press, 2021.
Allard, Jean. "Destroying Riel's Message." *Winnipeg Free Press*, 19 July 1994, p. A9.
Allard, Jean, and Peter Holting. "Demanding a Place of Honour for Louis Riel." CBC TV, 13 Dec. 1966, https://www.cbc.ca/archives/entry/demanding-a-place-of-honour-for-louis-riel. Accessed 23 Feb. 2020.
Andersen, Chris. "From Nation to Population: The Racialisation of 'Métis' in the Canadian Census." *Nations and Nationalism*, vol. 14, no. 2, 2008, pp. 347–68.
Andersen, Chris. *"Métis": Race, Recognition, and the Struggle for Indigenous Peoplehood*. UBC Press, 2014.
Anderson, Benedict. *Imagined Communities: Reflections on the Origin and Spread of Nationalism*. Revised ed., Verso, 2006.
André, Alexis. "A Letter of Father André to His Friend F.X. Lemieux," 20 Nov. 1885. *The Shadow of Riel*, by Emil Tremblay, Icon Press, 1984, pp. 137–43.
Anthony, Geraldine. *John Coulter*. Twayne Publishers, 1976.
Appréciateur C. Letter. University of Alberta Archives, Louis Riel Project, Accession No. 84-95. Box 1, No. 6, 7 pp.
Arnold, Andrew D. "Keeping It 'Riel'." *Time*, 12 Apr. 2004, http://content.time.com/time/arts/article/0,8599,609686,00.html. Accessed 26 Mar. 2021.
Assessor B. Letter. University of Alberta Archives, Louis Riel Project, Accession No. 84-95. Box 1, No. 6, 2 pp.

Assessor D. Letter. University of Alberta Archives, Louis Riel Project, Accession No. 84-95. Box 1, No. 6, 3 pp.

Assessor E. Letter. University of Alberta Archives, Louis Riel Project, Accession No. 84-95. Box 1, No. 6, 6 pp.

Assessor F. Letter. University of Alberta Archives, Louis Riel Project, Accession No. 84-95. Box 1, No. 6, 2 pp.

Association of Métis and Non-Status Indians of Saskatchewan. *Louis Riel: Justice Must Be Done*. Manitoba Métis Federation Press, 1979.

Atwood, Margaret. *Survival: A Thematic Guide to Canadian Literature*. 1972. McClelland and Stewart, 2004.

Atwood, Margaret. *The Testaments*. McClelland and Stewart, 2019.

Bahuaud, Daniel. "La cloche de Batoche, en chanson." *La Liberté*, 1 Aug. 2013, p. 31, https://www.la-liberte.ca/2013/08/01/la-cloche-de-batoche-en-chanson. Accessed 26 Mar. 2021.

Bahuaud, Daniel. "Saint Riel?" *La Liberté*, 19. Jan. 2011, http://peel.library.ualberta.ca/newspapers/LBT/2011/01/19/31/. Accessed 30 Mar. 2021.

Balfour, Andrew. "Empire Étrange—An Oratorio Based on the Death of Louis Riel." *Camerata Nova*, 6 May 2013, http://cameratanova.com/16/empire-etrange-an-oratorio-based-on-the-death-of-louis-riel. Accessed 13 Apr. 2019.

Begg, Alexander. "The Red River Journal of Alexander Begg." 1869–1870. *Alexander Begg's Red River Journal and Other Papers Relative to the Red River Resistance of 1869–1870*, edited by W.L. Morton, Champlain Society, 1956, pp. 149–394.

Bélanger, Damien-Claude. *Prejudice and Pride: Canadian Intellectuals Confront the United States, 1891–1945*. University of Toronto Press, 2011.

Bell, John. *Invaders from the North: How Canada Conquered the Comic Book Universe*. Dundurn Group, 2006.

Benjamin, Walter. "The Storyteller: Reflections on the Works of Nikolai Leskov (1936)." *Illuminations: Essays and Reflections*, edited by Hannah Arendt and translated by Harry Zohn, Shocken Books, 1969, pp. 83–109.

Bennett, Carolyn. "Statement by Minister Carolyn Bennett on Louis Riel Day." Crown-Indigenous Relations and Northern Affairs Canada, 16 Nov. 2018, https://www.canada.ca/en/crown-indigenous-relations-northern-affairs/news/2018/11/statement-by-minister-carolyn-bennett-on-louis-riel-day.html. Accessed 19 Apr. 2019.

Berger, Thomas. "Louis Riel and the New Nation." *Fragile Freedoms: Human Rights and Dissent in Canada*, Clarke, Irwin and Company, 1981, pp. 26–57.

Bethell, Tom. *The Noblest Triumph: Property and Prosperity through the Ages*. St. Martin's Press, 1998.

Bilan, R.P., and Sam Solecki. "Two Reviews of *The Scorched-Wood People.*" *A Voice in the Land: Essays by and about Rudy Wiebe*, edited by W.J. Keith, NeWest Press, 1981, pp. 171–78.

Birney, Earle. "Can. Lit." 1947. *Ghost in the Wheels: Selected Poems*, McClelland and Stewart, 1977, p. 49.

Blodgett, E.D. "Comparative Literature in Canada: A Case Study." *Canadian Review of Comparative Literature*, vol. 40, no. 3, 2013, pp. 308–20.

Blodgett, E.D. *Five-Part Invention: A History of Literary History in Canada.* University of Toronto Press, 2003.

Bocquel, Bernard. *Les fidèles à Riel: 125 ans d'évolution de l'Union nationale métisse Saint-Joseph du Manitoba.* Éditions de La Fourche, 2012.

Boss, Allan. *Identifying Mavor Moore: A Historical and Literary Study.* Playwrights Canada Press, 2011.

Bouchard, Michel, Sébastien Malette, and Guillaume Marcotte. *Bois-Brûlés: The Untold Story of the Métis of Western Québec.* UBC Press, 2020.

Bourget, Ignace. "Lettre d'Ignace Bourget à Louis Riel, (14 July 1875)." *Collected Writings*, vol. 1, Louis Riel, University of Alberta Press, 1985, pp. 491–92.

Bouvette Mason, Carrie. *"My Boy" Louis Riel [Volume 3]: The Heart-Wrenching Story as Told by a Metis Woman.* Legaia Books, 2019.

Bouvier, Rita. *papîyahtâk.* Thistledown Press, 2004.

Bower, Shannon. "'Practical Results': The Riel Statue Controversy at the Manitoba Legislative Building." *Manitoba History*, vol. 42, 2001–2002, pp. 30–38.

Bowler, Gerry. "Why Honour Those Who Fought Against Canada?" *Winnipeg Sun*, 24 Jan. 2020, https://winnipegsun.com/opinion/columnists/bowler-why-honour-those-who-fought-against-canada. Accessed 20 Feb. 2020.

Bowsfield, Hartwell. "Foreword." *Strange Empire*, by Joseph Kinsey Howard, Swan Publishing, 1965, pp. 5–7.

Bowsfield, Hartwell, editor. *Louis Riel: Rebel of the Western Frontier or Victim of Politics and Prejudice?* Copp Clark Publishing, 1969.

Bowsfield, Hartwell, editor. *Louis Riel: Selected Readings.* Copp Clark Pitman, 1988.

Bowsfield, Hartwell. "The Republic of Manitobah." *Manitoba Pageant*, vol. 7, no. 1, 1961, http://www.mhs.mb.ca/docs/pageant/07/republicofmanitobah.shtml. Accessed 20 Feb. 2020.

Boyden, Joseph. *Louis Riel and Gabriel Dumont.* Penguin Canada, 2010.

Brady, J.P. [James]. "Hero of the North West: Louis Riel's Place in History." Transcribed by David Morin, Gabriel Dumont Institute, pp. 1–3, http://www.metismuseum.ca/media/document.php/03841.LouisRiel.History.pdf. Accessed 22 Aug. 2021.

Brady, J.P. [James]. "The Trial and Execution of Louis Riel." 1952. Transcribed by David Morin, Gabriel Dumont Institute, www.metismuseum.ca/resource.php/03840. Accessed 22 Aug. 2021.

Brandt, Di. "Di Brandt at City Hall." *Winnipeg Arts Council*, 25 Apr. 2019, http://winnipegarts.ca/wac/news-article/di-brandt-at-city-hall. Accessed 9 Aug. 2019.

Braz, Albert. "The Continentalist Classic: Joseph Kinsey Howard's *Strange Empire*, Louis Riel, and Canada," *American Review of Canadian Studies*, vol. 50, no. 2, 2020, 137–50, https://www.tandfonline.com/doi/full/10.1080/02722011.2020.1756361.

Braz, Albert. "The Duelling Authors: Settler Imperatives and Agnes Laut's Denigration of Pierre Falcon." *Home Ground and Foreign Territory: Essays on Early Canadian Literature*, edited by Janice Fiamengo, University of Ottawa Press, 2014, pp. 157–73.

Braz, Albert. "The End of Hybridity: Self-Indigenization in Métis Literature." *Interfaces Brasil/Canadá*, vol. 16, no. 3, 2016, pp. 60–82, https://pdfs.semanticscholar.org/de65/852e47cb90811a3652b85bd961bd68197d5f.pdf. Accessed 26 Mar. 2020.

Braz, Albert. *The False Traitor: Louis Riel in Canadian Culture*. University of Toronto Press, 2003.

Braz, Albert. "Louis Riel's Trial from 135 Years Ago Continues Today with Competing Cultural Stories and Icons." *The Conversation*, 16 July 2020, https://theconversation.com/louis-riels-trial-from-135-years-ago-continues-today-with-competing-cultural-stories-and-icons-133049. Accessed 16 July 2020.

Braz, Albert. "The Orange Devil: Thomas Scott and the Canadian Historical Novel." *National Plots: Historical Fiction and Changing Ideas of Canada*, edited by Andrea Cabajsky and Brett Josef Grubisic, Wilfrid Laurier University Press, 2010, pp. 39–52.

Braz, Albert. "The Prairie Adam: Dumont's Displacement of Riel in Contemporary Literature." *Histoires et identités métisses: hommage à Gabriel Dumont / Métis Histories and Identities: Homage to Gabriel Dumont*, edited by Denis Gagnon, Denis Combet, and Lise Gaboury-Diallo, Presses universitaires de Saint-Boniface, 2009, pp. 39–55.

Braz, Albert. "United in Oppression: Religious Strife and Group Identity in *The Cavan Blazers*." *Literature and Theology*, vol. 16, no. 2, 2002, pp. 160–71.

Braz, Albert. "Western Canada's Man: Rudy Wiebe, Maria Campbell, and the De-Frenchification of Louis Riel." *Les représentations de la Nouvelle-France et de l'Amérique du Nord*, edited by Sophie Linon-Chipon, Raymonde Litalien, and Hélène Richard, Éditions du Comité des travaux historiques et scientifiques, 2013, pp. 113–26.

Braz, Albert. "Whitey in the Woodpile: The Problem of European Ancestry in Métis Literature." *Trans/American, Trans/Oceanic, Trans/lation: Issues in International American Studies*, edited by Susana Araújo, João Ferreira Duarte, and Marta Pacheco Pinto, Cambridge Scholars, 2010, pp. 151–61.

Brown, Chester. *I Never Liked You: A Comic-Strip Narrative*. Drawn and Quarterly, 1994.

Brown, Chester. *The Little Man: Short Strips 1980–1995*. Drawn and Quarterly, 1998.

Brown, Chester. *Louis Riel: A Comic-Strip Biography*. Drawn and Quarterly, 2003.

Brown, Chester. *Mary Wept over the Feet of Jesus*. Drawn and Quarterly, 2016.

Brown, Chester. *Paying for It: A Comic-Strip Memoir about Being a John*. Drawn and Quarterly, 2011.

Brown, Chester. *The Playboy*. Drawn and Quarterly, 1992.

Brown, Chester, and Sue Carter. "Q&A: Chester Brown on the 10th Anniversary of Louis Riel." *Quill & Quire*, 12 Nov. 2013, https://quillandquire.com/authors/2013/11/12/qa-chester-brown-on-the-10th-anniversary-of-louis-riel. Accessed 16 July 2020.

Brown, Chester, and Darrell Epp. "Two-Handed Man Interviews Cartoonist Chester Brown." 22 Apr. 2002, http://www.twohandedman.com/Interviews/Chester/Index.html. Accessed 16 July 2020.

Brown, Chester, and Dave Gilson. "The Pickup Artist: An Interview with Chester Brown." *Mother Jones*, 26 May 2011, http://www.motherjones.com/media/2011/05/chester-brown-prostitution-comic-memoir. Accessed 6 Oct. 2012.

Brown, Jennifer S.H. "People of Myth, People of History: A Look at Recent Writings on the Metis." *Acadiensis*, vol. 17, no. 1, 1987, pp. 150–62, https://journals.lib.unb.ca/index.php/Acadiensis/article/view/12146/12990. Accessed 27 Aug. 2019.

Bruyneel, Kevin. "Exiled, Executed, Exalted: Louis Riel, *Homo Sacer* and the Production of Canadian Sovereignty." *Canadian Journal of Political Science*, vol. 43, no. 3, 2010, pp. 711–32.

Bryant, Wilbur F. *The Blood of Abel*. Gazette-Journal Company, 1887.

Bumsted, J.M. "Louis Riel and His Papers: The 'Mahdi' of Western Canada?" Review of *The Collected Writings of Louis Riel / Les écrits complets de Louis Riel*, by Louis Riel. *Beaver*, vol. 67, no. 4, 1987, pp. 47–54.

Bumsted, J.M. "Louis Riel and the United States." *American Review of Canadian Studies*, vol. 29, no. 1, 1999, pp. 17–41.

Bumsted, J.M. *Louis Riel v. Canada: The Making of a Rebel*. Great Plains Publications, 2001.

Bumsted, J.M., editor. *Reporting the Resistance: Alexander Begg and Joseph Hargrave on the Red River Resistance*. University of Manitoba Press, 2003.

Bumsted, J.M. *Thomas Scott's Body and Other Essays in Early Manitoba History*. University of Manitoba Press, 2000.

Bumsted, J.M. "The Trial of Ambroise Lépine." *Beaver*, vol. 77, no. 2, 1997, pp. 9–19.

Cain, Stephen. "Louis Riel." *American Standard / Canada Dry*. Coach House Books, 2005, p. 101.

Cameron, Christina. "Commemoration: A Moving Target?" *The Place of History: Commemorating Canada's Past / Les lieux de la mémoire: la commémoration du passé du Canada*, edited by Thomas H.B. Symons, Royal Society of Canada, 1997, pp. 27–34.

Campbell, Glen. "Les femmes dans la vie de Louis Riel: une perspective poétique." *La langue, la culture et la société des francophones de l'Ouest*, edited by Annette Saint-Pierre and Liliane Rodrigue, Cefco: Centre d'études franco-canadiennes de l'Ouest, 1985, pp. 23–34.

Campbell, Glen. "Introduction." *Collected Writings*, vol. 4, Louis Riel, University of Alberta Press, 1985, pp. xxxiii–xlviii.

Campbell, Glen. "Introduction." *Selected Poetry of Louis Riel*. Translated by Paul Savoie and edited by Glen Campbell, Exile Editions, 1993, pp. 9-12.

Campbell, Glen. "The Tormented Soul: Riel's Poetic Image of Himself." *Images of Louis Riel in Canadian Culture*, edited by Ramon Hathorn and Patrick Holland, Edwin Mellen Press, 1992, pp. 353–64.

Campbell, Glen, and Tom Flanagan. "Louis Riel's Romantic Interests." *Manitoba History*, no. 90, 2019, pp. 2–12.

Campbell, Maria, *Halfbreed*. 1973. Goodread Biographies, 1983.

Campbell, Maria. *Riel's People: How the Métis Lived*, illustrated by David Maclagan, Douglas and McIntyre, 1978.

Campbell, Maria, translator. *Stories of the Road Allowance People*, paintings by Sherry Farrell Racette, Theytus, 1995.

Campbell, Maria. "Strategies for Survival." *Give Back: First Nations Perspectives on Cultural Practice*, by Maria Campbell et al., Gallerie Publications, 1992, pp. 5–12.

Campbell, Maria, and Doris Hillis. "'You Have to Own Yourself': An Interview with Maria Campbell." *Prairie Fire*, vol. 9, no. 3, 1988, pp. 44–58.

Campbell, Maria, and Hartmut Lutz. "Maria Campbell." *Contemporary Challenges: Conversations with Canadian Native Authors*, edited by Hartmut Lutz, Fifth House Publishers, 1991, pp. 41–65.

Canada. *House of Commons: Official Report*. House of Common Debates, vol. 134, no. 84–2nd Session; 35th Parliament, 21. Oct. 1996, https://www.ourcommons.ca/Content/House/352/Debates/087/han087-e.pdf. Accessed 29 Feb. 2020.

Canada. "Section 35: Rights of the Aboriginal Peoples of Canada," *Constitution Act, 1982*, Part II. *The Constitution Acts, 1867 to 1982*, https://laws-lois.justice.gc.ca/eng/const. Accessed 7 Jan. 2019.

Cardinal-Schubert, Joane. "Flying with Louis." *Aboriginal Perspectives on Art, Art History, Critical Writing and Community*, edited by Lee-Ann Martin, Banff Centre, 2003, pp. 26–49.

Cariou, Warren. "Epistemology of the Woodpile." *University of Toronto Quarterly*, vol. 71, no. 4, 2002, pp. 909–17.

Cariou, Warren. *Lake of the Prairies: A Story of Belonging*. Doubleday Canada, 2002.

Caron, Maia. *Song of Batoche*. Ronsdale Press, 2017.

Caron, Maia, and Ariel Gordon. "In Conversation: Maia Caron." *Winnipeg Free Press*, 10 Feb. 2018, p. D3.

Cartier, George-Étienne. "Avant tout je suis Canadien." 1835. *L'Encyclopédie d'histoire du Québec / The Quebec History Encyclopedia*, 2004, http://faculty.marianopolis.edu/c.belanger/quebechistory/encyclopedia/cartieravanttout.htm. Accessed 23 Mar. 2021.

CBC News. "Louis Riel Poems Return to Manitoba." 27 Nov. 2008, https://www.cbc.ca/news/canada/manitoba/louis-riel-poems-return-to-manitoba-1.711926. Accessed 6 Dec. 2021.

Chabun, Will. "Icons in Exile: How Regina's Riel Statue and Other Monuments Disappeared from View." *Regina Leader-Post*, 10 Sept. 2016, https://leaderpost.com/news/local-news/icons-in-exile-how-reginas-riel-statue-and-other-monuments-disappeared-from-view. Accessed 6 Dec. 2021.

Chalmers, Floyd S. *Both Sides of the Street: One Man's Life in Business and the Arts in Canada*. Macmillan of Canada, 1983.

Chapleau, Joseph-Adolphe. Telegrams to John Macdonald, 16 Nov. 1885. *Correspondence of Sir John Macdonald: Selections from the Correspondence of the Right Honourable Sir John Alexander Macdonald, G.C.B., First Prime Minister of the Dominion of Canada*, edited by Joseph Pope, Oxford University Press, 1921, p. 366.

Charland, Maurice. "Newsworld, Riel, and the Métis: Recognition and the Limits of Reconciliation." *Canadian Journal of Communication*, vol. 32, no. 1, 2007, pp. 9–27.

Charlebois, Peter. *The Life of Louis Riel*. NC Press, 1975.

Chartrand, Paul L.A.H. "The Constitutional Status and Rights of the Métis People in Canada." *aboriginal policy studies*, vol. 6, no. 2, 2017, pp. 120–31, https://journals.library.ualberta.ca/aps/index.php/aps/article/view/29329/pdf. Accessed 4 Feb. 2021.

Chartrand, Paul L.A.H. *Pierriche Falcon: The Michif Rhymester—Our Métis National Anthem: The Michif Version*. Gabriel Dumont Institute, 2009.

Clark, Joe. *A Nation Too Good to Lose: Renewing the Purpose of Canada*. Key Porter Books, 1994.

Cleomati. "To One of the Absent." *Two Months in the Camp of Big Bear: The Life and Adventures of Theresa Gowanlock and Theresa Delaney*, by Theresa Gowanlock and Theresa Delaney, Parkdale Times, 1885, pp. 63–64.

COC Staff. "A Message from the Estates of Harry Somers and Mavor Moore: Replacing the 'Kuyas' Aria in *Louis Riel*." *Canadian Opera Company*, 6 Feb. 2020, https://learn.coc.ca/COC-news?EntryID=20813. Accessed 30 Mar. 2020.

[Collins, Joseph Edmund.] *The Story of Louis Riel the Rebel Chief*. 1885. Coles Canadiana Collection, 1970.

Communications Staff. "A Dialogue on Indigenous Law, Song and Opera." *Queen's Gazette*, 24 Apr. 2017, https://www.queensu.ca/gazette/stories/dialogue-indigenous-law-song-and-opera. Accessed 6 Aug. 2017.

"A Complete Edition of Louis Riel." *Western Canadiana Publications Project Newsletter*, no. 4, Sept. 1978, p. 1.

Conner, Shawn. "Team Cartoon Canada: Rebel Rag." *Globe and Mail*, 9 Oct. 1999, p. C20.

Cook, Ramsay. "The Confessions of St. Louis Riel." *Saturday Night*, vol. 92, no. 1, 1977, pp. 76–77.

Cook, Ramsay. *The Maple Leaf Forever: Essays on Nationalism and Politics in Canada*. Macmillan of Canada, 1971.

Cosh, Colby. "The Demise of History." *Alberta Report*, vol. 25, no. 27, 22 June 1998, p. 33.

Coulter, John. *The Crime of Louis Riel*. 1966. Playwrights Co-op, 1976.

Coulter, John. *In My Day*. Hounslow Press, 1980.

Coulter, John. *Riel*. 1950. Cromlech Press, 1972.

Coulter, John. *The Trial of Louis Riel*. Oberon Press, 1980.

Coyne, Andrew. "A Rigged Trial. A Stacked Jury. An Historic Injustice. Yes, the CBC's The Retrial of Louis Riel." *National Post*, 25 Oct. 2002, p. A9.

Crean, Susan. "Riel's Prophecy." *The Walrus*, vol. 4, no. 21, 12 Apr. 2008, https://thewalrus.ca/2008-04-theatre. Accessed 21 Feb. 2020.

Dafoe, Christopher. "An Abundance of Louis Riels." *Winnipeg Free Press*, 26 Apr. 1986, p. 6.

Dahl, Gregg. "A Half-breed's Perspective on Being Métis." *Metis in Canada: History, Identity, Law and Politics*, edited by Christopher Adams, Gregg Dahl, and Ian Peach, University of Alberta Press, 2013, pp. 93–139.

Danckert, Paula. "Louis Riel: History, Theatre, and a National Narrative—An Evolving...Story." *University of Toronto Quarterly*, vol. 87, no. 4, 2018, pp. 39–50.

Daniels, Douglas. "Addendum Three [Letter to Father Joseph Curcio]." *Riel: A Life of Revolution*, by Maggie Siggins. 1994. HarperPerennial, 1995, pp. 453–59.

Daniels, Harry W. *We Are the New Nation: The Metis and National Native Policy*. Native Council of Canada, 1979.

Daniels, Jo-Ann. Letter to Norman Wagner, 22 Nov. 1983. University of Alberta Archives, Louis Riel Project, Accession No. 84-95. Box 2, No. 18, 1 p.

Deane, Richard Burton. *Mounted Police Life in Canada: A Record of Thirty-one Years' Service*. 1916. Prospero Books, 2001.

Delaronde, Billyjo. "Louis Riel Deserves Better." *Winnipeg Free Press*, 31 May 1993, p. A7.

Désilets, Andrée. "Review of *The Collected Writings of Louis Riel / Les écrits complets de Louis Riel*." *Revue d'histoire de l'Amérique française*, vol. 40, no. 3, 1987, pp. 429–32.

Devine, Heather. "Ahead of His Time: Joseph Kinsey Howard and the Writing of *Strange Empire*." *Montana: The Magazine of Western History*, vol. 61, no. 4, 2011, pp. 54–72, 94–96.

"Devotion: Louis Riel Writes Home." University of Calgary Archives and Special Collections, 2023. https://asc.ucalgary.ca/louis-riel. Accessed 8 June 2023.

DeVoto, Bernard. "Joseph Kinsey Howard." *Strange Empire*, by J. Howard, Minnesota Historical Society Press, 1994, pp. 3–10.

DeVoto, Bernard. "Remainder Shelf." *Harper's Magazine*, vol. 205, 1952, pp. 65–68.

Diefenbaker, John G. *One Canada: Memoirs of the John G. Diefenbaker, the Crusading Years, 1859–1956*. Macmillan of Canada, 1975.

Dimaline, Cherie. *Red Rooms*. Theytus Books, 2007.

Dixon, Guy. "The Greatest Canadian." *The Globe and Mail*, 30 Nov. 2004, https://www.theglobeandmail.com/arts/the-greatest-canadian/article1144309. Accessed 8 Mar. 2021.

Dobbin, Murray. *The One-and-a-Half Men: The Story of Jim Brady and Malcolm Norris, Metis Patriots of the Twentieth Century*. New Star Books, 1981.

Donkin, John G. *Trooper and Redskin in the Far North-West: Recollections of Life in the North-West Mounted Police, Canada, 1884–1888*. Sampson Lowe, Marston, Searle, and Rivington, 1889.

Dorge, Lionel. *Louis Riel, Manitoban, 1844–1885*. Manitoba Centennial Corporation, 1971.

Dorion, Leah, and Darren R. Préfontaine, *The Metis: Our People, Our Story— Teacher's Guide*. Gabriel Dumont Institute, 2003, http://www.metismuseum.ca/media/db/01260. Accessed 21 Feb. 2020.

Doss, Erika. "The Process Frame: Vandalism, Removal, Re-Siting, Destruction." *A Companion to Public Art*, edited by Cher Krause Knight and Harriet F. Senie, John Wiley and Sons, 2016, pp. 403-21.

Doyle, David. *Louis Riel: Let Justice Be Done*. Ronsdale Press, 2017.

Dubé, Jean-Pierre. *Évangile de Louis Riel*. Éditions du Péricarde, 2017.

Dubuc, Alfred. "The Decline of Confederation and the New Nationalism." Translated by Peter C. Moes, *Nationalism in Canada*, edited by Peter Russell, McGraw-Hill, 1966, pp. 112-32.

Dubuc, Joseph. "Correspondance de Sir Joseph Dubuc: correspondance du Nord-Ouest." 1870. *Revue d'histoire de l'Amérique française*, vol. 20, no. 4, 1967, pp. 625-30.

Duffy, Dennis. "Wiebe's Real Riel? *The Scorched-Wood People* and Its Audience." *Rough Justice: Essays on Crime in Literature*, edited by M.L. Friedland, University of Toronto Press, 1991, pp. 200-13.

Dummitt, Christopher. "After Inclusiveness: The Future of Canadian History." *Contesting Clio's Craft: New Directions and Debates in Canadian History*, edited by Christopher Dummitt and Michael Dawson, Institute for the Study of the Americas, 2009, pp. 98-122.

Dummitt, Christopher. "In the Eye of the Historian: Three Takes on Riel." *Literary Review of Canada*, vol. 29, no. 1, 2001, pp. 24-26.

Dumont, Guy. "Why Not Two Riels?" *Winnipeg Free Press*, 19 July 1994, p. A9.

Dumont, Marilyn. *The Pemmican Eaters*. ECW Press, 2015.

Dumont, Marilyn. *A Really Good Brown Girl*. Brick Books, 1996.

Dumont, Marilyn. *that tongued belonging*. Kegedonce Press, 2007.

Dumontet, Monique. "Controversy in the Commemoration of Louis Riel." *Mnemographia Canadensis: Essays on Memory, Community, and Environment in Canada, with Particular Reference to London, Ontario*, edited by D.M.R. Bentley, Canadian Poetry Press, 1999, pp. 89-111.

Durnin, Katherine. *Mixed Messages: The Métis in Canadian Literature, 1816-2007*. 2008. University of Alberta, PHD dissertation.

Dusenberry, Verne. "Waiting for a Day That Never Comes: The Dispossessed Métis of Montana." *The New Peoples: Being and Becoming Métis in North America*, edited by Jacqueline Peterson and Jennifer S.H. Brown, University of Manitoba Press, 1985, pp. 119-36.

Eddington, Bryan. "The Kidnapping of Sister Sainte-Thérèse." *Beaver*, vol. 82, no. 6, 2002-2003, pp. 42-43.

Eisler, Dale. *Rumours of Glory: Saskatchewan and the Thatcher Years*. Hurtig Publishers, 1987.

Elliott, Robin. "The Genesis and First Production of *Louis Riel*." *University of Toronto Quarterly*, vol. 87, no. 4, 2018, pp. 10-21.

Ens, Gerhard J. Intervention at Katherine Durnin's PHD Defence. University of Alberta, 22 Aug. 2008.

Ens, Gerhard J. "Prologue to the Red River Resistance: Pre-liminal Politics and the Triumph of Riel." *Journal of the Canadian Historical Association*, vol. 5, no. 5, 1994, pp. 111–23.

Ens, Gerhard J., and Joe Sawchuk. *From New Peoples to New Nations: Aspects of Métis History and Identity from the Eighteenth to the Twenty-First Centuries*. University of Toronto Press, 2016.

Erickson, Lesley. "Repositioning the Missionary: Sara Riel, the Grey Nuns, and Aboriginal Women in Catholic Missions of the Northwest." *Recollecting: Lives of Aboriginal Women of the Canadian Northwest and Borderlands*, edited by Sarah Carter and Patricia A. McCormack, AU Press, 2011, pp. 115–34.

Eyland, Cliff. "Officialdumbing." *Border Crossings*, vol. 20, no. 2, 2001, pp. 122–23.

Falcon, Pierre. "La bataille des Sept Chênes." 1816. *Songs of Old Manitoba, with Airs, French and English Words, and Introductions*, edited by Margaret Arnett MacLeod, Ryerson Press, 1960, pp. 5–8.

Falcon, Pierre. "The Battle of Seven Oaks." Translated by James Reaney. *Songs of Old Manitoba, with Airs, French and English Words, and Introductions*, edited by Margaret Arnett MacLeod, Ryerson Press, 1960, pp. 7–9.

Farrell Racette, Sherry. "Metis Man or Canadian Icon: Who Owns Louis Riel?" *Rielisms*. Winnipeg Art Gallery, 2001, pp. 42–53.

Feldbrill, Victor. "Louis Riel." *Opera Canada*, vol. 9, no. 3, 1968, p. 31.

Ferland, Marcien, editor. *Au temps de la Prairie: L'histoire des Métis de l'Ouest canadien racontée par Auguste VERMETTE, neveu de Louis Riel*. Éditions du Blé, 2000.

Flanagan, Thomas. "Appendix: Did Louis Riel Father a Son by Marie-Julie Guernon." "Louis Riel's Romantic Interests," by G. Campbell and Flanagan. *Manitoba History*, no. 90, 2019, pp. 9–11.

Flanagan, Thomas. "Introduction." *The Birth of Western Canada: A History of the Riel Rebellions*, by George Stanley. 1936. University of Toronto Press, 1992, xi–xxiii.

Flanagan, Thomas. "Introduction." *The Diaries of Louis Riel*, edited and translated by Flanagan, Hurtig Publishers, 1976, pp. 7–20.

Flanagan, Thomas. *Louis "David" Riel: "Prophet of the New World."* Revised ed. University of Toronto Press, 1996.

Flanagan, Thomas. "Louis Riel: Icon of the Left." *Transactions of the Royal Society of Canada*, series 5, vol. 1, 1986, pp. 207–18.

Flanagan, Thomas. "On the Trail of the *Massinahican*: Louis Riel's Encounter with Theosophy." *Journal of the Canadian Church Historical Society*, vol. 37, 1995, pp. 89–98.

Flanagan, Thomas. *Persona Non Grata: The Death of Free Speech in the Internet Age.* McClelland and Stewart, 2014.

Flanagan, Thomas. "Review of *Strange Empire: Louis Riel and the Métis People*, by Joseph Kinsey Howard, and *The Queen v Louis Riel*, edited by Desmond Morton." *Canadian Journal of Political Science*, vol. 7, no. 4, 1974, pp. 738-39.

Flanagan, Thomas. *Riel and the Rebellion: 1885 Reconsidered.* Western Producer Prairie Books, 1983.

Foot, Richard, updated by Andrew McIntosh. "Editorial: The Stanley Flag and the 'Distinctive Canadian Symbol'." *Canadian Encyclopedia*, 14 Feb. 2014. Nov. 2019, https://www.thecanadianencyclopedia.ca/en/article/the-stanley-flag. Accessed 21 Mar. 2021.

Foster, John. "Some Questions and Perspectives on the Problem of Métis Roots." *The New Peoples: Being and Becoming Métis in North America*, edited by Jacqueline Peterson and Jennifer S.H. Brown, University of Manitoba Press, 1985, pp. 73-91.

Fox, Norman A. "Joseph Kinsey Howard: Writer." *Montana: The Magazine of Western History*, vol. 2, no. 2, 1952, pp. 41-44.

Freynet, Robert. *Louis Riel en bande dessinée.* Éditions des Plaines, 1990.

Friesen, Gerald. "The Political Thought of Louis Riel and John Norquay." *Canadian Issues / Thèmes canadiens*, Spring/Summer 2021, pp. 61-65.

Friesen, Gerald. "Review of *The Collected Writings of Louis Riel / Les écrits complets de Louis Riel.*" *Canadian Historical Review*, vol. 69, no. 1, 1988, pp. 89-93.

Friesen, Gerald. *River Road: Essays on Manitoba and Prairie History.* University of Manitoba Press, 1996.

Full Professors of Political Science (University of Calgary). Letter to Norman Wagner, 6 Dec. 1983. University of Alberta Archives, Louis Riel Project, Accession No. 84-95. Box 2, No. 18, 1 p.

Garay, Kathleen. "John Coulter's Riel: The Shaping of 'a Myth for Canada.'" *Images of Louis Riel in Canadian Culture*, edited by Ramon Hathorn and Patrick Holland, Edwin Mellen Press, 1992, pp. 279-310.

Garneau, David. "Contemporary Métis Art as *Métissage.*" *Histoires et identités métisses: Hommage à Gabriel Dumont / Métis Histories and Identities: Homage to Gabriel Dumont*, edited by Denis Gagnon, Denis Combet, and Lise Gaboury-Diallo, Presses universitaires de Saint-Boniface, 2009, pp. 377-97.

Garneau, David. "Contemporary Métis Art, Prophetic Obligation and the Individual Talent." *Close Encounters: The Next 500 Years*, edited by Candice Hopkins et al., Plug In Editions, 2011, pp. 106-13.

Garneau, David. "Extra-Rational Indigenous Performance: *Dear John; Louis David Riel.*" *Canadian Theatre Review*, vol. 178, 2019, pp. 72-76.

Garneau, David. *Online Portfolio.* http://uregina.ca/~garneaud/paintings.html. Accessed 17 Sept. 2020.

Garneau, R.D. (Dick). *Canadian History: A Distinct Viewpoint.* http://www.agt. net/public/dgarneau. Accessed 21 Sept. 2020.

Gaudry, Adam. "Building the Field of Métis Studies: Toward Transformative and Empowering Métis Scholarship." *A People and a Nation: New Directions in Contemporary Métis Studies,* edited by Jennifer Adese and Chris Andersen, UBC Press, 2021, pp. 213–29.

Gaudry, Adam. "The Métis-ization of Canada: The Process of Claiming Louis Riel, Métissage, and the Métis People as Canada's Mythical Origin." *aboriginal policy studies,* vol. 2, no. 2, 2013, pp. 64–87, https://journals. library.ualberta.ca/aps/index.php/aps/article/view/17889. Accessed 5 Sept. 2018.

Gaudry, Adam. "A Métis Night at the Opera: Louis Riel, Cultural Ownership, and Making Canada Métis." 18 May 2017, https://adamgaudry.wordpress. com/2017/05/18/a-metis-night-at-the-opera-louis-riel-cultural-ownership-and-making-canada-metis. Accessed 5 Sept. 2018.

Gauvreau, Michael. "Review of *The Collected Writings of Louis Riel / Les écrits complets de Louis Riel.*" *Manitoba History,* vol. 16, 1988, http://www.mhs. mb.ca/docs/mb_history/16/rielwritings.shtml. Accessed 7 Mar. 2017.

Gibbons, Lillian. *My Love Affair with Riel* [reprints from *The Winnipeg Tribune*]. Self-published, ca. 1969.

Gillmor, Alison. "Take It Outside: Public Art Has Power to Please and Provoke." *Winnipeg Free Press,* 2 Aug. 2016, p. A6, https://www.winnipegfreepress. com/arts-and-life/entertainment/arts/take-it-outside-388904731.html. Accessed 15 Feb. 2020.

Giroux, Monique. "'Giving Them Back Their Spirit': Multiculturalism and Resurgence at a Metis Cultural Festival." *MUSICultures,* vol. 43, no. 1, 2018, pp. 64–88, https://journals.lib.unb.ca/index.php/MC/article/ view/25260/29248. Accessed 8 Aug. 2018.

Giroux, Monique. "The Goddamn [Opera] Is Dead!" *CNQ: Canadian Notes & Queries,* 23 Jan. 2018, http://notesandqueries.ca/essays/the-goddamn-opera-is-dead. Accessed 8 Aug. 2018.

Goldring, Peter. "The Truth about Louis Riel." *SIB* 91A, 2009, https://www. petergoldring.ca/media/SIB%2091A%20-%20Louis%20Riel.pdf. Accessed 24 May 2023.

Gould, Stephen Jay. "Darwin's Delay." *Ever Since Darwin: Reflections in Natural History,* W.W. Norton, 1977, pp. 21–27.

Grace, Sherrill. *On the Art of Being Canadian.* UBC Press, 2009.

Granatstein, J.L. *Who Killed Canadian History?* 1998. HarperPerennial, 1999.

Grandin, Vital, et al. *Le véritable Riel, suivi d'extraits des Mandements de nos seigneurs les évêques concernant l'agitation Riel.* Imprimerie Générale, 1887.

Greenspan, Edward L. "Riel Was the Government's Scapegoat Series: The Retrial of Louis Riel." *National Post*, 22 Oct. 2002, p. A19.

Griffiths, Linda, and Maria Campbell. *The Book of Jessica: A Theatrical Transformation*. Coach House Press, 1989.

Gutteridge, Don. *Riel: A Poem for Voices*. Fiddlehead Books, 1968.

Gutteridge, Don. "Riel: Historical Man or Literary Symbol?" *Humanities Association Bulletin*, vol. 21, no. 3, 1968, pp. 3-15.

Gwyn, Richard. *Nation Maker: Sir John A. Macdonald: His Life, Our Times, Volume Two: 1867–1891*. Vintage Canada, 2012.

Hamon, M. Max. *The Audacity of His Enterprise: Louis Riel and the Métis Nation That Canada Never Was, 1840–1875*. McGill-Queen's University Press, 2019.

Hamon, M. Max, editor. *CHR Presents Louis Riel. Canadian Historical Review*, vol. 102, sup. 1, 2021.

Hamon, M. Max, "Re-presenting Riel: 100 Years in the Canadian Historical Review." *Canadian Historical Review*, vol. 102, sup. 1, 2021, pp. S1-S32.

Harrison, Dick. "Cultural Insanity and Prairie Fiction." *Figures in a Ground: Canadian Essays on Modern Literature Collected in Honor of Sheila Watson*, edited by Diane Bessai and David Jackel, Western Producer Prairie Books, 1978, pp. 278-94.

Hathorn, Ramon, and Patrick Holland. "Foreword." Hathorn and Holland, *Images of Louis Riel*, pp. 1-7.

Hathorn, Ramon, and Patrick Holland, editors. *Images of Louis Riel in Canadian Culture*. Edwin Mellen Press, 1992.

Hinton, Peter. "Director's Notes." *University of Toronto Quarterly*, vol. 87, no. 4, 2018, pp. 37-38.

Hinton, Peter, and *Opera Canada*. "Restaging Riel." *Opera Canada*, vol. 62, no. 4, 2017, pp. 30-33.

Historical Committee of the Union nationale métisse Saint-Joseph du Manitoba. "Appendix." *Hold High Your Heads (History of the Métis Nation in Western Canada)*, by Auguste-Henri de Trémaudan, translated by Elizabeth Maguet. Pemmican Publications, 1982, pp. 175-97.

Historical Committee of the Union nationale métisse Saint-Joseph du Manitoba. "Foreword to the French Edition." *Hold High Your Heads (History of the Métis Nation in Western Canada)*, by Auguste-Henri de Trémaudan, translated by Elizabeth Maguet, Pemmican Publications, 1982, pp. xii-xvii.

Howard, Henry. "Medical History of Louis David Riel during His Detention in Longue Pointe Asylum." *Canada Medical & Surgical Journal*, vol. 14, 1886, pp. 641-49.

Howard, Joseph Kinsey. *Montana: High, Wide, and Handsome*. 1943. University of Nebraska Press, 2003.

Howard, Joseph Kinsey. *Strange Empire: A Narrative of the Northwest*. 1952. Minnesota Historical Society Press, 1994.

Hoyt, Jyl. "Montana Writer Joseph Kinsey Howard: Crusader for the Worker, Land, Indian and Community." 1988. University of Montana, Master's thesis. https://scholarworks.umt.edu/cgi/viewcontent.cgi?referer=https://www.google.com/&httpsredir=1&article=6090&context=etd. Accessed 6 July 2019.

Huel, Raymond J.A. *Archbishop A.-A. Taché of St. Boniface: The "Good Fight" and the Illusive Vision*. University of Alberta Press, 2003.

Huel, Raymond J.A. "The Clergyman as Historian: The Rev. A.-G. Morice, O.M.I., and Riel Historiography." *Historical Studies*, vol. 52, 1985, pp. 83–96.

Huel, Raymond J.A. "Introduction." *Collected Writings*, by Louis Riel, vol. 1, University of Alberta Press, 1985, pp. xxxix–liii.

Huel, Raymond J.A. "Louis Schmidt: A Forgotten Métis." *Louis Riel and the Métis: Riel Mini-Conference Papers*, edited by A.S. Lussier, Pemmican Publications, 1979, pp. 87–94, 168.

Hutcheon, Linda, and Michael Hutcheon. "Identity Crisis." *Opera Canada*, vol. 62, no. 4, 2017, pp. 18–24.

Igartua, José E. *The Other Quiet Revolution: National Identities in English Canada, 1945-71*. UBC Press, 2006.

Innes, Robert Alexander. "John A. Macdonald Should Not Be Forgotten, nor Celebrated." *The Conversation*, 13 Aug. 2018, https://theconversation.com/john-a-macdonald-should-not-be-forgotten-nor-celebrated-101503. Accessed 23 Feb. 2020.

Isbister, Alexander Kennedy, et al. *A Few Words on the Hudson's Bay Company; with a Statement on the Grievances of the Native and Half-Caste Indians, Addressed to the British Government through Their Delegates Now in London*. C. Gilpin, 1847.

Johnson, Chris. "Riel in Canadian Drama." *Images of Louis Riel in Canadian Culture*, edited by Ramon Hathorn and Patrick Holland, Edwin Mellen Press, 1992, pp. 175–210.

Karr, Jack, Herbert Whittaker, Vincent Tovell, and John Coulter. "John Coulter: Riel." *Canadian Drama and the Critics*, edited by L.W. Conolly, Talonbooks, 1987, pp. 19–28.

Kaye, Frances W. "Any Important Form: Louis Riel in Sculpture." *Prairie Forum*, vol. 22, no. 1, 1997, pp. 103–33.

Kaye, Frances W. *Hiding the Audience: Viewing Arts and Arts Institutions on the Prairies*. University of Alberta Press, 2003.

Keith, W.J. *Epic Fiction: The Art of Rudy Wiebe*. University of Alberta Press, 1981.

Kennedy, Roderick, et al. "Petition of Inhabitants and Natives of the Settlement Situated on the Red River, in the Assiniboin Country, British North America. To the Honourable the Legislative Assembly of the Province of

Canada..., 1857." *The Prairie West to 1905: A Canadian Sourcebook*, edited by Lewis G. Thomas et al., Oxford University Press, 1975, pp. 59–61.

Kertzer, J.M. "Biocritical Essay." *The Rudy Wiebe Papers: First Accession*, edited by Jean F. Tener, Sandra Mortensen, Marlys Chevrefils, and Apollonia Steele, University of Calgary Press, 1926, pp. ix–xxvi.

Kertzer, Jonathan. *Worrying the Nation: Imagining a National Literature in English Canada*. University of Toronto Press, 1998.

Kittredge, William. "Introduction." *Montana: High, Wide, and Handsome*, by Joseph Kinsey Howard. 1943. University of Nebraska Press, 2003, pp. v–xi.

Knox, H. C. "Riel Memorial." *Winnipeg Tribune*, 24 Dec. 1948, p. 4, https://digitalcollections.lib.umanitoba.ca/islandora/object/uofm:1864759. Accessed 7 Feb. 2020.

Koncan, Frances. *Women of the Fur Trade*. 2020. Playwrights Canada Press, 2022.

Kroetsch, Robert. "Disunity as Unity: A Canadian Strategy." *The Lovely Treachery of Words: Essays Selected and New*, Oxford University Press, 1989, pp. 21–33.

Kroetsch, Robert. "Waiting for Riel." Review of *The Life of Louis Riel*, by Peter Charlebois, *NeWest Review*, vol. 1, no. 9, 1976, p. 3.

Krueger, Alice. "MMF Pulls Rug Out from under Riel Artist." *Winnipeg Free Press*, 3 May 1995, p. B1.

Kundera, Milan. *The Book of Laughter and Forgetting*. Translated by Aaron Asher, Perennial Classics, 1999.

Lalonde, Catherine. "Une grande scène pour l'art autochtone." *Le Devoir*, 1 May 2019, https://www.ledevoir.com/culture/553315/mot-cle-une-grande-scene-pour-l-art-autochtone. Accessed 7 Feb. 2020.

Langager, Ross. "History in the Gutters: A Critical Examination of Chester Brown's Louis Riel." 2006. University of Alberta, Master's thesis.

LaRocque, Emma. *When the Other Is Me: Native Resistance Discourse, 1850–1990*. University of Manitoba Press, 2010.

LaRocque [LaRoque], Emma, and Robert Enright. "Standing-in-Between: A Conversation with Métis Writer Emma LaRoque." *Arts Manitoba: A Quarterly Review of the Arts*, vol. 4, no. 3, 1985, pp. 45–46.

Laurier, Wilfrid. "To Build a Nation." 1886. *Louis Riel: Rebel of the Western Frontier or Victim of Politics and Prejudice?*, edited by Hartwell Bowsfield, Copp Clark Publishing, 1969, pp. 215–20.

Lavallée, Guy. *Prayers of a Métis Priest: Conversations with God on the Political Experiences of the Canadian Métis, 1992–1994*, Self-published, 1997.

Le Chevallier, Jules. "Aux Prises avec la tourmente: Les missionaires de la Colonie de Saint-Laurent-de Grandin durant l'insurrection métisse de 1885." *Batoche: Les missionaires du Nord-Ouest pendant les troubles de 1885*. Oeuvre de presse dominicaine, 1941, pp. 1–76.

Le Chevallier, Jules. *Batoche: Les missionaires du Nord-Ouest pendant les troubles de 1885*. Oeuvre de presse dominicaine, 1941.

Lee, Dennis. *Civil Elegies and Other Poems*. Anansi, 1972.

Lee, Sook-Yin. "My Book of the Year." *Globe and Mail*, 31 Dec. 2011, p. 18.

Legault, Stephen. *The Third Riel Conspiracy*. Touchwood Editions, 2013.

Lehman, Timothy. "Wrong Side Up: Joseph Kinsey Howard and the Wisdom of the Dispossessed." *Regionalists on the Left: Radical Voices from the American West*, edited by Michael C. Steiner, University of Oklahoma Press, 2013, pp. 209–27.

Leman, Dilys. *The Winter Count*. McGill-Queen's University Press, 2014.

Leonard, David W. "Introduction: Charles Mair and the Settlement of 1899." *Through the Mackenzie Basin: An Account of the Signing of Treaty No. 8 and the Scrip Commission, 1899* [1908], by Charles Mair, University of Alberta Press, 1999, pp. xv-xl.

Lesk, Andrew. "Redrawing Nationalism: Chester Brown's *Louis Riel*: A Comic Strip Biography." *Journal of Graphic Novels and Comics*, vol. 1, no. 1, 2010, pp. 63–81.

Lilburn, Tim. *The House of Charlemagne*. University of Regina Press, 2018.

Littmann, S.K. "A Pathography of Louis Riel." *Canadian Psychiatric Association Journal*, vol. 23, no. 7, 1978, pp. 449–62.

Loring, Kevin. "We Are Awake: Kevin Loring on Indigenous Theatre at the National Arts Centre." *Professional Association of Canadian Theatres*, 22 Mar. 2018, https://pact.ca/we-are-awake-kevin-loring. Accessed 7 Feb. 2020.

Louis Riel. Music by Harry Somers, libretto by Mavor Moore and Jacques Languirand, directed by Franz Kraemer, conducted by Victor Feldbrill, performed by Bernard Turgeon, Donald Rutherford, Joseph Rouleau, Patricia Rideout, Mary Morrison, and Roxolana Roslak, 1969. Centrediscs, 2011.

"Louis Riel." *Western Canadiana Publications Project Newsletter*, no. 17, Sept. 1985, pp. 1–2.

Low, Tim. "Metis to Regain Lost Spirit." *New Breed*, vol. 16, no. 3, 1985, pp. 4–5.

Lower, Arthur R.M. *Colony to Nation: A History of Canada*. Revised ed., Longmans Canada, 1964.

MacBeth, R.G. *The Making of the Canadian West: Being the Reminiscences of an Eye-Witness*. 1898. Coles Publishing, 1973.

Macdonald, John. *Correspondence of Sir John Macdonald: Selections from the Correspondence of the Right Honourable Sir John Alexander Macdonald, G.C.B., First Prime Minister of the Dominion of Canada*, edited by Joseph Pope, Oxford University Press, 1921.

Macdonald, John. "Half-Breed Claims." 1885. *Louis Riel: Rebel of the Western Frontier or Victim of Politics and Prejudice?*, edited by Hartwell Bowsfield, Copp Clark Publishing, 1969, pp. 124–25.

Macdonald, John. Letter to Alexandre-Antonin Taché, 16 Feb. 1870. *Memoirs of the Right Honourable Sir John Alexander Macdonald, G.C.B., First Prime Minister of the Dominion of Canada*, by Joseph Pope. 1894. Musson Book Company, 1930, pp. 750–51.

Macdonald, John. Letter to William McDougall, 20 Nov. 1869. *Memoirs of the Right Honourable Sir John Alexander Macdonald, G.C.B., First Prime Minister of the Dominion of Canada*, by Joseph Pope. 1894. Musson Book Company, 1930, pp. 407–09.

MacDonald, Tanis. "Voice of the Gutter: Comics in the Academy." *From Text to Txting: New Media in the Classroom*, edited by Clint Burnham and Paul Vincent Budra, Indiana University Press, 2012, pp. 41–68.

Machado de Assis, Joaquim Maria. *The Posthumous Memoirs of Brás Cubas*. 1881. Translated by Gregory Rabassa, Oxford University Press, 1997.

MacLeod, Margaret Arnett, editor. *Songs of Old Manitoba, with Airs, French and English Words, and Introductions*. Ryerson Press, 1960.

Macleod, R.C. "Introduction." *Reminiscences of a Bungle by One of the Bunglers and Two Other Northwest Rebellion Diaries*, edited by R.C. Macleod, University of Alberta Press, 1983, pp. xi–xlix.

Mailhot, Philippe. "The Priest Who Shaped a Province." *Canada's History*, vol. 99, no. 5, pp. 20–27.

Malakieh, Jamil. "Adult and Youth Correctional Statistics in Canada, 2017/2018." *Juristat*, 9 May 2019, https://www150.statcan.gc.ca/n1/pub/85-002-x/2019001/article/00010-eng.htm. Accessed 14 Mar. 2020.

Mallet, Edmond. "Appendix F: Letter to [Ferdinand] Gagnon, 24 Aug. 1885." *The Blood of Abel*, by Wilbur F. Bryant, Gazette-Journal Company, 1887, pp. 162–64.

Maly, Stephen. "Helena is missing an opportunity to capitalize on Canadian visitors." *helenair.com*, 17 Jan. 2020, https://helenair.com/opinion/columnists/helena-is-missing-an-opportunity-to-capitalize-on-canadian-visitors/article_140a165a-73c7-5b37-82b8-d9705e37bb6c.html. Accessed 13 Nov. 2020.

"The Man They Could Not Hang..." *At Guelph*, vol. 29, no. 38, 7 Nov. 1985, pp. 1–2, https://atrium.lib.uoguelph.ca/xmlui/bitstream/handle/10214/12507/ug_atguelphvol29_issue38_1985.pdf?sequence=1&isAllowed=y. Accessed 14 Apr. 2020.

Manitoba Government. "Assiniboine River Walkway Project Completion Announced," 12 May 1994, https://news.gov.mb.ca/news/

archives/1994/05/1994-05 assiniboine_river_walkway_project_
completion_announced.pdf. Accessed 6 Feb. 2020.

Manitoba Government. "New Louis Riel Statue." 12 May 1995, https://news.gov.mb.ca/news/archives/1994/05/1994-05-12-new_louis_riel_statue.pdf. Accessed 6 Feb. 2020.

Manitoba Government. "Riel Statue Design Chosen," 15 May 1970, https://news.gov.mb.ca/news/archives/1970/05/1970-05-15-riel_statue_design_chosen.pdf. Accessed 17 Sept. 2019.

Manitoba Government. "Riel Statue Is Unveiled," 30 Dec. 1971, https://news.gov.mb.ca/news/archives/1971/12/1971-12-30-riel_statue_is_unveiled.pdf. Accessed 4 Feb. 2020.

Manitoba Historical Society. "Historic Sites of Manitoba: Scott Memorial Orange Hall (216 Princess Street, Winnipeg)," www.mhs.mb.ca/docs/sites/scottmemorialhall.shtml. Accessed 16 Feb. 2020.

Manitoba Historical Society. "Historic Sites of Manitoba: The Volunteer Monument (Main Street, Winnipeg)," www.mhs.mb.ca/docs/sites/volunteermonument.shtml. Accessed 13 Feb. 2023.

Marchand, Philip. "Extraordinary Canadians." *Walrus*, 12 Apr. 2009, https://thewalrus.ca/2009-04-books. Accessed 26 Aug. 2019.

Martel, Gilles. "Introduction." *Collected Writings*, by Louis Riel, vol. 2, University of Alberta Press, 1985, pp. xxxiii–l.

Martel, Gilles. "Review of *Louis Riel: la fin d'un rêve* [*The Scorched-Wood People*], by Rudy Wiebe." *Recherches Sociographiques*, vol. 27, no. 2, 1986, pp. 320–21.

Martin, Ged. "Archival Evidence and John A. Macdonald Biography." *Journal of Historical Biography*, vol. 1, 2017, pp. 79–115.

Marx, Anthony W. *Faith in Nation: Exclusionary Origins of Nationalism*. Oxford University Press, 2003.

Mattes, Catherine. "David Garneau's Métis Self and I: A Work in Progress." *David Garneau Online Portfolio: What They Say*, 2003, http://uregina.ca/~garneaud/whattheysay_1.html. Accessed 18 Sept. 2020.

Mattes, Catherine. "Rielisms." *Rielisms*. Winnipeg Art Gallery, 2001, pp. 12–22.

Mattes, Catherine. "Whose Hero? Images of Louis Riel in Contemporary Art and Métis Nationhood." 1998. Concordia University, Master's thesis, http://www.collectionscanada.gc.ca/obj/s4/f2/dsk3/ftp04/mq43534.pdf. Accessed 2 Nov. 2017.

Maunder, Mike. "Riel Statue Unveiled at Legislature." *Winnipeg Tribune*, 3 Dec. 1971, pp. 1–2.

Mayer, Lorraine. "Negotiating a Different Terrain: Geographical and Educational Cross-Border Difficulties." *Across Cultures / Across Borders: Canadian Aboriginal and Native American Literatures*, edited by Paul

DePasquale, Renate Eigenbrod, and Emma LaRocque, Broadview Press, 2010, pp. 97–107.

Mayer, Lorraine. "The Survival of Métis Women: Through Poetry." *Histoires et identités métisses: hommage à Gabriel Dumont/ Métis Histories and Identities: Homage to Gabriel Dumont*, edited by Denis Gagnon, Denis Combet, and Lise Gaboury-Diallo, Presses universitaires de Saint-Boniface, 2009, pp. 341–63.

McCardle, Bennett. "Review of *The Collected Writings of Louis Riel / Les écrits complets de Louis Riel.*" *Archivaria*, vol. 24, 1987, pp. 139–44, https://archivaria.ca/index.php/archivaria/article/view/11422/12364. Accessed 7 Mar. 2017.

McCloud, Scott. *Understanding Comics*. Kitchen Sink Press, 1993.

McClung, Nellie L. *Clearing in the West: My Own Story*. 1965. Thomas Allen and Son, 1976.

McCrady, David G. "Louis Riel and Sitting Bull's Sioux: Three Lost Letters." *Prairie Forum*, vol. 32, no. 2, 2007, pp. 223–34.

McCullough, Alan. "Parks Canada and the 1885 Rebellion/Uprising/Resistance." *Prairie Forum*, vol. 27, no. 2, 2002, pp. 161–97.

McDougall, John. *Pathfinding on Plain and Prairie: Stirring Scenes of Life in the Canadian North-West*. William Briggs, 1898.

McLachlin, Beverley. "Louis Riel: Patriot Rebel." *Manitoba Law Journal*, vol. 35, no. 1, pp. 1–13, http://uoftmusicicm.ca/wp-content/uploads/2017/04/McLachlin-Riel_Patriot_Rebel-Manitoba-Law-Journal-351-2011.pdf. Accessed 25 Mar. 2019.

McLean, Don. *1885: Metis Rebellion or Government Conspiracy?* Pemmican Publications, 1985.

"Metis Head Critical of Riel Statue." *Winnipeg Tribune*, 12 Jan. 1972, p. 53, https://digitalcollections.lib.umanitoba.ca/islandora/object/uofm%3A2418304. Accessed 16 Feb. 2020.

Metzger, Bruce M. "Literary Forgeries and Canonical Pseudepigrapha." *Journal of Biblical Literature*, vol. 91, no. 1, 1972, pp. 3–24.

Miller, J.R. "From Riel to the Métis." 1988. *Reflections on Native-Newcomer Relations: Selected Essays*, University of Toronto Press, 2004, pp. 37–57.

Mitchell, Linda. "One Sculptor's Racy Revenge with an Embarrassingly Real Riel." *Maclean's*, vol. 82, no. 5, May 1969, p. 2.

Mitchell, W.O. "The Riddle of Louis Riel," Part 1. *Maclean's*, vol. 65, no. 3, 1 Feb. 1952, pp. 7–9, 43, 45.

Moissac, Élisabeth de. "Les Soeurs Grises et les événements de 1869–1870." *Sessions d'étude*, vol. 37, 1970, pp. 215–28.

Moore, Brian. *The Luck of Ginger Coffey*. McClelland and Stewart, 1972.

Moore, Mavor. *Reinventing Myself*. Stoddart Publishing, 1994.

Moore, Mavor. "Riel." Letter to the Editor. *Globe and Mail*, 23 Jan. 1975, p. 7.

Moore, Mavor. "The Theme Is Timeless." 1967. *Opera Canada*, vol. 62, no. 4, 2017, pp. 28-29.

Moore, Mavor, with Jacques Languirand. *Louis Riel*. Composed by Harry Somers, 1967, Toronto: Canadian Opera Company.

Moore, Terence. "Manitoba's Revised Statues." *Winnipeg Free Press*, 17 May 1993, p. A6.

Morice, Adrien-Gabriel. "Louis Riel." 1908. Boileau *Louis Riel et les troubles du Nord-Ouest: De la Rivière-Rouge à Batoche*, edited by Gilles Boileau, Éditions du Méridien, 2000, pp. 179-91.

Morice, Adrien-Gabriel. *La race métisse: étude critique en marge d'un livre récent*. Chez l'Auteur, 1938.

Morison, Scot, with Comments by Rudy Wiebe. "The Annotated Rudy Wiebe." *New Trail*, vol. 72, no. 2, 2016, pp. 18-27.

Morisset, Jean. "Louis Riel, écrivain des Amériques." *Nuit blanche*, vol. 18, 1987, pp. 59-63.

Morisset, Jean. "Postface: Louis Riel, écrivain des Amériques." *Louis Riel: Poèmes Amériquains*, by Mathias Carvalho, Éditions Trois-Pistoles, 1997, pp. 61-111.

Morrison, Sheila Jones. *Rotten to the Core: The Politics of the Manitoba Métis Federation*. J. Gordon Shillingford Publishing, 1995.

Morton, Desmond. "Introduction." *Queen v Louis Riel*. 1885, edited by Morton, University of Toronto Press, 1974, pp. vii-xxxv.

Morton, Desmond. "Is History Another Word for Experience? Morton's Confessions." *Canadian Historical Review*, vol. 92, no. 4, 2011, pp. 666-93.

Morton, Desmond. "Reflections on the Image of Louis Riel a Century after." *Images of Louis Riel in Canadian Culture*, edited by Ramon Hathorn and Patrick Holland, Edwin Mellen Press, 1992, pp. 47-62.

Morton, W.L. "The Battle at the Grand Coteau, July 13 and 14, 1851." *Historical Essays on the Prairie Provinces*, edited by Donald Swainson, McClelland and Stewart, 1970, pp. 45-59.

Morton, W.L. "Review of *Louis "David" Riel: "Prophet of the New World"* by Thomas Flanagan." *Canadian Historical Review*, vol. 12, no. 3, 1980, p. 162.

Mosionier, Beatrice. "April, Cheryl and Me." *Across Cultures / Across Borders: Canadian Aboriginal and Native American Literatures*, edited by Paul DePasquale, Renate Eigenbrod, and Emma LaRocque, Broadview Press, 2010, pp. 139-42.

Mosionier, Beatrice. *In Search of April Raintree*. 1983. Peguis Publishers, 1992.

Motut, Roger. "La langue écrite de Louis Riel et quelques aspects de la langue parlée par les Métis." *Collected Writings*, by Louis Riel, vol. 5, University of Alberta, 1985, pp. 47-60.

Mullin, Barry. "New Statues of Riel to Better Serve Legacy." *Winnipeg Free Press*, 23 Apr. 1986, p. 2.

Mumford, Jeremy Ravi. "Why Was Louis Riel, a United States Citizen, Hanged as a Traitor in 1885?" *Canadian Historical Review*, vol. 88, no. 2, 2007, pp. 237–62.

Murray, Annie. Email to Author. 17 Apr 2023.

Needler, G.H. *The Battleford Column: Versified Memories of a Queen's Own Corporal in the Northwest Rebellion 1885*. Provincial Publishing, 1957.

"New Louis Riel Opera Has Its World Premiere Saturday with Regina Symphony." *Winnipeg Sun*, 8 Mar. 2019, https://winnipegsun.com/news/news-news/new-louis-riel-opera-has-its-world-premiere-saturday-with-regina-symphony. Accessed 14 Mar. 2019.

Noël, Mélanie. "L'historienne Andrée Désilets n'est plus." *La Tribune numérique*, 18 May 2017, https://www.latribune.ca/actualites/estrie-et-regions/lhistorienne-andree-desilets-nest-plus-330135f53b9fec2576e0839929f49e83. Accessed 23 Dec. 2020.

O'Hagan, Howard. *Tay John*. 1939. New Canadian Library, 1989.

Oosterom, Nelle. "The Mighty Have Fallen." *Canada's History*, vol. 99, no. 3, 2019, pp. 62–66.

Orr, David R. *Encountering Riel*. Stonehouse Publishing, 2017.

Osachoff, Margaret Gail. "Riel on Stage." *Canadian Drama*, vol. 8, no. 2, 1982, pp. 129–44.

Osborne, Brian S. "Corporeal Politics and the Body Politic: The Re-presentation of Louis Riel in Canadian Identity." *International Journal of Heritage Studies*, vol. 8, no. 4, 2002, pp. 303–22.

Osler, E.B. *The Man Who Had to Hang: Louis Riel*. Longmans Green, 1961.

O'Toole, Darren. "Hero. Heretic. Nation Builder." *Canadian Geographic*, Sept./Oct. 2019, pp. 64–69.

Owram, Doug. "The Myth of Louis Riel." 1982. *Louis Riel: Selected Readings*, edited by Hartwell Bowesfield, Copp Clark Pitman, 1988, pp. 11–29. *Louis Riel*, Bowsfield, pp. 11–29.

Owram, Doug. *Promise of Eden: The Canadian Expansionist Movement and the Idea of the West, 1856–1900*. Revised ed., University of Toronto Press, 1992.

Owram, Doug. "The Riel Project: History, Myth, and Money." *Transactions of the Royal Society of Canada*, series 5, vol. 1, 1986, pp. 207–18.

Pannekoek, Frits. "Review of *The Collected Writings of Louis Riel / Les écrits complets de Louis Riel*." *Prairie Forum*, vol. 11, no. 1, 1986, pp. 120–23.

Pannekoek, Frits. *A Snug Little Flock: The Social Origins of the Riel Resistance 1869–70*. Watson and Dwyer, 1991.

Paquette, Claude. *Jacques Languirand: Biographie*. Libre Expression, 1998.

Parker-Jervis, N. Letter to George F.G. Stanley, 3 Nov. 1976. University of Alberta Archives, Louis Riel Project, Accession No. 84-95. Box 1, No. 14, 2 p.

Parker-Jervis, N. "The Western Canadiana Publications Project at the University of Alberta." *Papers of the Bibliographical Society of Canada*, vol. 17, 1978, pp. 49-52, https://jps.library.utoronto.ca/index.php/bsc/article/view/17258/14198. Accessed 3 Mar. 2019.

Payment, Diane. "Un autre son de cloche." *La Liberté*, 24 July 2013, p. 5, http://peel.library.ualberta.ca.login.ezproxy.library.ualberta.ca/newspapers/LBT/2013/07/24A/5. Accessed 29 Mar. 2021.

Payment, Diane. "'La vie en rose'? Métis Women at Batoche, 1870 to 1920." *Women of the First Nations: Power, Wisdom, and Strength*, edited by Christine Miller et al., University of Manitoba Press, 1996, pp. 19-37.

Peel, Bruce. *Early Printing in the Red River Settlement, 1859-1870, and Its Effect on the Riel Rebellion*. Peguis Publishers, 1974.

Peel, Bruce. "Falcon, Pierre." *Dictionary of Canadian Biography*, vol. 10, University of Toronto / Université Laval, 2003, http://www.biographi.ca/en/bio/falcon_pierre_10E.html. Accessed 8 Apr. 2020.

Perry, Adele. "Nation, Empire and the Writing of History in Canada in English." *Contesting Clio's Craft: New Directions and Debates in Canadian History*, edited by Christopher Dummitt and Michael Dawson, Institute for the Study of the Americas, 2009, pp. 123-40.

Pincus-Witten, Robert. *John Nugent: Modernism in Isolation*. Norman Mackenzie Art Gallery, 1983.

Poitras, Edward. "House of Charlemagne." *Close Encounters: The Next 500 Years*, edited by Candice Hopkins et al., Plug In Editions, 2011, pp. 116-18.

Pope, Joseph. *Memoirs of the Right Honourable Sir John Alexander Macdonald, G.C.B., First Prime Minister of the Dominion of Canada*. 1894. Musson Book Company, 1930.

Preliminary Investigation and Trial of Ambroise D. Lepine for the Murder of Thomas Scott, Being a full report of the proceedings in this case before the Magistrates' Court and several Courts of Queen's Bench in the Province of Manitoba. Reported and compiled by [George B.] Elliott and [Frederick] Brokovski, Burland-Desbarats Lithographic Company, 1874.

Prince, Henry. "Letter from an Indian Chief[,] Indian Settlement, Red River." 26 Mar. 1870. *Embedded: Two Journalists, a Burlesque Star, and the Expedition to Oust Louis Riel*, by Ted Glenn, Dundurn, 2020, pp. 107-09.

"The Proceedings in the Convention, February 3 to February 5, 1870." *Manitoba: The Birth of a Province*, edited by W.L. Morton, Manitoba Record Society Publications, vol. 1, 1965, pp. 5-24.

A Prophet in Exile: Louis Riel's Sojourn in Montana. Written, produced, and videographed by Stephen Maly, Helena Civic Television, 2011, 46:36, https://www.youtube.com/watch?v=zcTQhTBw7nQ. Accessed 12 Feb. 2020.

Puxley, Chinta. "Calling Louis Riel a 'Villain' Lands Conservative MP in Hot Water." *Globe and Mail*, 19 Feb. 2010. https://www.theglobeandmail.com/news/politics/calling-louis-riel-a-villain-lands-conservative-mp-in-hot-water/article4180143/. Accessed 24 May 2023.

Queen v Louis Riel. 1885. Edited by Desmond Morton, University of Toronto Press, 1974.

Reaume, Geoffrey. "The Place of Mad People and Disabled People in Canadian Historiography: Surveys, Biographies, and Specialized Fields." *Journal of the CHA* [Canadian Historical Association], vol. 28, no. 1, 2017, pp. 277-316.

Reid, Jennifer. *Louis Riel and the Creation of Modern Canada: Mythic Discourse and the Postcolonial State*. University of New Mexico Press, 2008.

Remis, Leonard. "James Ross, 1835-1871: The Life and Times of an English-Speaking Halfbreed in the Old Red River Settlement." 1981. University of Manitoba, Master's thesis, https://mspace.lib.umanitoba.ca/xmlui/handle/1993/3469. Accessed 19 Dec. 2022.

Renan, Ernest, *Qu'est-ce qu'une une nation? / What Is a Nation?* 1882. Translated by Wanda Romer Taylor, Tapir Press, 1996.

Richard, Mark Paul. "'Riel...vivra dans notre histoire': The Response of French Canadians in the United States to Louis Riel's Execution." *Journal of Canadian Studies*, vol. 51, no. 3, 2017, pp. 697-724.

Riel, Louis. *The Collected Writings of Louis Riel / Les écrits complets de Louis Riel*, vol. 1, 29 Dec. 1861-7 Dec. 1875. Edited by Raymond Huel and George F.G. Stanley. University of Alberta Press, 1985.

Riel, Louis. *The Collected Writings of Louis Riel / Les écrits complets de Louis Riel*, vol. 2, 8 Dec. 1875-4 June 1884. Edited by Gilles Martel and George F.G. Stanley. University of Alberta Press, 1985.

Riel, Louis. *The Collected Writings of Louis Riel / Les écrits complets de Louis Riel*, vol. 3, 5 June 1884-16 Nov. 1885. Edited by Thomas Flanagan and George F.G. Stanley. University of Alberta Press, 1985.

Riel, Louis. *The Collected Writings of Louis Riel / Les écrits complets de Louis Riel*, vol. 4, Poetry / Poésie. Edited by Glen Campbell and George F.G. Stanley. University of Alberta Press, 1985.

Riel, Louis. *The Collected Writings of Riel / Les écrits complets de Louis Riel*, vol. 5, Reference / Référence. Edited by George F.G. Stanley, Thomas Flanagan, and Claude Rocan. University of Alberta Press, 1985.

Riel, Louis. *The Diaries of Louis Riel*. Edited and translated by Thomas Flanagan. Hurtig Publishers, 1976.

Riel, Louis. "Letter to Eustache Prudhomme [Prud'homme], 14 Dec. 1869." "Newly Discovered Writings by Louis Riel," by Glen Campbell and Tom Flanagan. *Metis in Canada: History, Identity, Law and Politics*, edited by Christopher Adams, Gregg Dahl, and Ian Peach, University of Alberta Press, 2013, pp. 266–68.

Riel, Louis. "Letter to Julie Riel, 9 Aug. 1882." "Updating *The Collected Writings of Louis Riel*," by Thomas Flanagan and Glen Campbell. *From Rupert's Land to Canada: Essays in Honour of John E. Foster*, edited by Theodore Binnema, Gerhard J. Ens, and R.C. Macleod, University of Alberta Press, 2001, pp. 278–83.

Riel, Louis. "Letters to Henry Moore Black, 1880." "Louis Riel and Sitting Bull's Sioux: Three Lost Letters," by David G. McCrady. *Prairie Forum*, vol. 32, no. 2, 2007, pp. 227–31.

Riel, Louis. *Selected Poetry of Louis Riel*. Translated by Paul Savoie and edited by Glen Campbell, Exile Editions, 1993.

Riel, Louis. "Song of the Métis Maiden." Translated by L. Verrault. *Songs of Old Manitoba, with Airs, French and English Words, and Introductions*, edited by Margaret Arnett MacLeod, Ryerson Press, 1960, pp. 54–55.

Riel, Sara. "Letters." *To Louis, from Your Sister who Loves You, Sara Riel*, by Mary V. Jordan, translated by Rossel Vien, Griffin House, 1974.

Robin, Martin. "Introduction." *Strange Empire: Louis Riel and the Métis People*, by Joseph Kinsey Howard, James Lewis and Samuel, 1970, pp. 3–10.

Rocan, Claude. "Images of Riel in Contemporary School Textbooks." *Images of Louis Riel in Canadian Culture*, edited by Ramon Hathorn and Patrick Holland, Edwin Mellen Press, 1992, pp. 93–126.

Rocan, Claude. "Letter to George Stanley, 8 Dec. 1983." University of Alberta Archives, Louis Riel Project, Accession No. 84-95. Box 2, No. 18, 1p.

Roeder, Richard B. "Joseph Kinsey Howard: His Vision of the West." *Montana: The Magazine of Western History*, 30, no. 1, 1980, pp. 2–11.

Ross, Alexander. *The Red River Settlement: Its Rise, Progress, and Present State, with Some Account of the Native Races and Its General History to the Present Day*. 1856. Hurtig Publishers, 1972

Ross, James. "A Notebook of James Ross, December 1 to December 14, 1869." *Manitoba: The Birth of a Province*, edited by W.L. Morton, Manitoba Record Society Publications, vol. 1, 1965, pp. 436–45.

Roux, Jean-Louis. *Bois-Brûlés*. Éditions du Jour, 1968.

Russell, Frances. *The Canadian Crucible: Manitoba's Role in Canada's Great Divide*. Heartland Associates, 2003.

Salhany, Roger E. *A Rush to Judgment: The Unfair Trial of Louis Riel*. Dundurn, 2019.

Saul, John Ralston. *A Fair Country: Telling Truths about Canada*. 2008. Penguin Canada, 2009.

Saul, John Ralston. "Introduction." *Louis Riel and Gabriel Dumont*, by Joseph Boyden. Penguin Canada, 2010, pp. ix-xiv.

Saunders, Kelly L. "Métis Political Identity and the Symbolism of Louis Riel." *The Politics of Popular Culture: Negotiating Power, Identity, and Place*, edited by Tim Nieguth, McGill-Queen's University Press, 2015, pp. 65-82.

Schafer, R. Murray. *The Public of the Music Theatre—Louis Riel: A Case Study*. Universal Edition, 1972.

Schmidt, Louis. "Memoirs of Louis Schmidt, Secretary of the First Provisional Government, Chapter 5, 1868-1870." 1912. *Alexander Begg's Red River Journal and Other Papers Relative to the Red River Resistance of 1869-1870*, edited by W.L. Morton, Champlain Society, 1956, pp. 458-79.

Schultz, Margaret. "Fault Lines: Race and Gender in the Fur Trade Family of Alexander Ross." *Manitoba History*, no. 90, 2019, pp. 13-26.

Scofield, Gregory. *Louis: The Heretic Poems*. Nightwood Editions and Gabriel Dumont Institute, 2011.

Scofield, Gregory. *Thunder through My Veins: Memories of a Métis Childhood*. HarperFlamingoCanada, 1999.

Scofield, Gregory. *Witness, I Am*. Nightwood Editions, 2016.

Scruton, Roger. "Oikophobia." *Journal of Education*, vol. 175, no. 2, 1993, pp. 93-98.

Segato, Gianmarco. "Honouring Indigeneity in *Louis Riel* / Honorer l'indigénéité de *Louis Riel*." Louis Riel Program, National Arts Centre, 15 and 17 June 2017, pp. 16-18.

Senie, Harriet F. *Contemporary Public Sculpture: Tradition, Transformation, and Controversy*. Oxford University Press, 1992.

Sestak, Bessie. "Joseph Kinsey Howard Bibliography." *Montana: The Magazine of Western History*, vol. 2, no. 2, 1952, pp. 44-47.

Seth. "Foreword." *Invaders from the North: How Canada Conquered the Comic Book Universe*, by John Bell. Dundurn Group, 2006, pp. 9-10.

Shaw, Edward Charles. "Kennedy, William." *Dictionary of Canadian Biography*, vol. 11. University of Toronto / Université Laval, 1982, http://www.biographi.ca/en/bio/kennedy_william_11F.html. Accessed 24 Dec. 2022.

Sickert, Sophie J. "From Controversy to Celebration: How the 1995 Relocation of Marcien Lemay's Riel from the Manitoba Legislature to Saint Boniface Impacted Its Public Reception." University of Winnipeg's Institute of Urban Studies, Student Paper 35, 2022, pp. 1-18. https://winnspace.uwinnipeg.ca/handle/10680/2001. Accessed 23 May 2023.

Siggins, Maggie. *Riel: A Life of Revolution*. 1994. HarperPerennial, 1995.

"Silver Coin Marks 175th Anniversary of Louis Riel's Birth." *Canadian Coin Notes*, 22 Oct. 2019, https://canadiancoinnews.com/silver-coin-marks-175th-anniversary-of-louis-riels-birth. Accessed 20 Aug. 2020.

Simonot-Maiello, Colette. "'Decolonizing' Riel." *University of Toronto Quarterly*, vol. 87, no. 4, 2018, pp. 73–82.

Sinclair, Murray. "Senators' Statements—Reconciliation through the Arts." Senate of Canada, 2 May 2019, https://sencanada.ca/en/senators/sinclair-murray/interventions/521565/7. Accessed 22 Feb. 2020.

Sinclair, Niigaanwewidam James, and Warren Cariou. "Introduction." *Manitowapow: Aboriginal Writings from the Land of Water*, edited by Sinclair and Cariou, Highwater Press, 2011, pp. 1–6.

Smith, Donald A. "Donald A. Smith's Report." 12 Apr. 1870. *Manitoba: The Birth of a Province*, edited by W.L. Morton, Manitoba Record Society Publications, vol. 1, 1965, pp. 25–45.

Smith, Donald B. *Honoré Jaxon: Prairie Visionary*. Coteau Books, 2007.

Smith, Doug. "Remembering Riel." *Canadian Dimension*, vol. 28, no. 5, 1994, p. 4.

Somers, Harry. "Harry Somers on the Score." 1967. *Opera Canada*, vol. 62, no. 4, 2017, pp. 25–27.

Somers, Harry. *Secret Agent: The Selected Journals and Letters of Harry Somers*, edited by William Scoular, N. pub, 2009.

Sperdakos, Paula. *Dora Mavor Moore: Pioneer of the Canadian Theatre*. ECW Press, 1995.

Spinoza, Benedict de. *Ethics*. 1678. Edited and translated by Edwin Curley. Penguin Books, 1996.

Sprague, D.N. *Canada and the Métis, 1869–1885*. Wilfrid Laurier University Press, 1988.

Stanley, George F.G. *The Birth of Western Canada: A History of the Riel Rebellions*. 1936. University of Toronto Press, 1992.

Stanley, George F.G. "Foreword." *Collected Writings*, by Louis Riel, vol. 1, University of Alberta Press, 1985, pp. xxi–xxiv.

Stanley, George F.G. "General Editor's Remarks." *Collected Writings*, by Louis Riel vol. 5, University of Alberta Press, 1985, pp. 1–22.

Stanley, George F.G. "The Last Word on Louis Riel—The Man of Several Faces." 1986. *Louis Riel: Selected Readings*, edited by Hartwell Bowsfield, Copp Clark Pitman, 1988, pp. 42–60.

Stanley, George F.G. Letter [1] to Thomas Flanagan, 12 Dec. 1983. University of Alberta Archives, Louis Riel Project, Accession No. 84-95. Box 2, No. 18, 2 pp.

Stanley, George F.G. Letter [2] to Thomas Flanagan, 29 Dec. 1983. University of Alberta Archives, Louis Riel Project, Accession No. 84-95. Box 2, No. 18, 2 pp.

Stanley, George F.G. Letter to N. Parker-Jervis. 17 May 1976. University of Alberta Archives, Louis Riel Project, Accession No. 84-95. Box 1, No. 14, 2 pp.

Stanley, George F.G. "Louis Riel." *Revue d'histoire de l'Amérique française*, vol. 18, no. 1, 1964, pp. 14-26.

Stanley, George F.G. *Louis Riel*. Ryerson Press, 1963.

Stanley, George F.G. *Louis Riel: Patriot or Rebel?* Canadian Historical Association, Booklet no. 2, 1954.

Stanley, George F.G. "Review of *Strange Empire: A Narrative of the Northwest*, by Joseph Kinsey Howard." *Canadian Historical Review*, vol. 34, no. 1, 1953, pp. 65-66.

Stanley, George F.G. "The Riel Project." *Louis Riel and the Métis: Riel Mini-Conference Papers*, edited by A.S. Lussier, Pemmican Publications, 1979, pp. 15-18.

Stanley, George F.G. "Statement re Professor Flanagan's Riel and the Rebellion," 6 Dec. 1983. University of Alberta Archives, Louis Riel Project, Accession No. 84-95. Box 2, No. 18, 1 p.

Steele, Harvey. *Dear Old Rebel: A Priest's Battle for Social Justice*. Pottersfield Press, 1993.

Stegner, Wallace. *The Uneasy Chair: A Biography of Bernard DeVoto*. Doubleday, 1974.

Stegner, Wallace. *Wolf Willow: A History, a Story, and a Memory of the Last Plains Frontier*. 1962. Penguin Books, 1990.

Stonechild, Blair, and Bill Waiser. *Loyal till Death: Indians and the North-West Rebellion*. Fifth House Publishers, 1997.

Suzack, Cheryl. *Indigenous Women's Writing and the Cultural Study of Law*. University of Toronto Press, 2017.

Swainson, Donald. "Rieliana and the Structure of Canadian History." 1982. *Louis Riel: Selected Readings*, edited by Hartwell Bowesfield, Copp Clark Pitman, 1988, pp. 30-41.

Sweeny, Alastair. *George-Etienne Cartier: A Biography*. McClelland and Stewart, 1976.

Taché, Alexandre. "Lettre à MM. Louis Riel et Ambroise Lépine." 1872. *Louis Riel et les troubles du Nord-Ouest: De la Rivière-Rouge à Batoche*, edited by Gilles Boileau, Éditions du Méridien, 2000, pp. 204-06.

Taylor, C.J. "Some Early Problems of the Historic Sites and Monuments Board of Canada." *Canadian Historical Review*, vol. 64, no. 1, 1983, pp. 3-24.

Taylor, James Wickes. *The James Wickes Taylor Correspondence, 1859-1870*, edited by Hartwell Bowsfield, Manitoba Record Society Publications, 1968.

Taylor, James Wickes. "Letters of J.W. Taylor from Ottawa, April 19 to May 5, 1870." *Manitoba: The Birth of a Province*, edited by W.L. Morton, Manitoba Record Society Publications, vol. 1, 1965, pp. 47-65.

Tefs, Wayne A. "Rudy Wiebe: Mystery and Reality." *Mosaic: An Interdisciplinary Critical Journal*, vol. 11, no. 4, 1978, pp. 155-58.

Teillet, Jean. "Louis Riel and Canada: A New Relationship, 150 Years in the Making." *Canadian Issues / Thèmes canadiens*, Spring/Summer 2021, pp. 56-60.

Teillet, Jean. *The North-West Is Our Mother: The Story of Louis Riel's People, the Métis Nation*. Patrick Crean Editions, 2019.

Teillet, Jean. "Putting History in a Noose," *Globe and Mail*, 16 Nov. 2010, p. A17.

Teillet, Jean. "The Sermon from the Mount: The Messages in the Canadian Opera Company's Remount of the *Riel* Opera." *University of Toronto Quarterly*, vol. 87, no. 4, 2018, pp. 29-36.

Teillet, Jean. "The Winds of Change: Métis Rights after *Powley*, *Taku*, and *Haida*." *The Long Journey of a Forgotten People: Métis Identities and Family Histories*, edited by Ute Lischke and David T. McNab, Wilfrid Laurier University Press, 2007, pp. 55-78.

Tétreault, Matthew. "Reading Scofield through Riel: *Louis: The Heretic Poems* as Dissonance." *Studies in Canadian Literature*, vol. 45, no. 1, 2020, pp. 29-48.

Tétreault, Matthew. *Red River Poetics: Toward a Métis Literary History*. 2022. University of Alberta, PHD dissertation.

Thompson, W.P. "Public Sculpture in Winnipeg: A Selective Tale of Outdoor Woe." *Border Crossings*, vol. 5, no. 2, 1985, pp. 10-12.

Tippett, Maria. *Sculpture in Canada: A History*. Douglas and McIntyre, 2017.

Tousley, Nancy. "Chester Brown: Louis Riel's Comic Strip Biographer." *Canadian Art*, vol. 21, no. 23, 2004, pp. 126-29.

Toussaint, Ismène. *Louis Riel, le bison de cristal*. Stanké, 2000.

Toussaint, Ismène. "Présentation." *Louis Riel: journaux de guerre et de prison*, edited by Toussaint, Stanké, 2005, p. 19-30.

Trémaudan, Auguste-Henri de. "The Execution of Thomas Scott." *Canadian Historical Review*, vol. 6, no. 3, 1925, pp. 222-36.

Trémaudan, Auguste-Henri de. *Histoire de la nation métisse dans l'Ouest canadien*. Éditions Albert Lévesque, 1935 [1936].

Trémaudan, Auguste-Henri de. *Hold High Your Heads (History of the Métis Nation in Western Canada)*. Translated by Elizabeth Maguet, Pemmican Publications, 1982.

Trémaudan, Auguste-Henri de. "Louis Riel and the Fenian Raid of 1871." *Canadian Historical Review*, vol. 4, no. 2, 1923, pp. 132-44.

Trudeau, Justin. "Prime Minister Justin Trudeau's Address to the 72th Session of the United Nations General Assembly." 21 Sept. 2017, https://pm.gc.ca/eng/news/2017/09/21/prime-minister-justin-trudeaus-address-72th-session-united-nations-general-assembly. Accessed 29 Oct. 2017.

Trudeau, Justin. "Statement by the Prime Minister on Louis Riel Day," 16 Nov. 2021, https://pm.gc.ca/en/news/statements/2021/11/16/statement-prime-minister-louis-riel-day. Accessed 30 Dec. 2022.

Trudeau, Pierre Elliott. "...with Riel." *PM / Dialogue*, High Hill Publishing House, 1972, pp. 109–11.

Truth and Reconciliation Commission of Canada. *Final Report of the Truth and Reconciliation Commission of Canada, Volume One: Summary—Honouring the Truth, Reconciling for the Future*. James Lorimer, 2015.

Truth and Reconciliation Commission of Canada. *What We Have Learned: Principles of Truth and Reconciliation*. Truth and Reconciliation Commission of Canada, 2015.

Van Kirk, Sylvia. *"Many Tender Ties": Women in Fur-Trade Society, 1670–1870*. Watson and Dwyer Publishing, 1980.

Van Kirk, Sylvia. "'What if Mama is an Indian?' The Cultural Ambivalence of the Alexander Ross Family." *The New Peoples: Being and Becoming Métis in North America*, edited by Jacqueline Peterson and Jennifer S.H. Brown, University of Manitoba Press, 1985, pp. 207–17.

Vermette, Katherena. *river woman*. Anansi, 2018.

Vermette, Katherena. *The Strangers*. Hamish Hamilton, 2021.

Vermette, Katherena, Scott B. Henderson, and Donovan Yaciuk, *Northwest Resistance, A Girl Called Echo*, vol. 3. Highwater Press, 2020.

Vermette, Katherena, Scott B. Henderson, and Donovan Yaciuk. *Red River Resistance, A Girl Called Echo*, vol. 2. Highwater Press, 2018.

Verrette, Michel. "Trémaudan, Auguste-Henri de." *Dictionary of Canadian Biography*, vol. 15, University of Toronto / Université Laval, 2005, http://www.biographi.ca/en/bio/tremaudan_auguste_henri_de_15F.html?print=1. Accessed 15 May 2020.

Voisine, Nive. "Review of *The Collected Writings of Louis Riel / Les écrits complets de Louis Riel*." *University of Toronto Quarterly*, vol. 57, no. 1, 1987, pp. 174–77.

Voth, Daniel. "The Race Question in Canada and the Politics of Racial Mixing." *A People and a Nation: New Directions in Contemporary Métis Studies*, edited by Jennifer Adese and Chris Andersen, UBC Press, 2021, pp. 67–91.

Wade, Mason. *The French Canadians 1760–1967: Volume One 1760–1911*. Laurentian Library, 1975.

Wade, Mason. "Review of *Louis Riel*, by George F.G. Stanley." *Canadian Historical Review*, vol. 46, no. 2, 1965, pp. 152–54.

Walz, Eugene, Diane Payment, and Emma LaRocque [Laroque], "Review: Three Views of Riel." *Manitoba History*, vol. 1, 1981, http://www.mhs.mb.ca/docs/mb_history/01/threeviewsofriel.shtml. Accessed 13 May 2020.

Wayman, Tom. "Canadian Culture: Another Riel Poem." *Event*, vol. 17, no.3, 1988, pp. 30–31.

Weatherbe, Stephen. "Why Louis Riel Had to Die: An Alberta Professor Debunks the Myths and Riles the Metis." *Alberta Report*, vol. 10, no. 50, 5 Dec. 1983, pp. 32–37.

Weekes, Mary, as Told to Her by Norbert Welsh. *The Last Buffalo Hunter*. 1939. Fifth House Publishers, 1994.

Welch, Mary Agnes. "Winnipeg's Hidden (in Plain Sight) Monument: In Conversation with Matthew McRae." *Winnipeg Free Press*, 14 Feb. 2015, https://www.winnipegfreepress.com/local/in-conversation-with-matt-mcrae-291943901.html. Accessed 18 Sept. 2019.

"A Welcome to Our Readers." *Riel Project BULLETIN du Projet Riel*, vol. 1, Apr. 1979, p. 1.

Western Canadiana Publications Projects Committee, et al. Application for a Major Editorial Grant to Publish the Collected Papers of Louis Riel, 22 June 1977. University of Alberta Archives, Louis Riel Project, Accession No. 84-95. Box 1, No. 6, 115 pp.

Western Canadiana Publications Projects Committee, et al. Revised Submission of Application for a Major Editorial Grant to Publish the Collected Papers of Louis Riel, 25 Jan. 1978. University of Alberta Archives, Louis Riel Project, Accession No. 84-95. Box 1, No. 2, 11 pp., plus appendices.

White, Patrick. "Indigenous Women Make up Half of the Female Population in Canada's Federal Prisons." *Globe and Mail*, 5 May 2022, https://www.theglobeandmail.com/canada/article-morning-update-indigenous-women-make-up-half-of-the-female-population. Accessed 5 May 2022.

Wiebe, Rudy. *First and Vital Candle*. 1966. Fitzhenry and Whiteside, 2006.

Wiebe, Rudy. "In the West, Sir John A. Is a Bastard and Riel Is a Saint. Ever Ask Why?" *A Voice in the Land: Essays by and about Rudy Wiebe*, edited by W.J. Keith, NeWest Press, 1981, pp. 209–11.

Wiebe, Rudy. "Louis Riel: The Man They Couldn't Hang." 1992. *River of Stone: Fictions and Memories*, by Rudy Wiebe, Vintage Books, 1995, pp. 188–215.

Wiebe, Rudy. *Of This Earth: A Mennonite Boyhood in the Boreal Forest*. Good Books, 2007.

Wiebe, Rudy. *Peace Shall Destroy Many*. 1962. McClelland and Stewart, 1972.

Wiebe, Rudy. "Riel: A Possible Film Treatment." 1975. *A Voice in the Land: Essays by and about Rudy Wiebe*, edited by W.J. Keith, NeWest Press, 1981, pp. 158–62.

Wiebe, Rudy. *The Scorched-Wood People*. McClelland and Stewart, 1977.

Wiebe, Rudy. "The Skull in the Swamp." 1987. *River of Stone: Fictions and Memories*, by Rudy Wiebe, Vintage Books, 1995, pp. 249–73.

Wiebe, Rudy. "Western Canada Fiction; Past and Future." *Western American Literature*, vol. 6, no. 1, 1971, pp. 21–30.

Wiebe, Rudy. "Where Is the Voice Coming From?" 1971. *River of Stone: Fictions and Memories*, by Rudy Wiebe, Vintage Books, 1995, pp. 27-40.

Wiebe, Rudy, and Brian Bergman. "Rudy Wiebe: Storymaker of the Prairies." 1977. *A Voice in the Land: Essays by and about Rudy Wiebe*, edited by W.J. Keith, NeWest Press, 1981, pp. 163-69.

Wiebe, Rudy, Robert Kroetsch, and Shirley Neuman. "Unearthing Language: An Interview with Rudy Wiebe and Robert Kroetsch." *A Voice in the Land: Essays by and about Rudy Wiebe*, edited by W.J. Keith, NeWest Press, 1981, pp. 226-47.

Wiebe, Rudy, and Eli Mandel. "Where the Voice Comes From." 1974. *A Voice in the Land: Essays by and about Rudy Wiebe*, edited by W.J. Keith, NeWest Press, 1981, pp. 150-55.

Wiebe, Rudy, and George Melnyk. "The Western Canadian Imagination: An Interview with Rudy Wiebe." 1974. *A Voice in the Land: Essays by and about Rudy Wiebe*, edited by W.J. Keith, NeWest Press, 1981, pp. 204-08.

Wiebe, Rudy, Margaret Reimer, and Sue Steiner. "Translating Life into Art: A Conversation with Rudy Wiebe." 1973. *A Voice in the Land: Essays by and about Rudy Wiebe*, edited by W.J. Keith, NeWest Press, 1981, pp. 126-30.

Wiebe, Rudy, [and Claude Rocan]. "An Interview with Rudy Wiebe." *Riel Project* BULLETIN *du Projet Riel*, vol. 6, 1981, pp. 4-5.

Wiebe, Rudy, and Herb Wyile, "Walking Where His Feet Can Walk: Rudy Wiebe." *Speaking in the Past Tense: Canadian Novelists on Writing Historical Fiction*, edited by Herb Wyile, Wilfrid Laurier University Press, 2007, pp. 53-77.

Wilkin, Karen. "Introduction." *A Sculpture Reader: Contemporary Sculpture since 1920*, edited by Glenn Harper and Twylene Moyer, ISC, 2006, pp. 10-12.

Winnipeg Foundation. "Education is the New Bison." 26 June 2020. https://www.wpgfdn.org/arts/education-is-the-new-bison. Accessed 22 May 2023.

Winnipeg Foundation. "Public art piece recognizing importance of education, truth and reconciliation unveiled at The Forks." 25 June 2020. https://www.wpgfdn.org/arts/public-art-piece-recognizing-importance-of-education-truth-and-reconciliation-unveiled-at-the-forks/. Accessed 22 May 2023.

Winslow, Robert. *The Cavan Blazers*. Ordinary Press, 1993.

Woodcock, George. *Gabriel Dumont: The Métis Chief and His Lost World*. Hurtig Publishers, 1975.

Woodcock, George. "Grant, Cuthbert." *Dictionary of Canadian Biography*, vol. 8, University of Toronto / Université Laval, 2003, http://www.biographi.ca/en/bio/grant_cuthbert_1854_8E.html. Accessed 5 Feb. 2021.

Woodcock, George. "Prairie Writers and the Métis: Rudy Wiebe and Margaret Laurence." 1982. *Northern Spring: The Flowering of Canadian Literature*, Douglas and McIntyre, 1987, pp. 94-109.

Woodcock, George. "Riel & Dumont." Review of *The Scorched-Wood People*, by Rudy Wiebe. *Canadian Literature*, no. 77, 1978, pp. 98–100.

Zoran et Toufik. *Louis Riel, le père du Manitoba*. Éditions des Plaines, 1996.

Index

Acoose, Janice, 220, 249, 253
Alacoque, Marguerite-Marie, 10
Alberta Report (magazine), 145
Allard, Jean, 163, 166, 170
Almighty Voice, 104
Andersen, Chris, 250
Anderson, Benedict, xviii
André, Alexis
    accepts LR's adopting name David, 10
    edits "Autobiographical Notes," 4
    entrusted with care of LR's body, 25
    portrayal in *Louis Riel*, 82, 89
    portrayal in *Riel*, 46
    prediction on LR's popularity, 241–42
    sees LR in prison, 34
    treatment of in *Histoire de la nation métisse*, 209
Atwood, Margaret, 74–75, 175
The Audacity of His Enterprise (Hamon), 26–27
"Autobiographical Notes," 3, 4–6, 26

Balfour, Andrew, 242
Barnabé, Évelina, 14–16, 17–18, 227
Barnabé, Fabien, 14, 28, 31
Battle of Seven Oaks, xx, 104–05, 107, 109

Battle of the Grand Coteau, xx, 59
Begg, Alexander, 28
Bell, John, 191
Benjamin, Walter, 108
Berger, Thomas, 37, 118
Bethell, Tom, 196
Big Bear, 100, 237
Bilan, R.P., 107
bilingualism, 75–76, 86–88
Birney, Earle, 123
The Birth of Western Canada (Stanley), 132
Black, Henry, 62
Blodgett, E.D., 89–90, 248
The Blue Mountains of China (Wiebe), 103
Bocquel, Bernard, 205
Bois-Brûlés (Roux), 88
Boss, Allan, 85
Boucher, Louis, 227–28
Boucher, Marguerite, 227
Bourget, Ignace
    appointed by LR as Pope of New World, 36, 208
    and LR's adopting name David, 12
    LR's relationship with, 8–10
    LR's writing on in "Autobiographical Notes," 3
    portrayal in 2017 revival of *Louis Riel*, 95

portrayal in *Louis Riel*, 87
portrayal in *The Scorched-Wood People*, 114, 115
views on nudity, 175
Bouvier, Rita, 201
Bower, Shannon, 169-70, 172, 178
Bowler, Gerry, 172
Bowman, Brian, 172
Boyden, Joseph, 148, 149-50, 182
Boyle, John, 66
Brady, James, 148-49, 251
Brandt, Di, 19
Brown, Chester
    background and affinities with LR, 182-84
    change in his view of LR, 191-92, 195-97
    and *Louis Riel: A Comic-Strip Biography*, 181-82, 185-88, 189-90, 192-93, 197, 198, 199
Brown, Jennifer S.H., 68, 152
Bryant, Wilbur F., 63
Bumsted, J.M., 140

Cain, Stephen, 36
Cameron, Christina, xxv-xxvi
Campbell, Douglas, 162
Campbell, Glen, 13, 128, 134, 176-77
Campbell, Maria
    and artistic prophecy quote, 251, 253
    background, 211
    criticized for Métis particularism, 220
    discomfort with Métis traits, 216
    feelings about LR, 213-15, 216
    and *Halfbreed*, 211-13, 238, 253
    Halfbreed as dominant Métis vision today, 238
    and *Riel's People*, 213-14

    and *Stories of the Road Allowance People*, 214-15
Canada
    acceptance of Métis as Indigenous people, xxii
    appeal of continentalism in, 66-67, 71-72
    belated interest in Canadian plains by, 64-65
    bilingualism of, 75-76
    change of identity after WWII, 74
    and *The Collected Writings of Louis Riel*, 153
    and colonization, 194-95
    contributions of Indigenous peoples to, 90
    J.K. Howard's animus toward, 59
    LR's attitude toward, xxiii, 23-24, 38
    map of in 1867, xv
    M. Moore's narrow vision of, 90
    portrayal of in *Louis Riel* (opera), 79-80
    proclaimed a Métis nation by intellectuals, 147-48
    as real focus of LR memorialization, xxiii-xxiv, 195
    true state of Métis in, 157
    view of border with US, 67-68, 69-71
    view of in *Louis Riel: A Comic-Strip Biography*, 199
Canada, Government of
    acquisition of Rupert's Land, 43
    C. Brown's attitude toward, 186-88, 191-92
    and dilemma regarding trying LR, 111, 122, 232

fear of US as impetus for
  annexation of North-West,
  64–65
and LR amnesty, 77, 91
and MMF funding, 164
and North-West War, xxviii, 188
relationship with Indigenous
  peoples, xxx
relationship with Métis, 157
and seizure of territory, 121. See
  also Macdonald, John A.
Canada Council, 130–31, 132–35, 136,
  137
Canadian cultural intelligentsia,
  65–67, 71, 147–48
Canadianization of Riel. See Riel
  rehabilitation
Canadian Pacific Railway (CPR),
  xxvii–xxviii, 123, 186–88
Cardinal-Schubert, Joane, 249
Cariou, Warren, 252
Caron, Maia, 233–38
Caron, Marguerite D., 235–36
Carrière, Ida, 163
Cartier, George-Étienne
  LR evokes poem of, 21
  LR poems to, 20
  penmanship of, 26
  as perpetrator of North-West
    War, 52
  portrayal in *Louis Riel*, 81
  portrayal in *Riel*, 45
Catholic Church
  importance to LR of, 30, 114–15,
    229–30, 233
  and Julie Riel, 6, 228
  and LR's sainthood, 244
  M. Campbell's rejection of, 212–13
  and Métis history, 208
Cavan Blazers, 50

Chabun, Will, 157
Chalmers, Floyd, 75–76, 100
"La chanson de la Grenouillère," 69,
  104–05, 107
Chapleau, J.A., 111
Charlottetown Festival, 76
Chartrand, David, 26
Chartrand, Paul L.A.H., 2
Cherry, Don, 247
Christianity, 212–13
Christie, Margot, 48
Christie, Robert, 49
"Civil Elegies" (poem), 194
Clark, Joe, xxviii
Clarke, Lawrence, 188
Cleveland, Grover, xxiii, 64, 78
The Collected Writings of Louis Riel
  (Stanley)
  as arbiter of LR's place in history,
    248–49
  and artistic prophecy quote, 249,
    251
  and crisis of publication of *Riel
    and the Rebellion*, 144–47
  decision to limit editorial
    comment in, 143–44
  how they refute how LR is
    portrayed, 147–48
  how unread they are by modern
    scholars, 149–50, 152–53
  photo, 129
  publishing decisions on, 1, 127,
    128, 137–38, 152
  reviews of, 138–44, 150, 152
  what is included in, 135–37
colonization, 194–95
Columbus, Christopher, 37
Constitution Act (1982), xxii
continentalism, 53, 65–66, 71–72
Cook, Ramsay, 245

Coulter, John
- completes trilogy on LR, 51–53
- impact of his play on opera *Louis Riel*, 85–86
- and play *Riel*, 40–51, 67, 108
- and start of LR industry, 48
- *Cowboys and Indians (and Métis?)* (exhibition), 222–23

Coyne, Andrew, 247
The Crime of Louis Riel (Coulter), 52–53
cross-border studies, 56
cultural appropriation, 89, 104
Cusson, Ian, 89
Cuthand, Stan, 135

Dahl, Gregg, 216
Damiani, Joseph, 12
Daniels, Douglas, 36
Daniels, Harry, 90
Daniels, Jo-Ann, 144–45
Deane, Richard B., 32–33, 122, 207
Dear John: Louis David Riel (performance piece), 170–71
Delaronde, Billyjo, 166
Dennis, John S., 67
Désilets, Andrée, 138, 249
Desmeules, Raynald, 51
Devine, Heather, 56, 68–69
"Devotion: Louis Riel Writes Home" (exhibition), 249
DeVoto, Bernard, 54, 55, 68
The Diaries of Louis Riel (Flanagan), 131
Diefenbaker, John, xxviii, xxix
Dominion Institute, 246
Donkin, John, 122
Dorge, Lionel, 164
Douglas, Thomas (Lord Selkirk), 5
Douglas, Tommy, 247

Doyle, David, 66
Dubé, Jean-Pierre, 237, 252
Dubuc, Joseph, 11
Duffy, Dennis, 181
Dumas, Michel, 96
Dumont, Gabriel
- in J. Coulter's plays, 47, 53, 108
- in *Halfbreed*, 212
- lionization of in *Strange Empire*, 70–71
- LR reveals reason for travelling to Batoche to, 34
- modern Métis preference for over LR, 202
- portrayal in 2017 revival of *Louis Riel*, 95
- portrayal in *Louis Riel*, 90–91
- portrayal in *Louis Riel: A Comic-Strip Biography*, 185
- portrayal in *Riel's People*, 214
- portrayal in *Song of Batoche*, 234, 235, 237
- portrayal in *Stories of the Road Allowance People*, 215
- portrayal in *The Pemmican Eaters*, 232
- portrayal in *The Scorched-Wood People*, 108–09, 112, 115–16
- portrayal in *Thunder through My Veins*, 226

Dumont, Guy, 178
Dumont, Madeleine, 234, 237
Dumont, Marilyn, 230–33, 243
Durnin, Katherine, 105

Eberschweiler, Frederick, 9
Elliott, Robin, 90
Empire Étrange (oratorio), 242
Encountering Riel (Orr), 247
Ens, Gerhard, 205

Epp, Darrell, 195–96
Ethics (Spinoza), 236
Évangile de Louis Riel (Dubé), 237–38
Eyland, Cliff, 178

A Fair Country: Telling Truths about Canada (Saul), 124
Falcon, Pierre
    background, 104–05
    and "La chanson de la Grenouillère," 69
    as narrator of The Scorched-Wood People, 104, 105, 123
    omission of in Histoire de la nation métisse, 208
    as oral poet, 107
    portrayal in The Scorched-Wood People, 106–07, 108, 109–10, 115–17, 125–26
    Wiebe's contention P. Falcon wrote The Scorched-Wood People, 105–6
Favell, Rosalie, 221
Feldbrill, Victor, 89
Ferril, Thomas H., 54
First and Vital Candle (Wiebe), 103
First Nations
    and Canadian national identity in opposition to, 194–95
    how they perceived Métis, 118, 220, 231
    J.R. Saul's view of, 124
    LR's feelings towards, xxiii, 21, 93, 239
    M. Campbell's engagement with, 213
    Métis relations with, 93, 97
    as part of LR's identity, 36, 99
    in A Really Good Brown Girl, 231
    representation in North-West War, 79
    in In Search of April Raintree, 217–18, 219, 221
    subjugation of, 29
    treatment of in LR's writing, 60.
    See also Indigenous peoples
Fitzpatrick, Charles, 35–36, 92
Flanagan, Thomas
    and The Diaries of Louis Riel, 131
    on editing of "Autobiographical Notes," 4
    as editor of The Collected Writings of Louis Riel, 139
    F. Pannekoek on, 143
    impact on C. Brown's view of LR, 191–92
    and LR love child, 13–14
    on LR's ambition, 37–38
    on LR's conversations with God, 176
    on memorialization of LR, 40
    publishing of and reaction to Riel and the Rebellion, 144–47
    resistance to LR's pardon, 245
    role in Projet Riel Project, 128, 131, 134
    on Strange Empire, 56
    view of LR's immortality, 99–100
Fox, Rosalea, 55
Franco-Manitoban Cultural Centre, 165
Freynet, Robert, 190–91
Friesen, Gerald, 140–41, 143–44, 150
Funnell, Jeff, 66

Gaboury, Étienne, 162–64
Gaboury, Marie-Anne, 5, 18
Garneau, David
    affinity with LR, 221–22

background, 222
and design of silver dollar, 241
on Lemay's *Louis Riel*, 170–71
and LR's artistic prophecy quote, 249, 252
LR visual art of, 221–25
and M. Campbell, 238
Garneau, Richard, 222, 223
Gaudry, Adam, 148, 157
Gauvreau, Michael, 142, 152, 168
gay-bashing, 169
Gerussi, Bruno, 49
Ghostkeeper, Elmer, 146–47
Gillmor, Alison, 178
A Girl Called Echo (Vermette), 243–44
Giroux, Monique, 249
Goldring, Peter, 155
Grace, Sherrill, 249
Granatstein, J.L., 245
Grandin, Vital, 33
Grant, Cuthbert, 104, 109, 112
Grant, Ulysses S., 9, 27, 63, 78
The Greatest Canadian (TV show), 247
Greenspan, Edward, 246
Guernon, Léon-Noël-Ernest, 13–14
Guernon, Marie-Julie, 12–13, 227
Gutteridge, Don, 66–67
Gwynn, Richard, 84, 246

Halfbreed (Campbell), 211–13, 238, 253
Halfbreeds
and 2017 revival of *Louis Riel*, 93
as distinct from Métis, xii, 211, 215–16
M. Campbell's uses for her identity, 211
as taboo term, xxiii
Halpenny, Frances, 143
Hamon, M. Max, 26–27, 150
Hannon, David, 221

Harper, Stephen, xxviii–xxix
Harrison, Dick, 171
Harron, Don, 48
Hathorn, Ramon, xxix
Henderson, Scott B., 243
Herbert, J.D., xxiv
Hinton, Peter, 94–95, 97, 249
Histoire de la nation métisse dans l'Ouest canadien (Trémaudan), 204–06, 206–07, 209–11
historical truth, xxv, xxvi
Holland, Patrick, xxix
Howard, Joseph Kinsey
derides Canada-US border, 67–68
life of, 54–55
and *Strange Empire*, 53–72
Hudson's Bay Company (HBC), 61, 64, 186
Huel, Raymond, 1, 128, 135

incest, 15
Indigenous peoples
Canada's embrace of after WWII, 74
and Canadian colonization, 194–95
contributions to Canada, 90
cultural appropriation of, 89, 104
dispute non-Indigenous claim to LR, xix, xxix–xxx
effect on M. Campbell, 213
impact on 2017 revival of *Louis Riel*, 94–95
J.R. Saul's view of settlers relationship with, 124
LR's conception of religion and land rights of, 36–37
LR's inability to identify with, xxiii, 152
LR's lack of affinity for, 21, 59–60

and LR's vision, 251–52
Métis lack of affinity for, 59–61, 238–39
portrayal in *A Really Good Brown Girl*, 231
portrayal in *In Search of April Raintree*, 219, 220
portrayal in opera *Louis Riel*, 79
portrayal in *Peace Shall Destroy Many*, 121
R. Wiebe's concern for, 101, 103–04, 123–24
spirituality of in *Song of Batoche*, 237
views on private property, 196. *See also* First Nations; Métis
In Search of April Raintree (Mosionier), 216–21
Irvine, Acheson G., 32, 150–51
Isbister, Alexander K., 61
Isbister, James, 95

Jackel, David, 128
Jackson, Cicely, 29
Jackson, Will (Honoré Jaxon), 28–30
Johnson, Chris, 47
Joyal, Miguel, 156, 166, 167
Jukes, Augustus, 248

Kardash, William, 162
Karr, Jack, 49
Kaye, Frances W., 157, 172, 177
Kennedy, Roderick, 64
Kennedy, William, 64
Kertzer, Jonathan, xxx, 103
kidnapping of nuns in 1859, 5
Knox, H.C., 162
Koncan, Frances, 242–43, 251
Kraemer, Franz, 84
Kreisel, Henry, 130

Kroetsch, Robert, xxvii, 38, 101, 123
Kundera, Milan, 254
"Kuyas" (song), 89

Lagimodière, Jean-Baptiste, 5, 18
Lamennais, Félicité de, 138
Languirand, Jacques, 39, 75, 76, 86, 90
LaRocque, Emma, 149, 201
Lavallée, Guy, 244
Lavallée, Louis, 32
LeBlanc, Marie-Joseph, 227–28
Lee, Dennis, 194
Lee, John, 12, 27, 28
Lee, Lucie, 28
LeGatt, Albert, 244
Legault, Stephen, 247
Leman, Dilys, 248
Lemay, Marcien, 66, 162–64, 165–66, 168
Lemieux, François-Xavier, 241
Leo XIII, Pope, 114
Lépine, Ambroise-Dydime
    character, 110
    complicity in Scott's execution, 110–11
    LR's idea to rename Lake Winnipeg for, 37
    and North-West War, 97, 112
    portrayal in *The Scorched-Wood People*, 109–10, 112
    trial of, 110, 111, 112
libertarianism, 195
Li Keur: Riel's Heart of the North (opera), 242
Long, Timothy, 168
Louis Riel (1971) (sculpture)
    commissioning of, 161–63
    G. Dumont on, 178

how it accords with LR's writings,
 176-77
nudity of as main point of
 censure, 173-74
praise for, 168-69
reception of, 163-64, 171
removal of, 164-66
vandalism of, 169-70
Louis Riel (1996) (sculpture), 166, 167, 176
Louis Riel (opera)
 2017 revival, 73, 93-95, 97
 bilingualism of, 86-89
 and Britishness of Canada in, 79-80
 as Canadian milestone, 91-92
 characterization of Red River Resistance, 77-83
 described, 76-77
 draws equivalency between LR and Macdonald, 82, 83-84
 influence of play Riel on, 85-86
 inspiration for, 75-76, 100
 making of, 39, 73, 76, 90
 perceived flaws of, 90-91
 portrayal of LR as Canadian hero, 84, 92-93
 and question of Macdonald amnesty, 81, 91
 TV adaptation of, 84, 85
Louis Riel, le pére du Manitoba (Zoran and Toufik), 190, 191
Louis Riel: A Comic-Strip Biography (Brown)
 non-bilingualism of, 88
 organization of, 185
 paratextual information in, 198
 reviews, 182
 story of, 181-82, 185-88, 189-90, 192-93, 197, 198

Louis Riel and Gabriel Dumont (Boyden), 148, 149-50
Louis Riel en bande dessinée (Freynet), 190-91
Louis Riel Memorial (1968) (sculpture), 157-61, 166, 168, 173-74
Louis Riel: Patriot or Rebel? (Stanley), 132
Louis Riel Statue Committee, 163
Louis: The Heretic Poems (Scofield), 226-30
Low, Tim, 251
The Luck of Ginger Coffey (Moore), 75, 100
Lyon, Sterling, 170
MacBeth, R.G., 110
Macdonald, John A.
 and Greatest Canadian contest, 247
 LR sees his equivalence to, 82
 LR's feelings on, 24
 LR's letters to, 31-32
 LR's writing on, 65
 L. St. Laurent view of, xxiv
 M. Atwood's view of, 74
 and Métis amnesty, 77, 81, 91, 113, 114
 modern reaction to, 245-46
 as perpetrator of North-West War, 52
 portrayal in A Really Good Brown Girl, 231
 portrayal in Louis Riel, 79-80, 82-84, 86-87, 90
 portrayal in Louis Riel: A Comic-Strip Biography, 185-88, 197, 198
 portrayal in Louis: The Heretic Poems, 229

portrayal in *Riel*, 45-46, 48, 49
portrayal in *Riel: A Poem for Voices*, 67
portrayal in *Strange Empire*, 65
sculpture of, 170
trades places with LR in mythmaking, xxvii
view of LR by, 78, 241
MacKenzie Art Gallery, 161
Mair, Charles, 19, 67, 81-82
Mallet, Edmond, 9, 27, 28, 63-64, 93
Maly, Stephen, 244
Mandel, Eli, 123
Manitoba Metis Federation, 164, 166, 167, 173, 175-76
Manitowapow (Sinclair and Cariou), 252
Marion sisters, 12
Martel, Gilles, 10, 128, 134
Marx, Anthony, xxx
Mason, Bouvette, 251
Massinahican, Cree (Riel), 150
Masson, Sophie, 7
Mattes, Catherine
 and D. Garneau, 222
 and exclusive right of Métis to LR memorialization, 172
 and LR's artistic prophecy quote, 249
 on LR's Canadianization, 148
 on Métis confusion over LR memorialization, 173
 and *Strange Empire*, 65-66
McCardle, Bennett, 141-42, 152
McCloud, Scott, 193
McClung, Nellie, 122
McCullough, Alan, xxv
McDougall, Daniel, 6
McDougall, John, 197

McDougall, William, 63, 77, 79, 105, 106
McKay, Joe, 216
McLachlin, Beverley, xix
Mennonitism, 103, 114, 119-21
Métis
 ambivalent attitude toward LR, xviii, 201-02, 216, 239
 and amnesty from federal government, 77, 81, 91, 113, 114
 claim right to say how LR should be memorialized, 172-73, 248
 conundrum of having two sets of ancestors, 220-21
 depiction in *Peace Shall Destroy Many*, 119-21
 D. Garneau's art on LR, 221-24, 225
 as distinct from Halfbreeds, xii, 211, 215-16
 and execution of T. Scott, 112
 fight between associations over LR memorialization, 173
 and *A Girl Called Echo*, 243-44
 G. Scofield's art and LR, 224, 225-30
 and *Halfbreed*, 211-13, 238
 history of, xx-xxiii, 202, 210
 how LR's mental state effects, 25-26
 identifying with LR through his writings, 2-3
 importance of North-West War to, xx, xxii
 J.K. Howard's view of, 69
 and "La chanson de la Grenouillère," 104-05
 and lack of affinity for First Nations, 59-61, 238-39

lack of representation in Projet
Riel Project, 135
in *Louis Riel*, 90
LR asks for their adoption of new
patron saint, 33
and LR's artistic prophecy quote,
249–55
LR's connection to, 18, 19–20, 38
and LR sculpture, 161, 162–63,
164, 173–74
M. Dumont's poetry and, 230–33
neglected in 2017 revival of *Louis Riel*, 93
performance art by, 170–71
preference of G. Dumont to LR
by, 202
reconciliation with Catholic
Church, 244
rejection of Canadianization of
LR by, xix, 148–49, 157
response to *Riel and the Rebellion*,
144–45, 146–47
and *The Scorched-Wood People*,
106–7, 125–26
and *In Search of April Raintree*,
216–20
seen as soul of Canada by
intellectuals, 147–48
and *Song of Batoche*, 233–38
territorial rights of, 118–19
true state of their relationship to
Canada, 157
in United States, 23, 24
view of in *Strange Empire*, 57, 59,
68
and Winnipeg Rifles monument,
172
Metis Association of Alberta, 144–45
Middleton, Frederick, 206, 232
modern art, 156–57

Monet, Marguerite
LR marries, 12, 15, 16–17
portrayal in *Louis Riel*, 79, 89
portrayal in *Riel*, 46, 47
portrayed as Cree, 86
Moore, Dora Mavor, 41–42
Moore, Mavor
admiration for *Strange Empire*, 85
and *Louis Riel*, 39, 75, 76, 85, 89
narrow vision of Canada, 90
and New Play Society, 41
portrayal of LR, 49
Moore, Terence, 175–76
Morice, Adrien-Gabriel, 205, 208–09
Morisset, Jean, 138, 139–40
Morton, Desmond, xxvi
Morton, Oliver P., 63–64
Morton, W.L., 51
Mosionier, Beatrice, 216–21, 238
Motut, Roger, 136, 139

nationalism, xxx, xxx–xxxi
National Library, 128
nation-building, xviii–xix
New, Chester W., 182
New Breed (magazine), 251
New Play Society, 41–42
The Noblest Triumph: Property and Prosperity (Bethell), 196
Nolin, Charles, 192
non-Indigenous Canadians
appeal of LR to, xix, 99–100
and connection to Indigenous
through *Strange Empire*, 66
modern reaction to LR-
Macdonald debate, 246
rationale for rehabilitating LR,
xxix–xxx
R. Wiebe's attempt to legitimize
presence of, 123–24

view of LR as Indigenous way of
being, 36
view of North-West War to, 122
Noose/Fist (Metis Flag) (Garneau),
223, 225
Norquay, John, 117, 118, 216
Norris, Malcolm, 251
The North-West Is Our Mother (Teillet),
2
Northwest Mounted Police, 62
North-West Mounted Police
Museum, xxiv
North-West War
A. McCullough's study of Parks
Canada interpretation of, xxv
and *The Crime of Louis Riel*, 52–53
in *Halfbreed*, 212
and Lépine's absence from, 112
in *Louis Riel: A Comic-Strip
Biography*, 185, 186–88
and LR's reason for travelling to
Batoche in 1884, 34–35
LR's role in, xx
LR's view of what caused, 31–32
and L. Schmidt, 97
memorials for, 171–72
M. Max Hamon's view of, 26
as pivotal Métis event, xx, xxii
portrayal in *A Girl Called Echo*, 243
portrayal in *Louis Riel*, 79
portrayal in *Riel*, 47
portrayal in *Stories of the Road
Alllowance People*, 214–15
portrayal in *Strange Empire*, 70–71
portrayal in *The Scorched-Wood
People*, 115–16
recent novels on, 247
S. Harper's view of, xxviii–xxix
in Trémaudan history, 204,
206–07

Western Canadians attitude
towards, 122
Nugent, John, 66, 157–61, 168
nuns, kidnapping of in 1859, 5

O'Donoghue, William
in *Louis Riel*, 80
and Red River Resistance, 42,
43–44, 45, 46
and US expansionism, 78
O'Hagan, Howard, 187
oikophobia, 246
Orr, David D., 247
O'Toole, Darren, 27
Ouellette, Moïse, 96
Owram, Doug, 84, 149

Painchaud, Robert, 135
Pannekoek, Frits, 142–43
Parisien, Norbert, 190
Parker-Jervis, Noël, 128, 129, 131, 137
Parks Canada, xxv–xxvi
Patrimony (Garneau), 223
Paying for It (Brown), 184
Payment, Diane, 237, 244
Peace Shall Destroy Many (Wiebe),
102, 103, 119–21, 122
Peel, Bruce, 130
The Pemmican Eaters (Dumont), 231–
33
Petursson, Philip, 161, 163
Pius IX, Pope, 115
Poésies de jeunesse (1977), 131
Poitras, Edward, 249, 251
Poitras, Henriette, 33–34
Poitras, Jane A., 221
The Posthumous Memoirs of Brás Cubas
(Machado de Assis), 105
Poundmaker, 79, 95
Primrose, Alexander, 40

Primrose, Olive C., 40
profit vandalism, 169
Projet Riel Project
    assessment of application for by Canada Council, 132–35
    and Flanagan's *Riel and the Rebellion*, 144–47
    how it came to be, 127–31
    and publishing decisions on *The Collected Writings of Louis Riel*, 137–38
    reviews of *The Collected Writings of Louis Riel*, 138–43
    what is included in *The Collected Writings of Louis Riel*, 135–37
A Prophet in Exile: Louis Riel's Sojourn in Montana (documentary), 244
Prud'homme, Eustache, 21
pseudepigrapha, 254
public art
    facets of, 156
    idealization of, 175–76
    pros and cons of, 177–79
    vandalism of, 169–70

La race métisse: étude critique (Morice), 208
Racette, Farrell, 194–95, 221
RCMP museum, 248
A Really Good Brown Girl (Dumont), 231
Red River, 20
Red River Resistance
    and amnesty for Métis, 91, 113, 114
    in *Louis Riel: A Comic-Strip Biography*, 185
    LR's part in, xix
    in LR's writings, 3

Parks Canada change in brochure information on, xxv–xxvi
    as pivotal Métis event, xx
    portrayal in *A Girl Called Echo*, 243
    portrayal in *Louis Riel*, 77–83
    portrayal in *Riel*, 42–46
    portrayal in *The Scorched-Wood People*, 108–09
Reid, Jennifer, 147–48
religious syncretism, 213
Renan, Ernest, xviii, 246, 248, 249, 254
Renooy, Ray, 250
The Retrial of Louis Riel (TV show), 246–47
Riel (Coulter)
    compared to *Strange Empire*, 67
    influence on *Louis Riel* of, 85–86
    M. Moore's tie to, 76
    story of, 40–51
Riel, Joseph, 32, 113, 202, 209, 253
Riel, Julie Lagimodière
    background, 5
    helps LR with money, 31
    impact on LR, 228
    intense Catholic belief of, 6, 228
    LR informs of his marriage, 16
    LR requests that she bless him, 33–34
    LR writes to, 19
    portrayal in *Louis Riel*, 87
    portrayal in *Riel*, 49
Riel, Louis
    academics view of in 1950s, 51
    admiration for Columbus, 37
    adopts the name David, 10–12
    appeals to US authorities, 9, 61–62, 63

apprehensions regarding
Indigenous peoples, 59–60,
239
arranges for his mother's blessing
of him, 33–34
belief he will become leader of
Confederation, 32–33
belief in his own resurrection,
25–26, 32
bullying nature of, 82–83
burial of compared to T. Scott's
end, 111
confined to Québec asylums, 8–9,
11, 28
connection to Métis of, 18, 38,
59–60, 125
contradictory nature of, 37–38
effect of father's death on, 30
evidence his views were not anti-
colonial, 37
and execution of T. Scott, 83,
110–11, 189
financial problems, 18, 31
as Francophile, 21, 37, 117
friendship with L. Schmidt, 96–
97
God appears to him, xx, 8–10, 27
groups he indentifies with, xxiii,
19–23, 63, 64
his opinion of his writing, 10,
150–51
importance of Catholic religion
to, 30, 114–15, 229–30, 233
lack of identification with
Canada, 23–24, 38
lack of self-knowledge by, 16, 38
lambastes Macdonald over
amnesty, 114
marries M. Monet, 12, 16, 86
megalomania of, 35–36

and New World church of, xx,
xxviii, 8, 30, 36–37, 49, 79, 176,
207–08, 233
and N-J Ritchot, 112–13
photos of, xxi, xxii
politics of, 118
possible love child of, 13–14
prudishness of, 229
questions about his mental state,
xxix, 8–9, 25–31, 132
romantic entanglements, 12–18
sees equivalence between himself
and Macdonald, 82
summary of public life, xix–xx
support for US expansion, 63–64,
65, 78
tie to A.-A. Taché, 113–14
trial of, xxii, 64, 110–11, 122
use of his writing to make money,
151–52
view of egalitarian religion, 36
view of Lépine, 110
view of what caused North-West
War, 31–32, 34–35
and W. Jackson, 29–30. *See also*
Riel memorialization; Riel
rehabilitation; Riel visual art;
Riel's writings
Riel, Sara, 7, 10–11, 35
Riel, Sr., Louis, 5, 6, 27, 30
Riel: A Life of Revolution (Siggins), 185
*Riel and the Rebellion: 1885
Reconsidered* (Flanagan), 144–
47, 191–92
Riel: A Poem for Voices (Gutteridge),
66, 67, 74, 88
Riel memorialization
in 2017 revival of *Louis Riel*, 94–95
aborted TV film on, 108
campaign for sainthood for, 244

compared to Macdonald and
CPR, xxvii–xxviii
complexity of LR defies, xi, 254
by D. Garneau, 221–25
and different identities he
embodies, 99–100
and difficulty of act of
remembering, 254
and effacement of his being a
Métis, 93
E. Mallet's prediction of, 93
and execution of T. Scott, 227
fictional v. non-fictional
representations of, 181
by G. Scofield, 224, 226–30
Guelph conference on, xxvi–xxvii
and his appeal to Canadians, 99
of his mental state, 116, 192, 222–23, 234–35, 248
of his treatment of Taché in
Histoire de la nation métisse,
210
important time markers of, 39
important works of, 40
longevity of, 241–42
in *Louis Riel*, 79, 80, 82, 83–84,
87–88, 90, 91
in *Louis Riel: A Comic-Strip
Biography*, 186, 192–93, 195–99
Louis Riel Day declared, 39
and LR's belief in heaven, 229–30
of LR's death, 47–48, 83–84, 87–88, 233
by M. Campbell, 211, 213–14, 216
in M. Dumont's poetry, 230–33
Métis claim exclusive right to,
172–73, 248
modern Métis resistance to, 201–02, 239, 242
opponents of, 169–70, 172

portrayal in *Strange Empire*, 67,
69–71
portrayal in *The Scorched-Wood
People*, 106, 111, 114, 115–16, 121
portrayal of trial, 47–48, 51
and Projet Riel Project, 127–35
recent examples of, 241–44
recognized as founder of
Manitoba, 39
as reflection of Canada, xxiii–xxiv,
195
in *Riel*, 40–51, 67
in R. Wiebe's early novels, 103
and sanitizing his image, 176, 177,
178
in *In Search of April Raintree*, 218,
221
in *Song of Batoche*, 233–35, 237–38
sources for, 255–56
and tracking artistic prophecy
quote, 249–55
why modern Métis still feel they
need LR, 239
by writers and scholars, 71
Riel rehabilitation
alluded to in *The Collected
Writings of Louis Riel*, 142–43,
147
into Canadian hero, xvii–xviii, 65,
73, 84–85, 86, 92–93
into Canadian icon, 53
Canadianization of, xi, xii, 155
into champion of Prairie West,
116–19
and decision of Canada Council
to fund scholarship project
on, 131–32
as defender of Canadian values,
xix

and effect of J. Coulter's two plays
of 1960s on, 51–52
and Flanagan's *Riel and the
Rebellion*, 144–47, 191–92
G.F.G. Stanley role in starting
myth of LR blamelessness, 132
of his mental illness in *Histoire de
la nation métisse*, 209
how little connected it is to LR's
writings, 149–50, 254
lack of resistance to, 155
into leader of pan-Indigenous
alliance, 79, 93, 94–95
as method of strengthening
nationalism, xxx–xxxi
and Métis control of, 248
Métis rejection of LR's
Canadianization, 148–49, 157
into non-British subject, 46
non-Indigenous Canadians
rationale for, xxix–xxx
opponents of, xxviii–xxix, 74–75,
169–70, 172, 245–46
recent novels dealing with, 247
and reservations about LR's
Canadianness by advocates
of, 181
split on view of from elites and
general public, 247
and St. Laurent speech, xxiv
on TV broadcasts, 246–47
by Union nationale métisse St-
Joseph du Manitoba, 202–07
Riel's Last Portraits (Mug Shots)
(Garneau), 223
Riel's People (Campbell), 213–14
Riel's writings
artistic prophecy quote, 249–55
Batoche "Journal," 24–25
effect of fear of afterlife on, 229

as final arbiter of his place in
history, 248–49
gaps in, 2, 4–5, 35
on his early life in
"Autobiographical Notes," 3–4
his view of Métis, 19–20, 59–60,
214
how little read they are, 38, 95, 97,
147–50, 152–53, 254
how *Louis Riel* sculpture accords
with, 176–77
identification as Métis through,
2–3
importance of Taché to LR in, 5–8
on J.A. Macdonald, 65
Keeseville poems, 122
"La Métisse," 19
"L'Archevêque de Saint Boniface,"
6
"Les Métis du Nord-Ouest," 121,
141
letters, 31–32, 33–34, 62, 78, 207–
08
limitations of his poetry, 35–36
love poems, 13, 14–15, 16, 17
LR's opinion of, 150–51
LR's use of to make money, 151–52
Massinahican, 150
during North-West War, 34–35
"O Québec," 20
poem "Alexandre-le-grand," 113
Regina "Journals," 114
shaped by R. Wiebe, 123
spiritual confessions in, 176–77,
253
and tie to French Canada, 20–21
on US, 22–25
view of Indigenous heritage in,
228
view of nudity/statues, 174–75

what is learned from, 1-2. *See also*
"Autobiographical Notes"; *The Collected Writings of Louis Riel*; Projet Riel Project
Riel/Van Gogh (Garneau), 222-23
Riel visual art
   commissioning of *Louis Riel* (1971), 161-66
   and D. Garneau, 221-23, 225
   examples of negative representations, 155-56
   and *Louis Riel* (1996), 166, 167
   and *Louis Riel Memorial*, 157-61
   mural in Moose Jaw, 250
   and nudity, 173-74
   praise for, 166, 168-69
   preference for commonplace over expressive, 175-76
   reasons for its controversial nature, 157
   V. Vint sculpture, 250
   what is learned from, 178-79
   and who gets to speak for LR, 156
   W. Jackson bust, 30
Ritchot, Noël-Joseph, 112-13
Robinson, Christopher, 53
Robinson, Dylan, 89
Robinson, John B., 53
Rocan, Claude, 128, 146-47, 249
Ross, Alexander, 232
Ross, James, 60-61, 83, 238-39
Ross, William, 61

Salter, F.M., 102
Saskatchewan Arts Board, 157
Saul, John Ralston, 124, 147, 148
Sawchuk, Joe, 205
Sayer affair, xx, 112
Schafer, R. Murray, 89
Schmidt, Louis
   on Lépine, 110
   life of, 96-97
   lack of support for LR, 35
   portrayal in 2017 revival of *Louis Riel*, 95-96
   portrayal in *Song of Batoche*, 235
   studies for priesthood, 6
Schreyer, Edward, 163, 164, 170, 171
Schultz, John C., 67, 77, 83, 190
Scofield, Gregory, 224, 225-30, 238
The Scorched-Wood People (Wiebe)
   criticism of, 101, 105, 107, 181
   described, 106
   details divide between LR and Church, 112-15
   elegiac tone of, 125-26
   portrayal of G. Dumont, 108-09, 112, 115-16
   portrayal of LR, 111, 115-17, 121
   view of Métis in, 106-07, 125-26
   Wiebe's use of P. Falcon as narrator/author of, 104, 105-06, 107, 108, 123
Scott, Thomas
   execution of, xix, 5, 28, 83, 110-11, 112, 132, 209, 226-27, 234
   LR's feelings on, 189
   memorials to, 171
   and Métis amnesty, 91
   non-burial of, 110, 111, 243-44
   portrayal in *Louis Riel*, 77-78, 88
   portrayal in *Louis Riel: A Comic-Strip Biography*, 189-90
   portrayal in *Louis: The Heretic Poems*, 229
   portrayal in other media, 190-91
   portrayal in *Riel*, 43, 44, 48, 86
   portrayal in *Women of the Fur Trade*, 242

transformed into racist demon, 188-89
trial of, 111
Scruton, Roger, 246
sectarianism, 49-50
Segato, Gianmarco, 95
Senie, Harriet, 156
Seth (graphic novellist), 182
settlers/colonizers, 123-24. *See also* non-Indigenous Canadians
Settlers Rights Association, 29
Siggins, Maggie, 4-5, 16-17, 28, 185, 228
Simonot-Maiello, Colette, 81, 90
Sinclair, James, 252
Sinclair, Murray, 250
Sitting Bull, 61-62, 100
Smith, C. Rhodes, 163
Smith, Donald A., 80, 82, 209
Solecki, Sam, 101
Somers, Harry
    as composer of *Louis Riel*, 39, 75, 76
    dying statement about *Louis Riel*, 89
    musical choices for *Louis Riel*, 90, 92
    and TV adaptation of *Louis Riel*, 84
Song of Batoche (Caron), 233-38
Spinoza, Baruch, 236
Stanley, George F.G.
    as editor of *The Collected Writings of Louis Riel*, 1, 127, 136, 137, 138, 139, 143, 153
    fear that he created myth of blameless LR, 132
    his biography of LR as inspiration for *Louis Riel*, 75
    on LR as prairie champion, 117-18

    on memorialization of LR, 40
    predicts LR statue in Winnipeg, 162
    on Québec ultramontanes, 8
    response to Flanagan book, 145-46
    role in Projet Riel Project, 128, 131, 145-46
    on statues, 175
    on *Strange Empire*, 56, 57
Steele, Harvey, 50
Steele, Suzanne, 242
Stegner, Wallace, 58, 68
Stephen, George, 187
St. Laurent, Louis, xxiv, xxv, 162
Stories of the Road Allowance People (Campbell), 214-15
Strange Empire: A Narrative of the Northwest (Howard)
    Canadian cultural intelligentsia's love of, 65-67
    continentalism of, 65-66, 71-72
    coverage of US annexationism in, 62, 63-65
    criticism of, 56-57, 58, 67
    political ideas of, 53-54
    portrayal of LR in, 61, 62, 69-71, 84-85
    view of Métis in, 59, 68, 69
    view of Red River Resistance, 62
    view of US-Canada border in, 67-68, 69-71
    writing of, 55-56, 57, 68-69
The Strangers (Vermette), 244
Stutsman, Enos, 62-63
Survival: A Thematic Guide to Canadian Literature (Atwood), 74-75
Suzack, Cheryl, 220
Swainson, Donald, 101

Taché, Alexandre-Antonin
    accepts LR's taking name David, 11–12
    appointed by LR as Pope of New World, 36
    in *Histoire de la nation métisse*, 209, 210
    importance to LR in writings, 3, 5–8
    LR's correspondence to on new faith, 208
    and LR's madness, 192
    LR's tie to, 113–14
    and L. Schmidt, 96, 97
    portrayal in *Louis Riel*, 80, 81, 82, 86–87, 90–91
    portrayal in *Riel*, 45
    portrayal in *The Scorched-Wood People*, 112–13
Tatlin, Vladimir, 168
Taylor, James W., 12, 63, 78
Teillet, Jean
    on *Louis Riel*, 82
    on *Louis Riel* (1996), 176
    on LR's mental state, 25–26
    and *The North-West Is Our Mother*, 2, 150
The Temptations of Big Bear (Wiebe), 103–04
Tétreault, Matthew, 228
Thatcher, Ross, 158, 161, 177
The Third Riel Conspiracy (Legault), 247
Thompson, W.P., 164
Through the Mackenzie Basin (Mair), 67
Thunder through My Veins: Memories of a Métis Childhood (Scofield), 224, 226
Tippett, Maria, 168

Tovell, Vincent, 50
Trémaudan, Auguste-Henri de, 203–06
Trémaudan, Madeleine de, 205
The Trial of Louis Riel (Coulter), 51
Trudeau, Justin, xxx–xxxi, 194
Trudeau, Pierre, xxiii–xxiv, 52, 158, 161
Truth and Reconciliation Commission (TRC), 94

Union nationale métisse, 164, 202–07
United States
    downplaying of annexationism in *Louis Riel*, 78–79
    fear of as impetus for Canada's annexation of North-West, 64–65
    J.K. Howard's view as true home of Métis, 68
    LR's criticism of, 24–25
    LR's tie to, xx, xxiii, 4, 12, 22–23, 24
United States, Government of, 24, 61–62, 64
Université de Saint-Boniface, 166

Vanderhaeghe, Guy, 147
Vermette, Auguste, 189
Vermette, Katherena, 124, 243–44
Vint, Val T., 250
Voisine, Nive, 138–39
Volunteer Monument, 171

Wagner, Norman, 144
Wallace, William S., 51
Wandering Spirit, 79
Waterston, Elizabeth, xxvii
Wayman, Tom, 169
Weisensel, Neil, 242

Welsh, Norbert, 215
Western Canadiana Publications
    Project, 128-31
What Is a Nation? (Renan), 246
"when Louis Riel went crazy"
    (poem), 243
*When the Other Is Me: Native
    Resistance Discourse*
    (LaRocque), 149
"Where Is the Voice Coming From?"
    (short story), 104
Whittaker, Herbert, 47
Who Killed Canadian History?
    (Granatstein), 245
Wiebe, Rudy
    background, 101-02
    concern for Indigenous peoples,
        101, 123-24
    description of early novels, 102-
        04
    and "Louis Riel: The Man They
        Couldn't Hang," 122
    review of *The Collected Writings of
        Louis Riel*, 141
    and *The Scorched-Wood People*, 101,
        105-09, 111-17, 121, 125-26
    as shaper of LR's words, 123
    similarity of LR's view of
        democratic church to his own,
        36
    use of P. Falcon in *The Scorched-
        Wood People*, 105-06, 107
William Morrow (publisher), 68
Williams, Margaret, 130
Winnipeg, 171-72
Winnipeg Rifles, 171, 172
The Winter Count (Leman), 248
Wolfit, Donald, 41
Wolseley, Garnet, 45, 46, 52, 81
Women of the Fur Trade (Koncan),
    242-43
Woodcock, George
    criticism of *The Scorched-Wood
        People*, 105
    and *Gabriel Dumont: The Métis
        Chief and His Lost World*, 181
    on non-Indigenous rehabilitation
        of LR, xxix
    and *Strange Empire*, 70
    on Western Canadiana advisory
        board, 130
    on Wiebe's portrayal of G.
        Dumont, 109

Yaciuk, Donovan, 243

Zoran and Toufik (cartoonists), 190,
    191

www.ingramcontent.com/pod-product-compliance
Lightning Source LLC
Chambersburg PA
CBHW021122170725
29492CB00038B/191